introduction

It's breakfast time—and I need something sweet. My taste buds crave a piece of Danish. It's three in the afternoon—time for a coffee break, and I cut a slice of sour cream coffee cake. It's ten o'clock at night—and my sweet tooth wants "just a bite." Nestled away in a corner of my pantry is my secret stash of brownies.

I spend the better part of my life surrounded by sweets. If I'm not having a "baking moment" in my kitchen, I am sharing my knowledge with my students in a classroom. What makes me chuckle is their curiosity about my personal dessert preferences. Since I am always on the lookout for subjects to write about, wouldn't they be surprised to learn that I am equally curious about their favorites? Why? It's because they provide me with material for my books. When it comes to desserts, at the top of my personal list of favorites are the "homey" sweets, like a slice of babka, a brownie, or a warm blueberry muffin topped with my favorite streusel. Through informal conversations with my family, friends, and students, I have learned that these types of satisfying pastries are at the top of their lists as well.

The style of pastries in this book is one that I have wanted to write about for years, and I am pleased to now have the opportunity to do so. *Great Coffee Cakes, Sticky Buns, Muffins & More* includes nine chapters filled with enticing recipes, many of which can be made quickly, for people on the run. With good planning, a variety of pastries can be partially prepared and finished when you have a few moments to bake. Many muffin batters can be made ahead and baked as needed. Those who are passionate about baking will relish spending time preparing my recipe for authentic Danish, sure to be savored by anyone fortunate enough to sample a piece.

Each recipe has an icon to designate the level of difficulty. One measuring cup indicates recipes that are the easiest to make and the least time-consuming. Two measuring cups stand for recipes that have a moderate level of difficulty, with procedures that take more time. Recipes that have three measuring cups are for the more experienced baker who welcomes a challenge. I do not believe in listing the preparation time for each recipe because everyone works at his or her own pace.

In Chapter 1, "Perfect Pound Cakes," there are more than a dozen recipes for velvety pound cakes. Here you will find favorites like Lemon Cream Cheese, Blueberry, and

marbled Black and White, along with new recipes like Plum-Topped Pound Cake Squares and Nut-Crusted Orange Pound Cake. In Chapter 2, "Home-Style Coffee Cakes," there is a selection of sour cream coffee cakes, as well as Bundt cakes like Banana Chocolate Chip, Caramel-Glazed Blackberry Jam Cake, and Toasted Pecan Eggnog Ring.

Chapter 3, "Muffins & Quick Breads," may easily become the chapter you turn to most. Whether you fancy "Too Good to Be True" Bran Muffins, Ultra-Rich Corn Muffins, or a Pumpkin Pecan Loaf, this chapter has something to please every palate. Bring out the bread basket for Chapter 4, "Biscuits & Scones." There are Old-Fashioned Buttermilk Biscuits, along with a tempting array of other biscuits including Cinnamon Pull-Apart and Naughty Sweet Cream. If you've never eaten homemade scones, you are in for a treat. Try your hand at Country Cherry Honey Scones, Cinnamon Apple Scones, and a treasured find, Sedona Cream Scones.

The chapter that I am the most excited about, and the one that is unique, is Chapter 5, "Easy Does It Yeasted Coffee Cakes." Many of these recipes were adapted from those that were so popular during the 1940s and '50s. During that era, they were shared among good bakers from coast to coast. Over the years, they disappeared owing to the hustle and bustle of modern-day living. Bakers will soon discover that there is nothing complex about making these wonderful cakes.

Here you will find two easy master dough recipes that can be used interchangeably for making favorites like Sticky Buns and Crumb Buns, along with new treats like Strawberry Dimple Sugar Cake and Rustic Cinnamon Walnut Horns. Not only are they "easy does it," but most can also be prepared the day before, refrigerated, and baked the next day. Included here is my treasured recipe for Streusel-Topped Babka, filled with cinnamon, nuts, and raisins and topped with lots of buttery crumbs.

Chapter 6, "Brioche, Croissants & Danish," is written for those for who appreciate European classics. Breakfast brioche begins the chapter, featuring a master recipe for Classic Brioche with toothsome variations like a Chocolate Duet and Brioche Buns with Dried Pears and Camembert. Next are Flaky Croissants—a treat whether served plain or transformed into delectable Pain au Chocolat or Flaky Apple and Cherry Puffs.

No one I know can resist classic Danish pastries, and the varieties included here are certainly no exception. Tempt your family and friends with such recipes as traditional Grandmother's Cake, flaky Apricot Twists, and Pineapple Cheese Bow Ties.

Chapter 7, "Strudel: Then and Now," features a recipe for Hand-Pulled Strudel Dough. Preparing the dough from scratch is easy and a baking experience you won't want to miss. I often suggest to my students that they host a strudel-stretching party—

it's a fun way to spend a Saturday night or a Sunday afternoon with a few of your cooking buddies.

For a quick alternative, you can use phyllo pastry, the ready-made, paper-thin dough that is available frozen in most supermarkets and sold fresh in Middle Eastern stores. Both hand-pulled and ready-made phyllo dough can be used for making classic Old-Fashioned Apple Walnut Strudel and the ever-popular Sour Cherry Cheese Strudel.

For that little "something" to munch on when snack time rolls around, turn to Chapter 8, "Coffee Break Bites." Nut-Crusted Rugelach, Powdered Sugar Italian Slices, Chocolate Pistachio Thumbprints, and Lemon Shortbread are but a few of the sweets that will satisfy your craving!

Chapter 9, "Streusels, Glazes, Frostings & Spreads," includes wonderful recipes for streusel, the addictive buttery crumbs that so many find irresistible. Here you will find toppings like Toasted Coconut, Rustic Maple Pecan, and even a recipe for Chocolate Streusel. In addition, there are simple glazes in flavors like Applejack, Caramel, Orange, Midnight Chocolate, and of course Vanilla. And don't forget to check out spreads like Orange Honey Butter and Crystallized Ginger and Macadamia Nut Cream Cheese, along with my favorite, Apple Cider Caramel.

To ensure successful results, be sure to read "About Equipment" (page 370) and "About Ingredients & Techniques" (page 376). Here is where the teacher in me goes to work. These sections contain a wealth of information that should not be overlooked. "About Ingredients & Techniques" discusses the many types of flours that are available, as well as the proper way to measure. Also contained here is valuable information about sugar and eggs, the enrichments that are so important to these types of pastries. Among the many techniques explained are the proper way to fold, to work with eggs, and to handle chocolate.

In "About Equipment," I advise you about the items that have served me well through my years of baking. I tell you what bakeware I think is essential and discuss proper measuring equipment, useful whisks, and spatulas. Each chapter includes an "About" page that provides tips and hints, as well as sidebars that zero in on specialized techniques.

Great Coffee Cakes, Sticky Buns, Muffins & More updates many of the recipes of yesteryear to fit today's contemporary lifestyles, and includes new ones that are soon to become family favorites. Baking is a wonderful activity—it's a relaxing outlet from daily stress, it's a project to share with children, it's fun, and best of all, the rewards make everyone smile. My baking kitchen is a happy kitchen. Open this book and make your kitchen happy, too.

perfect pound cakes

ABOUT POUND CAKES

Pound cakes, known for their velvety, fine-grain texture, are rich in butter and eggs. The batters use only a small amount of leavening and very little liquid. These cakes are usually domed on top and typically have a wide crack on the surface. In fact, toward the end of the baking period, professional bakers often slash the surface of the cake with a sharp knife to ensure that it will have that classic split across the top.

• Pay strict attention to the temperature of the butter and eggs when preparing a pound cake batter. If these ingredients are too warm or too cold, the consistency of the batter will be affected (see page 34).

• The batter for a pound cake usually needs to be very well beaten. Dry ingredients are generally added at a higher speed and are beaten for a longer period.

• Pound cakes are often baked in flat-bottomed angel food pans, which hold a large amount of batter. If you wish to make smaller cakes, most batters can be baked in two 8½ x 4½-inch loaf pans. The baking time may need to be reduced slightly. When you detect an aroma coming from the oven, the cake will soon be done.

• The purpose of baking pound cakes in a tube pan is to permit the oven heat to circulate through the funnel. This ensures that the center will cook through.

• Since pound cake batters are very dense, it is better to bake them at a lower temperature. This helps the center of the cake to bake completely without overbrowning the exterior.

• If the top of a pound cake is browning before the inside is done, lay a piece of aluminum foil loosely over the surface.

• During baking, it is common for beads of moisture to form on the crack of the pound cake. When testing the cake for doneness, test it in an area close to the middle, but not where the beads of moisture have formed.

• When testing for doneness, use a thin wooden skewer. This enables you to reach farther into the cake; a toothpick would be too short. Metal cake testers are not recommended, as the surface is slippery and uncooked batter often will not cling.

• Allow enough cooling time before removing pound cakes from their pans. These cakes are dense and need more time than usual to rest after baking.

• Pound cakes should be thinly sliced, using a serrated knife and a sawing motion.

• Sliced pound cake is wonderful when toasted. Place a slice on a piece of aluminum foil and pop it in the toaster oven until lightly browned.

MARBLING MATTERS

MARBLING IS A TECHNIQUE used to mingle different flavors or various fillings through a batter. The object is to combine the two components in a way that allows each of them to be visible throughout, creating an attractive effect when the cake is sliced. The most common combination of batters is vanilla and chocolate. Spice and sugar fillings, as well as streusels, nuts, and jams, are also popular and can be woven through a batter.

As a rule, most cakes that are marbled are baked in deep tube pans, such as a Bundt pan or an angel food pan. Thick batters such as those for pound cakes, those made with sour cream, or those not too fluid make the best candidates. Because the outside of a cake bakes before the center, heavy ingredients such as nuts, streusels, and chocolate chips will sink to the bottom of the pan. Chocolate batter is even heavier than vanilla. Therefore, if your fillings are sinking, it is often better to fill the pan halfway to two-thirds full before introducing any heavy ingredients. This creates a buffer or a thick base to support the heavier mixture.

Each of these marbling techniques will result in a different appearance.

• For the least amount of marbling, alternate layers of batter and filling. This technique is especially popular when making sour cream coffee cakes.

• To achieve an average marbled effect, alternate layers of two different flavored batters, or a batter and filling, then run a table knife two or three times around the pan.

• For finer marbling results, use a table knife to cut into the batter and fold it over on itself several times around the pan.

• Layering alternating spoonfuls of chocolate and vanilla batter results in a spotted effect.

Don't be concerned if your batter is skimpy on the top layer and some of the filling is exposed. When all is said and done, no matter what result you achieve, marbling a cake is a lot of fun, and the first slice is always a surprise.

powdered sugar pound cake

MAKES ONE 10-INCH CAKE, 16 TO 20 SERVINGS

If you are looking for a really terrific pound cake, you can stop here. Kept in my recipe box for years, this pound cake recipe was inspired by Nell Slagle, a dear friend from Fort Worth, Texas. Nell was a marvelous baker, and any recipe she ever recommended was always special.

The cake is made with powdered sugar, which gives it an extremely velvety texture. In Nell's day, cakes were sweeter, but I took the liberty of reducing some of the sugar. I also replaced a small amount of the butter with canola oil, which gives the cake added moistness. Be sure to drizzle in the oil slowly to retain the emulsion of the butter, and also follow the directions for adding the sugar slowly. This little extra touch will be well worth the effort. With one bite of this pound cake, I'm sure you will love it as much as I do.

> **AT A GLANCE**
> **PAN:** 10-inch angel food cake pan
> **PAN PREP:** Butter generously/line with parchment/ butter
> **OVEN TEMP:** 325°F
> **BAKING TIME:** 1 hour, 20 to 25 minutes
> **DIFFICULTY:** ♟

4 cups sifted cake flour, spooned in and leveled

2 teaspoons baking powder

½ teaspoon salt

6 large eggs

1½ cups (3 sticks) unsalted butter, slightly firm

¼ cup canola or vegetable oil

3½ cups strained powdered sugar, spooned in and leveled, plus extra for dusting

2 teaspoons pure vanilla extract

⅛ teaspoon lemon oil

1. Position the rack in the lower third of the oven. Heat the oven to 325°F. Generously butter a 10-inch angel food cake pan, line the bottom with baking parchment, then butter the parchment. Set aside.

2. In a large bowl, thoroughly whisk together the flour, baking powder, and salt. Set aside.

3. Place the eggs in a medium bowl and whisk until well blended. Set aside.

4. Cut the butter into 1-inch pieces and place in the bowl of an electric mixer fitted with the paddle attachment. Mix on medium speed until smooth and lightened in color, about 2 minutes. Slowly drizzle in the canola oil, taking about 1 minute, then beat for 2 minutes longer. Scrape down the side of the bowl.

5. Reduce the mixer speed to medium-low. *If your mixer has a splatter shield attachment, now is a good time to use it.* Add the powdered sugar, 2 to 3 tablespoons at a time, taking 8 to 10 minutes. Gradually add ½ cup of the eggs and beat for 2 minutes longer, scraping down the side of the bowl as needed. Blend in the vanilla and lemon oil.

6. Add the flour mixture alternately with the remaining eggs, dividing the flour into four parts and the eggs into three parts, beginning and ending with the flour, mixing until well blended after each addition. Scrape down the side of the bowl as needed.

7. Empty the batter into the prepared pan and smooth the top with the back of a large soupspoon. Bake for 1 hour and 20 to 25 minutes. The cake is done when the top is golden brown and firm to the touch, and a wooden skewer inserted deeply in the center comes out clean.

8. Remove the cake from the oven and let stand on a cooling rack for 25 to 30 minutes. Holding the tube, lift the cake from the outer ring and place it on the cooling rack. Let stand for another 20 to 30 minutes. Cover the cake with a cooling rack, invert, and carefully lift off the tube section of the pan and the parchment paper. Cover with another rack and turn the cake top side up to finish cooling. Dust with powdered sugar before serving.

STORAGE: Store under a glass cake dome or tightly covered with plastic wrap for up to 5 days. This cake may be frozen.

"Some desserts are just down-home, sweet comfort food evocative of warm childhood memories."
GEOFFREY ZAKARIAN

sour cream pound cake

MAKES ONE 10-INCH CAKE, 12 TO 16 SERVINGS

Every baker should have a good recipe for a sour cream pound cake in his or her repertoire. Here is one that was passed on to me by my aunt Blanche, whose reputation for being a fabulous baker was well deserved. In her home, a meal never ended without two or three desserts—no wonder I used to love to eat there!

AT A GLANCE
PAN: 10-inch angel food cake pan
PAN PREP: Butter generously/line with parchment/ butter
OVEN TEMP: 325°F
BAKING TIME: 1 hour, 10 to 15 minutes
DIFFICULTY: 🍴

3 cups sifted cake flour, spooned in and leveled

½ teaspoon salt

¼ teaspoon baking soda

1 cup (2 sticks) unsalted butter, slightly firm

2¼ cups superfine sugar

6 large eggs

1 teaspoon pure vanilla extract

1 cup sour cream

Powdered sugar, for dusting

1. Position the rack in the lower third of the oven. Heat the oven to 325°F. Generously butter a 10-inch angel food cake pan, line the bottom with baking parchment, then butter the parchment. Set aside.

2. In a large bowl, thoroughly whisk together the flour, salt, and baking soda. Set aside.

3. Cut the butter into 1-inch pieces and place in the bowl of an electric mixer fitted with the paddle attachment. Mix on medium speed until smooth and lightened in color, about 2 minutes. Add the sugar, 1 to 2 tablespoons at a time, taking 8 to 10 minutes. Blend in the eggs, one at a time, beating thoroughly after each addition. Scrape down the side of the bowl as needed, then add the vanilla.

4. Reduce the mixer speed to low. Add the dry ingredients alternately with the sour cream, dividing the flour mixture into four parts and the sour cream into three parts, beginning and ending with the flour. Scrape down the side of the bowl again.

5. Spoon the batter into the prepared pan and smooth the top with the back of a large soupspoon. Bake for 1 hour and 10 to 15 minutes. The cake is done when the top is golden brown and firm to the touch, and a wooden skewer inserted deeply in the center comes out clean.

6. Remove the cake from the oven and let stand on a cooling rack for 25 to 30 minutes. Holding the tube, lift the cake from the outer ring and place it on the cooling rack. Let stand for another 20 to 30 minutes. Cover the cake with a cooling rack, invert, and carefully lift off the tube section of the pan and the parchment paper. Cover with another rack and turn the cake top side up to finish cooling. Dust with powdered sugar before serving.

STORAGE: Store under a glass cake dome or tightly covered with plastic wrap for up to 7 days. This cake may be frozen.

VARIATION

crystallized ginger pound cake

For a modern twist on this old-fashioned recipe, try folding ½ cup chopped crystallized ginger into the batter after the flour and sour cream have been added in Step 4.

neil's whipped cream pound cake

MAKES ONE 9-INCH BUNDT CAKE, 10 TO 12 SERVINGS

If you've never tried a cake made with whipped cream instead of butter, you are missing a special treat. Just ask my grandson Neil—it's his most requested cake. Thickly whipped cream, folded throughout the vanilla batter, imparts an especially delicate flavor and fine texture. When you whip the cream, be sure to chill the bowl and the mixer's whip attachment beforehand. It's also a good idea to place a carton of cream in the freezer for 15 minutes before whipping to ensure that it is well chilled.

Check out the variations listed below. Shaved bittersweet chocolate added to the batter offers a marvelous flavor contrast to the sweetness of the cream. The cinnamon-nut variation will please those who love nuts and like a little spice in their life.

> **AT A GLANCE**
> PAN: 9-inch Bundt pan
> PAN PREP: Butter generously/flour
> OVEN TEMP: 350°F
> BAKING TIME: 55 to 60 minutes
> DIFFICULTY: 🍵

I cup heavy cream, well chilled

I ½ cups sifted all-purpose flour, spooned in and leveled

I ½ teaspoons baking powder

⅛ teaspoon salt

4 large eggs, at room temperature

I ⅓ cups superfine sugar

I teaspoon pure vanilla extract

Powdered sugar, for dusting

MAKE THE WHIPPED CREAM

1. In a chilled bowl with a chilled whip attachment, whip the cream on medium-low speed until firm peaks form. *Take care not to overwhip the cream, or it will become grainy and will not blend smoothly into the batter.*

MAKE THE BATTER

2. Position the rack in the lower third of the oven. Heat the oven to 350°F. Generously butter a 9-inch Bundt pan, dust with flour, then invert it over the kitchen sink and tap firmly to remove the excess flour. Set aside.

3. In a medium bowl, thoroughly whisk together the flour, baking powder, and salt. Set aside.

4. In the large bowl of an electric mixer fitted with the whip attachment, beat the eggs on medium-high speed for 5 minutes. Add the sugar, 1 tablespoon at a time, taking

about 4 minutes, then blend in the vanilla. Reduce the mixer speed to low and add the dry ingredients in two additions, mixing just until blended. Scrape down the side of the bowl as needed.

5. Remove the bowl from the mixer. Using an oversize rubber spatula, fold in the whipped cream, one-third at a time. Be sure the cream is thoroughly folded through the batter.

FINISH THE CAKE

6. Spoon the batter into the prepared pan and smooth the top with the back of a large soupspoon. Bake for 55 to 60 minutes. The cake is done when the top is golden brown and firm to the touch, and a wooden skewer inserted deeply in the center comes out clean.

7. Remove the cake from the oven and place on a cooling rack for 20 minutes. Invert the pan onto the rack and carefully lift it off. Let the cake cool completely. Dust lightly with powdered sugar before serving.

STORAGE: Store under a glass cake dome or covered with plastic wrap for up to 5 days. This cake may be frozen.

VARIATIONS

whipped cream pound cake with shaved chocolate
At the end of Step 4, gently fold in 1 (3.5-ounce) shaved bar fine-quality bittersweet chocolate, such as Lindt (see pages 387–388). Proceed with the recipe as written.

whipped cream pound cake with cinnamon and nuts
Place ¾ cup walnuts, 2 tablespoons sugar, ½ teaspoon ground cinnamon, and ⅛ teaspoon ground mace or nutmeg in the bowl of a food processor fitted with the steel blade. Process until the nuts are finely chopped. Fold the mixture gently into the batter at the end of Step 4. Proceed with the recipe as written.

black and white pound cake

I can't imagine a collection of pound cake recipes without one for a marble cake. This is a cake that everybody loves: buttery vanilla batter entwined with rich, robust chocolate is a timeless favorite. I guarantee that this cake will be the first one to disappear from a dessert buffet.

AT A GLANCE
PAN: 10-inch angel food cake pan
PREP: Butter generously/line with parchment
OVEN TEMP: 325°F
BAKING TIME: 1 hour, 20 minutes
DIFFICULTY: ☕

4 ounces fine-quality bittersweet chocolate, such as Lindt, coarsely chopped (see pages 387–388)

⅓ cup hot water

3 tablespoons *strained* Dutch-process cocoa powder

1 tablespoon light corn syrup

4 cups sifted cake flour, spooned in and leveled

2 teaspoons baking powder

½ teaspoon salt

6 large eggs

½ cup milk

2 teaspoons pure vanilla extract

1½ cups (3 sticks) unsalted butter, slightly firm

¼ cup canola or vegetable oil

3½ cups strained powdered sugar, spooned in and leveled, plus extra for dusting

¼ teaspoon baking soda

1. Position the rack in the lower third of the oven. Heat the oven to 325°F. Generously butter a 10-inch angel food cake pan with a removable bottom and line the bottom with baking parchment. Set aside.

MAKE THE CHOCOLATE MIXTURE

2. Combine the chocolate, hot water, cocoa powder, and corn syrup in a medium, heatproof bowl. Place the bowl over a pot of simmering water and heat just until the chocolate is melted. Stir to combine and set aside.

MAKE THE BATTER

3. In a large bowl, thoroughly whisk together the flour, baking powder, and salt.

4. Whisk the eggs in a medium bowl. Blend in the milk and vanilla.

5. Cut the butter into 1-inch pieces and place in the bowl of an electric mixer fitted with the paddle attachment. Mix on medium speed until smooth and lightened in

color, about 2 minutes. Slowly drizzle in the oil, taking about 1 minute, then beat for 1 minute longer. Scrape down the side of the bowl.

6. Reduce the speed to medium-low. *If your mixer has a splatter shield attachment, now is a good time to use it.* Add the powdered sugar, 2 to 3 tablespoons at a time, taking 8 to 10 minutes, scraping down the side of the bowl as needed. Slowly pour in ½ cup of the egg mixture and mix for 2 minutes longer.

7. Add the dry ingredients alternately with the remaining egg mixture, dividing the flour into four parts and the egg mixture into three parts, beginning and ending with the flour. Scrape down the side of the bowl as needed.

8. Remove 2 generous cups of the batter and place in a 2-quart bowl. Stir the baking soda into the *tepid* chocolate, then add the chocolate mixture to the 2 cups of batter, gently folding together.

9. Using two large clean spoons, alternate placing large spoonfuls of the chocolate and vanilla batters in the prepared pan, carefully spreading the flavors so they touch. Make a second layer of batter, this time placing spoonfuls of vanilla batter on the chocolate and the chocolate batter on the vanilla. Repeat, alternating the flavors, making about four layers. Insert a kitchen knife into the batter starting about 1 inch from the funnel and circle the pan twice. Do not overwork the batters. Firmly tap the pan two or three times on the counter to level the batter.

FINISH THE CAKE

10. Bake for about 1 hour and 20 minutes. The cake is done when the top is golden brown and firm to the touch, and a wooden skewer inserted deeply in the center comes out clean.

11. Remove the cake from the oven and let stand on a cooling rack for 25 to 30 minutes. Holding the tube, lift the cake from the outer ring and place it on the cooling rack. Let stand for another 20 to 30 minutes. Cover the cake with a cooling rack, invert, and carefully lift off the tube section of the pan and the parchment paper. Cover with another rack and turn the cake top side up to finish cooling. Dust with powdered sugar before serving.

STORAGE: Store under a glass cake dome or covered with plastic wrap for up to 5 days. This cake may be frozen.

vanilla bean pound cake

MAKES ONE 9-INCH BUNDT CAKE, 10 TO 12 SERVINGS

In this elegant Bundt cake, tiny flecks of vanilla bean are scattered throughout a zesty cream cheese batter. If you have the willpower to let the cake stand overnight—admittedly, not an easy feat—you will find that the flavor of the vanilla bean intensifies. Whether paired with fresh fruit or ice cream, or served au naturel, this cake will win you rave reviews.

> **AT A GLANCE**
> **PAN:** 9-inch Bundt pan
> **PAN PREP:** Butter generously/flour
> **OVEN TEMP:** 325°F
> **BAKING TIME:** 1 hour, 10 to 15 minutes
> **DIFFICULTY:** 🍵

1 (6- to 7-inch) vanilla bean

1⅔ cups granulated sugar

2⅓ cups sifted cake flour, spooned in and leveled

½ teaspoon baking powder

½ teaspoon salt

¼ teaspoon baking soda

1 cup (2 sticks) unsalted butter, slightly firm

4 ounces cream cheese, at room temperature, cut into 1-inch pieces

4 large eggs

⅓ cup milk

1 teaspoon pure vanilla extract

Powdered sugar, for dusting

1. Position the rack in the lower third of the oven. Heat the oven to 325°F. Place the vanilla bean on a small cookie sheet and toast for 8 to 10 minutes. Remove from the oven and let cool. Break into 1-inch pieces. *Note:* If the vanilla bean is already brittle, it does not have to be toasted.

2. Place the granulated sugar and vanilla bean pieces in the work bowl of a food processor fitted with the steel blade. Pulse 3 to 4 times, then process for 1 minute. Pulse another 3 to 4 times and process for another minute. Pass the mixture through a fine strainer, discarding any particles of vanilla bean, and set aside.

3. Generously butter a 9-inch Bundt pan, dust with flour, then invert it over the kitchen sink and tap firmly to remove the excess flour. Set aside.

4. In a large bowl, thoroughly whisk together the flour, baking powder, salt, and baking soda. Set aside.

5. In the bowl of an electric mixer fitted with the paddle attachment, process the butter on medium speed until smooth, about 1 minute. Add the cream cheese, 1 piece at a time, and continue to mix until smooth and creamy. Add the sugar, 2 tablespoons

at a time, taking 6 to 8 minutes, scraping down the side of the bowl as needed. Add 2 of the eggs, one at a time, beating for 1 minute after each addition.

6. Whisk the remaining eggs with the milk and vanilla until well blended. Set aside. Reduce the mixer speed to low, and add the dry ingredients alternately with the egg/ milk mixture, dividing the flour mixture into four parts and the liquid into three parts, beginning and ending with the flour. Scrape down the side of the bowl and mix for 10 seconds longer.

7. Spoon the batter into the prepared pan and smooth the top with the back of a large soupspoon. Bake for 1 hour and 10 to 15 minutes. The cake is done when the top is golden brown and firm to the touch, and a wooden skewer inserted deeply in the center of the cake comes out clean.

8. Remove from the oven and place the cake on a cooling rack for about 20 minutes. Invert the pan onto the rack and carefully lift it off. Let the cake cool completely. Dust with powdered sugar before serving.

STORAGE: Store under a glass cake dome or covered with plastic wrap for up to 5 days. This cake may be frozen.

"Plain vanilla is very much like that little black cocktail dress—always welcome, simply chic, so quietly dramatic."
LISA YOCKELSON

butter pecan pound cake

MAKES ONE 9-INCH BUNDT CAKE, 10 TO 12 SERVINGS

The scent of pecans toasting in the oven always causes my taste buds to tingle. For me, the combination of these crunchy nuts, rich, sweet butter, and dark brown sugar is irresistible. Be sure to use Lyle's Golden Syrup for this recipe. This honeylike syrup, so popular in England, adds moistness, color, and a unique flavor to this delectable cake.

AT A GLANCE
PAN: 9-inch Bundt pan
PAN PREP: Butter generously/flour
OVEN TEMP: 325°F
BAKING TIME: 1 hour, 5 to 10 minutes
DIFFICULTY: 🥄

2¼ cups sifted cake flour, spooned in and leveled

¾ teaspoon baking powder

½ teaspoon salt

¼ teaspoon baking soda

1 cup (2 sticks) unsalted butter, slightly firm

2 tablespoons Lyle's Golden Syrup (see page 376)

¾ cup superfine sugar

¾ cup (lightly packed) *very fresh* dark brown sugar

3 large eggs

¾ teaspoon pure vanilla extract

¾ teaspoon caramel extract

½ cup sour cream

1½ cups toasted pecans, coarsely chopped (see pages 391–392)

1. Position the rack in the lower third of the oven. Heat the oven to 325°F. Generously butter a 9-inch Bundt pan, dust with flour, then invert it over the kitchen sink and tap firmly to remove the excess flour. Set aside.

2. In a large bowl, thoroughly whisk together the flour, baking powder, salt, and baking soda. Set aside.

3. Cut the butter into 1-inch pieces and place in the bowl of an electric mixer fitted with the paddle attachment. Mix on medium speed until smooth and lightened in color, about 2 minutes. Stop the machine, add the syrup, and blend for about 2 minutes.

4. Add the superfine sugar, 1 to 2 tablespoons at a time, taking 3 to 4 minutes. Blend in the dark brown sugar, taking another 3 to 4 minutes. Add the eggs, one at a time, about 1 minute apart, scraping down the side of the bowl as needed. Blend in the vanilla and caramel extracts.

5. Reduce the mixer speed to low. Add the flour mixture alternately with the sour cream, dividing the flour into three parts and the sour cream into two parts, beginning and ending with the flour, mixing just until blended after each addition. Scrape down the side of the bowl and mix for about 10 seconds longer.

6. Remove the bowl from the machine, and using a large rubber spatula, fold in the pecans. Empty the batter into the prepared pan and smooth the top with the back of a large soupspoon. Bake for 1 hour and 5 to 10 minutes, or until the top is firm to the touch and a wooden skewer inserted deeply in the center comes out clean.

7. Remove the cake from the oven and place on a cooling rack for 20 minutes. Invert the pan onto the rack and carefully lift it off. Let the cake cool completely.

STORAGE: Store under a glass cake dome or covered with plastic wrap for up to 5 days. This cake may be frozen.

"*Nothing good was ever achieved without enthusiasm.*"

RALPH WALDO EMERSON

chocolate crown pound cake

MAKES ONE 9-INCH BUNDT CAKE, 10 TO 12 SERVINGS

Deep, dark, and decadent, this cake is loaded with chocolate flavor. Be sure to use fine-quality chocolate in this recipe—it will make a difference. Chose the accompaniment of your choice—a frosty glass of milk or a scoop of vanilla ice cream—and enjoy.

> **AT A GLANCE**
> **PAN:** 9-inch Bundt pan
> **PAN PREP:** Butter generously/flour
> **OVEN TEMP:** 350°F
> **BAKING TIME:** 55 to 60 minutes
> **DIFFICULTY:** ♨

6 ounces fine-quality bittersweet chocolate, such as Lindt, chopped (see pages 387–388)

1 tablespoon espresso powder

¼ cup boiling water

2 tablespoons honey

2 cups sifted all-purpose flour, spooned in and leveled

⅓ cup sifted Dutch-process cocoa powder, spooned in and leveled

¾ teaspoon baking powder

½ teaspoon salt

¼ teaspoon baking soda

⅔ cup (1⅓ sticks) unsalted butter, slightly firm

1¼ cups superfine sugar

3 large eggs

1½ teaspoons pure vanilla extract

¾ cup sour cream

Midnight Chocolate Glaze (page 363), optional (see **Note**)

1. Position the rack in the lower third of the oven. Heat the oven to 350°F. Generously butter a 9-inch Bundt pan, dust with flour, then invert it over the kitchen sink and tap firmly to remove the excess flour. Set aside.

2. Place the chocolate in a medium, heatproof bowl. Dissolve the espresso in the boiling water and add it to the chocolate along with the honey. Place the bowl over a pot of simmering water, making sure the bottom of the bowl does not touch the water. Heat until the chocolate is melted, stirring occasionally to blend. Remove the pot from the heat, keeping the bowl over the hot water. (The mixture should remain warm.)

3. In a large bowl, thoroughly whisk together the flour, cocoa powder, baking powder, salt, and baking soda. Set aside.

4. Cut the butter into 1-inch pieces and place in the bowl of an electric mixer fitted with the paddle attachment. Mix on medium speed until smooth and lightened in color, about 2 minutes. Add the sugar, 1 to 2 tablespoons at a time, taking 6 to 8 min-

utes. Add the eggs, one at a time, about 1 minute apart, scraping down the side of the bowl as needed. Blend in the vanilla.

5. Stop the machine and add the warm chocolate mixture, then mix on medium-low speed until blended, scraping down the side of the bowl as needed.

6. Add the dry ingredients alternately with the sour cream, dividing the flour into three parts and the sour cream into two parts, beginning and ending with the flour, mixing well after each addition. Scrape down the side of the bowl again as needed.

7. Empty the batter into the prepared pan and smooth the top with the back of a large soupspoon. Bake for 55 to 60 minutes. The cake is done when the top is firm to the touch and a wooden skewer inserted deeply in the center comes out clean.

8. Remove the cake from the oven and let stand on a cooling rack for 20 minutes. Invert the pan onto the rack and carefully lift it off. While the cake is cooling, make the glaze.

9. While the cake is slightly warm, set the rack on a rimmed cookie sheet lined with wax paper. Spoon the glaze on top of the cake, letting it trickle down the side at random. Let the cake stand until the glaze has completely set.

STORAGE: Store under a glass cake dome or tented with aluminum foil for up to 5 days. This cake may be frozen before glazing.

NOTE: If you wish to omit the glaze, when ready to serve, dust the top with powdered sugar.

"Chocolate is not a privilege: it is a right. As such, it must be provided as a readily available service in every state, in every community, on every block."

SANDRA BOYNTON

lemon cream cheese pound cake

MAKES ONE LARGE LOAF CAKE, 8 TO 10 SERVINGS

Take the zing of lemon, the tang of cream cheese, and the sweetness of sugar and you have an addictive trio of flavors. When you make the batter, be sure the cream cheese is soft; otherwise, it will not blend smoothly with the butter. Serve this dynamite loaf cake for brunch or afternoon tea, or enjoy a slice on the sly when everyone has gone to bed.

AT A GLANCE
PAN: 9 x 5 x 2¾-inch loaf pan
PAN PREP: Butter generously/line with parchment/ butter
OVEN TEMP: 325°F
BAKING TIME: 1 hour, 10 to 15 minutes
DIFFICULTY: 🥄

1¾ cups sifted cake flour, spooned in and leveled

1 teaspoon baking powder

½ teaspoon salt

¾ cup (1½ sticks) unsalted butter, slightly firm

4 teaspoons freshly grated lemon zest

¼ teaspoon lemon oil

4 ounces cream cheese, at room temperature, cut into 1-inch pieces

1¼ cups superfine sugar

3 large eggs, separated

2 tablespoons fresh lemon juice

1 teaspoon pure vanilla extract

⅛ teaspoon cream of tartar

1. Position the rack in the lower third of the oven. Heat the oven to 325°F. Generously butter a 9 x 5 x 2¾-inch loaf pan, line the bottom with baking parchment, then butter the parchment. Set aside.

2. In a medium bowl, thoroughly whisk together the flour, baking powder, and salt. Set aside.

3. Cut the butter into 1-inch pieces and place in the bowl of an electric mixer fitted with the paddle attachment. Add the lemon zest and lemon oil, and mix on medium speed until smooth. Add the cream cheese, one piece at a time, and continue to mix until smooth and creamy. Blend in the sugar, 1 tablespoon at a time, taking 6 to 8 minutes. Add the egg yolks, one at a time, beating well after each addition, scraping down the side of the bowl as needed.

4. Combine the lemon juice and vanilla in a small bowl. Reduce the mixer speed to low and mix in one-half of the dry ingredients, then the lemon juice mixture, and then the remaining dry ingredients, mixing just to incorporate. Empty into a large bowl.

5. In a clean bowl of an electric mixer fitted with the whisk attachment, beat the egg whites on medium speed until frothy. Add the cream of tartar and continue to beat until soft peaks form. Using an oversize rubber spatula, fold one-third of the egg whites into the batter, using about 20 strokes to blend. Fold in the remaining whites, one-half at a time, using about 40 strokes to incorporate.

6. Spoon the batter into the prepared pan and smooth the top with the back of a large soupspoon. Bake for 1 hour and 10 to 15 minutes. The cake is done when the top is golden brown and firm to the touch, and a wooden skewer inserted deeply in the center comes out clean.

7. Remove the cake from the oven and let stand on a cooling rack for 20 minutes. Turn the loaf pan on its side and carefully ease the cake from the pan. When the cake is cool enough to handle, remove the parchment paper, turn the loaf top side up, and cool completely on the rack.

STORAGE: Store under a glass cake dome or tightly covered with plastic wrap for up to 5 days. This cake may be frozen.

VARIATION

poppy seed lemon cream cheese pound cake

Whisk 3 tablespoons poppy seeds into the flour mixture in Step 2 and proceed with the recipe.

blueberry pound cake

MAKES ONE 9-INCH BUNDT CAKE, 10 TO 12 SERVINGS

Sweet blueberries are mingled through a creamy lemon-scented batter in this delicious pound cake. As with most pound cakes, I like the cake to mature overnight to allow the flavor of the berries to permeate the delicate crumb. Be sure to follow the directions carefully for layering the batter and berries, and don't get overzealous with the amount of berries that you use. Too much of a good thing is not always a good thing.

AT A GLANCE
PAN: 9-inch Bundt pan
PAN PREP: Butter generously/flour
OVEN TEMP: 325°F
BAKING TIME: 1 hour, 15 to 20 minutes
DIFFICULTY: ☕

2⅓ cups plus 2 teaspoons sifted all-purpose flour, spooned in and leveled

½ teaspoon baking powder

¼ teaspoon salt

4 large eggs

1 cup (2 sticks) unsalted butter, slightly firm

2 teaspoons freshly grated lemon zest

3 tablespoons canola or vegetable oil

2¾ cups strained powdered sugar, spooned in and leveled

1½ teaspoons pure vanilla extract

1½ cups fresh blueberries, washed and well dried (see page 390)

1. Position the rack in the lower third of the oven. Heat the oven to 325°F. Generously butter a 9-inch Bundt pan, dust with flour, then invert it over the kitchen sink and tap firmly to remove the excess flour. Set aside.

2. In a large bowl, thoroughly whisk together 2⅓ cups of the flour, the baking powder, and salt. Set aside.

3. Place the eggs in a medium bowl and whisk until well blended. Set aside.

4. Cut the butter into 1-inch pieces and place in the bowl of an electric mixer fitted with the paddle attachment. Add the lemon zest and mix on medium speed until smooth and lightened in color, about 2 minutes. Slowly drizzle in the oil, taking about 1 minute, then mix for 2 minutes longer. Scrape down the side of the bowl.

5. Reduce the mixer speed to medium-low. *If your mixer has a splatter shield attachment, now is a good time to use it.* Add the powdered sugar, 2 to 3 tablespoons at a time, taking 6 to 8 minutes, then blend in the vanilla. Gradually beat in ¼ cup of the eggs. Scrape down the side of the bowl.

6. Reduce the mixer speed to low and add the flour mixture alternately with the remaining eggs, dividing the dry ingredients into three parts and the eggs into two parts, beginning and ending with the flour, mixing until well blended after each addition. Scrape down the side of the bowl again as needed.

7. Spread one-fourth of the batter in the prepared pan. Gently toss the blueberries with the remaining 2 teaspoons flour, then sprinkle ⅓ cup of the berries evenly over the batter, pressing them in gently. To layer the remaining batter and blueberries, spread about one-fourth of the batter to barely cover the first layer of berries, then press in one-third of the remaining blueberries. Alternate the remaining batter and blueberries, using just enough batter to cover the berries each time. You should have about five layers of batter and four layers of berries.

8. Bake for 1 hour and 15 to 20 minutes. The cake is done when the top is golden brown and springy to the touch, and a wooden skewer inserted deeply in the center comes out clean.

9. Remove the cake from the oven and place on a cooling rack for about 20 minutes. Invert the pan onto the rack and gently lift it off. Let the cake cool completely.

STORAGE: Store under a glass cake dome or tightly covered with aluminum foil for up to 3 days. This cake may be frozen.

dried cherry almond pound cake

MAKES ONE 10-INCH BUNDT CAKE, 10 TO 12 SERVINGS

This pound cake is loaded with really good stuff! The sour cream batter, made with almond paste and orange zest, is studded with Amaretto-plumped dried cherries and crunchy toasted almonds. You will find that the flavors become even better as this cake mellows with age.

AT A GLANCE
PAN: 10-inch Bundt pan
PAN PREP: Butter generously/flour
OVEN TEMP: 325°F
BAKING TIME: 1 hour, 10 minutes
DIFFICULTY: 🥄

1 cup sliced unblanched almonds, toasted (see page 391)

⅔ cup dried cherries (not organic)

3 tablespoons Amaretto liqueur

2 cups sifted all-purpose flour, spooned in and leveled

½ teaspoon baking powder

¼ teaspoon salt

⅛ teaspoon baking soda

1 cup (2 sticks) unsalted butter, slightly firm

2 teaspoons freshly grated navel orange zest

½ cup (2½ ounces) shredded almond paste (see page 391)

1¼ cups superfine sugar

4 large eggs

1 teaspoon pure vanilla extract

¼ teaspoon pure almond extract

½ cup sour cream

Powdered sugar, for dusting

1. Position the rack in the lower third of the oven. Heat the oven to 325°F. Generously butter a 10-inch Bundt pan, dust with flour, then invert it over the kitchen sink and tap firmly to remove the excess flour. Set aside.

2. Place the toasted almonds in a medium bowl and crumble them with your hands. Sprinkle 2 to 3 tablespoons of the crumbled nuts evenly on the bottom of the pan. Set the remaining almonds aside.

3. Place the cherries in a small bowl. Add enough boiling water to cover the cherries and let stand for 5 minutes to soften. Drain and blot dry on paper towels. Coarsely chop the cherries, then return to the bowl and add the Amaretto. Cover the bowl and let steep while preparing the batter.

4. In a medium bowl, thoroughly whisk together the flour, baking powder, salt, and baking soda. Set aside.

5. Cut the butter into 1-inch pieces and place in the bowl of an electric mixer fitted with the paddle attachment. Add the orange zest and mix on medium speed until smooth. Add the almond paste in three additions and beat until smooth and lightened in color, about 2 minutes.

6. Add the sugar, 2 to 3 tablespoons at a time, taking 4 to 6 minutes and scraping down the side of the bowl as needed. Add the eggs, one at a time, beating thoroughly after each addition, then blend in the extracts.

7. Reduce the mixer speed to low. Add the dry ingredients alternately with the sour cream, dividing the flour into three parts and the sour cream into two parts, beginning and ending with the flour, mixing just until blended after each addition. Scrape down the side of the bowl again.

8. Remove the bowl from the machine, and using a large rubber spatula, fold in the almonds and well-drained cherries. Empty the batter into the prepared pan and smooth the top with the back of a large soupspoon. Bake for about 1 hour and 10 minutes. The cake is done when the top is golden brown and firm to the touch, and a wooden skewer inserted deeply in the center comes out clean.

9. Remove the cake from the oven and place on a cooling rack for about 20 minutes. Invert the pan onto the rack and carefully lift it off. Let the cake cool completely. Dust with powdered sugar before serving.

STORAGE: Store under a glass cake dome or tightly covered with plastic wrap for up to 5 days. This cake may be frozen.

"As far as I'm concerned, a meal is not complete without a sweet thing or two at the end."

CHARLIE TROTTER

nut-crusted orange pound cake

MAKES ONE 10-INCH BUNDT CAKE, 10 TO 12 SERVINGS

Nothing beats the refreshing flavor of orange blended with sweet, creamy butter. And that is just what we have here. The batter—with lots of freshly grated orange zest—is poured into a nut-crusted pan. As the cake bakes, the sugar melts and forms a crunchy nut surface, a perfect contrast to the velvety texture of the pound cake.

> **AT A GLANCE**
> **PAN:** 10-inch Bundt pan
> **PAN PREP:** Butter generously
> **OVEN TEMP:** 350°F
> **BAKING TIME:** 55 to 60 minutes
> **DIFFICULTY:** 🥄 🥄

¾ cup walnuts

2 tablespoons granulated sugar

3 cups sifted cake flour, spooned in and leveled

½ teaspoon baking soda

½ teaspoon salt

5 large eggs

1¼ cups (2½ sticks) unsalted butter, slightly firm

2 tablespoons freshly grated navel orange zest

3 cups strained powdered sugar, spooned in and leveled

1½ teaspoons pure vanilla extract

⅓ cup fresh navel orange juice

1. Position the rack in the lower third of the oven. Heat the oven to 350°F.

2. Place the walnuts and granulated sugar in the work bowl of a food processor fitted with the steel blade. Pulse 6 to 8 times to medium-fine pieces. Do not overprocess; the nuts should retain some texture.

3. Generously butter a 10-inch Bundt pan. Working with 1 tablespoon of the nut mixture at a time, tilt the pan, hold the spoon on the rim, and let the nut mixture run down the side into the pan. Continue the process while rotating the pan until the entire pan is coated with nuts. Be sure to coat the side of the funnel as well. Chill the pan while preparing the batter, taking care not to jar the nut crust. It's okay if some of the nuts drop down to the bottom of the pan.

4. In a large bowl, thoroughly whisk together the flour, baking soda, and salt. Set aside.

5. Place the eggs in a medium bowl and whisk until well blended. Set aside.

6. Cut the butter into 1-inch pieces and place in the bowl of an electric mixer fitted with the paddle attachment. Add the lemon zest and mix on medium speed until smooth and lightened in color, about 2 minutes.

7. Reduce the mixer speed to medium-low. *If your mixer has a splatter shield attachment, now is a good time to use it.* Add the powdered sugar, 1 to 2 tablespoons at a time, taking 6 to 8 minutes. Add the beaten eggs in four additions, taking 4 to 5 minutes. Mix well after each addition. Blend in the vanilla and mix for another 2 minutes.

8. On low speed, add the dry ingredients alternately with the orange juice, dividing the flour mixture into three parts and the liquid into two parts, starting and ending with the flour. Spoon the batter into the prepared pan, being careful not to disturb the nut crust, and smooth the top with the back of a large soupspoon. Bake for 55 to 60 minutes, or until the top is golden brown and firm to the touch, and a wooden skewer inserted deeply in the center comes out clean.

9. Remove the cake from the oven and place on a cooling rack for 10 to 15 minutes. Invert the hot cake onto the rack and carefully lift off the pan. Let the cake cool completely.

STORAGE: Store under a glass cake dome or tightly covered with aluminum foil for up to 1 week. This cake may be frozen.

plum-topped pound cake squares

MAKES ONE 9 X 13 X 2-INCH CAKE, TWENTY 2 X 2¼-INCH SERVINGS

These enticing squares are made with overlapping slices of rosy pink plums that rest on a dreamy pound cake layer, drizzled with vanilla glaze. When serving the plum cake squares, warm them slightly, and don't forget to take out the vanilla ice cream. You'll be in for quite a treat!

AT A GLANCE
PAN: 9 x 13 x 2-inch baking pan
PAN PREP: Butter generously
OVEN TEMP: 350°F
BAKING TIME: 50 to 55 minutes
DIFFICULTY: 🍮 🍮

1¾ pounds dark-skinned plums, such as Princess, Santa Rosa, or Black Diamond (about 8 medium)

BATTER

2 cups sifted cake flour, spooned in and leveled

1 teaspoon baking powder

¼ teaspoon salt

3 large eggs

¾ cup (1½ sticks) unsalted butter, slightly firm

2 tablespoons canola or vegetable oil

1¾ cups strained powdered sugar, spooned in and leveled, plus extra for dusting

1 teaspoon pure vanilla extract

7 to 8 drops lemon oil

2 teaspoons fresh lemon juice

4 teaspoons granulated sugar

½ teaspoon ground cinnamon

1 large recipe Vanilla Glaze (page 359), substituting half-and-half or milk for the water

PREPARE THE PLUMS

1. Wipe the plums with moistened paper towels. Cut them in half lengthwise and remove the pits. Lay the halves skin side up on a cutting board, and using a serrated knife, cut them crosswise (across the pit cavity) into ⅜-inch slices.

MAKE THE BATTER

2. Position the rack in the middle of the oven. Heat the oven to 350°F. Generously butter a 9 × 13 × 2-inch pan and set aside.

3. In a medium bowl, thoroughly whisk together the flour, baking powder, and salt. Set aside.

4. Place the eggs in a medium bowl and whisk until well blended.

5. Cut the butter into 1-inch pieces and place in the bowl of an electric mixer fitted with the paddle attachment. Mix on medium speed until smooth and lightened in color, about 2 minutes. Slowly drizzle in the canola oil, taking about 1 minute, then beat for 2 minutes longer. Scrape down the side of the bowl.

6. Reduce the mixer speed to medium-low. *If your mixer has a splatter shield attachment, now is a good time to use it.* Add the powdered sugar, 2 to 3 tablespoons at a time, taking 4 to 6 minutes. Gradually add ¼ cup of the eggs and beat for 2 minutes longer, scraping down the side of the bowl as needed. Blend in the vanilla and lemon oil.

7. Add the flour mixture alternately with the remaining eggs, dividing the flour into three parts and the eggs into two parts, mixing until well blended after each addition. Scrape down the side of the bowl as needed. Empty the batter into the prepared pan and smooth the top with a small offset spatula.

8. Arrange the plum slices, slightly overlapping, making five rows across the wide side of the pan. Sprinkle the lemon juice over the plums.

FINISH THE CAKE

9. In a small bowl, combine the granulated sugar and ground cinnamon. Sprinkle the mixture evenly over the plums and bake for 50 to 55 minutes. The cake is done when the top of the cake shows signs of browning and a toothpick inserted in the center comes out clean. While the cake is baking, make the glaze.

10. Remove the cake from the oven and let stand on a cooling rack. While the cake is slightly warm, drizzle the top with glaze. When ready to serve, cut into 2 × 2¼-inch squares. This cake is best enjoyed the day it is made.

STORAGE: Store lightly covered with aluminum foil for up to 1 day. This cake may be frozen.

home-style coffee cakes

Classic Sour Cream Cinnamon and Nut Coffee Cake

Banana Chocolate Chip Cake

VARIATION: *Banana Nut Cake*

Butter Crumb Coffee Cake

Sour Cream Coffee Cake with Chocolate and Nuts

Chocolate Chocolate Streusel Squares

Sour Cream Marble Cake

Pineapple Squares with Toasted Coconut Streusel

Apple Walnut Caramel Kuchen

Blueberry Buckle

Brown Butter Almond Cake

Fruit and Nut Applesauce Cake

Caramel-Glazed Blackberry Jam Cake

Carrot Honey Cake

Honey Spice Squares

Toasted Pecan Eggnog Ring

Irish Whiskey Cake

Golden Apple Upside-Down Gingerbread Cake

Greek Semolina Coffee Cake with Orange Syrup

ABOUT HOME-STYLE COFFEE CAKES

Most home-style coffee cakes fall under a category known as "creamed butter cakes," a method of mixing butter that dates as far back as the colonial days. *Creaming* means to beat or mix air into the butter until it becomes very light in color, sometimes almost white, resulting in a finely textured cake.

For these types of cakes, it is essential that the butter be at a temperature that air can be incorporated into it without the butter breaking down and becoming too soft. Butter that is too soft loses the ability to hold air, resulting in a heavy-textured cake. My motto is "What starts out wrong, ends up wrong"; so, always be mindful of the temperature of the butter when you begin your cake.

Batters can also be made with oils made from vegetables, fruits, or nuts. These oils are used exclusively or are combined with butter. Because oils are fluid, they lack the ability to hold air, and the method of incorporating them differs. Cakes that are made with oil have a texture that is moist, rather than velvety.

Here are some tips to ensure successful home-style coffee cakes:

• Determine the correct temperature of the butter. If you are using an electric mixer, the butter should be slightly firm. You should be able to leave an imprint when you press it with your fingertips. If you are making the batter by hand, the butter should be soft enough to spread.

• When beating or mixing butter in an electric mixer, cut the sticks of butter into 1-inch chunks. For batters that are made by hand, cut the butter into ½-inch dice.

• Adding sugar gradually, over an extended period of time, is crucial to the success of a butter-style cake. If sugar is added too quickly, the mixture does not receive enough aeration and the structure of the batter will be affected. The cake will not rise as high, and the crumb or texture will be coarse.

• If the butter/sugar mixture becomes too soft during the mixing process, use *cold* eggs, milk, or other liquids as specified in the recipe. This will help firm up the consistency of the batter.

• Pay attention to the time specified in individual recipes for adding the dry ingredients. They should be blended just until incorporated to prevent the formation of gluten, which toughens the cake.

• If mixing a batter in a stand mixer, be sure to stop the machine and scrape frequently around the side of the bowl and under the paddle attachment. It is important that all of the ingredients in the bowl be thoroughly combined.

- It's okay to modify the flavor of a vanilla batter by adding spices, flavor extracts, or citrus zests. These additions will not affect the consistency of the batter, and you can create flavors to your own taste.

- Stand mixers with a paddle attachment can be used for blending in coarse ingredients such as nuts and dried fruits into batters. However, these ingredients must be mixed briefly. Overmixing some fruits, such as dried cherries or figs, can change the color of the batter.

- To easily remove a baked cake from a warm pan, it is helpful to wear rubber gloves. They give a firmer grip, which prevents the pan from slipping and will protect your hands.

- When inverting a cake with a streusel topping, to remove the pan, place a 12-inch strip of aluminum foil over the top of the cake and cup it around the pan. Invert the cake onto a rack, remove the pan, invert it again, and carefully remove the aluminum foil.

- It is better to dust a cake with powdered sugar just before serving. When cakes are garnished ahead of time, the sugar often melts into the cake. This is especially true in warm or humid weather.

- To achieve a clean cut when slicing most butter-style cakes, use a knife with a serrated blade, such as a bread knife. Move the knife back and forth in a sawing motion, rather than cutting straight down.

classic sour cream cinnamon and nut coffee cake

MAKES ONE 10-INCH CAKE, 16 TO 20 SERVINGS

When I began this book, this was one recipe that I knew I wanted to include. It was given to me by my good friend Mariette Bronstein, a superb cook and baker. The memory of my first taste of this cake in her home stayed with me for years. The brown sugar and toasted pecans form a crunchy crust that is absolutely addictive. Although many recipes for this type of cake exist, I think this one is extra special.

AT A GLANCE
PAN: 10-inch angel food cake pan
PAN PREP: Butter generously/line with parchment/ butter
OVEN TEMP: 350°F
BAKING TIME: 1 hour, 10 to 15 minutes
DIFFICULTY: 🥄

1½ cups sour cream

1 teaspoon baking soda

NUT MIXTURE

1¼ cups toasted pecans (see page 391)

3 tablespoons granulated sugar

2 tablespoons dark brown sugar

½ teaspoon ground cinnamon

BATTER

3 cups sifted all-purpose flour, spooned in and leveled

2 teaspoons baking powder

1 teaspoon salt

1 cup (2 sticks) unsalted butter, slightly firm

1¾ cups superfine sugar

3 large eggs

1 teaspoon pure vanilla extract

1. In a small bowl, stir together the sour cream and baking soda. Let stand at room temperature for 1 hour.

2. Position the rack in the lower third of the oven. Heat the oven to 350°F. Generously butter a 10-inch angel food cake pan, line the bottom with baking parchment, then butter the parchment. Set aside.

MAKE THE NUT MIXTURE

3. Place the pecans, granulated and dark brown sugars, and cinnamon in the work bowl of a food processor fitted with the steel blade. Pulse 5 to 6 times, or until the nuts are medium chopped. Set aside.

Great COFFEE CAKES,
STICKY BUNS, MUFFINS & MORE

contents

For **KATHIE FINN-REDDEN**
My clever, smart, and mischievous
culinary partner and dear friend,
who filled my days with laughter.
Love ya, gal.
F.

All rights reserved.
Published in the United States by Clarkson Potter/Publishers,
an imprint of the Crown Publishing Group,
a division of Random House, Inc., New York.
www.crownpublishing.com
www.clarksonpotter.com

Clarkson N. Potter is a trademark and Potter and colophon
are registered trademarks of Random House, Inc.

Library of Congress Cataloging-in-Publication Data
Walter, Carole.
    Great coffee cakes, sticky buns, muffins & more :
200 anytime treats and special sweets for morning to
midnight / Carole Walter.
    Includes index.
    1. Baking.   2. Coffee cakes.   I. Title.
    TX765.W33   2007
    641.8'15—dc22   2007006730

ISBN 978-0-307-23755-2

Printed in the U.S.A.

Design by Maggie Hinders
Photographs by Duane K. Winfield
Illustrations by Meredith Hamilton

10 9 8 7 6 5 4 3 2 1

First Edition

Great COFFEE CAKES, STICKY BUNS, MUFFINS & MORE

200 ANYTIME TREATS AND SPECIAL SWEETS FOR MORNING TO MIDNIGHT

Carole Walter

CLARKSON POTTER/PUBLISHERS
NEW YORK

MAKE THE BATTER

4. In a large bowl, thoroughly whisk together the flour, baking powder, and salt, and set aside.

5. Cut the butter into 1-inch pieces and place in the bowl of an electric mixer fitted with the paddle attachment. Mix on medium speed until smooth and lightened in color, about 2 minutes. Add the superfine sugar, 1 to 2 tablespoons at a time, taking 6 to 8 minutes. Add the eggs, one at a time, beating for 1 minute after each addition, scraping down the side of the bowl as needed. Blend in the vanilla.

6. Reduce the mixer speed to low. Add the flour mixture alternately with the sour cream, dividing the flour into four parts and the sour cream into three parts, beginning and ending with the flour, mixing until just blended after each addition. Scrape down the side of the bowl again.

7. Spoon two-thirds of the batter into the prepared pan. Sprinkle one-half of the nut mixture evenly over the batter. Cover the mixture with the remaining batter, distributing it evenly over the nuts. Smooth the batter with the back of a large soupspoon or a small offset spatula, spreading it to the side of the pan first, before spreading it toward the center. (*To prevent the nut mixture from being disturbed, do not pick up the spoon as the batter is spread.*) Sprinkle with the remaining nut mixture, pressing it gently into the batter with a clean soupspoon.

FINISH THE CAKE

8. Bake for 1 hour and 10 to 15 minutes. The cake is done when the top is golden brown and springy to the touch, and a wooden skewer or toothpick inserted deeply in the center comes out clean.

9. Remove the cake from the oven and let stand on a cooling rack for 25 to 30 minutes. Holding the tube, lift the cake from the outer ring and place it on the cooling rack. Let stand for another 20 to 30 minutes. To remove the cake from the tube section, cut a 2-inch hole in the center of a 12-inch piece of aluminum foil and place it directly on top of the cake, cupping the foil around the side to hold the topping in place. Cover with a cooling rack, invert the cake, and carefully lift off the tube section and the parchment paper. Cover with another rack and invert again. Remove the aluminum foil and cool right side up.

STORAGE: Store under a glass cake dome or tightly covered with plastic wrap for up to 5 days. This cake may be frozen.

banana chocolate chip cake

MAKES ONE 10-INCH BUNDT CAKE, 10 TO 12 SERVINGS

One of my assistants, Judy Epstein, has two teens with
terrific taste buds. After we sent home various cakes for them
to sample, Cory and Hannah wanted to know when I was
finally going to make their favorite, a Banana Chocolate
Chip Cake. When I did, it passed muster with flying colors,
and that was good enough for me.

AT A GLANCE
PAN: 10-inch Bundt pan
PAN PREP: Butter generously/flour
OVEN TEMP: 350°F
BAKING TIME: 55 to 60 minutes
DIFFICULTY: 🍴

Be sure to use mini chips because larger ones will sink to the bottom of the pan. And, for an even-textured
cake, take the time to strain the pureed bananas. The finished cake will be so much better. Just ask Cory and
Hannah!

2½ cups sifted cake flour, spooned in and leveled	1 teaspoon pure vanilla extract
1 teaspoon baking soda	¾ teaspoon banana extract
½ teaspoon salt	¾ cup (1½ sticks) unsalted butter, slightly firm
½ teaspoon mace	1¼ cups superfine sugar
2 large, very ripe bananas	3 large eggs
1 teaspoon lemon juice	½ cup mini chocolate chips
¾ cup sour cream	1 large recipe Vanilla Glaze (page 359)

1. Position the rack in the lower third of the oven. Heat the oven to 350°F. Generously butter a 10-inch Bundt pan, dust with flour, then invert it over the kitchen sink
and tap firmly to remove the excess flour. Set aside.

2. In a large bowl, thoroughly whisk together the flour, baking soda, salt, and mace.
Set aside.

3. Cut the bananas into 1-inch pieces and place with the lemon juice in the work
bowl of a food processor fitted with the steel blade. Process for 30 seconds, then stop
the machine and scrape down the side of the bowl. Process for another 10 seconds, or
until the bananas are pureed. Strain the puree through a medium-gauge strainer. You
should have a generous cupful. Stir the sour cream and extracts into the bananas and
set aside.

4. Cut the butter into 1-inch pieces and place in the bowl of an electric mixer fitted with the paddle attachment. Mix on medium speed until smooth and lightened in color, about 2 minutes. Add the sugar, 1 to 2 tablespoons at a time, taking 6 to 8 minutes. Blend in the eggs, one at a time, beating thoroughly after each addition, scraping down the side of the bowl as needed.

5. Reduce the mixer speed to low and add the dry ingredients alternately with the banana/sour cream mixture, dividing the flour mixture into four parts and the liquid into three parts, beginning and ending with the flour. Scrape down the side of the bowl, then mix for 10 to 15 seconds longer. Remove the bowl from the machine, and using a large rubber spatula, fold in the mini chocolate chips.

6. Spoon the batter into the prepared pan. Smooth the surface with the back of a large soupspoon and bake for 55 to 60 minutes. The cake is done when the top is golden brown and firm to the touch, and a wooden skewer inserted deeply in the center comes out clean.

7. Remove the cake from the oven and let stand on a cooling rack for 10 minutes. Invert the pan onto the rack and carefully lift it off. As the cake is cooling, prepare the vanilla glaze. While the cake is still warm, place a piece of parchment or wax paper under the rack and spoon the glaze onto the cake. The glaze will harden as the cake cools.

STORAGE: Store under a glass cake dome or tightly covered with aluminum foil for up to 7 days. This cake may be frozen before glazing.

VARIATION

banana nut cake
Omit the mini chips and fold in ½ to ¾ cup medium-chopped pecans or walnuts.

"Cuisine is when things taste like themselves."
MAURICE SAILLAND, AKA CURNONSKY

butter crumb coffee cake

MAKES ONE 10-INCH CAKE, 10 TO 12 SERVINGS

This simple cake is one that you will make over and over again. The batter is made by hand in one bowl, then scraped into a springform pan and topped with lots of streusel crumbs. The scent of the cinnamon and butter as the cake bakes is almost as enticing as the sugary, plump crumbs sitting atop the finished cake.

AT A GLANCE
PAN: 10-inch springform pan
PAN PREP: Butter generously/line with parchment/ butter
OVEN TEMP: 350°F
BAKING TIME: 40 to 45 minutes
DIFFICULTY: 🍵

1 large recipe **Carole's Favorite Streusel** (page 350)

2 cups sifted **all-purpose flour, spooned in and leveled**

¾ cup **granulated sugar**

1 tablespoon **baking powder**

½ teaspoon **salt**

½ cup (1 stick) **unsalted butter, cut into ½-inch cubes, at room temperature**

1 large **egg**

⅔ cup **milk**

1 teaspoon **pure vanilla extract**

Powdered sugar, for dusting

1. Prepare a large recipe of Carole's Favorite Streusel. Set aside.

2. Position the rack in the lower third of the oven. Heat the oven to 350°F. Generously butter a 10-inch springform pan, line the bottom with baking parchment, then butter the parchment. Set aside.

3. In a large bowl, thoroughly whisk together the flour, granulated sugar, baking powder, and salt. Add the butter and work with your fingertips until fine crumbs are formed.

4. In a medium bowl, whisk together the egg, milk, and vanilla. Make a well in the center of the flour mixture and add the liquid. Using a wooden spoon, gradually push the crumbs into the liquid, beginning with the crumbs in the center of the bowl and gradually working toward the edge of the bowl. Beat for about 1 minute, or until the batter is smooth. (Note: the batter will be thick.)

5. Scrape the batter into the prepared pan and smooth the top with the back of a large soupspoon or an offset spatula. Take a handful of the streusel crumbs and squeeze gently to form a large clump. Then break the clump apart, and sprinkle the crumbs onto the batter. Repeat until all of the streusel mixture has been used. Lightly press the streusel onto the batter.

6. Set the pan on a 12-inch strip of aluminum foil and bake the cake for 40 to 45 minutes, or until the top is golden brown and firm to the touch, and a toothpick inserted in the center comes out clean.

7. Remove the cake from the oven and let stand on a cooling rack for 20 to 25 minutes, then remove the outer ring. Place a 12-inch piece of aluminum foil directly on top of the cake, cupping it around the side to hold the topping in place. Cover with a cooling rack, invert the cake, and carefully lift off the bottom of the pan and peel off the parchment paper. Cover with another rack, invert again, remove the aluminum foil, and cool right side up. Just before serving, dust with powdered sugar.

STORAGE: Store under a glass cake dome or tightly covered with aluminum foil for up to 5 days. This cake may be frozen.

sour cream coffee cake with chocolate and nuts

MAKES ONE 10-INCH BUNDT CAKE, 10 TO 12 SERVINGS

For those of you who like your sour cream coffee cakes made with chocolate as well as cinnamon and nuts, this is the cake for you. Instead of cocoa powder in the filling, I use high-quality ground chocolate. The flavor of the chocolate marries extremely well with the buttery batter and the rich tang of the sour cream.

AT A GLANCE
PAN: 10-inch Bundt pan
PAN PREP: Butter generously/flour
OVEN TEMP: 350°F
BAKING TIME: 55 to 60 minutes
DIFFICULTY: 🍶 🍶

CHOCOLATE MIXTURE

2 ounces fine-quality, bittersweet chocolate, such as Lindt (see page 387)

1 cup walnuts or pecans

¼ cup granulated sugar

3 tablespoons light brown sugar

1 teaspoon ground cinnamon

BATTER

1¼ cups sour cream

½ teaspoon baking soda

2½ cups sifted cake flour, spooned in and leveled

1½ teaspoons baking powder

½ teaspoon salt

¾ cup (1½ sticks) unsalted butter, slightly firm

1¼ cups superfine sugar

4 large eggs, separated

1½ teaspoons pure vanilla extract

¼ cup milk

Powdered sugar, for dusting

1. Position the rack in the lower third of the oven. Heat the oven to 350°F. Generously butter a 10-inch Bundt pan, dust with flour, then invert it over the kitchen sink and tap firmly to remove the excess flour. Set aside.

MAKE THE CHOCOLATE MIXTURE

2. Break the chocolate into 1-inch pieces and place in the work bowl of a food processor fitted with the steel blade. Pulse until the chocolate is finely chopped. Add the walnuts, granulated and light brown sugars, and cinnamon, and pulse again until the nuts are finely chopped, 6 to 7 times. Set aside.

MAKE THE BATTER

3. In a small bowl, stir together the sour cream and baking soda.

4. In a large bowl, whisk together the flour, baking powder, and salt. Set aside.

5. Cut the butter into 1-inch pieces and place in the bowl of an electric mixer fitted with the paddle attachment. Mix on medium speed for 2 minutes, then add 1 cup of the sugar, 1 to 2 tablespoons at a time, taking 4 to 6 minutes. Add the egg yolks, two at a time, beating for 30 seconds after each addition. Scrape down the side of the bowl. Blend in the vanilla.

6. Reduce the mixer speed to low. Stir the milk into the sour cream mixture and add it alternately with the flour, dividing the flour into three parts and the sour cream into two parts, beginning and ending with the flour, mixing until just blended after each addition. Scrape down the side of the bowl as needed.

7. In a clean bowl of an electric mixer fitted with the whip attachment, beat the egg whites on medium speed until frothy. Increase the mixer speed to medium high and whip until soft peaks form. Add the remaining ¼ cup superfine sugar, 1 tablespoon at a time, taking about 15 seconds. Beat for another 15 seconds.

8. Using a large rubber spatula, fold one-third of the whites into the batter, taking about 20 turns to incorporate. Fold in the remaining whites, taking about 40 more turns.

FINISH THE CAKE

9. Spoon about one-third of the batter into the prepared pan. Sprinkle one-third of the chocolate mixture evenly over the top. Cover the mixture with half of the remaining batter, distributing it evenly. Smooth the top with the back of a large soupspoon or a small offset spatula, spreading the batter to the side of the pan first, before spreading it toward the center. (*To prevent the chocolate layer from being disturbed, do not pick up the spoon as the batter is spread.*) Sprinkle the remaining chocolate mixture over the top, then cover it with the rest of the batter.

10. To marbleize the batter, use a table knife, and cut into the batter *almost* to the bottom of the pan. Gently lift the knife up and over, about eight times, folding the batter and filling together while rotating the pan.

11. Bake the cake for 55 to 60 minutes. The cake is done when the top is golden brown and springy to the touch, and a wooden skewer inserted deeply in the center comes out clean. Remove the cake from the oven and let stand on a cooling rack for 20 minutes. Cover with a cooling rack, invert the cake, and carefully lift off the pan. Just before serving, dust with powdered sugar.

STORAGE: Store under a glass cake dome or tightly covered with plastic wrap for up to 5 days. This cake may be frozen.

chocolate chocolate streusel squares

This chocolate-packed coffee cake is a chocoholic's dream. Rich sour cream pairs with cocoa powder and unsweetened chocolate to make a cake with a tender, melt-in-your-mouth crumb. In keeping with the chocolate theme, I top the batter with buttery chocolate streusel and then add mini chocolate chips and chopped walnuts for a bit of pizzazz.

AT A GLANCE

PAN: 9 x 13 x 2-inch baking pan

PAN PREP: Butter generously

OVEN TEMP: 350°F

BAKING TIME: 30 to 35 minutes

DIFFICULTY: 🍮

---

1 recipe **Chocolate Streusel (page 354)**

1¼ cups sifted all-purpose flour, spooned in and leveled

¼ cup strained Dutch-process cocoa powder

¾ teaspoon baking powder

¼ teaspoon salt

3 ounces unsweetened chocolate, coarsely chopped

6 tablespoons (¾ stick) unsalted butter

2 tablespoons canola or vegetable oil

2 large eggs

⅔ cup granulated sugar

⅓ cup (lightly packed) *very fresh* dark brown sugar

1 teaspoon pure vanilla extract

¾ cup sour cream

FINISHING

⅓ cup mini chocolate chips

½ cup medium-chopped walnuts (see page 392)

---

1. Prepare the Chocolate Streusel. Set aside.

2. Position the rack in the middle of the oven. Heat the oven to 350°F. Generously butter a 9 × 13 × 2-inch pan and set aside.

3. In a medium bowl, thoroughly whisk together the flour, cocoa powder, baking powder, and salt. Set aside.

4. Place the chocolate, butter, and oil in a medium, heatproof bowl and set over a pot of simmering water. (The bottom of the bowl should not touch the water.) Heat until the chocolate is melted, stirring occasionally. Keep warm.

5. Place the eggs in the bowl of an electric mixer fitted with the whip attachment. Beat on medium-high speed for 2 minutes. Add the granulated sugar, then the dark brown sugar, 1 to 2 tablespoons at a time, taking 2 minutes for each. Add the vanilla and beat for 1 minute longer. The mixture should be thick.

6. Reduce the speed to medium and add the warm chocolate mixture, mixing for 2 minutes to blend. Scrape down the side of the bowl as needed.

7. Reduce the mixer speed to low. Add the dry ingredients alternately with the sour cream, dividing the flour mixture into three parts and the sour cream into two parts, beginning and ending with the flour. Scrape down the side of the bowl.

8. Spread the batter evenly into the prepared pan. Take a handful of the streusel mixture and squeeze gently to form a large clump. Then break the clump apart, and sprinkle the crumbs onto the batter. Repeat until all of the streusel mixture has been used. *Gently* press the crumbs onto the top of the batter, sprinkle with the mini chips and walnuts, and press *gently* again.

9. Bake for 30 to 35 minutes. The cake is done when a toothpick inserted in the center comes out clean and the sides begin to pull away from the pan.

10. Remove the cake from the oven and let stand on a cake rack until cool. When ready to serve, cut into 2-inch squares.

STORAGE: Store in the pan, well wrapped with aluminum foil, for up to 5 days. This cake may be frozen.

sour cream marble cake

MAKES ONE 9-INCH BUNDT CAKE, 10 TO 12 SERVINGS

Weaving together swirls of deep chocolate and creamy vanilla, this sour cream marble cake is an irresistible taste combination any time your sweet tooth calls. It never ceases to amaze me that so many people are drawn to these contrasts of flavors and colors. To achieve a beautiful marbled affect, be sure to follow the directions carefully. If the batter is overworked, the layers of chocolate and vanilla will not be clearly defined.

> **AT A GLANCE**
> PAN: 9-inch Bundt pan
> PAN PREP: Butter generously/flour
> OVEN TEMP: 350°F
> BAKING TIME: 55 to 60 minutes
> DIFFICULTY: ♕ ♕ ♕

MARBLING

3 ounces fine-quality bittersweet chocolate, such as Lindt, coarsely chopped (see pages 387–388)

4 teaspoons unsalted butter

3 tablespoons Dutch-process cocoa powder

2 tablespoons light corn syrup

3 tablespoons water

¼ teaspoon baking soda

BATTER

2½ cups sifted cake flour, spooned in and leveled

1½ teaspoons baking powder

½ teaspoon baking soda

½ teaspoon salt

1¼ cups sour cream

¼ cup milk

1½ teaspoons pure vanilla extract

¾ cup (1½ sticks) unsalted butter, slightly firm

1½ cups superfine sugar

4 large eggs

Powdered sugar, for dusting

1. Position the rack in the lower third of the oven. Heat the oven to 350°F. Generously butter a 9-inch Bundt pan, dust with flour, then invert the pan over the kitchen sink and tap firmly to remove the excess flour. Set aside.

MAKE THE MARBLING

2. Melt the chocolate and butter in a 2-quart bowl set over a pot of simmering water. (The bottom of the bowl should not touch the water.) Stir in the cocoa powder, corn syrup, and water, mixing until smooth. Remove from the heat and blend in the baking soda. Keep the chocolate mixture warm over the water bath while you prepare the batter.

MAKE THE BATTER

3. In a large bowl, thoroughly whisk together the flour, baking powder, baking soda, and salt and set aside.

4. In a medium bowl, combine the sour cream, milk, and vanilla. Set aside.

5. Cut the butter into 1-inch pieces and place in the bowl of an electric mixer fitted with the paddle attachment. Mix on medium speed for 2 minutes, then add the superfine sugar, 1 to 2 tablespoons at a time, taking 6 to 8 minutes. Scrape down the side of the bowl as needed. Add the eggs, one at a time, at 30-second intervals, scraping down the side of the bowl again.

6. Reduce the mixer speed to low. Add the dry ingredients alternately with the sour cream mixture, dividing the flour into three parts and the sour cream into two parts. Mix just until blended after each addition. Scrape down the side of the bowl as needed.

7. Remove the marbling mixture from the water bath. Measure 1½ cups of the batter, and add it to the marbling mixture, folding the two mixtures together gently.

FINISH THE CAKE

8. Spoon one-half of the vanilla batter into the prepared pan and smooth the top with the back of a large soupspoon. Using about one-third of the chocolate batter, distribute spoonfuls evenly over the vanilla batter, smoothing it carefully to the edge and covering as much vanilla batter as possible. Spoon one-half of the remaining vanilla batter over the chocolate batter. Spread the remaining chocolate batter over the vanilla, then finish with the remaining vanilla batter. As each layer of vanilla batter is spread, cover as much of the chocolate as you can.

9. Insert a table knife almost to the bottom of the pan and gently lift the knife up, over, and down again to fold the batters together, making about 15 folds as you rotate the pan. Smooth the top of the batter with the back of a large soupspoon.

10. Bake for 55 to 60 minutes. The cake is done when the top is golden brown and firm to the touch, and a wooden skewer inserted in the center comes out clean.

11. Remove the cake from the oven and let stand on a cooling rack for 15 to 20 minutes. Cover with a cooling rack, invert the cake, and carefully lift off the pan. Cool the cake completely on the rack. Just before serving, dust the top with powdered sugar.

STORAGE: Store under a glass cake dome or covered with plastic wrap for up to 5 days. This cake may be frozen.

pineapple squares with toasted coconut streusel

MAKES ONE 9 X 13 X 2-INCH CAKE, 2 DOZEN 2-INCH SERVINGS

If you love pineapple as much as I do, be sure to try these tasty, streusel-topped squares. The citrus-scented batter is laced with sweet pineapple, which gives the cake a wonderful moistness. These pretty crumb cake squares with their generous coating of chewy, buttery streusel make a refreshing tropical treat at any time of the year.

AT A GLANCE
PAN: 9 x 13 x 2-inch baking pan
PAN PREP: Butter generously
OVEN TEMP: 350°F
BAKING TIME: 30 to 35 minutes
DIFFICULTY: ☕

Toasted Coconut Streusel (page 355)

1 (8-ounce) can crushed pineapple in pineapple juice, well drained

1¾ cups sifted cake flour, spooned in and leveled

1 teaspoon baking powder

¼ teaspoon baking soda

¼ teaspoon salt

½ cup (1 stick) unsalted butter, slightly firm

1 teaspoon freshly grated navel orange zest

1 teaspoon freshly grated lemon zest

⅔ cup plus 3 tablespoons superfine sugar

2 large eggs, separated

⅓ cup sour cream

3 tablespoons fresh navel orange juice

¾ teaspoon pure vanilla extract

1. Prepare the Toasted Coconut Streusel. Set aside.

2. Position the rack in the middle of the oven. Heat the oven to 350°F. Generously butter a 9 × 13 × 2-inch pan and set aside.

3. Place the pineapple in the work bowl of a food processor fitted with the steel blade. Process for 10 seconds, or until finely chopped.

4. In a large bowl, thoroughly whisk together the flour, baking powder, baking soda, and salt. Set aside.

5. Cut the butter into 1-inch pieces and place in the bowl of an electric mixer fitted with the paddle attachment. Add the orange and lemon zests and mix on medium speed until smooth and lightened in color, about 2 minutes. Add ⅔ cup of the sugar, 1 tablespoon at a time, taking 4 to 6 minutes.

6. Add the egg yolks, one at a time, beating until blended after each addition and scraping down the side of the bowl as needed. Reduce the mixer speed to low and blend in the pineapple.

7. Combine the sour cream, orange juice, and vanilla in a small bowl. Add the dry ingredients alternately with the sour cream mixture, dividing the flour into three parts and the sour cream into two parts, beginning and ending with the flour, scraping down the side of the bowl as needed. Mix just to incorporate after each addition.

8. Place the egg whites in the bowl of an electric mixer fitted with the whip attachment. Whip on medium speed until soft peaks form, then add the remaining 3 tablespoons sugar, 1 tablespoon at a time, and beat for 30 seconds until thoroughly blended. Do not overbeat.

9. Using an oversize rubber spatula, fold about one-third of the whipped egg whites into the batter, taking about 20 turns. Fold in the remaining egg whites, taking about 40 turns. Scrape the batter into the prepared pan. Smooth the top with the back of a large soupspoon. Distribute the streusel evenly over the batter, patting lightly to adhere.

10. Bake for 30 to 35 minutes. The cake is done when the top is golden brown and springy to the touch, and a toothpick inserted in the center comes out clean.

11. Remove the cake from the oven and let stand on a cooling rack for about 20 minutes. Place a 15-inch strip of aluminum foil directly on top of the cake, cupping it around the sides to hold the topping in place. Cover with a cooling rack, invert the cake, and carefully lift off the pan. Cover with another rack, invert again, remove the foil, and cool right side up. (Alternatively, the cake may be stored in the pan and cut directly into 2-inch squares.)

STORAGE: Store in the pan, well wrapped with aluminum foil, for up to 5 days. This cake may be frozen.

apple walnut caramel kuchen

MAKES ONE 9-INCH CAKE, 8 TO 10 SERVINGS

Apples, walnuts. and caramel—what could be bad? Here is a cake made with a nutty press-in pastry that is filled with layers of caramel-coated sliced apples and toasted walnuts. The cake is finished with a topping of buttery streusel crumbs. Be sure to serve this cake slightly warm.

AT A GLANCE

PAN: 9-inch springform pan
PAN PREP: Butter generously/line with parchment
OVEN TEMP: 350°F
BAKING TIME: 55 to 60 minutes
DIFFICULTY: 🥤 🥤 🥤

CRUST

1¼ cups all-purpose flour, spooned in and leveled

⅓ cup walnuts, lightly toasted (see page 391)

⅔ cup sugar

1½ teaspoons baking powder

¼ teaspoon salt

½ cup (1 stick) unsalted butter, cut into ½-inch cubes, partially frozen

2 large egg yolks

3 tablespoons milk

1 teaspoon pure vanilla extract

½ teaspoon freshly grated lemon zest

CRUMB TOPPING

⅔ cup all-purpose flour, spooned in and leveled

¼ cup sugar

½ teaspoon ground cinnamon

Pinch of salt

¼ cup unsalted butter, melted and cooled to tepid

FILLING

3 medium Granny Smith apples (about 1 pound), peeled, halved, and cored

½ teaspoon freshly grated lemon zest

1 tablespoon fresh lemon juice

¼ cup water

⅔ cup sugar

¼ teaspoon salt

⅓ cup heavy cream

1 cup coarsely chopped, lightly toasted walnuts (see pages 391–392)

½ teaspoon pure vanilla extract

Powdered sugar, for dusting

1. Position the rack in the middle of the oven. Heat the oven to 350°F. Generously butter a 9-inch springform pan, line the bottom with parchment, and place in the refrigerator until ready to use.

MAKE THE CRUST

2. Place the flour, walnuts, sugar, baking powder, and salt in the work bowl of a food processor fitted with the steel blade. Pulse 8 to 10 times. Add the chilled but-ter, pulse 10 to 12 times, then process for 5 to 7 seconds, or until fine crumbs are formed.

3. In a small bowl, whisk together the egg yolks, milk, vanilla, and lemon zest. Add to the processor and pulse 6 to 8 times, or just until the mixture begins to gather together and form a ball.

SHAPE THE CRUST

4. Remove the dough from the work bowl and place it on a lightly floured surface. With lightly floured hands, pat it into a disk. Place the disk into the chilled baking pan and with a floured hand, press the dough into the bottom of the pan, working from the center out. Then press the dough against the side of the pan, forcing it upward to form a wall ½ inch thick and ¾ inch deep. Because the dough has a tendency to be thick at the crease of the pan, bend your index finger and press against the crease of the pan. Then press the bottom of the pan to smooth the surface. Check the dough for evenness by inserting the tip of a small knife at intervals around the pan. Refrigerate the dough while preparing the topping and filling.

MAKE THE CRUMB TOPPING

5. In a medium bowl, whisk together the flour, sugar, cinnamon, and salt. Add the melted butter and stir with a kitchen fork until small crumbs form. Set aside.

MAKE THE FILLING

6. Cut the apples into scant ¼-inch slices and place them in a large bowl. Toss them with the lemon zest and 2½ teaspoons of the lemon juice. Set aside.

7. Place the water in a 2-quart heavy saucepan measuring 7 inches across the top. Add the sugar, the remaining ½ teaspoon lemon juice, and the salt, and stir gently. Cook on medium-low heat until the liquid comes to a boil. If some sugar crystals remain on the bottom of the saucepan, gently stir the syrup to dissolve them. On low heat, continue to cook until the mixture turns a medium amber color. (This can take from 5 to 15 minutes, depending on the thickness of the saucepan.) *When the color of the sugar begins to change, watch carefully, as it can burn in a matter of seconds.*

recipe continues

continued from previous page

8. Remove the caramel syrup from the heat, immediately add the heavy cream (the mixture will bubble up), then stir until the caramel is smooth. Return to the heat and simmer for 3 to 4 minutes, or until big bubbles begin to form on the surface. *Watch carefully or the caramel will become too dark.* Off the heat, stir in the chopped walnuts and vanilla. Let cool for 5 minutes.

9. Fold the caramel/nut mixture into the apples; it's okay if some of the nuts cluster together. Spoon the fruit and nuts carefully into the dough-lined pan, arranging the apples and nuts to fill in the spaces, slightly mounding them in the center.

10. Take a handful of the streusel crumbs and squeeze gently to form a large clump. Then break the clump into smaller pieces and sprinkle them evenly over the filling. Repeat until all of the crumbs have been used and the apples are covered.

FINISH THE CAKE

11. Place the pan on a strip of heavy-duty aluminum foil and mold the foil around the pan to catch any leakage. Bake for 55 to 60 minutes. The cake is done when it begins to pull away from the side of the pan and the crumbs are golden brown.

12. Remove the cake from the oven and let stand on a cooling rack for 20 minutes. Release and remove the side of the pan and let cool for 30 minutes longer. To remove the bottom of the pan and the parchment, place a 12-inch strip of aluminum foil directly on top of the cake, cupping the foil around the side to hold the topping in place. Cover with a cooling rack, invert the cake, and carefully lift off the bottom of the pan and remove the parchment. Immediately cover with another rack, invert again, and remove the foil. This cake is best served slightly warm.

STORAGE: Store under a glass cake dome or tightly covered with aluminum foil for up to 2 days. For longer storage, refrigerate for up to 5 days. Reheat before serving in a 325°F oven for 15 minutes, or until slightly warm. This cake may be frozen.

blueberry buckle

MAKES ONE 9-INCH CAKE, 8 TO 10 SERVINGS

When checking out a variety of recipes in my quest for a classic blueberry buckle, I noted that while the basic ingredients and method of preparation were similar, the recipe names were different. Some recipes called the buckle a coffee cake, some referred to it as a kuchen, and the description I loved the best was "one giant blueberry muffin." All of the recipes started with a simple butter cake that was loaded with fresh blueberries and always finished with a generous streusel crumb topping. This cake is perfect for every occasion and promises to become a favorite.

> **AT A GLANCE**
> **PAN:** 9-inch spingform pan
> **PAN PREP:** Butter generously/line with parchment
> **OVEN TEMP:** 350°F
> **BAKING TIME:** 50 to 55 minutes
> **DIFFICULTY:** 🍵

The name "buckle" refers to the surface of the cake buckling under the weight of the crumb topping. I am sure that the amount of blueberries in the batter has something to do with it as well. When you serve this cake warm out of the oven, if the top of the cake doesn't buckle, with one taste, the knees of your guests surely will, making the name apt nevertheless.

STREUSEL

6 tablespoons (¾ stick) unsalted butter

¾ cup all-purpose flour, spooned in and leveled

⅓ cup sugar

¾ teaspoon ground cinnamon

⅛ teaspoon salt

BATTER

1¾ cups sifted all-purpose flour, spooned in and leveled

1 teaspoon baking powder

½ teaspoon salt

½ cup (1 stick) unsalted butter, slightly firm

½ teaspoon freshly grated lemon zest

¾ cup sugar

2 large eggs

1 teaspoon pure vanilla extract

¼ cup milk

2 cups (1 dry pint) blueberries, washed and well dried (see page 390)

1. Position the rack in the lower third of the oven. Heat the oven to 350°F. Generously butter a 9-inch springform pan and line the bottom with a parchment circle. Set aside.

PREPARE THE STREUSEL

2. Melt the butter in a medium saucepan. Remove from the heat and cool to tepid. In a small bowl, whisk together the flour, sugar, cinnamon, and salt and add it to the melted butter. Stir the mixture with a fork and set aside.

recipe continues

continued from previous page

MAKE THE BATTER

3. In a large bowl, thoroughly whisk together the flour, baking powder, and salt. Set aside.

4. Cut the butter into 1-inch pieces and place in the large bowl of an electric mixer fitted with the paddle attachment. Add the lemon zest and mix on medium speed until smooth and lightened in color, $1\frac{1}{2}$ to 2 minutes.

5. Add the sugar, 1 tablespoon at a time, taking 5 to 6 minutes to blend it in well. Scrape the side of the bowl occasionally. Add the eggs, one at a time, 1 minute apart. Beat for 1 minute longer, scraping down the side of bowl as necessary. Blend in the vanilla.

6. Reduce the mixer speed to low. Add the flour mixture alternately with the milk, dividing the dry ingredients into three parts and the milk into two parts, starting and ending with the flour. Beat just until incorporated after each addition. Scrape the side of the bowl and mix for 10 seconds longer.

7. Carefully fold the blueberries into the batter using a rubber spatula, then scrape the mixture into the pan. (Note: This is a very thick batter.) Spread the batter evenly using a small offset or rubber spatula, or the back of a large soupspoon, leveling the surface as best you can.

8. Take a handful of the crumb mixture and squeeze gently to form a large clump. Then break the clump into coarse crumbs and sprinkle them evenly over the filling. Repeat until all of the crumbs have been used and the batter is completely covered. Pat the streusel gently into the batter.

FINISH THE CAKE

9. Bake for 50 to 55 minutes. The cake is done when the streusel topping is golden brown and the cake begins to pull away from the side of the pan. A toothpick inserted into the center should come out clean.

10. Remove the cake from the oven and let stand on a cooling rack for 20 minutes. Remove the side of the pan and let cool for 30 minutes longer. To remove the bottom of the pan, place a 12-inch strip of aluminum foil directly on top of the cake, cupping the foil around the side to hold the topping in place. Cover with a cooling rack, invert the cake, and carefully lift off the bottom of the pan. Cover with another rack, invert again, and remove the foil.

STORAGE: Cover with aluminum foil and store at room temperature for the first day after baking. For longer storage, refrigerate for up to 3 additional days. Before serving, reheat in a 325°F oven for 10 to 15 minutes, or until slightly warm.

"[The wild blueberry has] a tartness which takes the edge off its sweetness and makes it more interesting, like a beauty spot on the face of a plain woman."

WAVERLY ROOT

brown butter almond cake

MAKES ONE 10-INCH CAKE, 10 TO 12 SERVINGS

This cake receives its rich flavor from nutty browned butter and lots of ground almonds. My recipe is a play on the popular French pastries known as financiers—little cakes that are baked in bar-shaped molds. These sponge-type cakes are commonly made with all egg whites and no leavening. Here I have chosen to enrich the batter with a couple of egg

AT A GLANCE
PAN: 10-inch springform pan
PAN PREP: Butter generously/line with parchment
OVEN TEMP: 350°F
BAKING TIME: 35 to 40 minutes
DIFFICULTY: 🥄 🥄

yolks and lighten it with some baking powder. For ease of preparation, I bake this cake in a springform pan rather than as individual cakes. Be sure to brown the butter in a heavy saucepan to prevent it from burning.

While this cake can stand alone, it also makes a terrific cool-weather treat topped with a mélange of stewed fruits (page 306). In summer, don't hesitate to serve this almond cake with sliced fresh peaches, along with a scoop of vanilla ice cream.

¾ cup (1½ sticks) unsalted butter

1 to 2 tablespoons dark rum, such as Meyer's

1 teaspoon pure vanilla extract

1½ cups strained powdered sugar, spooned in and leveled

1 cup (4 ounces) toasted slivered almonds (see page 391)

1 cup all-purpose flour, spooned in and leveled

1½ teaspoons baking powder

6 large egg whites (about ¾ cup)

2 large eggs

¼ teaspoon salt

½ cup superfine sugar

2 tablespoons sliced blanched almonds

MAKE THE BROWN BUTTER

1. Place the butter in a heavy 2-quart saucepan and melt over low heat. Continue to simmer, skimming the foam from the top as it forms; this will take 10 minutes or more, depending on the weight of the pan. The butter is finished when the color is a rich golden brown and has a "nutty" fragrance. *Watch carefully to avoid burning.* Blend in the rum and vanilla and cool to tepid.

MAKE THE BATTER

2. Position the rack in the lower third of the oven. Heat the oven to 350°F. Generously butter a 10-inch springform pan and line the bottom with baking parchment. Set aside.

3. Place the powdered sugar, slivered almonds, flour, and baking powder in the work bowl of a food processor fitted with the steel blade. Pulse 5 to 6 times, then process for 50 to 60 seconds, or until the mixture forms fine meal. Set aside.

4. Place the egg whites, whole eggs, and salt in the bowl of an electric mixer fitted with the whip attachment. Beat the eggs on medium speed until frothy. Gradually increase the speed to medium high and continue to whip for about 2 minutes, until very light and foamy. Add the superfine sugar, 1 tablespoon at a time, taking about 30 seconds, then beat for 1 minute longer.

5. Reduce the mixer speed to medium and pour the *tepid* butter down the side of the bowl in a slow, steady stream, also adding the browned bits from the bottom of the pan. Add the nut/flour mixture in three additions and mix just to combine.

FINISH THE CAKE

6. Scrape the batter into the prepared pan, smooth the top with the back of a large soupspoon, and sprinkle with the sliced almonds. Bake for 35 to 40 minutes. The cake is done when the top is golden brown, firm to the touch, and begins to release from the side of the pan.

7. Remove the cake from the oven and let stand on a cooling rack for 15 minutes. Carefully release and remove the side of the pan, invert onto a cooling rack, and remove the bottom of the pan and the parchment paper. Cover with another rack, invert again, and cool right side up.

STORAGE: Store under a glass cake dome or tightly covered with plastic wrap for up to 5 days. This cake may be frozen.

fruit and nut applesauce cake

MAKES ONE 9 X 13 X 2-INCH CAKE, 2 DOZEN 2-INCH SERVINGS

If you like applesauce cake, you must try this recipe. The batter is made with fresh apples, raisins, and dried cranberries accented with cinnamon and nutmeg. Don't be tempted to substitute jarred applesauce because it is too watery and the end result will not be the same. Fresh apples add superior flavor and just the right amount of moisture.

> **AT A GLANCE**
> **PAN:** 9 x 13 x 2-inch baking pan
> **PAN PREP:** Butter generously
> **OVEN TEMP:** 350°F
> **BAKING TIME:** 35 to 40 minutes
> **DIFFICULTY:** 🍵 🍵

APPLESAUCE

3 Granny Smith apples (about 1 pound), peeled, halved, and cored

2 tablespoons unsalted butter

¼ cup water

1 teaspoon fresh lemon juice

BATTER

2½ cups sifted all-purpose flour, spooned in and leveled

1½ teaspoons ground cinnamon

1 teaspoon baking soda

½ teaspoon baking powder

½ teaspoon ground nutmeg

½ teaspoon salt

½ cup (1 stick) unsalted butter, slightly firm

1 teaspoon freshly grated lemon zest

¾ cup granulated sugar

¾ cup (lightly packed) *very fresh* dark brown sugar

2 large eggs

1 teaspoon pure vanilla extract

½ cup low-fat plain yogurt or buttermilk

1 cup medium-chopped walnuts (see page 392)

½ cup golden raisins, plumped (see page 389)

¼ cup dried cranberries (not organic), plumped and coarsely chopped (page 389)

Applejack Glaze (page 360)

MAKE THE APPLESAUCE

1. Using a food processor fitted with the medium shredding disk, shred the apples. (Alternatively, the apples can be shredded on the half-moon side of a box grater.) Melt the butter in a heavy 10-inch sauté pan. Stir in the apples, water, and lemon juice. Cover the pan and reduce the heat to low; cook the apples until tender, about 25 minutes. (The apples should retain some texture.) Empty from the pan and set aside to cool. You should have about 1 cup of applesauce.

MAKE THE BATTER

2. Position the rack in the lower third of the oven. Heat the oven to 350°F. Generously butter a 9 × 13 × 2-inch pan and set aside.

3. In a large bowl, strain together the flour, cinnamon, baking soda, baking powder, nutmeg, and salt. Set aside.

4. Cut the butter into 1-inch pieces and place it in the bowl of an electric mixer fitted with the paddle attachment. Add the lemon zest and mix on medium speed until smooth and lightened in color, about 2 minutes. Add the granulated sugar, 1 tablespoon at a time, taking 2 to 3 minutes, then add the brown sugar, taking another 2 to 3 minutes. Beat for 1 minute longer. Add the eggs, one at a time, beating for 1 minute after each addition, then mix in the vanilla. Scrape down the side of the bowl as needed.

5. Reduce the mixer speed to medium-low and blend in the applesauce. Add the dry ingredients alternately with the yogurt, dividing the flour mixture into three parts and the yogurt into two parts, beginning and ending with the flour. Scrape down the side of the bowl.

6. Remove the bowl from the machine, and using an oversize rubber spatula, fold in the walnuts, raisins, and cranberries. Spoon the batter into the prepared pan and smooth the top with the bottom of a large soupspoon.

FINISH THE CAKE

7. Bake for 35 to 40 minutes. The cake is done when the top is springy to the touch and a toothpick inserted deeply in the center comes out clean. Remove the cake from the oven and place on a cooling rack. Fifteen minutes before the cake is done, prepare the glaze.

8. While the cake is still hot, *immediately* pour the glaze over the cake, spreading evenly with an offset spatula. The glaze will harden within minutes. Cool the cake completely on the rack.

STORAGE: Store lightly covered with aluminum foil for up to 5 days. This cake may be frozen before glazing.

caramel-glazed blackberry jam cake

MAKES ONE 9-INCH BUNDT CAKE, 10 TO 12 SERVINGS

If you are looking for a spice cake with a bit of a twist, try this tasty version made with blackberry preserves, buttermilk, and pecans. I tested this cake first with blackberry jam, called for in most recipes. The second time I tested the recipe, I used blackberry preserves and loved the results even more—the finished cake was deeper in color and richer in flavor. You can use either and while I prefer preserves, it just seemed odd to call what is traditionally known as jam cake "preserves cake."

AT A GLANCE
PAN: 9-inch Bundt pan
PAN PREP: Butter generously/flour
OVEN TEMP: 325°F
BAKING TIME: 1 hour, 15 to 20 minutes
DIFFICULTY: ♨

2½ cups sifted all-purpose flour, spooned in and leveled

1 teaspoon ground cinnamon

½ teaspoon ground nutmeg

½ teaspoon ground allspice

½ teaspoon salt

¼ teaspoon ground cloves

¾ cup buttermilk

¾ teaspoon baking soda

1 cup (2 sticks) unsalted butter, slightly firm

1 cup superfine sugar

½ cup (lightly packed) very *fresh* dark brown sugar

3 large eggs

¾ cup seedless blackberry preserves or jam

1 teaspoon pure vanilla extract

1 cup coarsely chopped toasted pecans (see pages 391–392), plus 2 tablespoons for garnish

Caramel Glaze (page 361)

1. Position the rack in the lower third of the oven. Heat the oven to 325°F. Generously butter a 9-inch Bundt pan, dust with flour, then invert it over the kitchen sink to remove the excess flour. Set aside.

2. In a large bowl, thoroughly whisk together the flour, cinnamon, nutmeg, allspice, salt, and cloves. Set aside.

3. Combine the buttermilk and baking soda and let stand for 7 to 8 minutes.

4. Cut the butter into 1-inch pieces and place in the bowl of an electric mixer fitted with the paddle attachment. Mix on medium speed for 2 minutes, until smooth and lightened in color, about 2 minutes. Add the superfine sugar, 1 to 2 tablespoons at a time, taking 3 to 4 minutes, then add the brown sugar, taking 2 to 3 minutes. Scrape down the side of the bowl.

5. Add the eggs, one at a time, beating for 1 minute after each addition, then blend in the preserves and vanilla. (The mixture will appear curdled, but will come together when the flour is added.)

6. Reduce the mixer speed to low and add the flour mixture alternately with the buttermilk mixture, dividing the flour into three parts and the buttermilk into two parts, beginning and ending with the flour. Mix just until blended after each addition. Scrape down the side of the bowl as needed. Remove the bowl from the machine and gently fold in 1 cup of the pecans using an oversize rubber spatula.

7. Spoon the batter into the prepared pan, smooth the top with the back of a large soupspoon, and bake for 1 hour and 15 to 20 minutes. The cake is done when the top is firm to the touch, the side begins to release, and a wooden skewer inserted in the center comes out clean. Remove from the oven and place on a cooling rack for about 20 minutes.

8. While the cake is standing, prepare the glaze. When ready to glaze the cake, invert it onto the rack, gently lift off the pan, and place the rack on a rimmed cookie sheet.

9. Immediately pour the glaze over the warm cake, then sprinkle the remaining 2 tablespoons chopped pecans over the top. Work quickly; the glaze begins to harden as soon as it is poured onto the cake.

STORAGE: Store under a glass cake dome or loosely covered with aluminum foil for up to 3 days. This cake may be frozen before glazing.

carrot honey cake

MAKES ONE 9 X 9-INCH CAKE, SIXTEEN 2¼-INCH SERVINGS

The addition of honey to carrot cake not only adds flavor but also gives the cake a very moist texture. Cinnamon, cardamom, and orange zest complement the sweetness of the carrots and honey, making a cake that promises to please.

When you prepare the batter, be sure to have your cake pan ready and your oven preheated because this is a batter that cannot stand after mixing.

AT A GLANCE
PAN: 9 x 9 x 2-inch square baking pan
PAN PREP: Butter generously
OVEN TEMP: 350°F
BAKING TIME: 40 to 45 minutes
DIFFICULTY: 🍵

3 large carrots (about 8 ounces), peeled and trimmed

1½ cups all-purpose flour, spooned in and leveled

2 teaspoons ground cinnamon

1 teaspoon baking soda

¾ teaspoon ground cardamom

½ teaspoon salt

3 large eggs

½ cup granulated sugar

½ cup (lightly packed) *very fresh* light brown sugar

1 teaspoon freshly grated navel orange zest

¾ cup canola oil

¼ cup honey

1 teaspoon pure vanilla extract

½ cup medium-chopped toasted pecans (see pages 391–392)

1 large recipe Cream Cheese Frosting (page 364)

1. Position the rack in the middle of the oven. Heat the oven to 350°F. Generously butter a 9 x 9 x 2-inch square pan and set aside.

SHRED THE CARROTS

2. To shred the carrots in a food processor: Fit the machine with the medium shredding disk. Cut the carrots into 1-inch chunks and place in the feeder tube. Shred using very light pressure. Remove the shredding disk and insert the steel blade. Pulse 4 to 5 times, then process for 5 to 6 seconds. (You should have 1½ to 1⅔ cups.) Set aside.

2. To shred the carrots by hand: Finely shred the carrots using the smallest (scant ⅛-inch) half-moon side of a box grater. (You should have 1½ to 1⅔ cups.) Set aside.

MAKE THE BATTER

3. In a medium bowl, thoroughly whisk together the flour, cinnamon, baking soda, cardamom, and salt. Set aside.

4. Place the eggs in the bowl of an electric mixer fitted with the whip attachment. Beat for 2 minutes on medium speed, then add the granulated sugar, 1 tablespoon at a time, taking 2 to 3 minutes. Add the brown sugar, 1 tablespoon at a time, taking another 2 to 3 minutes, then beat in the orange zest.

5. Using a small whisk, mix together the oil, honey, and vanilla in a 1-quart mixing bowl, beating until the honey is thoroughly incorporated with the oil. Immediately pour into the egg/sugar mixture in a steady stream and beat well. Reduce the speed to medium-low and mix in the carrots. Add the dry ingredients in two additions, mixing only to blend after each addition. Scrape down the side of the bowl as needed. Then, quickly mix in the pecans. Note: This batter cannot stand before baking because the oil and honey will settle to the bottom of the bowl.

FINISH THE CAKE

6. Immediately pour the batter into the prepared pan and bake for 40 to 45 minutes. The cake is done when it is firm to the touch, the sides begin to release, and a toothpick inserted in the center comes out clean.

7. While the cake is baking, prepare the frosting.

8. Remove the cake from the oven and place on a cooling rack. When the cake is cool, spread with the frosting, swirling it with the bottom of a soupspoon. Cut into sixteen 2¼ × 2¼-inch squares.

STORAGE: Refrigerate for up to 7 days. The frosted cake may be frozen.

honey spice squares

MAKES 2 DOZEN 2-INCH SQUARES

Here is a cake that is ideal to serve on those blustery, winter days when your taste buds are longing for something a little spicy to give you a boost. This cake is moistened with an orange-honey syrup that makes it the perfect accompaniment to an afternoon cup of tea or, if you've just come in from the slopes, a hot toddy.

AT A GLANCE
PAN: 9 x 13 x 2-inch baking pan
PAN PREP: Butter generously
OVEN TEMP: 350°F
BAKING TIME: 22 to 25 minutes
DIFFICULTY: ☕

THE BATTER

2¼ cups all-purpose flour, spooned in and leveled

½ teaspoon ground cinnamon

½ teaspoon ground nutmeg

½ teaspoon baking powder

¼ teaspoon baking soda

¼ teaspoon salt

¾ cup (1½ sticks) unsalted butter

¼ cup honey

1½ teaspoons freshly grated navel orange zest

2 large eggs

1 cup (lightly packed) *very fresh* dark brown sugar

1 teaspoon pure vanilla extract

¼ cup sour cream

1 cup medium-chopped toasted sliced almonds (see pages 391–392)

THE SYRUP

⅓ cup honey

⅓ cup orange juice

⅓ cup water

1. Position the rack in the lower third of the oven. Heat the oven to 350°F. Generously butter a 9 × 13 × 2-inch pan and set aside.

MAKE THE BATTER

2. In a large bowl, thoroughly whisk together the flour, cinnamon, nutmeg, baking powder, baking soda, and salt. Set aside.

3. Melt the butter with the honey and the orange zest. Cool until tepid.

4. In the bowl of an electric mixer fitted with the whip attachment, beat the eggs on medium-high speed until lightened, about 1 minute. Add the brown sugar, 1 to 2 tablespoons at a time, taking about 2 minutes. Scrape down the side of the bowl, then beat for 1 minute more.

5. Reduce the speed to medium-low and slowly pour in the butter mixture, mixing for 30 seconds. The mixture will thicken. Then add the vanilla. The mixture will look curdled.

6. Reduce the mixer speed to low. Add one-half of the dry ingredients, then the sour cream, and then the remaining flour, mixing just to combine after each addition. Remove the bowl from the machine. Crush the almonds into smaller pieces with your hand and fold in ¾ cup of the almonds with a large rubber spatula. Spread the batter evenly in the prepared pan and smooth the top with a small offset spatula or the back of a large soupspoon. Sprinkle the remaining almonds over the top.

7. Bake the cake for 22 to 25 minutes, or until the top feels springy to the touch and a toothpick inserted in the center comes out clean.

MAKE THE SYRUP

8. Combine the honey, orange juice, and water in a heavy 1-quart saucepan and bring to a slow boil over medium heat. Reduce the heat to low and simmer for 5 minutes.

FINISH THE CAKE

9. Remove the cake from the oven, and while it is still warm, poke the surface at 1-inch intervals with a wooden skewer or toothpick. Spoon the warm syrup very slowly and evenly over the top of the cake, continuing until all the syrup is absorbed. Place the pan on a cooling rack and let stand for 2 to 3 hours before cutting into 2-inch squares.

STORAGE: Store in an airtight container, layered between strips of waxed paper, for up to 3 weeks. Freezing is not recommended.

toasted pecan eggnog ring

MAKES ONE 9-INCH BUNDT CAKE, 10 TO 12 SERVINGS

Who doesn't look forward to indulging in a glass of rich eggnog? The creamy texture, hint of nutmeg, and of course occasional splash of bourbon ring in the holiday season for me. So I included these wonderful flavors in this toasted pecan eggnog ring. Not only will you enjoy this cake on your holiday dessert table, it's a terrific way to use up that extra cup of eggnog.

AT A GLANCE
PAN: 9-inch Bundt pan
PAN PREP: Butter generously/flour
BAKING TIME: 1 hour, 10 to 15 minutes
OVEN TEMP: 325°F
DIFFICULTY: ☕

2½ cups plus 1 tablespoon sifted cake flour, spooned in and leveled

½ teaspoon ground nutmeg

½ teaspoon baking soda

½ teaspoon salt

1 cup premium-quality eggnog

¼ cup bourbon, such as Jack Daniel's

¾ cup (1½ sticks) unsalted butter, slightly firm

1½ cups (lightly packed) *very fresh* light brown sugar

3 large eggs

1 teaspoon pure vanilla extract

1 cup (4 ounces) coarsely chopped toasted pecans (see pages 391–392)

EGGNOG GLAZE

1 cup strained powdered sugar, spooned in and leveled

2 tablespoons warm eggnog

1 tablespoon light corn syrup

---

1. Position the rack in the lower third of the oven. Heat the oven to 325°F. Generously butter a 9-inch Bundt pan, dust with flour, then invert it over the kitchen sink and tap firmly to remove the excess flour. Set aside.

MAKE THE BATTER

2. In a large bowl, whisk together 2½ cups of the flour, the nutmeg, baking soda, and salt. Set aside.

3. In a small bowl, combine the eggnog and bourbon. Set aside.

4. Cut the butter into 1-inch pieces and place in the bowl of an electric mixer fitted with the paddle attachment. Mix on medium speed until smooth and lightened in color, about 2 minutes. Add the brown sugar, 1 to 2 tablespoons at a time, taking 6 to 8 minutes.

5. Add the eggs, one at a time, mixing for 1 minute after each addition. Blend in the vanilla. Scrape down the sides of the bowl as needed.

6. Reduce the mixer speed to low. Add the dry ingredients alternately with the eggnog mixture, dividing the flour mixture into three parts and the liquid into two parts, starting and ending with the flour.

7. In a small bowl, toss the pecans with the remaining tablespoon of flour. Remove the bowl from the mixer, and using a large spatula, fold in the nuts. Spoon the batter into the prepared pan, smooth the top with the back of a large soupspoon, and bake for 1 hour and 10 to 15 minutes. The cake is done when the top is firm to the touch and a wooden skewer inserted in the center comes out clean.

8. Remove from the oven and let stand on a cooling rack for 20 minutes. Invert the cake onto the rack and carefully lift off the pan. Turn the cake right side up onto a cooling rack, and place it over a rimmed cookie sheet. While the cake is cooling, make the glaze.

MAKE THE GLAZE

9. Whisk the powdered sugar, eggnog, and corn syrup together until smooth.

FINISH THE CAKE

10. Using a fork or a whisk, drizzle the glaze over the cake while it is still warm. Let stand at room temperature until the glaze is set.

STORAGE: Store under a glass cake dome or covered with aluminum foil for up to 5 days. This cake may be frozen.

"Over the years since I left home, I have kept thinking about the people I grew up with and about our way of life. I realize how much the bond that held us together had to do with food."
EDNA LEWIS

irish whiskey cake

MAKES ONE 9-INCH BUNDT CAKE, 10 TO 12 SERVINGS

During lunch with my cousin Elsa Sobo, a senior member of
my family who still appreciates a fine piece of cake, the
conversation turned to this book. She asked me if I had a
recipe for Irish whiskey cake, and I replied that I didn't. "Oh,
you must!" she said. And before the day was over, she made
sure I had her recipe in hand. I couldn't wait to test it, and

AT A GLANCE
PAN: 9-inch Bundt pan
PAN PREP: Butter generously/flour
OVEN TEMP: 325°F
BAKING TIME: 1 hour, 15 to 20 minutes
DIFFICULTY: ♛

upon tasting the first slice, I concluded that she was absolutely right. Elsa was also right when she told me
that this cake gets better with age.

3 cups sifted cake flour, spooned in and leveled

½ teaspoon salt

½ teaspoon baking soda

1 cup (2 sticks) unsalted butter, slightly firm

2 cups superfine sugar

3 large eggs

3 tablespoons very fresh instant coffee crystals,
   dissolved in 1 tablespoon boiling water

1 teaspoon pure vanilla extract

¼ cup Scotch whiskey

1 cup sour cream

Powdered sugar, for dusting, or Midnight
   Chocolate Glaze (page 363)

1. Position the rack in the lower third of the oven. Heat the oven to 325°F.
Generously butter a 9-inch Bundt pan, dust with flour, then invert it over the kitchen
sink and tap firmly to remove the excess flour. Set aside.

2. In a large bowl, thoroughly whisk together the flour, salt, and baking soda.
Set aside.

3. Cut the butter into 1-inch pieces and place in the bowl of an electric mixer fitted
with the paddle attachment. Mix on medium speed until smooth and lightened in
color, about 2 minutes. Add the superfine sugar gradually, 1 to 2 tablespoons at a time,
taking 6 to 8 minutes. Add the eggs, one at a time, about 1 minute apart, scraping the
side of the bowl as needed. Blend in the dissolved coffee and the vanilla.

4. Reduce the mixer speed to low. Stir the Scotch into the sour cream and add the
mixture alternately with the dry ingredients, dividing the flour into three parts and the
sour cream mixture into two parts, beginning and ending with the flour. Mix just until
blended after each addition. Scrape the side of the bowl and mix for 10 seconds longer.

5. Spoon the batter into the prepared pan, smooth the top with the bottom of a large soupspoon, and bake for 1 hour and 15 to 20 minutes. The cake is done when the top is springy to the touch and a wooden skewer inserted deeply in the center comes out clean.

6. Remove the cake from the oven and let stand on a cooling rack for 20 minutes. Invert the cake onto the rack, gently lift off the pan, and cool the cake completely. When ready to serve, dust with powdered sugar. If using the glaze, while the cake is on the cooling rack, make the glaze. Place the cake over a rimmed cookie sheet, and glaze while it is still warm. If desired, after glazing, sprinkle the top with a few chocolate shavings.

STORAGE: Store under a glass cake dome or covered with aluminum foil for up to 5 days. This cake may be frozen.

"The black stove, stoked with coal and firewood, glows like a lighted pumpkin. Eggbeaters whirl, spoons spin round in bowls of butter and sugar, vanilla sweetens the air, ginger spices it; melting nose-tingling odors saturate the kitchen. . . . In four days our work is done. Thirty-one cakes, dampened with whiskey, bask on window sills and shelves."

TRUMAN CAPOTE, *A CHRISTMAS MEMORY*

golden apple upside-down gingerbread cake

MAKES ONE 9 X 9-INCH CAKE, 8 TO 10 SERVINGS

This recipe comes from Kathie Finn Redden, whose input in this book has been invaluable—so much so that this book is dedicated to her. Kathie, a cooking teacher and caterer, was blessed with an extraordinary sense of taste. Her recipe for this zesty gingerbread is complemented by a topping of sweet sautéed apples. When the cake is inverted, the juices of the fruit enhance the tender crumb of the cake. Be sure to serve this with a scoop of vanilla ice cream.

APPLES

5 tablespoons unsalted butter

5 medium Golden Delicious apples (about 2¼ pounds), peeled, cored, and cut into eighths

¼ cup (lightly packed) dark brown sugar

¼ cup Calvados or applejack brandy

CAKE

1½ cups all-purpose flour, spooned in and leveled

2 teaspoons ground ginger

1 teaspoon baking soda

1 teaspoon ground cinnamon

½ teaspoon salt

¼ teaspoon ground nutmeg

¼ teaspoon ground cloves

½ cup (1 stick) unsalted butter, slightly firm

½ cup (lightly packed) *very fresh* dark brown sugar

2 large eggs

½ cup light molasses

¼ cup crystallized ginger, cut into ¼-inch pieces

¼ cup milk

1. Position the rack in the middle of the oven. Heat the oven to 350°F. Generously butter a 9-inch square (preferably nonstick) pan and set aside.

PREPARE THE APPLES

2. Melt 2 tablespoons of the butter in a heavy 12-inch frying pan. Arrange half of the apples cut side down in a single layer, and sauté over medium heat until lightly browned. Using a thin metal spatula, turn the apples and brown on the other side. Have ready a large rimmed cookie sheet lined with a double thickness of paper towels. When the apples are done, using the metal spatula, transfer them to the rimmed cookie sheet. Add 1 more tablespoon of butter to the frying pan, sauté the remaining apples, and

transfer them to the rimmed cookie sheet. (It's okay to add a bit more butter to the pan if needed.)

3. Add the remaining 2 tablespoons of butter, the brown sugar, and the brandy to the frying pan. Cook over medium heat until the sugar is melted. Simmer for 2 to 3 minutes, or until large bubbles and a thick syrup form. Pour the syrup into the prepared cake pan and tilt it to distribute evenly. (It's okay if the liquid does not cover the entire bottom of the pan.) Arrange the apples in rows on top of the syrup.

MAKE THE BATTER

4. In a medium bowl, whisk together the flour, ginger, baking soda, cinnamon, salt, nutmeg, and cloves. Set aside.

5. Cut the butter into 1-inch pieces and place in the bowl of an electric mixer fitted with the paddle attachment. Mix on medium speed until smooth, 1½ to 2 minutes. Add the brown sugar and mix until well blended. Add the eggs, one at a time, about 1 minute apart. With the machine off, add the molasses and the crystallized ginger. Scrape down the side of the bowl.

6. With the mixer on low speed, blend in half of the dry ingredients, add the milk, then add the remaining dry ingredients. Mix just until blended after each addition. Pour the batter over the apples and smooth the top with a small offset spatula.

FINISH THE CAKE

7. Bake for 50 to 55 minutes, or until the top of the gingerbread is springy to the touch and begins to release from the side of the pan. Remove the cake from the oven and place on a cooling rack for 10 minutes. Run a knife around the side of the pan, then set aside until ready to serve. Serve warm.

NOTE: Since upside-down cakes are best served shortly after inverting, do not invert the cake until you are ready to serve it. If you make this cake early in the day, reheat the cake in a 350°F oven for 10 to 15 minutes to melt the juices again. Invert the cake onto a serving platter. To allow the caramelized juices to coat the top of the cake, do not remove the pan for a few minutes. When you remove the pan, if any apples remain, replace them on top of the cake.

STORAGE: Store loosely wrapped in aluminum foil for up to 2 days. Freezing is not recommended.

greek semolina coffee cake with orange syrup

MAKES ONE 9 X 13 X 2-INCH CAKE, 2 DOZEN 2-INCH SQUARES

I was introduced to a Greek semolina cake at Periyali, a fine Greek restaurant in New York City, and I instantly fell in love with it. A large square of the golden cake was served topped with rich Greek yogurt and a drizzle of honey. It was heavenly.

Greek semolina is available at Middle Eastern or specialty food stores. Italian semolina, which may be used as well, can be found in the flour section of most supermarkets. These semolinas are derived from durum wheat and are more coarsely ground than ordinary wheat flours. Leftover semolina should be stored in the freezer for future use.

AT A GLANCE
PAN: 9 x 13 x 2-inch baking pan
PAN PREP: Butter generously
OVEN TEMP: 350°F
BAKING TIME: 28 to 32 minutes
DIFFICULTY: 🥄 🥄

ORANGE SYRUP

1 cup sugar

1 cup water

¼ teaspoon cream of tartar

3 (3-inch) pieces lemon zest

3 (3-inch) pieces navel orange zest

2 tablespoons light rum

CAKE

1 cup sifted all-purpose flour, spooned in and leveled

½ cup slivered almonds

1 tablespoon baking powder

¼ teaspoon salt

¾ cup semolina, preferably Greek (see headnote)

6 large eggs

1 cup (2 sticks) unsalted butter, slightly firm

1 teaspoon freshly grated navel orange zest

¾ cup sugar

1 teaspoon pure vanilla extract

MAKE THE SYRUP

1. Combine the sugar, water, cream of tartar, and zests in a heavy 2-quart saucepan. Bring to a boil and simmer for 10 minutes. Remove from the heat and stir in the rum. Set aside to cool.

2. Position the rack in the middle of the oven. Heat the oven to 350°F. Generously butter a 9 x 13 x 2-inch pan and set aside.

MAKE THE BATTER

3. Combine the flour, almonds, baking powder, and salt in the work bowl of a food processor fitted with the steel blade. Process until the almonds are finely chopped, about 1½ minutes. Add the semolina and pulse 3 to 4 times to blend. Set aside.

4. Place the eggs in a medium bowl and whisk until well blended. Set aside.

5. Cut the butter into 1-inch pieces and combine with the lemon and orange zests in the bowl of an electric mixer fitted with the paddle attachment. Mix on medium speed until smooth and lightened in color, about 2 minutes. Add the sugar, about 1 tablespoon at a time, taking 3 to 4 minutes, scraping down the side of the bowl as needed. Beat in ½ cup of the eggs, taking about 1 minute, and blend in the vanilla.

6. Reduce the mixer speed to low and add the dry ingredients alternately with the remaining eggs, dividing the flour into four parts and the eggs into three parts, beginning and ending with the flour. Scrape down the side of the bowl as needed.

FINISH THE CAKE

7. Empty the batter into the prepared pan and smooth the top with the bottom of a large soupspoon. Bake for 28 to 32 minutes. The cake is done when the top is golden brown and firm to the touch, and a toothpick inserted in the center comes out clean.

8. Remove the cake from the oven and place on a cooling rack for 5 minutes. Spoon the cooled syrup over the *hot cake. Do this slowly so the syrup thoroughly absorbs into the crumb of the cake.* Let stand for at least 3 hours before cutting into 2-inch squares.

STORAGE: Store in the pan, tightly covered with aluminum foil, for up to 1 week. This cake may be frozen.

"Only dull people are brilliant before breakfast."
OSCAR WILDE

muffins
& quick breads

Orange Cream Cheese Muffins with Pepita Crunch

Rhubarb Upside-Down Muffins

Maple Pecan Sweet Potato Muffins

Crumb-Topped Whole Wheat Peach Muffins

"Too Good to Be True" Bran Muffins

Whole Wheat Sunflower Seed Muffins

QUICK BREADS

Irish Soda Bread

Grandma Jennie's Date and Nut Bread

Pumpkin Pecan Loaf

Zucchini Loaf with Apricots and Dates

Candied Maple Walnut Pancake Loaf

ABOUT MUFFINS AND QUICK BREADS

Muffins and quick breads are a pleasure to make and fun to eat. The difference between the two is that the texture of a muffin is more cakelike, while the structure of a quick bread is usually somewhat moist. When you eat a muffin, it is usually broken apart with your fingertips. Therefore, muffins make perfect candidates for chunkier additions to the batter. Quick breads, on the other hand, are always sliced. They have more moisture, and because of this they hold their shape when sliced and have a long shelf life. These breads always benefit from resting overnight.

Once the ingredients are assembled for muffins and quick breads, the mixing can be done in no time. There are two methods for making muffins. The first is the One Bowl or Quick Method, whereby all of the dry ingredients are placed in a large bowl. The wet ingredients are added to a well in the center and the two are combined with a rubber spatula. With this method, the batter is not mixed completely smooth; in fact, a somewhat lumpy batter creates a lighter muffin.

The second method is the Standard Creaming Method, based on the technique used for mixing butter cakes. Here, the butter is mixed until smooth and creamy, which results in a finished muffin with a finer texture. Although muffins may seem similar to cupcakes, they are usually less rich and often finished with crumb toppings. Sometimes muffins have a simple glaze, but with the exception of cream cheese frosting, thick icings are not to be found.

The method that I use for making quick breads differs from that for muffin batters. I start with well-beaten eggs to which sugar is added, followed by oil or melted butter. The dry ingredients and other flavor enhancements are added quickly at the end. These batters are usually more fluid. Because of this, nuts and fruits are generally cut into smaller pieces to prevent them from sinking to the bottom of the batter.

Here are more pointers for making better muffins and quick breads.

• Muffin and quick bread batters made in an electric mixer require less mixing time than do those for cupcakes.

• When adding oil or melted butter to a batter made in an electric mixer, in order to maintain the volume of the beaten eggs, it is important that these fats be poured slowly, in a steady stream down the side of the bowl.

• Muffins will have a better shape if portioned with an ice cream scoop. For this book, a no. 16 (¼-cup capacity) ice cream scoop was used.

- If you don't have a no. 16 ice cream scoop, fill each muffin pan cavity three-quarters full with batter.

- Since muffins are usually made without thick frostings, they will have more "oomph" if the tins are generously filled.

- If you have only one muffin pan, extra batter may be baked in buttered custard cups as a snack for the cook.

- When only three or four cavities of a muffin pan are to be filled, the muffins will bake more evenly if you place the batter in the cups closer to the center of the pan. It is unnecessary to fill empty muffin cups with water.

- When making corn muffins, if you choose to preheat the pan with butter and/or oil, each cavity must be filled with batter to prevent smoking during baking. Take care to portion the batter accordingly.

- When applying crumb toppings, use a small pastry brush to remove any crumbs that may fall onto the muffin pan. This will keep them from burning during baking.

- When more than one pan is being baked at the same time, rotate the pans from front to back and top to bottom toward the end of baking time for even baking.

- Quick breads commonly have a split across the top where beads of moisture form. Despite this, the loaf may still be done. Therefore, check for doneness on either side of the split.

- Because muffins generally contain less fat than cupcakes, they have a shorter shelf life and are best eaten the day they are made.

- Leftover muffins should be reheated in a 325°F oven for 6 to 8 minutes or until warmed through. When they come out of the oven, let them cool to tepid for 5 to 10 minutes, depending on the muffin.

- Covering quick breads made with dried fruits with plastic wrap will keep them moist and make them easier to slice.

blueberry corn muffins

MAKES 16 MUFFINS

It's midsummer and guests are coming for the weekend. I can't think of a nicer treat for Sunday brunch than warm corn muffins filled with blueberries. Because blueberries are so plump, I like to chop some of the berries just enough to break them up, and add them to the batter along with the whole berries. This way I can incorporate more berries in the batter.

AT A GLANCE

PANS: Two standard muffin pans
PAN PREP: Butter/oil
OVEN TEMP: 400°F
BAKING TIME: 20 to 25 minutes
DIFFICULTY: 🍴

Batter for Ultra-Rich Corn Muffins (page 82), but increase the canola oil to ⅓ cup when preparing the pans

1¼ cups fresh blueberries, washed and dried

1. Position the racks in the upper and lower thirds of the oven. Heat the oven to 400°F. Follow the pan preparation instructions for Ultra-Rich Corn Muffins (page 82), using two pans.

2. Prepare the muffin batter with the change noted above.

3. Place ¾ cup of blueberries in the work bowl of a food processor fitted with a steel blade. Pulse 3 to 4 times, until very coarsely chopped. *Immediately* fold the chopped and remaining whole berries into the batter using an oversize rubber spatula.

4. Portion level scoops of the batter into the muffin cups using a no. 16 ice cream scoop (¼-cup capacity).

5. Bake for 20 to 25 minutes, or until the muffins are golden brown and the tops are springy to the touch. To ensure even baking, toward the end of baking time, rotate the pans top to bottom and front to back. Remove from the oven and place on a rack to cool.

STORAGE: Store at room temperature, tightly wrapped in aluminum foil, for up to 3 days. These muffins may be frozen.

sweet yankee corn muffins

MAKES 12 MUFFINS

North, south, east, west—which corn muffins do you like the best? The recipe for these corn muffins came to me from my childhood friend Sondra Ballin, who hails from Memphis, Tennessee. It is curious that this recipe, which contains sugar, came to me from the South, since it is not in keeping with a Southern-style corn muffin, which does not contain sugar.

AT A GLANCE
PAN: Standard muffin pan
PAN PREP: Butter/oil
OVEN TEMP: 400°F
BAKING TIME: 18 to 20 minutes
DIFFICULTY: ☕

That's why I think of it as a "Yankee" recipe. The muffins are often baked in preheated pans that contain a small amount of fat, usually bacon drippings. When the batter is portioned in the hot fat, it sizzles. I have also found that excellent results are produced without preheating the pan; in fact, the muffins rise even higher. I have been making these corn muffins for years and I no longer preheat the pan. Not only do I enjoy them for breakfast and snacks, but they make a perfect addition to my cornbread stuffing recipe at Thanksgiving. Sometimes I add toasted pecans, which give the muffins a tantalizing crunch.

6 tablespoons (¾ stick) unsalted butter

2 tablespoons canola oil

1 cup all-purpose flour, spooned in and leveled

1 cup stone-ground yellow cornmeal, spooned in and leveled

⅓ cup sugar

1 tablespoon baking powder

¾ teaspoon salt

2 large eggs

1 cup milk

¾ teaspoon pure vanilla extract

1. Position the rack in the lower third of the oven. Heat the oven to 400°F.

2. Place the butter in a heavy 1-quart saucepan and melt over low heat. Continue to simmer, skimming the foam from the top as it forms. The butter is ready when it is a rich golden brown and has a nutty fragrance. This will take 5 to 7 minutes or more, depending on the weight of the pan. *Watch carefully to avoid burning.* Pour the browned butter into a glass measuring cup and add the oil. Spoon a generous ½ teaspoon of the butter/oil mixture into each cup of a muffin pan.

3. In a large bowl, whisk together the flour, cornmeal, sugar, baking powder, and salt.

4. In a medium bowl, combine the eggs, milk, and vanilla.

5. Make a well in the center of the dry ingredients and add the liquids, along with the remaining butter/oil mixture. Using an oversize rubber spatula, incorporate the

dry ingredients into the liquids by pushing them from the side of the bowl toward the center. *Do not overmix.* The batter will be loose and slightly lumpy.

6. Portion the batter into the muffin cups using a no. 16 ice cream scoop (¼-cup capacity). Fill the cups until almost full.

7. Bake for 18 to 20 minutes, or until the muffins are golden brown and the tops are springy to the touch. To ensure even baking, toward the end of baking time, rotate the pans top to bottom and front to back. Remove from the oven and place on a rack to cool.

STORAGE: Store at room temperature, tightly covered with plastic wrap, for up to 3 days. These muffins may be frozen.

VARIATION

pecan corn muffins

Prepare the Sweet Yankee Corn Muffin batter as directed in the recipe. In Step 3, whisk ½ cup of medium-chopped, toasted pecans (see pages 391–392) into the dry ingredients. Proceed with the recipe as written.

ultra-rich corn muffins

MAKES 12 MUFFINS

After creating the recipe for this corn muffin, I put it at the top of the list as my favorite. Its velvety crumb, which comes from the addition of cream-style corn and sour cream, is contrasted by the crunch of stone-ground cornmeal.

AT A GLANCE
PAN: Standard muffin pan
PAN PREP: Butter/oil
OVEN TEMP: 400°F
BAKING TIME: 20 to 22 minutes
DIFFICULTY: 🍵

⅓ cup (⅔ stick) unsalted butter

¼ cup canola oil

1¼ cups stone-ground cornmeal, spooned in and leveled

¾ cup all-purpose flour, spooned in and leveled

⅓ cup sugar

1 tablespoon baking powder

¾ teaspoon salt

¼ teaspoon baking soda

1 cup canned yellow cream-style corn

½ cup sour cream

3 large eggs

2 tablespoons milk

1 teaspoon pure vanilla extract

1. Position the rack in the lower third of the oven. Heat the oven to 400°F.

2. Place the butter in a heavy 2-quart saucepan and melt over low heat. Continue to simmer, skimming the foam from the top as it forms. The butter is ready when it is a rich golden brown and has a nutty fragrance. This will take 5 to 7 minutes or more, depending on the weight of the pan. *Watch carefully to avoid burning.* Pour the browned butter into a glass measuring cup and add the oil. Spoon a scant 1 teaspoon of the tepid butter/oil mixture into each cup of a muffin pan.

3. In a large bowl, whisk together the cornmeal, flour, sugar, baking powder, salt, and baking soda.

4. In a medium bowl, combine the corn, sour cream, eggs, milk, and vanilla.

5. Make a well in the center of the dry ingredients and add the liquids, along with the remaining butter/oil mixture. Using an oversize rubber spatula, incorporate the dry ingredients into the liquids by pushing them from the side of the bowl toward the center. *Do not overmix.* It's okay if the batter is slightly lumpy.

6. Portion level scoops of the batter into the muffin cups using a no. 16 ice cream scoop (¼-cup capacity).

7. Bake for 20 to 22 minutes, or until the muffins are golden brown and the tops are springy to the touch. To ensure even baking, toward the end of baking time, rotate the pans top to bottom and front to back. Remove from the oven and place on a rack to cool.

STORAGE: Store at room temperature, tightly covered with plastic wrap, for up to 3 days. These muffins may be frozen.

MUFFINS IN MINUTES

MUFFIN BATTERS refrigerate beautifully, so the batter may be made ahead and the muffins baked as needed. In fact, I have found that muffin batter that has been refrigerated often produces muffins with a better dome on top.

After you make the batter, you may either keep it in a bowl to scoop out as needed or, alternatively, portion it into muffin tins ready for baking. The batter will keep for up to 3 days, well covered with plastic wrap. If portioning into muffin tins in advance, I like to use aluminum foil liners because they are stronger and the batter does not seep through the bottom as it does with paper liners.

Muffin batters that have been made ahead can go from refrigerator to oven. Simply add a few additional minutes to the baking time.

rustic corn muffins

MAKES 14 MUFFINS

If you like texture in your corn muffins, this is the recipe to make. The batter is made with stone-ground cornmeal and whole wheat flour along with caramelized kernels of fresh corn. The sweetness of the corn is tempered by the tang of the buttermilk. Although I like to make these muffins with fresh sweet corn, it's okay to substitute frozen kernels. When ready to eat, just spoon on some of your favorite preserves and bite into this tasty treat.

AT A GLANCE

PAN: Two standard muffin pans
PAN PREP: Butter/oil
OVEN TEMP: 400°F
BAKING TIME: 18 to 22 minutes
DIFFICULTY: ☕

CARAMELIZED CORN

1 tablespoon unsalted butter

⅓ cup *very fresh* light brown sugar

1 cup fresh corn kernels (1 large or 2 small ears of corn)

¼ cup water

Pinch of salt

BATTER

⅓ cup (⅔ stick) unsalted butter

⅓ cup canola oil

1½ cups stone-ground cornmeal, spooned in and leveled

¾ cup stone-ground whole wheat flour, spooned in and leveled

¼ cup sugar

2 teaspoons baking powder

1 teaspoon salt

½ teaspoon baking soda

½ teaspoon chili powder

2 large eggs

1 cup buttermilk

1 teaspoon pure vanilla extract

1. Position the racks in the upper and lower thirds of the oven. Heat the oven to 400°F.

MAKE THE CARAMELIZED CORN

2. Have ready a flat pan lined with a sheet of buttered aluminum foil. Melt the butter in a 10-inch, heavy-bottomed skillet over medium-low heat. Add the brown sugar and stir to blend. Cook until the mixture is syrupy, then add the corn, water, and pinch

of salt. Break up any lumps of sugar with a spoon. Cover and cook for 5 minutes longer. Remove the cover, and continue to cook over medium-low heat for another 12 to 15 minutes, or until the liquid is evaporated and the corn is golden brown. Remove from the heat and spread the kernels in a single layer on the prepared pan.

MAKE THE BATTER

3. Place the butter in a heavy 1-quart saucepan and melt over low heat. Continue to simmer, skimming the foam from the top as it forms. The butter is ready when it is a rich golden brown and has a nutty fragrance. This will take 5 to 7 minutes or more, depending on the weight of the pan. *Watch carefully to avoid burning.* Pour the browned butter into a glass measuring cup and add the oil. Spoon a scant teaspoon of the tepid butter/oil mixture into fourteen muffin cups.

4. In a large bowl, whisk together the cornmeal, flour, sugar, baking powder, salt, baking soda, and chili powder. Add the cooled corn mixture and work through with your fingertips until all the clusters of corn are broken up. Set aside.

5. In a medium bowl, combine the eggs, buttermilk, and vanilla. Make a well in the center of the dry ingredients and add the liquids, along with the remaining butter/oil mixture. Using an oversize rubber spatula, incorporate the dry ingredients into the liquids by pushing them from the side of the bowl toward the center. The batter will be loose and slightly lumpy.

BAKE THE MUFFINS

6. Portion level scoops of the batter into the muffin cups using a no. 16 ice cream scoop (¼-cup capacity).

7. Bake for 18 to 22 minutes, or until the muffins are golden brown and the tops are springy to the touch. To ensure even baking, toward the end of baking time, rotate the pans top to bottom and front to back. Remove from the oven and place on a rack to cool.

STORAGE: Store at room temperature, tightly covered with plastic wrap, for up to 3 days. These muffins may be frozen.

favorite vanilla muffins

MAKES 12 MUFFINS

Here is a vanilla muffin that children will surely love. This tender textured muffin has a top that glistens with crunchy sugar crystals. Those of you who favor chocolate should not overlook the chocolate chunk variation—fine-quality chocolate is cut into ¼-inch chunks and folded throughout the batter. Whether you like your muffins plain or with chocolate or almond crunch, these are bound to become a family favorite.

AT A GLANCE
PAN: Standard muffin pan
PAN PREP: Line with paper or foil cupcake liners
OVEN TEMP: 375°F
BAKING TIME: 23 to 25 minutes
DIFFICULTY: 🍶

1½ cups all-purpose flour, spooned in and leveled

¾ teaspoon baking powder

½ teaspoon salt

¼ teaspoon baking soda

½ cup (1 stick) unsalted butter, slightly firm

2 teaspoons pure vanilla extract

1 cup granulated sugar

2 large eggs

½ cup sour cream

3 to 4 teaspoons sparkling sugar (see page 380)

1. Position the rack in the lower third of the oven. Heat the oven to 375°F. Line a muffin pan with paper or foil cupcake liners.

2. In a large bowl, thoroughly whisk together the flour, baking powder, salt, and baking soda. Set aside.

3. Cut the butter into 1-inch pieces and place in the bowl of an electric mixer fitted with the paddle attachment. Add the vanilla and mix on medium speed until smooth and lightened in color, about 1 minute.

4. Add the granulated sugar in four additions and mix for 1 minute longer. Scrape down the side of the bowl. Blend in the eggs, one at a time, and mix for another minute.

5. Reduce the mixer speed to low and add the flour mixture alternately with the sour cream, dividing the dry ingredients into two parts, starting and ending with the flour. Mix just until blended after each addition.

6. Portion the batter into the prepared pan using a no. 16 ice cream scoop (¼-cup capacity). Sprinkle the top of each muffin with about ¼ teaspoon of the sparkling sugar.

7. Bake for 23 to 25 minutes, or until the muffins are golden brown and the tops are springy to the touch. To ensure even baking, toward the end of baking time, rotate the pans top to bottom and front to back. Remove from the oven and place on a rack to cool.

STORAGE: Store at room temperature, tightly wrapped in aluminum foil, for up to 3 days. These muffins may be frozen.

VARIATION

chocolate chunk vanilla muffins

1 (3.5 ounce) bar fine-quality bittersweet chocolate,
   such as Lindt, cut into ¼-inch dice

In Step 5, when the bowl is removed from the mixer, fold in the chocolate chunks using an oversize rubber spatula. Proceed with Step 6 of the recipe.

VARIATION

almond crunch muffins

Almond Crunch Streusel (page 351)
1 large egg mixed with 1 teaspoon of water, for egg wash

In Step 5, when the bowl is removed from the mixer, sprinkle half of the almond crunch streusel over the top of the batter, but do not mix through. Proceed with step 6 of the recipe and brush the tops of the muffins with the egg wash. Distribute 1 tablespoon of the remaining streusel over each muffin, pressing lightly with your fingertips.

jeff's chocolate-glazed midnight muffins

MAKES 12 MUFFINS

Ever since my grandson Jeffrey was a little boy his love of chocolate has never waned, and that was quite evident when he tasted these muffins. Since chocolate is my weakness as well, I guess Jeffrey is a chocolate chip off the old block.

If you wish, these deep, dark chocolate muffins can be studded with toasted walnuts that add a marvelous crunch. Be sure to add the nuts in two additions. This will ensure that the nuts will be evenly distributed when the batter is portioned.

AT A GLANCE
PAN: Standard muffin pan
PAN PREP: Line with paper or foil cupcake liners
OVEN TEMP: 350°F
BAKING TIME: 20 to 25 minutes
DIFFICULTY: ☕

²⁄₃ cup strained cocoa powder, spooned in and leveled

6 tablespoons hot water

½ cup sour cream

½ cup canola oil

2 large eggs

1 teaspoon pure vanilla extract

1¾ cups all-purpose flour, spooned in and leveled

1¼ cups sugar

½ teaspoon baking soda

½ teaspoon baking powder

¼ teaspoon salt

¾ cup broken toasted walnuts (see page 391), optional

Midnight Chocolate Glaze (page 363)

1. Position the rack in the lower third of the oven. Heat the oven to 350°F. Line a muffin pan with paper or foil cupcake liners.

2. In a medium bowl, blend the cocoa powder and hot water to form a smooth paste. Stir in the sour cream. Whisk in the oil in four additions, then add in the eggs and vanilla, whisking until smooth.

3. In a large bowl, thoroughly whisk together the flour, sugar, baking soda, baking powder, and salt.

4. Make a well in the center of the dry ingredients. Add the chocolate mixture, and using an oversize rubber spatula, incorporate the dry ingredients into the liquids by pushing them from the side of the bowl toward the center. If using walnuts, blend in ½ cup as you fold.

5. Portion level scoops of the batter into the prepared pan using a no. 16 ice cream scoop (¼-cup capacity). As you reach the batter in the bottom of the bowl, fold in the remaining optional walnuts (see headnote).

6. Bake for 20 to 25 minutes, or until the tops of the muffins are springy to the touch. To ensure even baking, toward the end of baking time, rotate the pans top to bottom and front to back. Remove from the oven and place on a rack. While the muffins are slightly warm, drizzle with Midnight Chocolate Glaze. Leftover glaze may be refrigerated for up to several weeks, or frozen.

STORAGE: Store at room temperature, tightly wrapped in aluminum foil, for up to 3 days. These muffins may be frozen before glazing.

"There is a charm in improvised eating which a regular meal lacks."
GRAHAM GREENE

sam's oodles of apple muffins with country crumb topping

MAKES 16 MUFFINS

My granddaughter Samantha, a terrific baker in her own right, loves apples. When creating recipes for this book, what better muffin to make for Sam than one loaded with all the flavors that she loves. The batter is filled with chopped apples, brown sugar, honey, and spices, and accented with raisins and pecans. The crumb topping is made with a buttery mixture of white and whole wheat flours, along with oatmeal, brown sugar, and cinnamon. When Sam took her first bite, the twinkle in her eye told me that this muffin was a winner.

AT A GLANCE
PANS: Two standard muffin pans
PAN PREP: Line with paper or foil cupcake liners
OVEN TEMP: 375°F
BAKING TIME: 20 to 25 minutes
DIFFICULTY: 🥄

Country Crumb Topping (page 356)

3 medium McIntosh apples (about 1 pound), peeled, cored, and cut into eighths

1¾ cups all-purpose flour, spooned in and leveled

1 teaspoon baking powder

1 teaspoon ground cinnamon

½ teaspoon ground nutmeg

½ teaspoon baking soda

½ teaspoon salt

2 large eggs

1 cup *very fresh* dark brown sugar

2 tablespoons honey

1 teaspoon pure vanilla extract

¼ cup (½ stick) unsalted butter, melted and cooled

2 tablespoons canola oil

½ cup dark raisins, plumped (see page 389)

½ cup medium-chopped toasted pecans (see pages 391–392)

1. Prepare the Country Crumb Topping. Set aside.

2. Position the racks in the upper and lower thirds of the oven. Heat the oven to 375°F. Line sixteen muffin cups with paper or foil cupcake liners.

3. Place the apples in the work bowl of a food processor fitted with a steel blade and pulse 8 to 10 times, or until the apples are chopped into ¼-inch pieces.

4. In a medium bowl, thoroughly whisk together the flour, baking powder, cinnamon, nutmeg, baking soda, and salt. Set aside.

5. In the bowl of an electric mixer fitted with the whip attachment, beat the eggs on medium-high speed until lightened in color, about 2 minutes. Add the brown

sugar, 1 to 2 tablespoons at a time, taking about 2 minutes, and beat the mixture for 1 minute longer.

6. *Stop the machine* and add the honey and vanilla. Turn the mixer on to medium speed and mix to combine. In a small bowl, whisk together the melted butter and oil and pour it into the egg mixture in a steady stream, taking about 1 minute. Add the apples and blend well.

7. Reduce the mixer speed to medium-low and add the dry ingredients all at once, blending just until incorporated. Remove the bowl from the mixer, and using an over-size rubber spatula, fold in the raisins and pecans.

8. Portion the batter into the prepared pans using a no. 16 ice cream scoop (¼-cup capacity). Top each muffin with a few tablespoons of topping, pressing it gently into the batter.

9. Bake for 20 to 25 minutes, or until the streusel is golden brown. To ensure even baking, toward the end of baking time, rotate the pans top to bottom and front to back. Remove from the oven and place on a rack to cool.

STORAGE: Store at room temperature, tightly wrapped in aluminum foil, for up to 5 days. These muffins may be frozen.

apricot and dried pineapple muffins

MAKES 14 MUFFINS

Apricots and pineapple make a terrific combination. Here we have tangy bites of dried apricots combined with the sweetness of sugary dried pineapple. The fruit is folded through a vanilla batter that is highlighted with the zest of orange and lemon. I like to sprinkle the tops of the muffins with granulated sugar. After baking, the sugar forms a marvelous crunchy topping.

AT A GLANCE

PANS: Two standard muffin pans
PAN PREP: Line with paper or foil cupcake liners
OVEN TEMP: 375°F
BAKING TIME: 22 to 25 minutes
DIFFICULTY: ☕

---

2 cups all-purpose flour, spooned in and leveled

2 teaspoons baking powder

$\frac{1}{2}$ teaspoon baking soda

$\frac{1}{2}$ teaspoon salt

$\frac{1}{2}$ cup (1 stick) unsalted butter, slightly firm

$1\frac{1}{2}$ teaspoons finely grated navel orange zest

1 teaspoon finely grated lemon zest

$\frac{3}{4}$ cup superfine sugar

2 large eggs

1 teaspoon pure vanilla extract

1 cup plain yogurt

$\frac{1}{2}$ cup dried, sugared pineapple chunks (not organic), cut into $\frac{1}{4}$-inch dice

$\frac{1}{3}$ cup *very fresh* dried apricots (not organic), cut in eighths, plumped for $\frac{1}{2}$ hour (see page 389)

$1\frac{1}{2}$ to 2 tablespoons granulated sugar, for sprinkling

1. Position the racks in the upper and lower thirds of the oven. Heat the oven to 375°F. Line fourteen muffin cups with paper or foil cupcake liners.

2. In a medium bowl, thoroughly whisk together the flour, baking powder, baking soda, and salt. Set aside.

3. Cut the butter into 1-inch pieces and place in the bowl of an electric mixer fitted with the paddle attachment. Add the orange and lemon zests and mix on medium speed until smooth and lightened in color, about 1 minute. Add the superfine sugar, 2 to 3 tablespoons at a time, taking 2 to 3 minutes. Scrape down the side of the bowl as needed. Add the eggs, one at a time, beating well after each addition. Add the vanilla and mix until combined.

4. Reduce the mixer speed to low and add the flour mixture alternately with the yogurt, dividing the flour into three parts and the yogurt into two parts, starting and ending with the flour. Mix just until blended after each addition. Scrape down the side

of the bowl as needed. Remove the bowl from the mixer, and using an oversize rubber spatula, fold in the pineapple and apricots.

5. Portion level scoops of the batter into the prepared pans using a no. 16 ice cream scoop (¼-cup capacity). Sprinkle the top of each muffin with about ½ teaspoon granulated sugar.

6. Bake for 22 to 25 minutes, or until the muffins are golden brown and the tops are springy to the touch. To ensure even baking, toward the end of baking time, rotate the pans top to bottom and front to back. Remove from the oven and place on a rack to cool.

STORAGE: Store at room temperature, tightly wrapped in aluminum foil, for up to 3 days. These muffins may be frozen.

banana date muffins

MAKES 14 MUFFINS

If you've never tried the combination of bananas and dates, you are in for a treat. The freshness of the dates is of the utmost importance. They should be moist, tender, and extremely sweet. In these muffins, they blend beautifully with mashed bananas. Ground cardamom and nutmeg round out the flavors, while chopped pecans provide crunchy texture.

AT A GLANCE
PANS: Two standard muffin pans
PAN PREP: Line with paper or foil cupcake liners
OVEN TEMP: 375°F
BAKING TIME: 25 to 28 minutes
DIFFICULTY: 🍵

---

2 very ripe, medium bananas

1 teaspoon fresh lemon juice

1¾ cups all-purpose flour, spooned in and leveled

½ cup granulated sugar

1 teaspoon baking powder

1 teaspoon ground cardamom

¾ teaspoon salt

½ teaspoon baking soda

½ teaspoon ground nutmeg

½ cup *very fresh*, pitted, hand-cut dates (¼-inch dice)

½ cup toasted pecans, coarsely chopped (see pages 391–392)

½ cup (1 stick) unsalted butter, melted and cooled to tepid

½ cup *very fresh* dark brown sugar

½ cup low-fat plain yogurt

2 large eggs, lightly beaten

1 teaspoon pure vanilla extract

1. Position the racks in the upper and lower thirds of the oven. Heat the oven to 375°F. Line fourteen muffin cups with paper or foil cupcake liners.

2. Cut the bananas into 1-inch chunks and place them in a medium bowl. Mash with a potato masher or a fork. You should have about 1 cup banana pulp. Stir in the lemon juice and set aside.

3. In a large bowl, thoroughly whisk together the flour, granulated sugar, baking powder, cardamom, salt, baking soda, and nutmeg. Toss the dates and nuts through the dry ingredients, separating the pieces of dates with your fingertips.

4. In a medium bowl, whisk together the tepid butter and brown sugar. Blend in the bananas, yogurt, eggs, and vanilla.

5. Make a well in the center of the dry ingredients and add the banana-egg mixture. Using an oversize rubber spatula, incorporate the dry ingredients into the liquids by

pushing them from the side of the bowl toward the center. *Do not overmix.* It's okay if a few streaks of flour remain.

6. Portion generous scoops of the batter into the prepared pans using a no. 16 ice cream scoop (¼-cup capacity).

7. Bake for 25 to 28 minutes, or until the muffins are golden brown and the tops are springy to the touch. To ensure even baking, toward the end of baking time, rotate the pans top to bottom and front to back. Remove from the oven and place on a rack to cool.

STORAGE: Store at room temperature, tightly covered with plastic wrap, for up to 3 days. These muffins may be frozen.

"Muffins are the simpletons of the cake world. No fancy tricks required."
NANCY SILVERTON

peanut butter banana muffins

MAKES 14 MUFFINS

Here we have a muffin featuring that dynamic duo—peanut butter and banana—accented with mini chocolate chips and chopped Spanish peanuts. Be sure to seek out the little, oval Spanish peanut variety; their thin red skins add marvelous flavor and a touch of color to the muffins.

When you make the muffin batter, the butter should be very soft so it will blend smoothly with the peanut butter. I don't recommend using "natural-style" peanut butter as the finished muffin will have a drier texture.

> **AT A GLANCE**
> **PANS:** Two standard muffin pans
> **PAN PREP:** Line with paper or foil cupcake liners
> **OVEN TEMP:** 375°F
> **BAKING TIME:** 25 to 27 minutes
> **DIFFICULTY:** 🥄

1½ cups all-purpose flour, spooned in and leveled

1 teaspoon baking powder

½ teaspoon salt

¼ teaspoon baking soda

⅓ cup (⅔ stick) unsalted butter, *very soft*

⅓ cup smooth peanut butter

½ cup very fresh dark brown sugar

⅓ cup granulated sugar

1 large egg

1 teaspoon pure vanilla extract

½ cup plain yogurt

½ cup mashed banana (about 1½ medium, very ripe bananas)

⅓ cup medium chopped salted Spanish peanuts

½ cup mini chocolate chips

4 teaspoons sparkling sugar (see page 380)

1. Position the racks in the upper and lower thirds of the oven. Heat the oven to 375°F. Line fourteen muffin cups with paper or foil cupcake liners.

2. In a medium bowl, thoroughly whisk together the flour, baking powder, salt, and baking soda.

3. Combine the butter and peanut butter in the bowl of an electric mixer fitted with the paddle attachment. Mix on medium speed until smooth, about 1 minute.

4. Add the brown sugar, then the granulated sugar, and mix on medium speed for 2 minutes, scraping down the side of the bowl as needed. Add the egg and vanilla and mix for about 1 minute.

5. Combine the yogurt with the banana. Reduce the mixer speed to low and add the dry ingredients alternately with the yogurt/banana mixture, dividing the flour into

three parts and the yogurt mixture into two parts, starting and ending with the flour. *Do not overmix.*

6. Set aside 2 tablespoons of the peanuts for garnishing. Remove the bowl from the mixer. Using a rubber spatula, fold the remaining peanuts and the mini chocolate chips into the batter.

7. Portion level scoops of the batter into the prepared pans using a no. 16 ice cream scoop (¼-cup capacity). Sprinkle the top of each muffin with a scant ½ teaspoon of chopped peanuts and about ¼ teaspoon of sparkling sugar.

8. Bake for 25 to 27 minutes, or until the muffins are golden brown and the tops are springy to the touch. To ensure even baking, toward the end of baking time, rotate the pans top to bottom and front to back. Remove from the oven and place on a rack to cool.

STORAGE: Store at room temperature, tightly wrapped in aluminum foil, for up to 3 days. These muffins may be frozen.

zach's blueberry buttermilk muffins with streusel topping

MAKES 14 MUFFINS

Until I created this chapter, I never realized that blueberry muffins were so popular. When I announced to my grandson Zach that I was writing a book that contained a chapter on muffins, he said, "You are putting in a recipe for blueberry, aren't you? It's my favorite!" Zach is not alone. Blueberry muffins are at the top of many people's list.

AT A GLANCE
PANS: Two standard muffin pans
PAN PREP: Line with paper or foil cupcake liners
OVEN TEMP: 375°F
BAKING TIME: 25 to 30 minutes
DIFFICULTY: 🍮

These blueberry muffins are absolutely heavenly. They are flavored with a hint of lemon zest and are topped with a thick layer of buttery streusel crumbs. To overcome the problem of the berries sinking to the bottom of the muffins, instead of folding the berries through the batter, I top the batter with a handful of berries. Then I cover the berries with a generous handful of streusel. The blueberry muffin lovers in your life are in for a real treat.

I small recipe Carole's Favorite Streusel (page 350)

1¾ cups all-purpose flour, spooned in and leveled

½ teaspoon baking powder

½ teaspoon salt

¼ teaspoon baking soda

⅔ cup (1⅓ sticks) unsalted butter, slightly firm

2 teaspoons finely grated lemon zest

¾ cup sugar

1 large egg

1 teaspoon pure vanilla extract

½ cup buttermilk

1½ cups fresh blueberries, washed and well dried (see page 390)

1. Prepare a small recipe of Carole's Favorite Streusel. Set aside.

2. Position the racks in the upper and lower thirds of the oven. Heat the oven to 375°F. Line fourteen muffin cups with paper or foil cupcake liners.

3. In a large bowl, thoroughly whisk together the flour, baking powder, salt, and baking soda. Set aside.

4. Cut the butter into 1-inch pieces and place in the bowl of an electric mixer fitted with the paddle attachment. Add the lemon zest and mix on medium speed until smooth and lightened in color, about 1 minute. Add the sugar in a steady stream, then blend in the egg and vanilla, scraping down the side of the bowl as needed.

5. Reduce the mixer speed to low and add the flour mixture alternately with the buttermilk, dividing the flour into three parts and the buttermilk into two, starting and ending with the flour. Mix just until blended after each addition.

6. Portion half scoops of the batter into the prepared pans using a no. 16 ice cream scoop (¼-cup capacity). Place a layer of blueberries evenly over the batter, then place a dollop of batter on top of the blueberries. It's okay for the berries to show. Take a handful of the streusel topping and crumble it over the batter and berries, completely covering the tops of the muffins with the crumbs. Press gently to adhere. Brush any stray crumbs from the top of the muffin pans using a small pastry brush.

7. Bake for 25 to 30 minutes, or until the streusel topping is golden brown. To ensure even baking, toward the end of baking time, rotate the pans top to bottom and front to back. Remove from the oven and place on a rack to cool.

STORAGE: Store at room temperature, tightly wrapped in aluminum foil, for up to 3 days. These muffins may be frozen.

VARIATION

raspberry buttermilk muffins with streusel topping

I small recipe Carole's Favorite Streusel
(page 350)

Batter for Zach's Blueberry Buttermilk
Muffins (page 98)

2 (6-ounce) packages fresh raspberries,
washed and well dried (see page 390)

Follow the recipe for the blueberry muffins, replacing the blueberries in Step 6 with raspberries. Proceed with the recipe as written.

old-fashioned carrot muffins

MAKES 14 MUFFINS

Of the many muffin varieties, carrot muffins are certainly one of the most popular. Sweet carrots, crushed pineapple, and raisins form a tasty trio that blends perfectly with the spice-accented batter. Be sure to use canned crushed pineapple, not fresh; fresh pineapple must be cooked before using in baked goods. Check out the Cream Cheese Frosting (page 364), the favorite topping for these muffins. You can frost them ahead of time and store them in the refrigerator or freezer.

AT A GLANCE
PANS: Two standard muffin pans
PAN PREP: Line with paper or foil cupcake liners
OVEN TEMP: 375°F
BAKING TIME: 25 to 28 minutes
DIFFICULTY: ☕

8 ounces (about 3) carrots, peeled

1½ cups all-purpose flour, spooned in and leveled

1 teaspoon baking powder

1 teaspoon ground cinnamon

¾ teaspoon ground cardamom

½ teaspoon baking soda

½ teaspoon salt

¼ teaspoon ground nutmeg

Pinch of ground cloves

⅓ cup (⅔ stick) unsalted butter, slightly firm

⅓ cup canola oil

½ cup very *fresh* dark brown sugar

¼ cup granulated sugar

2 large eggs

1 teaspoon pure vanilla extract

½ cup canned crushed pineapple, drained

¾ cup walnuts, medium chopped (see page 392)

¼ cup golden raisins, plumped (see page 389)

1 small recipe Cream Cheese Frosting (page 364)

1. Cut the carrots into 1-inch chunks. Shred the carrots in a food processor fitted with the medium shredding disk using little or no pressure on the pusher. (This will give you a finer shred.) Change to the steel blade and pulse the carrots 10 to 12 times, until finely cut. You should have about 1 cup carrots. Set aside.

2. Position the racks in the upper and lower thirds of the oven. Heat the oven to 375°F. Line fourteen muffin cups with paper or foil cupcake liners.

3. In a medium bowl, thoroughly whisk together the flour, baking powder, cinnamon, cardamom, baking soda, salt, nutmeg, and cloves. Set aside.

4. Cut the butter into 1-inch pieces and place in the bowl of an electric mixer fitted with the paddle attachment. Mix on medium speed until smooth and lightened in color, about 1 minute. Drizzle in the oil, taking about 1 minute, scraping down the

side of the bowl as needed. Add the brown sugar in three or four additions, then pour in the granulated sugar and mix until well blended, about 1 minute. Add the eggs, one at a time, mixing well after each addition. Scrape down the side of the bowl again. Blend in the vanilla.

5. Reduce the mixer speed to low and blend in the carrots and pineapple. Add the dry ingredients in two additions, mixing just until combined. Remove the bowl from the mixer. Using a rubber spatula, fold in the nuts and raisins.

6. Portion the batter into the prepared pans using a no. 16 ice cream scoop ($\frac{1}{4}$-cup capacity). Fill the cups until *almost* full. Bake for 25 to 28 minutes, or until the tops show signs of browning and are springy to the touch. To ensure even baking, toward the end of baking time, rotate the pans top to bottom and front to back. Remove from the oven and place on a rack to cool.

7. While the muffins are baking, prepare the frosting. When the muffins are cool, spread the tops with frosting, applying it with the bottom of a teaspoon.

STORAGE: Refrigerate, tightly wrapped in aluminum foil, for up to 5 days. These muffins may be frozen.

cape cod cranberry muffins

MAKES 14 MUFFINS

Several years ago, I took cooking lessons at a bed-and-breakfast in New England. Dave, my cooking partner and a chef from Cape Cod, shared with me his marvelous cranberry muffin recipe.

AT A GLANCE
PANS: Two standard muffin pans
PAN PREP: Line with paper or foil cupcake liners
OVEN TEMP: 375°F
BAKING TIME: 18 to 20 minutes
DIFFICULTY: ☕

5 ounces (1¼ cups) fresh or frozen cranberries

2¼ cups all-purpose flour, spooned in and leveled

1½ teaspoons baking powder

½ teaspoon baking soda

½ teaspoon salt

3 tablespoons unsalted butter, melted

3 tablespoons canola oil

¾ cup sugar

2 large eggs, lightly beaten

⅔ cup orange juice

¾ cup coarsely chopped toasted walnuts (see pages 391–392)

1. Position the racks in the upper and lower thirds of the oven. Heat the oven to 375°F. Line fourteen muffin cups with paper or foil cupcake liners.

2. Coarsely chop the berries in the food processor using the steel blade.

3. In a large bowl, whisk together the flour, baking powder, baking soda, and salt.

4. Heat the butter and oil in a small saucepan until the butter melts. Remove from the heat and blend in the sugar. The sugar will not dissolve.

5. Using a wooden spoon, stir together the eggs and orange juice in a large bowl. Blend in the warm sugar mixture. Add the dry ingredients and stir just until moistened. When the flour is *almost* incorporated, gently fold in the nuts and cranberries.

6. Portion the batter into the prepared pans using a no. 16 ice cream scoop (¼-cup capacity). Fill the cups until *almost* full. Bake the muffins for 18 to 20 minutes, or until the muffins are golden brown and the tops are springy to the touch. To ensure even baking, toward the end of baking time, rotate the pans top to bottom and front to back. Remove from the oven and place on a rack to cool.

STORAGE: Store at room temperature, tightly wrapped in aluminum foil, for up to 3 days. These muffins may be frozen.

oatmeal raisin muffins

MAKES 12 MUFFINS

Oatmeal raisin muffins are one of the most popular of all varieties, and for good reason, since they are one of the more healthful muffins. If you wish to skip the nuts, simply increase the raisins.

AT A GLANCE
PAN: Standard muffin pan
PAN PREP: Paper or foil cupcake liners
OVEN TEMP: 375°F
BAKING TIME: 23 to 25 minutes
DIFFICULTY:

1¼ cups all-purpose flour, spooned in and leveled

1¼ cups old-fashioned oats

1 teaspoon baking powder

1 teaspoon baking soda

¾ teaspoon salt

1½ teaspoons ground cinnamon

½ teaspoon ground nutmeg

¼ teaspoon ground allspice

2 large eggs

¾ cup (lightly packed) dark brown sugar

1 cup buttermilk

½ cup canola oil

1 teaspoon pure vanilla extract

½ cup dark raisins, plumped, drained, and patted dry (see page 389)

½ cup coarsely chopped toasted walnuts (see pages 391–392)

1. Position the rack in the lower third of the oven. Heat the oven to 375°F. Line a muffin pan with paper or foil cupcake liners.

2. Combine the flour, ¾ cup of the oats, the baking powder, baking soda, salt, cinnamon, nutmeg, and allspice in the bowl of a food processor fitted with the steel blade. Pulse 10 times. Empty into a large bowl and add ½ cup oats. Make a well in the center.

3. In a medium bowl, whisk together the eggs and brown sugar, then add the buttermilk, oil, and vanilla and pour the mixture into the well. Using an oversize rubber spatula, incorporate the mixtures by pushing them from the side of the bowl toward the center. Fold in the raisins and nuts. Let stand for 5 minutes.

4. Portion the batter into the prepared pan using a no. 16 ice cream scoop (¼-cup capacity). The batter should be filled to slightly below the top of the paper liner (about three-fourths full). Bake for 23 to 25 minutes, or until the muffins are golden brown and the tops are springy to the touch. To ensure even baking, toward the end of baking time, rotate the pans top to bottom and front to back. Remove from the oven and place on a rack to cool.

STORAGE: Store at room temperature, tightly wrapped in aluminum foil, for up to 5 days. These muffins may be frozen.

lemon poppy seed muffins

MAKES 14 MUFFINS

The combination of lemon and poppy seeds is a traditional favorite. In this recipe, using the juice as well as the zest enhances the lemon flavor, while buttermilk provides extra tang. Pair this muffin with a cup of warm tea for a cool-weather pick-me-up, or complement it with a glass of lemonade when the temperature begins to climb. Either way, it's a special treat.

AT A GLANCE
PANS: Two standard muffin pans
PAN PREP: Line with paper or foil cupcake liners
OVEN TEMP: 375°F
BAKING TIME: 25 to 30 minutes
DIFFICULTY: 🍵

2 cups all-purpose flour, spooned in and leveled

3 tablespoons poppy seeds

½ teaspoon baking powder

½ teaspoon baking soda

½ teaspoon salt

½ cup (1 stick) unsalted butter, slightly firm

4 teaspoons freshly grated lemon zest

3 tablespoons canola oil

1 cup superfine sugar

2 large eggs

½ cup buttermilk

¼ cup fresh lemon juice

1 teaspoon pure vanilla extract

4 teaspoons granulated sugar, for garnish

1. Position the racks in the upper and lower thirds of the oven. Heat the oven to 375°F. Line fourteen muffin cups with paper or foil cupcake liners.

2. In a medium bowl, thoroughly whisk together the flour, poppy seeds, baking powder, baking soda, and salt. Set aside.

3. Cut the butter into 1-inch pieces and place in the bowl of an electric mixer fitted with the paddle attachment. Add the lemon zest and mix on medium speed until smooth and lightened in color, about 1 minute. Drizzle in the oil, taking about 1 minute, then mix for 1 minute longer. Add the superfine sugar, 2 to 3 tablespoons at time, taking 2 to 3 minutes. Scrape down the side of the bowl as needed. Add the eggs, one at a time, mixing well after each addition.

4. In a small bowl, combine the buttermilk, lemon juice, and vanilla. Reduce the mixer speed to low and add the flour mixture alternately with the liquids, dividing the flour into three parts and the buttermilk into two parts, starting and ending with the flour. Mix just until blended after each addition. Scrape down the side of the bowl as needed.

5. Portion the batter into the prepared pans using a no. 16 ice cream scoop (¼-cup capacity). Fill the cups until almost full. Sprinkle the top of each muffin with a scant ½ teaspoon of granulated sugar.

6. Bake for 25 to 30 minutes, or until the muffins are golden brown and the tops are springy to the touch. To ensure even baking, toward the end of baking time, rotate the pans top to bottom and front to back. Remove from the oven and place on a rack to cool.

STORAGE: Store at room temperature, tightly wrapped in aluminum foil, for up to 3 days. These muffins may be frozen.

"I'll be with you in the squeezing of a lemon."
OLIVER GOLDSMITH

orange cream cheese muffins with pepita crunch

MAKES 14 MUFFINS

Here is a twist on a popular combo—sweet butter and tangy cream cheese. Together with a puree of fresh orange—rind and all—they make a tender, delectable muffin that is crowned with a crunchy topping of toasted, sugary pepitas. You won't know which to eat first—the muffin or the topping! They're both terrific.

AT A GLANCE
PANS: Rimmed cookie sheet/two standard muffin pans
PAN PREP: Line with paper or foil cupcake liners
OVEN TEMP: 350°/375°F
BAKING TIME: 17 to 18 minutes for Pepita Crunch
22 to 25 minutes for muffins
DIFFICULTY: 🥄 🥄

PEPITA CRUNCH

1 large egg white (reserve yolk)

2 tablespoons plus 1 teaspoon granulated sugar

½ cup pepitas

MUFFINS

½ small navel orange, cut into 6 to 8 pieces (zest, pith, and flesh)

4 ounces cream cheese, at room temperature, broken into 3 to 4 pieces

2 cups all-purpose flour, spooned in and leveled

½ teaspoon baking powder

½ teaspoon salt

¼ teaspoon baking soda

½ cup (1 stick) unsalted butter, slightly firm

1 cup superfine sugar

2 large eggs

1 large egg yolk (reserved from Pepita Crunch)

1 teaspoon pure vanilla extract

1. Position the racks in the upper and lower thirds of the oven. Heat the oven to 350°F. Spray a rimmed cookie sheet with nonstick cooking spray.

MAKE THE PEPITA CRUNCH

2. In a small bowl, whisk together the egg white and 1 tablespoon of the granulated sugar. Add the pepitas, tossing to coat well with the egg/sugar mixture. Pour into the prepared cookie sheet and spread evenly in a single layer. Sprinkle 1 more tablespoon of the sugar over the pepitas. Bake for 7 to 8 minutes, stir the pepitas with a fork, and bake for another 7 minutes. Remove from the oven, stir the pepitas, sprinkle with the remaining 1 teaspoon of sugar, and bake for another 3 minutes. Remove from the oven and allow to cool. Break up any clusters with your fingertips and set aside.

MAKE THE BATTER

3. Increase the oven temperature to 375°F. Line fourteen muffin cups with paper or foil cupcake liners.

4. Fit a food processor with the steel blade. With the machine on, drop the orange pieces through the feeder tube. Process until finely chopped, then measure ¼ cup pulp and return it to the processor bowl. (Discard any remaining orange.) Add the cream cheese and process in three 10-second intervals, scraping down the side of the bowl after each process. The mixture should retain some orange texture.

5. In a large bowl, thoroughly whisk together the flour, baking powder, salt, and baking soda. Set aside.

6. Cut the butter into 1-inch pieces and place in the bowl of an electric mixer fitted with the paddle attachment. Mix on medium speed until smooth and lightened in color, about 1 minute. Stop the machine and add the cream cheese/orange mixture, then mix on medium speed for 1 minute. Add the superfine sugar in a steady stream, then blend in the eggs, the reserved yolk, and the vanilla.

7. Reduce the mixer speed to low and add the flour mixture in three additions, mixing just until blended after each addition.

BAKE THE MUFFINS

8. Portion level scoops of the batter into the prepared pans using a no. 16 ice cream scoop (¼-cup capacity). Sprinkle the top of each muffin with 1 tablespoon of the Pepita Crunch. Be sure to use any sugar that remains in the pan.

9. Bake for 22 to 25 minutes, or until the muffins are golden brown and the tops are springy to the touch. To ensure even baking, toward the end of baking time, rotate the pans top to bottom and front to back. Remove from the oven and place on a rack to cool.

STORAGE: Store at room temperature, tightly wrapped in aluminum foil, for up to 3 days. These muffins may be frozen.

rhubarb upside-down muffins

MAKES 14 MUFFINS

Pretty and delicious is how I would describe these muffins. Chunks of fresh rhubarb are sautéed in a sugar syrup and then spooned into buttered muffin cups. A tasty sour cream batter flavored with a bit of cinnamon and nutmeg tops the sweet-tart rhubarb. After baking, the muffin pans are inverted and the sweet syrup glistens atop the pink rhubarb. Eat these muffins warm on the day they are baked.

AT A GLANCE
PANS: Two standard muffin pans, preferably nonstick
PAN PREP: Butter generously
OVEN TEMP: 375°F
BAKING TIME: 23 to 25 minutes
DIFFICULTY: ♨

Be sure to use fresh rhubarb for these muffins. There are two varieties of rhubarb: hothouse and field grown. Field grown has a more tart flavor and a deeper red color, while the hothouse variety is a lighter shade of pink with stringy stalks, which should be peeled. Rhubarb leaves are toxic and must not be eaten either raw or cooked. Frozen rhubarb should not be used, as it is too watery.

RHUBARB

¼ cup (½ stick) unsalted butter

¾ cup *very fresh* light brown sugar

I teaspoon freshly grated navel orange zest

I pound fresh rhubarb, cut into ¾-inch chunks

MUFFINS

1½ cups all-purpose flour, spooned in and leveled

I teaspoon baking powder

½ teaspoon baking soda

½ teaspoon salt

½ teaspoon ground cinnamon

⅛ teaspoon ground nutmeg

½ cup (I stick) unsalted butter, slightly firm

½ cup *very fresh* light brown sugar

¼ cup granulated sugar

I large egg

I teaspoon pure vanilla extract

¾ cup sour cream

2 tablespoons milk

1. Position the racks in the upper and lower thirds of the oven. Heat the oven to 375°F. Generously butter fourteen muffin cups and set aside.

COOK THE RHUBARB

2. In a heavy 12-inch skillet, melt the butter over low heat. Add the brown sugar and stir until dissolved. Mix in the orange zest and cook over medium heat until bubbly. Add the rhubarb, arranging in a single layer, stirring to coat with the syrup.

Cook the rhubarb for 7 to 8 minutes, until transparent and easily pierced with the tip of a sharp knife. Be careful not to overcook the rhubarb or it will begin to shred.

3. Remove the rhubarb from the pan with a slotted spoon. Spread in a single layer on a rimmed cookie sheet and let cool. Cook the remaining syrup over medium heat until it is reduced to about $\frac{1}{2}$ cup, then pour into a heatproof glass measuring cup. Pour 1 teaspoon of the syrup into each muffin cup, then evenly distribute the rhubarb among the cups. Distribute whatever syrup remains over the rhubarb. (*Note:* If the syrup has become too thick to pour, reheat in the microwave for 10 to 15 seconds.)

MAKE THE BATTER

4. In a medium bowl, thoroughly whisk together the flour, baking powder, baking soda, salt, cinnamon, and nutmeg. Set aside.

5. Cut the butter into 1-inch pieces and place in the bowl of an electric mixer fitted with the paddle attachment. Mix on medium speed until smooth and lightened in color, about 1 minute. Add the brown sugar, 1 to 2 tablespoons at a time, taking about 1 minute, then pour in the granulated sugar and mix for 1 minute longer.

6. Blend in the egg and vanilla, scraping down the side of the bowl as needed, then mix for 1 minute longer.

7. Reduce the mixer speed to low and add one-half of the dry ingredients, then the sour cream, mixing just until blended. Remove the bowl from the mixer, and using an oversize rubber spatula, fold in the remaining dry ingredients with the milk.

BAKE THE MUFFINS

8. Portion the batter into the prepared pans using a no. 16 ice cream scoop ($\frac{1}{4}$-cup capacity). Bake for 23 to 25 minutes, or until the muffins are golden brown and the tops are springy to the touch. To ensure even baking, toward the end of baking time, rotate the pans top to bottom and front to back.

9. Place a large cooling rack over a sheet of wax paper. Remove the muffins from the oven and let stand for 5 minutes on the rack. Invert the pan onto the rack and let rest for 5 minutes longer to allow the syrup to coat the rhubarb. Carefully remove the pan. If any of the mixture sticks to the bottom of the muffin pan, remove it with a spoon and replace it on the muffin. Cool the muffins on the rack.

STORAGE: Store at room temperature, tightly wrapped in aluminum foil, for 1 day. Freezing is not recommended.

maple pecan sweet potato muffins

MAKES 20 MUFFINS

These streusel-topped sweet potato muffins make quite an impressive statement with their crunchy topping of broken pecans mixed with buttery brown sugar crumbs. The batter and crumbs are flavored with maple, which is a marvelous complement to sweet potatoes. While either a sweet potato or yam can be used, I like to use a yam, which is pinker and more rich in color and whose flavor is sweeter. Be sure the sweet potato is baked until very soft, and the pulp is well mashed.

AT A GLANCE
PANS: Two standard muffin pans
PAN PREP: Line with paper or foil cupcake liners
OVEN TEMP: 375°F
BAKING TIME: 20 to 25 minutes
DIFFICULTY: ☕

Rustic Maple Pecan Streusel (page 357)

I large sweet potato or yam, baked, peeled, and mashed to measure I cup

2²/₃ cups all-purpose flour, spooned in and leveled

2¹/₂ teaspoons baking powder

³/₄ teaspoon salt

¹/₂ teaspoon baking soda

¹/₈ teaspoon ground allspice

²/₃ cup sour cream

3 tablespoons pure maple syrup

³/₄ teaspoon imitation maple extract

³/₄ teaspoon pure vanilla extract

²/₃ cup (1¹/₃ sticks) unsalted butter, slightly firm

1¹/₂ teaspoons freshly grated lemon zest

²/₃ cup granulated sugar

²/₃ cup *very fresh* dark brown sugar

2 large eggs

Powdered sugar, for dusting (optional)

1. Prepare the Rustic Maple Pecan Streusel.

2. Position the racks in the upper and lower thirds of the oven. Heat the oven to 375°F. Line twenty muffin cups with paper or foil cupcake liners.

3. In a medium bowl, thoroughly whisk together the flour, baking powder, salt, baking soda, and allspice. Set aside.

4. In a small bowl, whisk together the sour cream, maple syrup, maple extract, and vanilla. Set aside.

5. Cut the butter into 1-inch pieces and place in the bowl of an electric mixer fitted with the paddle attachment. Add the lemon zest and mix on medium speed until smooth and lightened in color, about 1 minute. Add the granulated sugar, in three or four additions, then the brown sugar in three or four additions, and mix until well blended, about 1 minute.

6. Add the eggs, one at a time, scraping down the side of the bowl as needed. Blend in the sweet potato. The batter will look curdled.

7. Reduce the mixer speed to low and add one-third of the dry ingredients, mixing just to combine. Blend in the sour cream mixture. Add the remaining dry ingredients all at once, scraping down the side of the bowl again. *Do not overmix.* This is a very dense batter.

8. Portion the batter into the prepared pans using a no. 16 ice cream scoop (¼-cup capacity). The batter should be filled to slightly below the top of the paper liner. Gently press a healthy handful of the streusel onto the surface of each muffin.

9. Set each muffin pan on a 12-inch strip of aluminum foil and bake for 20 to 25 minutes, or until the streusel is golden brown. To ensure even baking, toward the end of baking time, rotate the pans top to bottom and front to back.

10. Remove from the oven and place on a rack to cool. If desired, dust the tops of the muffins lightly with powdered sugar just before serving.

STORAGE: Store at room temperature, tightly wrapped in aluminum foil, for up to 3 days. These muffins may be frozen.

crumb-topped whole wheat peach muffins

MAKES 16 MUFFINS

When summer comes around, my daughter-in-law, Marla, especially loves fresh peaches, so when I bake a batch of these crumb-topped muffins, she is more than happy to indulge her sweet tooth. The muffins are made with whole wheat flour, which provides a nutty background flavor for the sweetness of the fruit.

A crunchy streusel made with oatmeal and brown sugar, along with whole wheat flour, is the perfect complement. Because of the moistness of the peaches, these muffins are best eaten the day they are baked.

Brown Sugar Whole Wheat Streusel (page 352)

2 to 3 ripe peaches (about 8½ ounces)

1 cup all-purpose flour, spooned in and leveled

¾ cup stone-ground whole wheat flour, spooned in and leveled

½ cup quick-cooking oats

1 teaspoon baking powder

½ teaspoon baking soda

½ teaspoon salt

½ cup (1 stick) unsalted butter, slightly firm

2 tablespoons honey

2 teaspoons finely grated navel orange zest

¾ cup *very fresh* light brown sugar

2 large eggs

1 teaspoon pure vanilla extract

½ cup buttermilk

½ cup coarsely chopped toasted pecans (see pages 391–392), optional

1. Prepare the Brown Sugar Whole Wheat Streusel. Set aside.

2. Position the racks in the upper and lower thirds of the oven. Heat the oven to 375°F. Line sixteen muffin cups with paper or foil cupcake liners.

3. Peel and pit the peaches. Cut into ½-inch pieces. You should have about 1½ cups. Set aside.

4. In the work bowl of a food processor fitted with the steel blade, combine the all-purpose and whole wheat flours, oats, baking powder, baking soda, and salt. Pulse 4 times to blend. Set aside.

5. Cut the butter into 1-inch pieces and place in the bowl of an electric mixer fitted with the paddle attachment. Add the honey and orange zest and mix on medium speed for about1 minute. Add the brown sugar and mix for 1 minute longer. Blend in

the eggs, one at a time, mixing well after each addition, then add the vanilla. Scrape down the side of the bowl.

6. Reduce the mixer speed to low and add the dry ingredients alternately with the buttermilk, dividing the flour into three parts and the buttermilk into two parts, beginning and ending with the flour. Be careful not to overmix. Remove the bowl from the machine, and using an oversize rubber spatula, fold in the optional pecans.

7. Portion *half* scoops of the batter into the prepared pans using a no. 16 ice cream scoop (¼-cup capacity). Place a layer of peaches evenly over the batter, then place a dollop of batter on top of the fruit. It's okay for the peaches to show. Take a handful of the streusel topping and crumble it over the batter and peaches, completely covering the top of each muffin with the crumbs. Press gently to adhere. Brush any stray crumbs from the top of the muffin pans using a small pastry brush.

8. Bake for 22 to 25 minutes, or until the streusel topping is golden brown. To ensure even baking, toward the end of baking time, rotate the pans top to bottom and front to back. Remove from the oven and place on a rack to cool.

STORAGE: Store at room temperature, tightly wrapped with aluminum foil, for up to 2 days. Freezing is not recommended.

"too good to be true" bran muffins

MAKES 12 MUFFINS

When I tested the recipe for these bran muffins, my assistant
and I sampled them when they came out of the oven. After
our first bite, we both had the same reaction: "These muffins
are too good to be true!"

Here we have a batter with lots of spices heightened by
the addition of cocoa powder. Brown sugar, Lyle's Golden

Syrup, and molasses add a wonderful depth of sweetness, while dark raisins and coarsely chopped nuts provide
texture.

¾ cup wheat bran, spooned in and leveled

¾ cup boiling water

½ cup dark raisins, plumped (see page 389)

2 cups all-purpose flour, spooned in and leveled,
    plus I teaspoon for raisins

1½ teaspoons baking powder

I teaspoon baking soda

½ teaspoon salt

2 tablespoons unsweetened cocoa powder

1½ teaspoons ground cinnamon

I teaspoon ground ginger

¾ teaspoon ground nutmeg

⅛ teaspoon ground allspice

2 large eggs

¾ cup *very fresh* dark brown sugar

¼ cup Lyle's Golden Syrup (see page 379)

2 tablespoons molasses

½ cup canola oil

I teaspoon pure vanilla extract

½ cup buttermilk

½ cup coarsely chopped pecans or walnuts (see
    page 392), optional

1. Position the rack in the lower third of the oven. Heat the oven to 375°F. Line a
muffin pan with paper or foil cupcake liners.

2. In a medium bowl, combine the wheat bran and boiling water. Set aside. Mix the
raisins with the 1 teaspoon of flour and set aside.

3. In a large bowl, thoroughly whisk together the 2 cups flour, baking powder,
baking soda, salt, cocoa powder, and spices. Set aside.

4. In the bowl of an electric mixer fitted with the whip attachment, beat the eggs
on medium-high speed for 2 minutes, or until lightened in color. Add the brown
sugar, 1 to 2 tablespoons at a time, taking about 2 minutes.

5. In a small bowl, whisk together the syrup and molasses. Gradually whisk in the oil. Reduce the mixer speed to medium and slowly add the liquid in a steady stream. Add the bran and vanilla and mix until combined.

6. Reduce the mixer speed to low and add the dry ingredients alternately with the buttermilk, dividing the flour into three parts and the buttermilk into two parts, starting and ending with the flour, mixing just until combined. Remove the bowl from the mixer, and using a rubber spatula, fold in the raisins and optional nuts.

7. Portion generous scoops of the batter into the prepared pan using a no. 16 ice cream scoop (¼-cup capacity). The batter should be filled to slightly below the top of the paper liner.

8. Bake for 18 to 20 minutes, or until the tops of the muffins are springy to the touch. To ensure even baking, toward the end of baking time, rotate the pans top to bottom and front to back. Remove from the oven and place on a rack to cool.

STORAGE: Store at room temperature, tightly covered in plastic wrap, for up to 3 days. These muffins may be frozen.

whole wheat sunflower seed muffins

MAKES 12 MUFFINS

Sunflower seeds make a wonderful addition to baked goods. Here the crunchy little morsels are blended through a lightly spiced muffin batter made with a touch of cornmeal, yogurt, and sweet, shredded apple. The apple adds moisture and is the perfect complement to the nuttiness of the whole wheat flour. Use a box grater to shred the apple—it works perfectly.

1¼ cups stone-ground whole wheat flour, spooned in and leveled

½ cup all-purpose flour, spooned in and leveled

½ cup very *fresh* dark brown sugar

¼ cup granulated sugar

⅓ cup plus 3 tablespoons salted sunflower seeds, toasted (see page 393)

2 tablespoons stone-ground cornmeal

1 tablespoon wheat germ

1½ teaspoons ground cinnamon

¾ teaspoon ground ginger

¾ teaspoon salt

½ teaspoon baking powder

½ teaspoon baking soda

½ teaspoon ground nutmeg

2 large eggs

¾ cup plain yogurt (not low-fat)

½ cup canola oil

1 teaspoon pure vanilla extract

1 teaspoon freshly grated lemon zest

1 medium (5 to 6 ounces) McIntosh or Golden Delicious apple, peeled, cored, and grated (about ⅔ cup)

1. Position the rack in the lower third of the oven. Heat the oven to 375°F. Line a muffin pan with paper or foil cupcake liners.

2. In a large bowl, thoroughly whisk together the whole wheat and all-purpose flours, the brown and granulated sugars, the ⅓ cup sunflower seeds, the cornmeal, wheat germ, cinnamon, ginger, salt, baking powder, baking soda, and nutmeg. Set aside.

3. In a medium bowl, whisk together the eggs, yogurt, oil, vanilla, and zest. Make a well in the center of the dry ingredients and add the liquids and the apple. Using an oversize rubber spatula, incorporate the dry ingredients into the liquids by pushing them from the side of the bowl toward the center. Stir just to blend.

4. Portion the batter into the prepared pan using a no. 16 ice cream scoop (¼-cup capacity). Fill the cups until almost full. Sprinkle a generous ½ teaspoon of sunflower seeds evenly over the top of each muffin.

5. Bake for 22 to 25 minutes, or until the muffins are golden brown and the tops are springy to the touch. To ensure even baking, toward the end of baking time, rotate the pans top to bottom and front to back. Remove from the oven and place on a rack to cool.

STORAGE: Store at room temperature, tightly wrapped in aluminum foil, for up to 3 days. These muffins may be frozen.

MAKING MUFFINS INTO QUICK BREADS

Most muffin batters can easily be turned into quick breads. Batters that make the best candidates are those that do not contain large pieces of dried fruits and nuts. Since quick breads are sliced rather than broken apart, as in muffins, the texture is important. If the muffin recipe you want to convert contains large pieces of dried fruits and nuts, be sure to cut them a little smaller. After baking, cover the quick bread in plastic wrap to retain moisture and allow it to mature at least one day before serving. Use a serrated knife to cut beautiful even slices.

Choose a 9 x 5 x 2½-inch loaf pan as your baking pan. Butter it generously and line the bottom with a piece of baking parchment. If the batter is very textured, butter the parchment as well. Bake the loaf in a 325°F oven for 55 to 65 minutes. When done, the top should be springy to the touch, the bread should begin to release from the sides, and a wooden skewer inserted near the center should come out clean. (See "About Muffins and Quick Breads," page 77.)

To get you started, here are a few suggestions for muffins that are good candidates to become quick breads: Apricot and Dried Pineapple Muffins, Cape Cod Cranberry Muffins, and Lemon Poppy Seed Muffins

irish soda bread

MAKES TWO 8-INCH ROUNDS, 6 TO 8 SERVINGS PER BREAD

Every March, before St. Patrick's Day, I look forward to preparing this simple-to-make Irish soda bread. It is absolutely the best that I have ever come across. This recipe came to me by way of Ellen Meehen, whose family hails from the Emerald Isle.

AT A GLANCE
PANS: Two 8-inch round layer cake pans
PAN PREP: Butter generously
OVEN TEMP: 375°F
BAKING TIME: 45 to 50 minutes
DIFFICULTY: 🍵

The characteristic cross that appears on top of Irish soda bread is made by cutting deeply into the round of dough before it is baked. This is best done with the blade of a single-edge razor blade, available in most drug stores. A sharp, thin-bladed paring knife will do in a pinch, but it tears the dough and you won't achieve the same result.

4 cups sifted, unbleached all-purpose flour, spooned in and leveled, plus 2 to 3 tablespoons for kneading

¼ cup sugar

1 tablespoon caraway seeds

2 teaspoons baking powder

½ teaspoon salt

½ cup (1 stick) unsalted butter, cut into ½-inch cubes, at room temperature

1 to 2 cups dark raisins, plumped (see page 389)

1⅓ cups buttermilk

1 teaspoon baking soda

2 large eggs

1 large egg white

1 large egg yolk

1 teaspoon water

1. Position the rack in the lower third of the oven. Heat the oven to 375°F. Generously butter two 8-inch layer cake pans and set aside.

2. In a large bowl, thoroughly whisk together the flour, sugar, caraway seeds, baking powder, and salt.

3. Add the butter to the flour mixture, and using a pastry blender, work the butter into the dry ingredients until the mixture resembles coarse meal. Stir in the raisins.

4. In a small bowl, blend together the buttermilk, baking soda, whole eggs, and egg white. Stir the liquids into the flour mixture, blending together with a fork. When the liquids are absorbed, turn the batter onto a floured work surface. The mixture will be sticky. With floured hands, knead lightly just until the dough is smooth.

5. Divide the dough in half. Working with one piece of dough at a time, lightly flour the cut side and shape into a ball. Place into a prepared pan and flatten slightly.

Using a single-edge razor blade or a sharp knife held at a 25° angle, cut a 4-inch cross, about ½-inch deep, in the center of each ball.

6. Combine the egg yolk with the water and brush over the surface of the dough, brushing from the bottom up. Bake for 45 to 50 minutes, or until golden brown. Remove from the oven and place on a rack to cool. To slice, cut the soda bread in half with a serrated knife. Working with one half at a time, place the cut side down on a cutting board and slice across into ½- to ¾-inch pieces.

STORAGE: Store at room temperature, tightly wrapped in aluminum foil, for up to 3 days.

"Bread deals with living things, with giving life, with growth, with the seed, the grain that nurtures. It is not coincidence that we say bread is the staff of life."

LIONEL POILÂNE

grandma jennie's date and nut bread

MAKES 4 ROUND BREADS, 3 TO 4 SERVINGS PER BREAD, OR 2 MEDIUM LOAVES, 6 TO 8 SERVINGS PER LOAF

I came across this 1940s recipe quite by accident when shopping in a local handbag store. I was discussing my latest venture with Bernice Frankel, my saleswoman, who enthusiastically recalled her Grandma Jennie's delectable date and nut bread.

During that era, date and nut breads were often baked in cans with the lids removed. When unmolded, the finished bread revealed the ridges of the can. If you want to re-create the original look of this bread, be sure to use 19-ounce cans (such as those used for Progresso canned products). Avoid cans with pop-top lids, as they do not work, and be sure to butter the cans extremely well. As an alternative, Grandma Jennie's bread can be baked in loaf pans.

AT A GLANCE
PANS: Four empty 19-ounce cans (not pop-top) with tops removed or two 8½ x 4½ x 2¾-inch loaf pans
PAN PREP: Generously butter/line with parchment/butter
OVEN TEMP: 350°F
BAKING TIME: 60 to 65 minutes for loaves
50 to 55 minutes for cans
DIFFICULTY: 🍞

1 pound pitted dates, cut into ½-inch pieces

2 cups boiling water

2 teaspoons baking soda

3 cups sifted all-purpose flour, spooned in and leveled

½ teaspoon salt

½ teaspoon ground allspice

½ cup (1 stick) unsalted butter, slightly firm

1 teaspoon grated navel orange zest

¾ cup granulated sugar

½ cup (lightly packed) *very fresh* dark brown sugar

2 large eggs

1 teaspoon pure vanilla extract

1¼ cups walnuts, cut into ½-inch pieces

1. Position the rack in the lower third of the oven. Heat the oven to 350°F. Generously butter four 19-ounce tin cans using a pastry brush, line the bottoms with baking parchment circles, then butter the parchment. Or generously butter two 8½ x 4½ x 2¾-inch loaf pans, line the bottoms with baking parchment, then butter the parchment.

2. Place the dates in a 2-quart bowl. Stir in the boiling water and the baking soda. Set aside.

3. In a large bowl, thoroughly whisk together the flour, salt, and allspice. Set aside.

4. Cut the butter into 1-inch pieces and place in the bowl of an electric mixer fitted with the paddle attachment. Add the orange zest and mix on medium speed until

lightened in color, 1½ to 2 minutes. Add the granulated sugar, 1 to 2 tablespoons at a time, taking about 2 minutes, then add the brown sugar, taking another 2 minutes, scraping down the side of the bowl as necessary, and mix for 1 minute longer.

5. Add the eggs, one at a time, mixing for 1 minute after each addition, then blend in the vanilla. Scrape down the side of the bowl.

6. Reduce the mixer speed to low and add the flour mixture alternately with the date mixture, dividing the flour into four parts and the dates into three parts, beginning and ending with the flour. Remove the bowl from the mixer, and using an oversize rubber spatula, fold in the walnuts.

7. If baking in tin cans, fill each can with 1½ cups of batter. Tap the cans firmly on the counter to level the batter. Bake for 50 to 55 minutes. (Alternatively, divide the batter between the prepared loaf pans and bake for 60 to 65 minutes.) The bread is done when it is firm to the touch, the sides begin to release, and a toothpick inserted in the center comes out clean.

8. Remove from the oven and let cool on racks for about 20 minutes. Invert each bread onto a rack and gently lift off the cans or pans and the parchment. When the breads are cool enough to handle, carefully turn them right side up.

STORAGE: Store at room temperature, tightly covered with plastic wrap, for up to 5 days, or refrigerate for up to 10 days. These breads may be frozen.

"I do like a bit of butter to my bread."
A. A. MILNE, *WINNIE THE POOH*

pumpkin pecan loaf

MAKES 1 LARGE LOAF, 8 TO 10 SERVINGS

Here is a terrific recipe for a pumpkin quick bread. The pleasantly spiced batter has orange and lemon zests, which enhance the flavor of pumpkin. Be sure to use pure pumpkin puree, not ready-made pumpkin pie filling; a popular brand is Libby's. This is a quick bread that gets better with age. However, in my experience, it is always devoured in the blink of an eye.

AT A GLANCE
PAN: 9 x 5 x 2½-inch loaf pan
PAN PREP: Butter generously/line with parchment/butter
OVEN TEMP: 325°F
BAKING TIME: 60 to 65 minutes
DIFFICULTY: ☕

1¾ cups all-purpose flour, spooned in and leveled

1½ teaspoons ground cinnamon

1 teaspoon baking powder

1 teaspoon baking soda

½ teaspoon salt

½ teaspoon ground nutmeg

¼ teaspoon ground allspice

2 large eggs

¾ cup (lightly packed) *very fresh* dark brown sugar

⅓ cup granulated sugar

2 teaspoons freshly grated navel orange zest

1 teaspoon freshly grated lemon zest

½ cup canola oil

1¼ cups canned pure pumpkin puree

½ cup medium-chopped toasted pecans (see pages 391–392)

1. Position the rack in the middle of the oven. Heat the oven to 325°F. Generously butter a 9 × 5 × 2½-inch loaf pan, line the bottom with baking parchment, then butter the parchment. Set aside.

2. Combine the flour, cinnamon, baking powder, baking soda, salt, nutmeg, and allspice in a medium bowl and whisk until thoroughly combined. Set aside.

3. In the bowl of an electric mixer fitted with the whip attachment, beat the eggs on medium-high speed for 2 minutes, or until lightened in color. Add the brown sugar, 1 to 2 tablespoons at a time, taking about 2 minutes, and the granulated sugar, taking about 1 minute. Add the orange and lemon zests and beat for 1 minute longer. Scrape down the side of the bowl as needed.

4. Reduce the mixer speed to medium-low and drizzle in the oil in a steady stream, taking about 2 minutes. Reduce the mixer speed to low and add the pumpkin puree. Mix until thoroughly combined. Add the dry ingredients in two additions and blend

for 10 to 15 seconds, just until incorporated. Remove the bowl from the mixer, and using a large rubber spatula, fold in the pecans.

5. Spoon the batter into the prepared pan and bake for 60 to 65 minutes, or until the top feels springy to the touch, or a wooden skewer or a toothpick inserted deeply into the center comes out clean.

6. Remove from the oven and place on a cooling rack. When the loaf is almost cool, invert it onto the rack. Remove the pan, peel off the parchment paper, and turn the loaf top side up. When ready to serve, cut with a serrated knife into $\frac{1}{2}$-inch slices.

STORAGE: Store at room temperature, tightly covered with plastic wrap, for up to 5 days. This loaf may be frozen.

zucchini loaf with apricots and dates

MAKES I MEDIUM LOAF, 6 TO 8 SERVINGS

Zucchini is a vegetable that marries well with other flavors because of its neutral taste. Here, the batter is mingled with tangy dried apricots, sweet dates, and a zesty assortment of spices. Toasted walnuts add a touch of crunch. When all of these flavors mellow, this becomes a marvelous tea loaf that you won't want to miss. When preparing the fruit, do not cut the pieces too large.

> **AT A GLANCE**
> **PAN:** 8½ x 4½ X 2¾-inch loaf pan
> **PAN PREP:** Butter generously/line with parchment/butter
> **OVEN TEMP:** 325°F
> **BAKING TIME:** 65 to 70 minutes
> **DIFFICULTY:** ☕

3 small zucchini (about I pound)

I teaspoon salt

¼ cup (about 2 ounces) dried apricots (not organic), cut into ¼-inch pieces, packed

1½ cups all-purpose flour, spooned in and leveled, plus 2 tablespoons for fruit and nuts

I teaspoon baking powder

I teaspoon ground cinnamon

½ teaspoon baking soda

½ teaspoon ground ginger

½ teaspoon ground coriander

2 large eggs

½ cup (lightly packed) *very fresh* dark brown sugar

½ cup granulated sugar

¼ cup (½ stick) unsalted butter, melted

¼ cup canola oil

I teaspoon pure vanilla extract

½ cup (about 4 ounces) diced dates, cut into ¼-inch pieces, packed

¾ cup coarsely chopped toasted walnuts (see pages 391–392)

1. Position the rack in the lower third of the oven. Heat the oven to 325°F. Generously butter an 8½ x 4½ x 2¾-inch loaf pan, line the bottom with baking parchment, then butter the parchment. Set aside

2. Scrub the zucchini well using a vegetable brush, trim the ends, but do not peel. Cut the zucchini into 1-inch chunks. Shred the zucchini in a food processor fitted with the medium shredder blade using light pressure on the pusher. You should have about 4 cups. (Alternatively, the zucchini may be shredded on the half-moon side of a box grater.)

3. Transfer the zucchini to a colander and sprinkle with the salt, working it through to distribute evenly. Place an 8-inch plate directly on top of the zucchini and weight it down with a heavy object, such as a large can of tomatoes. Let stand for 30 minutes to

exude the liquid, then take handfuls of the zucchini and squeeze firmly to remove additional liquid. Set aside.

4. Place the diced apricots in a microwave-safe bowl and add enough water to cover. Microwave on high power for 2 minutes. Empty into a strainer and rinse under cold water to cool. Drain well on paper towels.

5. In a large mixing bowl, whisk together 1½ cups of the flour, the baking powder, cinnamon, baking soda, ginger, and coriander. Set aside.

6. Place the eggs in the bowl of a standing mixer fitted with the whip attachment and beat on medium-high speed for 3 minutes. Scrape down the side of the bowl as needed.

7. Add the brown sugar, then the granulated sugar, 1 tablespoon at a time, taking 2 to 3 minutes for each one. Beat for 2 minutes longer, or until the mixture is thickened and lightened in color. Scrape the side of the bowl as needed.

8. Combine the butter and oil. With the mixer on, pour in the butter/oil mixture in a steady stream. Reduce the mixer speed to low and add the zucchini and vanilla. Add the flour mixture all at once, mixing just until incorporated. Remove the bowl from the machine.

9. Toss the apricots, dates, and walnuts with the remaining 2 tablespoons of flour. Using an oversize rubber spatula, fold gently into the batter.

10. Pour the batter into the prepared pan and bake for 65 to 70 minutes, or until the top is golden brown and springy to the touch. A wooden skewer or toothpick inserted into the center should come out clean.

11. Remove from the oven and place on a rack to cool. When the loaf is almost cool, invert onto the rack. Remove the pan, peel off the parchment paper, and turn the loaf top side up and cool completely. To serve, cut the loaf into ½-inch slices with a serrated knife, using a back-and-forth sawing motion.

STORAGE: Store at room temperature, tightly covered in aluminum foil or plastic wrap, for up to 5 days, or refrigerate for up to 10 days. This loaf may be frozen.

"Zucchini's name is Italian, a derivative of the word meaning 'sweetest.'"
BERT GREENE

candied maple walnut pancake loaf

MAKES 1 MEDIUM LOAF, 6 TO 8 SERVINGS

This terrific recipe comes from Yocheved Hirsch, my very talented friend who teaches cooking in Tel Aviv, Israel. I named the cake "Pancake Loaf" because the batter is made with self-rising flour, a flour often used for pancakes, and the finished loaf is soaked with maple syrup. A mixture of chunky walnuts and cinnamon is used as a topping, as well as laced through the batter.

AT A GLANCE
PAN: 8½ x 4½ x 2¾-inch loaf pan
PAN PREP: Butter generously/line with parchment/butter
OVEN TEMP: 325°F
BAKING TIME: 40 minutes
DIFFICULTY: ☕

Be sure to poke lots of holes in the top and apply the syrup several times to allow it to be absorbed through the buttery crumb. As the syrup is spooned, the nuts become glazed, giving the finished cake an addictive candied topping.

1 large egg

1 large egg yolk

1 cup sugar

1 teaspoon pure vanilla extract

¼ cup vegetable oil

1 cup self-rising cake flour, spooned in and leveled, sifted

6 tablespoons sour cream

⅔ cup coarsely chopped walnuts (see page 392)

½ teaspoon ground cinnamon

½ cup pure maple syrup

1. Position the rack in the middle of the oven. Heat the oven to 325°F. Generously butter an 8½ x 4½ x 2¾-inch loaf pan, line the bottom with baking parchment, then butter the parchment. Set aside.

2. In the bowl of an electric mixer fitted with the whip attachment, beat the whole egg and egg yolk on medium speed for 1 minute. Add the sugar, 1 to 2 tablespoons at a time, taking about 2 minutes, and continue to beat until thickened, about 2 minutes longer. Blend in the vanilla. Drizzle in the oil in a steady stream, taking about 30 seconds. Beat for 15 seconds longer.

3. Reduce the mixer speed to low. Add one-half of the flour, then blend in the sour cream, then the remaining flour, mixing only until combined after each addition. Remove the bowl from the mixer.

4. Combine the walnuts and cinnamon. Using a rubber spatula, fold ¼ cup of the nut mixture into the batter.

5. Spoon the batter into the prepared pan, smoothing the top with the back of a large soupspoon. Sprinkle the remaining walnut mixture over the top. Bake for about 40 minutes, or until the top of the loaf is golden brown and springy to the touch, and a toothpick inserted deeply in the center comes out clean. *Note:* This loaf will not rise to the top of the pan. The shallow cake allows the maple syrup to be fully absorbed.

6. Remove from the oven and place on a cooling rack. Poke the cake at 1-inch intervals using a wooden or metal skewer, or a toothpick (see headnote). Spoon the maple syrup over the top *very slowly* to allow the cake to absorb the syrup. Do this several times until all the syrup has been absorbed. Let stand for 30 minutes.

7. To remove the pan, place a 10-inch piece of aluminum foil directly on top of the loaf, cupping it around the side to hold the topping in place. Cover with the cooling rack, invert the cake, and carefully lift off the pan and the parchment paper. Cover with another rack, invert again, and cool right side up. To serve, cut the loaf into ½-inch slices using a serrated knife.

STORAGE: Store at room temperature, tightly wrapped in aluminum foil, for up to 3 days. This loaf may be frozen.

biscuits & scones

ABOUT MAKING BISCUITS AND SCONES

Every baker should have a good biscuit and scone recipe in his or her repertoire. Classically, biscuits and scones were made by hand using a method in which butter, vegetable shortening, or lard was rubbed into the dry ingredients to form flakelike particles. More contemporary methods incorporate the fats using either an electric mixer with the paddle attachment or a food processor. Each of these methods can produce excellent results, but care should be taken to follow the directions carefully for incorporating the fats into the flour.

Here are some tips for mixing, rolling, and baking perfect biscuits and scones:

• Choose a large bowl (about four quarts is perfect) for blending the fats into the flour.

• Always chill the butter and vegetable shortening before using. This makes it easier to form crumbs and prevents the mixture from becoming oily.

• Before working the butter and vegetable shortening into the flour, toss the pieces with flour to coat them. This will make them easier to cut in, because it prevents the pieces of fat from sticking to each other.

• When working the fats into the flour, be sure to use only your fingertips. Avoid rubbing the mixture between the palms of your hands.

• After cutting in the crumbs, rub your hands through the mixture to feel for any overly large pieces of fat that may not have been broken up.

• It's okay to have pea-size pieces of fat. This will create more tender pastries.

• Work with the side of the fork around the perimeter of the bowl toward the center when incorporating the liquid.

• Chilling the dough before rolling makes it easier to handle.

• Use a plastic palm-size plastic bowl scraper or oversize rubber spatula to help remove the dough from the bowl.

• Biscuit dough should be wet, so a well-floured surface (about 2 tablespoons of flour) will prevent it from sticking when kneading.

• Replace the flour on the kneading surface as it becomes too coarse (bits of dough will fall off into the flour as you knead and should not be reincorporated into the dough).

• Do not overhandle the dough, as it will make the biscuits tough.

• If you have warm hands, use a dough scraper to lift the dough.

- Roll the dough on a well-floured (about 2 tablespoons of flour) pastry cloth with a cloth-covered rolling pin. Flour the pin before rolling.
- Always cut biscuit dough with a straight-sided cutter. Move the cutter straight down into the dough and do not twist as you remove it.
- Flour the cutter before making each cut.
- Always cut as close to the previous biscuit as possible. It's helpful to premark the dough with the biscuit cutter.
- After the first biscuits are cut, the dough may be rerolled once. After the second rolling, the dough will become too elastic and will not rise properly.
- Invert the biscuits before placing them on cookie sheets. This will put the flat surface on top and give a better rise.
- Brush the unbaked dough with melted butter, egg, cream, or milk. Do not let the liquid run down the side of the biscuits, as it will prevent them from rising.
- Biscuits are best served immediately after baking. Biscuits made in advance (or frozen) should be warmed in a 300°F oven before serving.

old-fashioned buttermilk biscuits

MAKES 12 BISCUITS

What is more welcome at breakfast time than a basket of freshly baked biscuits, warm from the oven and slathered with butter and your favorite fruit preserves? These biscuits are made the classical way, a method whereby the butter is rubbed into flakelike particles by hand. This gives the biscuits an especially tender crumb. With your first bite, I am sure you will agree that the extra effort is well worth the reward.

> **AT A GLANCE**
> **PAN:** Large cookie sheet
> **PAN PREP:** None
> **OVEN TEMP:** 400°F
> **BAKING TIME:** 18 to 20 minutes
> **DIFFICULTY:** 🍵

When do-ahead planning is needed, I make a batch of the crumb mixture, pack it in an airtight resealable plastic bag, and store it in the refrigerator or freezer. The crumbs will keep up to 5 days in the refrigerator and about 1 month in the freezer. When I'm ready to bake a batch of biscuits, I empty the contents into a large bowl and let them stand until the buttery flakes begin to soften. Add the buttermilk, and, voilà! Mix, roll, bake, and enjoy!

3⅓ cups all-purpose flour, spooned in and leveled, plus additional for kneading and dusting

4½ teaspoons baking powder

1 teaspoon baking soda

1¼ teaspoons salt

¾ cup (1½ sticks) unsalted butter, chilled, plus 2 tablespoons melted

1⅔ cups buttermilk

1. Position the rack in the middle of the oven. Heat the oven to 400°F. Have ready a large, ungreased cookie sheet.

2. In a large bowl, thoroughly whisk together the flour, baking powder, baking soda, and salt.

3. Shave the chilled butter into ⅛-inch slices using a dough scraper or a sharp knife. Add the butter to the dry ingredients, one-third at a time, rubbing it between your fingertips to form flakelike pieces. Work gently and quickly so the butter does not become too warm. You should have both large and small pieces.

4. Add the buttermilk, pouring it around the edge of the bowl. Using a rubber spatula, push the mixture toward the center, working your way around the bowl to blend the buttermilk with the flakes. The mixture will be soft and resemble large curds of cottage cheese. Let stand for 2 or 3 minutes while you prepare the rolling surface.

5. Sprinkle a pastry board or other flat surface generously with flour, about 2 table-spoons. Empty the dough onto the board. *The dough will be sticky.* With the help of a dough scraper, lift the dough four or five times to coat it with flour. With floured hands, gently knead the dough six or eight times, or just until it forms a "skin" (see the sidebar on page 141). It's okay if larger particles of butter are visible. Do not over-work the dough or your biscuits will not be tender. When the dough is ready, slide it aside and clean the work surface.

6. Lay a pastry cloth (page 370) on the surface and fit a rolling pin with a pastry sleeve, or rolling pin cover (page 370). Rub an additional 2 to 3 tablespoons of flour into the pastry cloth and sleeve.

7. Place the dough on the cloth and pat it lightly with floured hands, shaping it into a rectangle. Roll the dough into a 10 × 14-inch rectangle, with the 10-inch side parallel to the edge of the counter. Fold the dough into thirds, like a business letter. To do this, lift the far side of the pastry cloth up and fold the top third of the dough over on itself. Press the dough to align the edges as best you can. Lift the lower edge of the pastry cloth and flip the bottom third of the dough over on itself, keeping the edges as best you can. You will now have three layers of dough. Press the top gently with your hands, then roll the dough into a 5 × 15-inch strip, with a thickness of a generous ½ inch.

8. Using a 2¼-inch straight-sided cookie cutter dipped in flour, cut straight down into the dough, without twisting the cutter, cutting two rows of six biscuits. Be sure to dip the cutter in flour before each cut and cut as close to the previous biscuit as possible. When placing on the cookie sheet, *invert* each biscuit, spacing them about 1½ inches apart. (See "What to Do with Bits and Pieces of Dough," page 151.)

9. Brush the tops with the melted butter and bake for 18 to 20 minutes, or until golden brown. Remove the biscuits from the oven and let cool for about 5 minutes before loosening with a thin metal spatula. Serve the biscuits warm. If baking ahead, warm the biscuits for a few minutes in a 300°F oven.

STORAGE: Store in an airtight plastic bag for up to 3 days. These biscuits may be frozen.

"Raising children is like making biscuits: it is as easy to raise a big batch as one,
while you have your hands in the dough."

E. W. HOWE

cinnamon pull-apart biscuits

Here is an interesting way to serve biscuits. The rounds of dough are baked in a springform pan, forming a cake. The biscuit dough is filled with lots of cinnamon and sugar, along with, if you would like, pieces of toasted pecans. After placing the rounds of dough in the pan, they are sprinkled with more cinnamon and sugar. This cake is a lot of fun to serve at a Sunday brunch or other festive occasions. There's no need to slice; your guests simply pull off a round. Serve these with Orange Honey Butter (page 367).

AT A GLANCE
PAN: 10-inch springform pan
PAN PREP: Butter
OVEN TEMP: 400°F
BAKING TIME: 24 to 26 minutes
DIFFICULTY: ♨

2⅔ cups all-purpose flour, spooned in and leveled, plus additional for dusting

4 tablespoons sugar

4 teaspoons baking powder

¾ teaspoon baking soda

¾ teaspoon salt

⅔ cup (1⅓ sticks) unsalted butter, cubed and chilled, plus 2 tablespoons melted

1¼ cups buttermilk, chilled

½ cup broken toasted pecans (see page 391), optional

1 teaspoon ground cinnamon

1. Position the rack in the middle of the oven. Heat the oven to 400°F. Butter a 10-inch springform pan and set aside.

2. Combine the flour, 2 tablespoons sugar, baking powder, baking soda, and salt in the work bowl of a food processor fitted with a steel blade. Chill for at least 30 minutes.

3. Pulse 3 to 4 times to blend. Add one-half of the chilled butter and pulse 6 times, then process for 10 seconds. Add the remaining chilled butter and pulse 6 to 7 times to form coarse crumbs.

4. Transfer the mixture to a large bowl and run your fingers through it to break any large pieces of butter into flakes. Add the buttermilk, pouring it around the edge of the bowl. Using a rubber spatula, push the mixture toward the center, working your way around the bowl to blend the buttermilk with the crumbs. Add the optional pecans, and work them gently into the dough.

5. Combine the remaining 2 tablespoons sugar and the cinnamon and set aside.

6. Empty the mixture onto a well-floured surface and, with the aid of a dough scraper, knead the dough six or eight times. It will not be smooth.

7. Cover a pastry board or other flat surface with a pastry cloth (page 370) and rub a generous amount of flour into it. Pat the dough out lightly with your hands.

8. Fit a pastry sleeve (page 370) onto the rolling pin, flour the pin, and roll the dough into a 12 × 9-inch rectangle with the 9-inch side parallel to the counter. Brush with the melted butter and sprinkle with 4 teaspoons of the sugar/cinnamon mixture. Fold the rectangle into thirds as if you were folding a letter. Press the top gently with your hands, then roll the dough into a 5 × 15-inch strip.

9. Using a 2¼-inch straight-sided cookie cutter dipped in flour, cut straight down into the dough, without twisting the cutter, forming 12 rounds. Be sure to dip the cutter in flour before cutting each biscuit. The biscuits should be inverted before being placed in the pan. Place 10 rounds around the perimeter of the pan and set the remaining two rounds aside. Gather the scraps of dough together and knead gently two or three times. Pat the dough into a ¾-inch-thick rectangle. Fold it in half and roll it into a ½-inch-thick rectangle. Cut two more biscuits. Fill in the center of the pan with the four cut biscuits, alternating the rounds from first and second roll. The rounds should barely touch each other. Discard the scraps.

10. Brush the tops with the melted butter and sprinkle with the remaining sugar/cinnamon mixture. Place the pan in the oven on a square of aluminum foil to catch any leakage. Bake the biscuits for 24 to 26 minutes, or until golden brown.

11. Remove the pan from the oven, place on a wire rack, and let the biscuits cool in the pan for about 10 minutes before removing the side of the pan. Invert the biscuits on the rack and carefully remove the bottom of the pan. Then invert on a napkin-lined serving platter. Serve the biscuits warm. If baking ahead, warm the cake in a 300°F oven.

STORAGE: Store in an airtight plastic bag for up to 3 days. These biscuits may be frozen.

cornmeal buttermilk biscuits

MAKES 12 BISCUITS

I am a big fan of mixing cornmeal with my biscuit dough. It adds an interesting crunch, which I love. These are especially tasty served with Cranberry Orange Spread (page 366).

AT A GLANCE

PAN: Large cookie sheet
PAN PREP: None
OVEN TEMP: 400°F
BAKING TIME: 18 to 20 minutes
DIFFICULTY: ☕

2⅓ cups all-purpose flour, spooned in and leveled, plus 4 tablespoons or more for dusting

⅔ cup stone-ground cornmeal, spooned in and leveled, plus 1 tablespoon for topping

4 teaspoons baking powder

½ teaspoon baking soda

½ teaspoon salt

¾ cup (1½ sticks) unsalted butter, cubed and chilled, plus 2 tablespoons melted

1½ cups buttermilk, chilled

1. Position the rack in the middle of the oven. Heat the oven to 400°F. Have ready a large, ungreased cookie sheet.

2. Place the flour, cornmeal, baking powder, baking soda, and salt in the bowl of a processor fitted with the steel blade. Process for 15 seconds.

3. Add one-half of the cubed butter to the bowl; pulse 5 times, then process for 5 seconds. Add the remaining butter; pulse 5 times, then process for 5 seconds. You should have both large and small pieces of butter.

4. Empty the crumb mixture into a large bowl and add the buttermilk, pouring it around the edge of the bowl. Using a rubber spatula, push the mixture toward the center, working your way around the bowl to blend the buttermilk with the crumbs. The mixture will be soft and resemble large curds of cottage cheese.

5. Sprinkle a pastry board or other flat surface generously with 2 tablespoons flour. Empty the dough onto the board with the help of a palm-size plastic bowl scraper or rubber spatula. With floured hands, gently knead the dough six or eight times, or just until it forms a "skin" (see the sidebar on page 141). The dough will not be smooth. Use a dough scraper to help lift the dough as needed. Do not overwork the dough or your biscuits will not be tender. When the dough is ready, move it aside and clean the work surface.

6. Lay a pastry cloth on the surface and fit a rolling pin with a pastry sleeve (page 370). Rub another 2 tablespoons of flour into the pastry cloth and sleeve.

7. Place the dough on the cloth and pat it lightly with floured hands, shaping it into an 8-inch square. Roll the dough into a 10 × 14-inch rectangle, with the 10-inch side parallel to the edge of the counter. Fold the dough into thirds like a business letter. To do this, lift the far side of the pastry cloth up and fold the top third of the dough over on itself. Press the dough to line up the edges as best you can. Lift the lower edge of the pastry cloth and flip the bottom third of the dough over on itself, evening the edges as best you can. You will now have three layers of dough. Press the top gently with your hands, then roll it into a 5 × 15-inch strip.

8. Using a 2¼-inch straight-sided cookie cutter dipped in flour, cut straight down into the dough, without twisting the cutter, cutting two rows of six biscuits. Be sure to dip the cutter in flour before each cut and cut as close to the previous biscuit as possible. When placing on the cookie sheet, invert each biscuit, spacing them about 1½ inches apart. (See "What to Do with Bits and Pieces of Dough," page 151.)

9. Brush the tops with the melted butter, sprinkle with the 1 tablespoon cornmeal, and bake for 18 to 20 minutes, or until golden brown. Remove the biscuits from the oven and let cool for about 5 minutes before loosening with a thin metal spatula. Serve the biscuits warm. If baking ahead, warm the biscuits for a few minutes in a 300°F oven.

STORAGE: Store in an airtight plastic bag for up to 3 days. These biscuits may be frozen.

"To try to cook without cornmeal in the South is a lost cause."
SALLIE F. HILL

naughty sweet cream biscuits

MAKES 12 BISCUITS

If you're looking for a sweet biscuit to use for a traditional strawberry shortcake, you can stop right here. These are perfect! The sweet biscuit dough is enriched with butter and bound with heavy cream. After baking, split the biscuit in half and fill the bottom with juicy macerated berries and a spoonful of whipped cream. Cover with the top of the biscuit and finish it off with, yes, more whipped cream. Yum!

> **AT A GLANCE**
> **PAN:** Large cookie sheet
> **PAN PREP:** None
> **OVEN TEMP:** 375°F
> **BAKING TIME:** 18 to 20 minutes
> **DIFFICULTY:** ☕

2¾ cups all-purpose flour, spooned in and leveled, plus additional for dusting

6 tablespoons granulated sugar

1 tablespoon baking powder

1 teaspoon salt

½ cup (1 stick) unsalted butter, chilled and cut into ½-inch cubes

1½ cups heavy cream

1 teaspoon pure vanilla extract

3 to 4 teaspoons sparkling sugar (see page 380), for sprinkling

1. Position the rack in the middle of the oven. Heat the oven to 375°F. Have ready a large, ungreased cookie sheet.

2. Place the flour, granulated sugar, baking powder, and salt in the work bowl of a food processor fitted with the steel blade. Pulse 3 to 4 times to blend.

3. Add one-half of the butter and pulse 5 times, then process for 8 seconds. Add the remaining butter, pulse 3 times, then process for 5 seconds. Empty the mixture into a large bowl. Rub the mixture between your fingertips to reduce any large pieces of butter into flakes.

4. Remove 2 tablespoons of heavy cream and set aside. Stir the vanilla into the remaining cream. Pour the liquid around the edge of the bowl. Using a rubber spatula, push the mixture toward the center, working your way around the bowl to blend the cream with the flour/butter mixture. The mixture will be soft and resemble large curds of cottage cheese.

5. Sprinkle a pastry board or other flat surface generously with flour, about 2 tablespoons. Empty the dough onto the board with the help of a palm-size plastic bowl scraper or a rubber spatula. *The dough will be sticky.* With floured hands, gently knead the

dough five or six times, or until it just forms a "skin" (see the sidebar on page 141). The dough will not be smooth. Use a dough scraper to help lift the dough as needed. Do not overwork the dough or your biscuits will not be tender. When the dough is ready, move it aside and clean the work surface.

6. Lay a pastry cloth on the surface and fit a rolling pin with a pastry sleeve (page 370). Rub another 2 tablespoons of flour into the pastry cloth and sleeve.

7. Place the dough on the cloth, and with floured hands, pat it lightly, shaping it into an 8-inch square. Roll the dough into a 10 × 14-inch rectangle with the 10-inch side parallel to the counter. Fold the dough into thirds like a business letter. To do this, lift the far side of the pastry cloth up and fold the top third of the dough over on itself. Press the dough to line up the edges as best you can. Lift the lower edge of the pastry cloth and flip the bottom third of the dough over on itself. You will now have three layers of dough. Press the top gently with your hands, then roll into a 5 × 15-inch strip.

8. Using a 2¼-inch straight-sided cookie cutter dipped in flour, cut straight down into the dough, without twisting the cutter, cutting two rows of six biscuits. Be sure to dip the cutter in flour before each cut and cut as close to the previous biscuit as possible. When placing on the cookie sheet, invert each biscuit, spacing them about 1½ inches apart. (See "What to Do with Bits and Pieces of Dough," page 151.)

9. Brush the top of each biscuit with some of the reserved cream and sprinkle with ¼ teaspoon of sparkling sugar. Bake for 18 to 20 minutes, or until golden brown. Remove the biscuits from the oven and let cool for about 5 minutes before loosening with a thin metal spatula. Serve the biscuits warm. If baking ahead, warm the biscuits for a few minutes in a 300°F oven.

STORAGE: Store in an airtight plastic bag for up to 3 days. These biscuits may be frozen.

"The morning bounties 'ere I left my home,
The biscuit, or confectionary plum."
WILLIAM COWPER

angel biscuits

Angel biscuits are traditionally made with yeast, which gives them an especially delicate texture. If you have never baked with yeast, try this easy recipe (see "Working with Yeast," page 186). Instead of baking these biscuits free-form, they are arranged in a pan. To serve, separate the biscuits and place them in a napkin-lined basket.

AT A GLANCE
PAN: 9 x 9-inch baking pan
PAN PREP: Butter
OVEN TEMP: 400°F
BAKING TIME: 25 to 30 minutes
DIFFICULTY: ♥ ♥

2 tablespoons sugar, plus 1 teaspoon

2 tablespoons warm water (110° to 115°F)

½ package active dry yeast

2¼ cups all-purpose flour, spooned in and leveled, plus more for kneading and shaping

1 teaspoon salt

¼ teaspoon baking soda

½ cup (1 stick) unsalted butter, cut into ½-inch cubes and chilled, plus 2 tablespoons melted

1 cup buttermilk

1. Rinse a small bowl in hot water to warm it. Add 1 teaspoon of the sugar and the water. Sprinkle the yeast over the water. *Do not stir.* Cover the bowl with a saucer and let the mixture stand for 5 minutes. Stir it briefly with a fork, cover again, and let it stand for 2 to 3 minutes, or until bubbly.

2. Place the flour, remaining 2 tablespoons sugar, the salt, and baking soda in the work bowl of a food processor fitted with the steel blade. Pulse 2 to 3 times to blend. Add the chilled butter and pulse until the mixture forms crumbs the size of small peas. Empty into a large bowl.

3. Combine the buttermilk with the yeast mixture and pour it around the edge of the bowl containing the crumbs. Using a rubber spatula, push the mixture toward the center, working your way around the bowl to blend the mixture with the crumbs.

4. Sprinkle a pastry board or other flat surface *generously* with flour. Empty the dough onto the board with the help of a palm-size plastic bowl scraper or a rubber spatula. *The dough will be sticky and soft.* With floured hands, gently knead the dough six to eight times, or just until it forms a "skin" (see the sidebar on page 141). Use a dough scraper to help lift the dough as needed. Do not overwork the dough or your biscuits will not be tender.

5. Using a dough scraper or a sharp knife, divide the dough into quarters, then divide each quarter into thirds, making a total of 12 pieces.

6. Butter a 9-inch square pan.

7. Place about ¼ cup of flour in a shallow dish, such as a pie plate. Working with one piece of dough at a time, roll it in the flour, coating it well on all sides. Gently shape it into an oval and place it in the prepared pan. Repeat with the remaining pieces of dough, making three rows across and four down. The ovals of dough do not have to touch each other, and it's okay if they are well coated with flour. Cover with a tea towel and set in a warmish place to rise until almost doubled, about 1 hour.

8. Fifteen minutes before baking, position the rack in the middle of the oven. Heat the oven to 400°F. Brush the tops of the biscuits generously with the melted butter and bake for 25 to 30 minutes, or until golden brown. Remove from the oven and let cool in the pan for 10 minutes. Serve the biscuits warm. If baking ahead, warm the biscuits for a few minutes in a 300°F oven.

STORAGE: Store in an airtight plastic bag for up to 3 days. These biscuits may be frozen.

FORMING A SKIN

When dough is prepared, it usually has a tacky surface. In order to bring it to a state where you can easily handle it, you must form a "skin" on the surface. To do this, place the dough on a floured surface. Most dough requires a lightly floured surface—that is, about 2 tablespoons of flour sprinkled over a wide area, about 16 inches round. For a well-floured surface, 4 tablespoons of flour should be used for the same area.

Empty the dough onto the floured surface, and with floured hands, knead it as many times as the recipe directs. A dough scraper (page 370) is a very helpful tool to have on hand. The object in kneading is to form a thin layer of flour on the surface. This layer of flour, referred to as a "skin," will prevent the dough from sticking.

When the dough has to be divided, whether into large pieces or small, each time it is cut, the skin is broken. The cut surface will be sticky and the dough must be kneaded again to form another skin.

sweet potato drop biscuits

MAKES 12 BISCUITS

If you have never tasted a pastry made with sweet potatoes, you are in for a treat. Here we have the mashed pulp of a baked sweet potato combined with brown sugar and cinnamon, made into a rustic drop biscuit dough. The soft texture of the biscuit is complemented by the crunch of the toasted pecans and sparkling sugar.

AT A GLANCE
PAN: Large cookie sheet
PAN PREP: Butter
OVEN TEMP: 400°F
BAKING TIME: 16 to 18 minutes
DIFFICULTY: ☕

I like to make these with yams rather than sweet potatoes. While either may be used, I prefer the sweetness and deep orange color of the yam to the more pale, less sweet flesh of the sweet potato.

3⅓ cups all-purpose flour, spooned in and leveled

2 tablespoons baking powder

1 teaspoon salt

Scant ½ teaspoon baking soda

¾ cup (1½ sticks) unsalted butter, cut into ½-inch pieces and chilled

¾ cup medium-chopped toasted pecans (see pages 391–392)

¾ cup mashed, cooked sweet potato

⅓ cup (well packed) *very fresh* dark brown sugar

1½ teaspoons ground cinnamon

¾ teaspoon ground ginger

⅛ teaspoon ground nutmeg

1¾ cups plus 2 tablespoons buttermilk

FINISHING

1 egg mixed with 2 teaspoons cold water, for egg wash

1 tablespoon sparkling sugar (see page 380)

1. Position the rack in the middle of the oven. Heat the oven to 400°F. Butter a large cookie sheet and set aside.

2. Combine the flour, baking powder, salt, and baking soda in the work bowl of a food processor fitted with the steel blade. Pulse to blend. Add one-half of the butter and pulse 6 times, then process for 8 seconds. Add the remaining butter and pulse 5 to 6 times. Empty into a large mixing bowl and add the nuts.

3. Place the sweet potato, brown sugar, cinnamon, ginger, and nutmeg in the processor bowl. Pulse 3 to 4 times until blended, then with the machine on, add the buttermilk through the feed tube in a steady stream. Process until combined.

4. Make a well in the center of the dry ingredients and add the sweet potato/buttermilk mixture. Using a spatula, gently draw the dry ingredients into the liquid to form a soft dough.

5. Using a tablespoon, drop the biscuits onto the prepared cookie sheet, spacing them about 2 inches apart, making 12 biscuits. Brush with the egg wash and sprinkle each biscuit with ¼ teaspoon of sparkling sugar. Bake for 16 to 18 minutes, or until firm to the touch.

6. Remove from the oven and let cool on the cookie sheet for 5 minutes. Loosen the biscuits with a thin-bladed metal spatula. Serve warm. If baking ahead, reheat the biscuits for a few minutes in a 300°F oven.

STORAGE: Store in an airtight plastic bag for up to 3 days. These biscuits may be frozen.

sedona cream scones

MAKES 12 SCONES

A few years ago, on a visit to Sedona, Arizona, I stopped for lunch at the well-known Shugrue's Hillside Grill. To my delight, a basket of scones was offered, and I can tell you, these were not ordinary scones. They had a golden crust and a crumb that melted in your mouth.

The baker's name was Ruth Titus, and I asked her if she would be kind enough to share her recipe with me. And that she did! She told me that the recipe was her grandmother's, who originally lived in Scotland. Here is my improvisation on Ruth's recipe.

AT A GLANCE
PAN: Large cookie sheet
PAN PREP: None
OVEN TEMP: 375°F
BAKING TIME: 16 to 18 minutes
DIFFICULTY:

2 cups sifted cake flour, spooned in and leveled

1⅓ cups all-purpose flour, spooned in and leveled, plus ¼ cup additional for kneading and rolling

6 tablespoons granulated sugar

4½ teaspoons baking powder

¾ teaspoon salt

½ cup (1 stick) unsalted butter, cut into ½-inch cubes and chilled

1 cup plus 2 tablespoons heavy cream

1 large egg

1 large egg yolk (reserve white for egg wash)

1 egg white beaten with 1 teaspoon cold water, for egg wash

1 tablespoon sparkling sugar (see page 380)

1. Position the rack in the middle of the oven. Heat the oven to 375°F. Have ready a large, ungreased cookie sheet.

2. Combine the cake and all-purpose flours, granulated sugar, baking powder, and salt in the bowl of an electric mixer fitted with the paddle attachment. Add the butter and mix for 2 to 2½ minutes, or until the mixture forms pea-size bits.

3. Whisk together the cream, egg, and egg yolk. Remove the paddle attachment and replace with the dough hook. With the machine off, add the cream/egg mixture to the flour mixture, then blend on low speed only until a dough is formed.

4. Sprinkle a pastry board or other flat surface with about 2 tablespoons of all-purpose flour. Empty the dough onto the board with the aid of a palm-size plastic bowl scraper or a rubber spatula. With floured hands, knead five or six times to form a "skin" (see the sidebar on page 141), then press into a square about 8 inches. With the aid of a dough scraper, move the dough aside and clean the work surface.

5. Lay a pastry cloth on the surface and fit a rolling pin with a pastry sleeve. Rub an additional 2 tablespoons of flour into the pastry cloth and sleeve.

6. Place the dough on the cloth and roll into a 9 × 12-inch rectangle, with the 9-inch side parallel to the edge of the counter. Fold the dough into thirds like a business letter. To do this, lift the far side of the pastry cloth and fold the top third of the dough over onto itself. Press the dough to align the edges as best you can. Lift the lower edge of the pastry cloth and flip the bottom third of the dough over on itself. You will now have three layers of dough. Press the top gently with your hands, then roll into a 15 × 5-inch strip.

7. Using a 2¼-inch straight-sided cookie cutter dipped in flour, cut straight down into the dough, without twisting the cutter, making six rounds across and two down. Be sure to dip the cutter in flour before cutting each round. When placing on the cookie sheet, invert each scone, spacing them about 1½ inches apart. Brush the tops with the egg wash and sprinkle with sparkling sugar. (See "What to Do with Bits and Pieces of Dough," page 151.)

8. Bake for 16 to 18 minutes, or until firm to the touch. Remove from the oven and let cool on the cookie sheet for about 5 minutes before loosening with a thin, metal spatula. Serve the scones warm. If baking ahead, warm the scones in a 300°F oven.

STORAGE: Store in an airtight plastic bag for up to 3 days. These scones may be frozen.

VARIATION

chocolate chip scones

Dough for Sedona Cream Scones (opposite)

½ **cup mini chocolate chips**

I **egg white lightly beaten with** I **teaspoon water, for egg wash**

I **tablespoon sparkling sugar (see page 380)**

In Step 2, blend the mini chips into the flour/butter mixture. Prepare and cut the dough as directed in the recipe. Before baking, brush the tops of the scones with the egg wash and sprinkle with sparkling sugar. Bake and store as directed.

cinnamon apple scones

MAKES 12 SCONES

These cinnamon-flavored scones with a subtle background of apple add a tasty twist to ordinary scones. I love to eat these with *Apple Cider Caramel Spread* (page 365).

AT A GLANCE
PAN: Large cookie sheet
PAN PREP: None
OVEN TEMP: 375°F
BAKING TIME: 18 to 20 minutes
DIFFICULTY: ☕

1 **Golden Delicious apple, peeled, cored, and cut into eighths**

2 **cups cake flour, spooned in and leveled**

1½ **cups all-purpose flour, spooned in and leveled, plus additional for kneading and rolling**

6 **tablespoons sugar**

4½ **teaspoons baking powder**

2 **teaspoons ground cinnamon**

¾ **teaspoon salt**

½ **cup (1 stick) unsalted butter, cut into ½-inch cubes and chilled**

1 **cup plus 2 tablespoons heavy cream**

1 **large egg**

1 **large egg yolk**

FINISHING

1 **tablespoon sugar**

½ **teaspoon ground cinnamon**

1 **large egg beaten with 1 teaspoon water, for egg wash**

1. Position the rack in the middle of the oven. Heat the oven to 375°F. Have ready a large, ungreased cookie sheet.

2. Place the apple in the work bowl of a food processor fitted with a steel blade and pulse 8 to 10 times, or until the apples are chopped into ¼-inch pieces.

3. Combine the cake and all-purpose flours, sugar, baking powder, cinnamon, and salt in the bowl of an electric mixer fitted with the paddle attachment. Add the butter and mix for 2 to 2½ minutes, or until the mixture forms pea-size bits. Blend in the apple.

4. Whisk together the cream, egg, and egg yolk. Remove the paddle attachment and replace with the dough hook. Add the egg/cream mixture to the flour mixture and blend on low speed just until a dough is formed.

5. Sprinkle a pastry board or other flat surface with about 2 tablespoons of flour. Empty the dough onto the board with the aid of a palm-size plastic bowl scraper or a

rubber spatula. Dust the dough lightly with flour. With floured hands, knead six to eight times to form a "skin" (see the sidebar on page 141), then press it into a square about 8 inches. With the aid of a dough scraper, move the dough aside and clean the work surface.

6. Lay a pastry cloth on the surface and fit a rolling pin with a pastry sleeve. Rub an additional 2 tablespoons of flour into the pastry cloth and sleeve.

7. Place the dough on the cloth and roll into a 10 × 12-inch rectangle, with the 10-inch side parallel to the edge of the counter. Fold the dough into thirds like a business letter. To do this, lift the far side of the pastry cloth and fold the top third of the dough over onto itself. Press the dough to align the edges as best you can. Lift the lower edge of the pastry cloth and flip the bottom third of the dough over on itself. You will now have three layers of dough. Press the top gently with your hands, then roll into a 5 × 15-inch strip.

8. Using a 2¼-inch straight-sided cookie cutter dipped in flour, cut straight down into the dough, without twisting the cutter, making six rounds across and two down. Be sure to dip the cutter in flour before cutting each round. When placing on the cookie sheet, invert each scone, spacing them about 1½ inches apart. Stir together the sugar and cinnamon. Brush the tops with the egg wash, then sprinkle with the sugar/cinnamon mixture. (See "What to Do with Bits and Pieces of Dough," page 151.)

9. Bake for 18 to 20 minutes, or until firm to the touch. Remove from the oven and let cool on the cookie sheet for about 5 minutes before loosening with a thin, metal spatula. Serve the scones warm. If baking ahead, warm the scones in a 300°F oven.

STORAGE: Store in an airtight plastic bag for up to 3 days. These scones may be frozen.

"For a tender, flaky scone, follow your grandmother's advice. Work quickly with gentle hands and once you've added your liquids, don't overmix."

NANCY SILVERTON

pearl bresev's scones

MAKES 12 SCONES

For many years, the *Anna Amendolara Nurse Brunch* was the kick-off event for *Beard Week*, when the James Beard Foundation held their annual awards. *Anna's brunch was a covered-dish event, worthy of a centerfold in the finest of food publications, in which New York's most talented chefs participated. Anna was also blessed with a few close friends*

AT A GLANCE
PAN: Rimmed baking sheet
PAN PREP: Line with parchment
OVEN TEMP: 350°F
BAKING TIME: 23 to 25 minutes
DIFFICULTY: 🍵

who were extraordinary cooks and bakers, and Pearl Bresev was one of them. Pearlie's claim to fame at this event was her fabulous scones, and she generously shared her recipe for your pleasure.

½ cup golden raisins, plumped (see page 389)

3 tablespoons Grand Marnier or other orange-flavored liqueur

2 cups all-purpose flour, spooned in and leveled, plus additional for kneading and rolling

¼ cup sugar

1 tablespoon baking powder

¾ teaspoon freshly grated navel orange zest

Pinch of salt

¼ cup (½ stick) unsalted butter, cut into ½-inch cubes and chilled

2 large eggs

1 large egg yolk (reserve white for egg wash)

¾ cup heavy cream

1 large egg white beaten with 1 teaspoon water, for egg wash

1. Combine the raisins and Grand Marnier. Let steep for 20 to 30 minutes.

2. Position the rack in the middle of the oven. Heat the oven to 350°F. Line a rimmed baking sheet with baking parchment and set aside.

3. Place the flour, sugar, baking powder, orange zest, and salt in the work bowl of a food processor fitted with the steel blade. Pulse to blend. Add the butter and pulse 8 to 10 times, or until the mixture resembles coarse crumbs. Empty into a large mixing bowl.

4. Combine the eggs, egg yolk, and cream, whisking thoroughly to blend. Pour the cream mixture around the edge of the bowl. Using a rubber spatula, work around the bowl toward the center to blend the liquid with the crumbs. The dough will be very wet.

5. Sprinkle a pastry board or other flat surface with about 2 tablespoons of flour. Empty the dough onto the board with the aid of a palm-size plastic bowl scraper or a

rubber spatula. With floured hands, pat the dough into an 8 × 10-inch rectangle. With the aid of a dough scraper, move it aside and clean the work surface.

6. Lay a pastry cloth on the surface and fit a rolling pin with a pastry sleeve. Rub an additional 2 tablespoons of flour into the pastry cloth and sleeve.

7. Drain the raisins well and pat them dry. Place the dough on the cloth and, with well floured hands, reshape the dough into an 8 × 10-inch rectangle, with the 8-inch side parallel to the counter. Sprinkle with one-half of the raisins. Lift the far side of the pastry cloth up and fold the top third of the dough over on itself, as if you were folding a business letter. Press one-half of the remaining raisins into the surface of the dough and align the edges as best you can. Lift the lower edge of the pastry cloth and flip the bottom third of the dough over on itself. Press the remaining raisins into the dough surface.

8. Roll the dough into a 7 × 11-inch rectangle about ½ inch thick. Using a 2¼-inch straight-sided cookie cutter dipped in flour, cut straight down into the dough, without twisting the cutter, making six rounds across and three down. Be sure to dip the cutter in flour before cutting each round. When placing on the cookie sheet, *invert* each scone, spacing them about 1½ inches apart. Brush the tops with the egg wash. (See "What to Do with Bits and Pieces of Dough," page 151.)

9. Bake for 23 to 25 minutes, or until firm to the touch. Remove from the oven and let cool on the cookie sheet for about 5 minutes before loosening with a thin, metal spatula. Serve the scones warm. If baking ahead, warm the scones in a 300°F oven.

STORAGE: Store in an airtight plastic bag for up to 3 days. These scones may be frozen.

a dilly of a cheese scone

MAKES 12 SCONES

Here is a delicious savory scone made with shredded Jarlsberg cheese and lots of finely chopped fresh dill. These are shaped into triangles, and are wonderful to serve for a brunch or lunch with chicken or fish. Be sure to use only fresh dill, not dried; it makes a vast difference. For buffet service, it's okay if you wish to divide the dough into smaller portions.

AT A GLANCE
PAN: Large cookie sheet
PAN PREP: Butter
OVEN TEMP: 400°F
BAKING TIME: 18 to 20 minutes
DIFFICULTY: 🥄

1¾ cups all-purpose flour, spooned in and leveled, plus additional for kneading and rolling

2 tablespoons sugar

1 tablespoon baking powder

½ teaspoon salt

Pinch of nutmeg

⅓ cup (⅔ stick) unsalted butter, cut into ½-inch cubes and chilled

¾ cup (about 3 ounces) shredded Jarlsberg cheese

3 tablespoons chopped fresh dill

1 large egg

¾ cup heavy cream, plus 1 tablespoon, for brushing

1. Position the rack in the middle of the oven. Heat the oven to 400°F. Butter a large cookie sheet and set aside.

2. Place the flour, sugar, baking powder, salt, and nutmeg in the work bowl of a food processor fitted with a steel blade. Pulse 2 to 3 times to combine. Add the butter and pulse 5 times, then process for 8 seconds. Add the cheese and dill, pulsing twice to blend. Empty into a large mixing bowl.

3. In a small bowl, whisk together the egg and ¾ cup cream. Make a well in the center of the dry ingredients and pour in the liquid. Using a rubber spatula, push the crumb mixture into the well, working your way around the bowl to form a rough dough. With lightly floured hands, knead the dough three or four times in the bowl. Divide the dough in half.

4. Lay a pastry cloth on a pastry board or other flat surface and fit a rolling pin with a pastry sleeve. Rub about 2 tablespoons of flour into the pastry cloth and sleeve.

5. Place one piece of dough on the cloth and, with floured hands, shape into a ball. Flatten the ball into a disk and roll into a 7-inch circle about ½ inch thick. Cut into six

wedges using a bench scraper or sharp knife. Place on the prepared cookie sheet. Repeat with the remaining dough.

6. Brush with 1 tablespoon heavy cream and bake for 18 to 20 minutes, or until lightly browned. Remove from the oven and cool slightly on the cookie sheet before loosening with a thin-bladed metal spatula. Serve warm. If baking ahead, reheat the scones in a 300°F oven.

STORAGE: Store in an airtight plastic bag for up to 3 days. These scones may be frozen.

WHAT TO DO WITH BITS AND PIECES OF DOUGH

MOST OF THE RECIPES in this chapter specify a yield of 12 biscuits or scones. That amount is based on the first cut of the dough. Since these types of doughs should be handled with a deft touch, the first cut gives the best rise. However, the leftover bits and pieces can be rerolled.

To do this, clean and reflour your pastry cloth or work surface. Gather the bits and pieces and lightly press them together into a rectangle. Roll the dough to a ¼-inch thickness and fold it in thirds. Give the dough a quarter turn and gently roll it again into a long strip, approximately ½ inch thick and 2½ to 3 inches wide. Dip the cutter into flour, then cut the rounds as close together as possible. Invert the rounds on the cookie sheet, and finish according to the recipe. Discard the remaining dough. These types of doughs should not be worked beyond the second cut.

country cherry honey scones

If you want to make a pretty scone, this is the recipe to choose. The dough is flavored with honey and orange zest, and has chopped dried cherries throughout. When you chop the cherries, make sure they are free of pits. The scones are cut into triangles and the tops are trimmed with sparkling sugar. If you have a long basket, these are beautiful served with the tips of the triangles angled in different directions.

> **AT A GLANCE**
> **PAN:** Large cookie sheet
> **PAN PREP:** Butter
> **OVEN TEMP:** 400°F
> **BAKING TIME:** 14 to 16 minutes
> **DIFFICULTY:** 🍵

2½ cups all-purpose flour, spooned in and leveled, plus additional for kneading and rolling

2 tablespoons *very fresh* light brown sugar

1 tablespoon baking powder

½ teaspoon salt

¼ teaspoon baking soda

1 teaspoon freshly grated navel orange zest

½ cup (1 stick) unsalted butter, cold

½ cup (about 2½ ounces) dried cherries (not organic), plumped (see page 389) and coarsely chopped

1 large egg

¼ cup honey

½ cup half-and-half

1 large egg lightly beaten with 1 teaspoon water, for egg wash

1 tablespoon sparkling sugar (see page 380)

1. Position the rack in the middle of the oven. Heat the oven to 400°F. Butter a large cookie sheet and set aside.

2. In a large bowl, thoroughly whisk together the flour, brown sugar, baking powder, salt, and baking soda. Add the orange zest and work it into the dry ingredients with your hands.

3. Shave the butter into ⅛-inch slices using a dough scraper or sharp knife. Add the butter to the dry ingredients, rubbing it between your fingertips until the mixture resembles coarse meal. It's okay if some larger flakes of butter are visible. Add the cherries and toss to coat with the crumbs.

4. In a small bowl, combine the egg, honey, and half-and-half. Make a well in the center of the dry ingredients and add the liquid. Using a rubber spatula, draw the crumbs into the center, working your way around the side of the bowl until a soft dough is formed. With floured hands, knead the dough gently five or six times to

form a "skin" (see the sidebar on page 141). Divide the dough in half and form a skin on the cut side, and set aside.

5. Lay a pastry cloth on a pastry board or other flat surface and fit a rolling pin with a pastry sleeve. Rub about 2 tablespoons of flour into the pastry cloth and sleeve.

6. Place 1 piece of dough on the cloth and, with floured hands, turn the dough two or three times to coat it with the flour. Pat the dough into a disk, then roll it into a 7-inch circle about ½ inch thick. Cut into six wedges using a dough scraper or sharp knife. Place on the prepared cookie sheet. Repeat with the remaining dough.

7. Brush with the egg wash and sprinkle each scone with ¼ teaspoon sparkling sugar. Bake for 14 to 16 minutes, or until lightly browned. Remove from the oven and cool slightly on the cookie sheet before loosening with a thin-bladed metal spatula. Serve warm. If baking ahead, reheat the scones in a 300°F oven.

STORAGE: Store in an airtight plastic bag for up to 3 days. These scones may be frozen.

cranberry pecan cream scones

MAKES 14 SCONES

This recipe is based on *Sedona Cream Scones* (page 144). The sweet-tart cranberries and crunchy pecans add just the right amount of flavor and texture. I like to serve these with *Orange Honey Butter* (page 367). The flavors of the scones and the butter make for a happy marriage.

AT A GLANCE
PAN: Cookie sheet
PAN PREP: None
OVEN TEMP: 375°F
BAKING TIME: 16 to 18 minutes
DIFFICULTY: ♨

---

2 cups cake flour, spooned in and leveled

1⅓ cups all-purpose flour, spooned in and leveled, plus additional for kneading and rolling

6 tablespoons sugar

4½ teaspoons baking powder

¾ teaspoon salt

½ cup (1 stick) unsalted butter, cut into ½-inch cubes and chilled

1 teaspoon freshly grated navel orange zest

½ cup sweetened dried cranberries (not organic), plumped (see page 389), patted dry

½ cup toasted broken pecans

1 cup plus 2 tablespoons heavy cream

1 large egg

1 large egg yolk (reserve white for egg wash)

1 teaspoon pure vanilla extract

1 egg white mixed with 1 teaspoon cold water, for egg wash

1. Position the rack in the middle of the oven. Heat the oven to 375°F. Have ready an ungreased cookie sheet.

2. Combine the cake and all-purpose flours, the sugar, baking powder, and salt in the bowl of an electric mixer fitted with the paddle attachment, and mix for 5 seconds. Add the butter and orange zest and mix on low speed for 2 to 2½ minutes, or until the mixture forms pea-size bits. Add the cranberries and mix for 5 seconds. Add the pecans and mix for 5 seconds more.

3. In a small bowl, whisk together the cream, egg, egg yolk, and vanilla. Remove the paddle attachment and replace with the dough hook. With the mixer off, add the liquids to the flour mixture. Then mix on low speed, scraping down the side of the bowl as needed. Mix until a rough dough is formed. *Note:* Discard any small particles remaining at the bottom of the bowl.

4. Sprinkle a pastry board or other flat surface with about 2 tablespoons of flour. Empty the dough onto the board with the aid of a palm-size plastic bowl scraper or

rubber spatula. With floured hands, knead the dough five or six times to form a skin (see the sidebar on page 141), then press it into a square. With the aid of a dough scraper, move the dough aside and clean the work surface.

5. Lay a pastry cloth on the surface and fit a rolling pin with a pastry sleeve. Rub an additional 2 tablespoons of flour into the pastry cloth and sleeve.

6. Place the dough on the cloth and roll into a 12-inch square. Fold the dough into thirds like a business letter. To do this, lift the far side of the pastry cloth and fold the top third of the dough over on itself. Press the dough to align the edges as best you can. Lift the lower edge of the pastry cloth and flip the bottom third of the dough over on itself. You will now have three layers of dough. Press the top gently with your hands, then roll into an 18 × 5-inch strip.

7. Using a straight-sided 2¼-inch cookie cutter dipped in flour, cut straight down into the dough, without twisting the cutter, making seven rounds across and two down. Be sure to dip the cutter in flour before cutting each round. When placing on the cookie sheet, invert each scone, spacing them about 1½ inches apart. Brush the tops with the egg wash. (See "What to Do with Bits and Pieces of Dough," page 151.)

8. Bake for 16 to 18 minutes, or until firm to the touch. Remove from the oven and let cool on the cookie sheet for about 5 minutes before loosening with a thin, metal spatula. Serve the scones warm. If baking ahead, warm the scones for a few minutes in a 300°F oven.

STORAGE: Store in an airtight plastic bag for up to 2 days. Freezing is not recommended.

easy does it yeasted coffee cakes

Simple Sweet Dough

Rich Sour Cream Dough

Crumb Buns

Cinnamon Buns

Swedish Tea Ring

Dried Plum Tea Ring

Holiday Stollen

Rustic Cinnamon Walnut Horns

Scalloped Chocolate Pecan Strip

Sticky Buns

VARIATION: *Sticky Bun Cake*

Sour Cherry Cream Kuchen

VARIATION: *Prune Plum Cream Kuchen*

Cheese Kuchen

Blueberry Pizza

Apple and Dried Cranberry Coffee Cake

Fig and Walnut Loaf

Woven Apricot-Almond Strip

Pineapple Cheese Braid

Golden Raisin Poppy Seed Twist

Golden Cinnamon Loaf

Dimpled Sugar Cake

VARIATION: Strawberry Dimpled Sugar Cake

Kugelhopf

Old-Fashioned Babka Dough

Carole's Streusel-Topped Babka

Apricot-Raisin Babka

Double Chocolate Walnut Babka

VARIATION: Double Chocolate Babka

Glazed Loaded-with-Nuts Babka

YEASTED CAKES, BABKAS, AND KUCHENS

When I began this chapter, I did considerable research for a great sweet bread dough to make a yeast-style coffee cake. I checked my recipe folder, and it was brimming with recipes that I had collected over the years. In my mother's day, these types of cakes were simply referred to as "yeast cakes." These were yeast-based cakes, made with dough that was rich with butter, eggs, and often sour cream. They were filled with cinnamon, nuts, and raisins and were usually baked in an angel food cake pan.

I approached a few of the bakers in my family, as well as friends and students, to find out what sweet bread recipes they had in their files. What I learned was that really fine recipes stand the test of time and, over years, make the rounds from baker to baker, as well as state to state. No matter the name—yeast cake, babka, or kuchen—the basic dough recipes were consistently the same.

The only differences were in shape, often dictated by the baking pan at hand and the kind of filling. Fillings included such treats as dried fruits, nuts, chocolate chips, or poppy seeds. The cakes were sweetened with white and brown sugars as well as preserves, and had flavorings like cinnamon, almond paste, or lemon or orange zest. They were often topped with irresistible buttery streusel crumbs.

No matter what the name, the shape, or the filling, these are satisfying cakes that will never go out of style and should be enjoyed for many years to come.

ABOUT YEASTED COFFEE CAKES

Making yeasted coffee cakes is easier than you think. While the process may appear daunting, there is very little that can go wrong. To build confidence, read through the following tips and hints. With a little bit of know-how you'll be on your way to making terrific yeasted coffee cakes.

MAKING THE DOUGH
• Eggs will incorporate more quickly and evenly into yeasted dough if they are lightly beaten before adding them to the dry ingredients.
• Kneading nuts, raisins, or other dried fruits into the dough can be easily done in a stand mixer during the final stage of mixing. However, be careful not to overwork the

dough. Darker dried fruits, such as cherries, can change the color of the dough if mixed too long.

• The purpose of kneading is to develop structure. However, with rich yeasted doughs, excessive kneading is unnecessary because of the high fat content in the mixture.

• Weather can be a contributing factor when it comes to making yeasted dough. Humidity at any time of year can affect the preparation. When the air is moist, it's not unusual for the dough to absorb more flour. If the dough becomes too soft and is difficult to handle, chill it briefly in the refrigerator—it's the best remedy! For ease of handling in the summer, it is essential to roll the dough while it is still chilled. In the winter, if the weather is especially dry and cold, the dough may have to stand at room temperature to soften a bit. To determine if the dough is ready to shape, when you press the top, you should be able to make a *slight* imprint.

ROLLING THE DOUGH

• There are two important pieces of equipment to have on hand to make rolling most yeasted dough easier. The first is a wooden pastry board, approximately 18 × 24 inches. A polyethylene cutting board of sufficient size makes a satisfactory alternative. The second piece of equipment is a tool called a dough scraper. This rectangular tool, measuring 6 × 4½ inches, has a plastic or wooden handle and a stainless steel edge that is sharp enough to cut through dough and scrape the work surfaces clean.

• When using a pastry board or large cutting board to roll dough, place a strip of wax paper partially under the left or right side of the board, leaving about 8 inches exposed. As you clean the work surface with a dough scraper, the wax paper is the perfect place to deposit particles of dough and excess flour.

• To keep the work surface clean, work from right to left when rolling dough. (If you are left handed, reverse the following procedure.) Keep a small bowl of clean flour to the right. The center should be kept clean for kneading and rolling, using only small amounts of flour as needed. Use the dough scraper to move loose bits of dough to the left, scraping the board clean from time to time.

• Flour your hands before touching the dough to prevent the dough from sticking. Be sure to reflour your hands several times during the kneading process.

• While rolling the dough, don't overflour your board because it is preferable for the dough to grasp the rolling surface. When the dough adheres to the board, it is easier to roll to the desired size and it is less likely to spring back.

SHAPING THE DOUGH

• Dough that is to be rolled and filled is easier to handle when it is cold. It also enables you to roll the dough thinner. Room-temperature dough is used when it must be pressed into a pan or shaped into individual balls; softer dough is easier to work with.

• When dividing dough, flour the exposed cut surface to form a thin covering. Knead the dough briefly until it is no longer sticky. As the dough is kneaded, a thin coating forms over the surface that is referred to as the skin. Each time the dough is cut, the skin is broken and before the dough can be rolled again, a new skin must be formed (see "Forming a Skin," page 141).

• When dough becomes too elastic or continually springs back when rolling, let it rest for 2 to 3 minutes. The more you handle the dough, the more elastic it will become; therefore, resting from time to time is helpful.

• Picking the dough up will help to roll the dough thinner. It also ensures that it has not adhered to the rolling surface.

• If when rolling dough you have difficulty achieving the proper dimension called for, it may be too elastic. In addition to resting it, pull the edges gently with your fingertips to stretch the dough, rather than using the rolling pin.

• When dough is topped with a filling and then rolled into a log, stretch the log *lengthwise* as you roll. This helps to distribute the filling, which has a tendency to accumulate in the center. After the cylinder is made, roll it back and forth to seal the layers.

• When filled dough is rolled into a log, as you start to roll, the filling may shift on the first turn. To prevent this from happening, turn a 1-inch edge of the dough over the filling and press it with your thumb, then continue rolling. This will keep the filling from moving.

• To divide a log into even pieces, refer to the recipe for how many pieces it should make. For example, if the recipe calls for dividing a 12-inch log into 1-inch pieces, make an indentation with a dough scraper or the back of a paring knife at the halfway point of the log (6 inches). Then divide each 6-inch piece in half, marking off four 3-inch pieces. Finally, mark each 3-inch piece at 1-inch intervals. Once the dough is marked, you can cut. You will have a total of twelve 1-inch pieces. (See "Playing with Dough," page 222.)

• After the dough is shaped, place it in a warm, draft-free environment to rise; the optimum temperature is about 100°F. The shaped dough will rise well wherever it is placed, as long as the optimum temperature is not exceeded. The At-a-Glance box will indicate the approximate rising time after shaping. Here are three easy ways to raise the dough:

1. Warm the oven for only one minute on the lowest temperature setting. Turn it off and place the shaped and covered dough inside. If baking space is limited, carefully remove the dough and let it continue rising at room temperature while the oven is heating.

2. Fill a large double-handle pot with 2 or 3 inches of very hot tap water. Place a rimmed cookie sheet over the pot, and rest the shaped and covered dough on top.

3. Place the shaped and covered dough in a draft-free spot in your kitchen. This is an excellent method, but will require a longer rising time. A slow rise is always better.

• Caution should be taken not to overrise the dough. You run the risk of the shaped dough collapsing because it is overrisen, and the flavor becomes very "yeasty" (sour).

• Extra yeast does not make the dough rise higher. It can speed the rising process, but does not affect the height of the finished product. Too much yeast spoils the flavor of the finished pastry.

• Covering the dough loosely with a dry towel for the final rise prevents it from being exposed to drafts and drying out. Avoid using dampened towels because they will stick to the dough as it rises.

• Many of the recipes in this chapter suggest baking in aluminum foil pans because many bakers do not have three medium metal loaf pans of the same size. A great advantage of using these disposable pans is that extra loaves can be frozen directly in them. They are also ideal for gift giving. If you own heavier weight loaf pans of similar size and choose to use them, by all means do so.

• When baking cakes in disposable aluminum foil pans, always place them on rimmed cookie sheets for ease of handling and better heat conductivity.

• If you have any filling preparations left over, such as chopped nuts, streusels, sugar combinations, or plumped dried fruits, they can be either refrigerated for short term or frozen for later use. Pastry cream can be refrigerated for up to 3 days, but should not be frozen.

two master doughs

You will find the following two yeasted sweet dough recipes a cinch to prepare. The directions are written for both stand mixer and hand methods. Making the dough takes less time than you think, especially if you use a stand mixer with a paddle attachment. Preparing the dough by hand can give equally marvelous results; however, the amount of flour must be increased slightly.

The recipes for Simple Sweet Dough (page 164) and Rich Sour Cream Dough (page 166) are interchangeable and both produce excellent pastries; the only difference is that the latter is richer. They can also be used for any of the babka recipes found in this chapter. Both dough recipes require overnight refrigeration because they are enriched with butter and eggs and are too soft to handle when freshly made. After the dough is chilled, it is easy to handle and a snap to roll and shape.

When you cube the butter, lay the butter on the open wrapper. Using a dough scraper or thin, sharp knife, halve the butter lengthwise, give it a quarter turn and cut it again lengthwise, forming four "sticks." Then cut across the sticks, making ½-inch cubes.

If the recipe you are preparing uses only half of the dough, prepare the full master recipe. This gives you the opportunity to make more than one variety, or to freeze half for later use (see "Freezing Yeasted Doughs," page 225).

simple sweet dough

MAKES 2 POUNDS OF DOUGH, ENOUGH FOR I LARGE OR 2 MEDIUM COFFEE CAKES,

OR 2 TO 3 DOZEN INDIVIDUAL COFFEE CAKES

PLAN AHEAD: Refrigerate overnight

4 tablespoons sugar

¼ cup warm water (110° to 115°F)

I package active dry yeast

3 cups unbleached all-purpose flour, spooned in
and leveled (plus ¼ cup for Hand Method)

I teaspoon salt

I cup (2 sticks) unsalted butter, cut into ½-inch
cubes (see "Two Master Doughs," page 163),
plus I teaspoon soft butter for brushing top
of dough

½ cup milk

3 large egg yolks

I teaspoon pure vanilla extract

1. Rinse a small bowl in hot water to warm it. Add 1 tablespoon of the sugar and the warm water to the bowl. Sprinkle the yeast over the water. *Do not stir.* Cover the bowl with a saucer and let the mixture stand for 5 minutes. Stir it briefly with a fork, cover again, and let it stand for 2 to 3 minutes more, or until bubbly. (See "Working with Yeast," page 186.)

MAKE THE DOUGH

Stand Mixer Method

2. In the bowl of an electric mixer fitted with the paddle attachment, mix on low speed the 3 cups of flour, remaining 3 tablespoons of sugar, and the salt. Add the *slightly* firm cubed butter and continue to mix until meal-size crumbs form, 2 to 4 minutes, depending upon the temperature of the butter. Stop the mixer.

3. Using a fork, in a separate bowl, mix the milk, egg yolks, and vanilla. Add the milk mixture to the flour, along with the dissolved yeast, and mix on low speed for about 15 seconds. Stop the mixer and scrape down the side of the bowl with a rubber spatula. Mix on low speed for another 30 seconds, or until a smooth dough is formed. *Note:* This is a soft dough.

Hand Method

2. In a large mixing bowl, whisk together the 3 cups of flour, remaining 3 tablespoons of sugar, and the salt. Add the *soft* cubed butter, and using a pastry blender or your fingertips, work in the butter until the mixture resembles fine meal.

3. Make a well in the center. Using a fork, blend together in a small bowl the milk, egg yolks, and vanilla. Pour the milk mixture into the well and add the dissolved yeast. With a wooden spoon, gradually work the crumbs into the liquids, mixing until all the crumbs are incorporated and a rough dough is formed. Sprinkle the work surface with about 2 tablespoons of the remaining flour. Turn the dough onto the floured surface and knead lightly, adding the remaining 2 tablespoons of flour, kneading until smooth. *Note:* This is a soft dough.

4. Lightly butter a medium bowl for storing the dough. Empty the dough into the prepared bowl, smoothing the top with lightly floured hands. Spread a thin layer of softened butter over the top. Cover tightly with plastic wrap and refrigerate overnight.

STORAGE: This dough may be kept in the refrigerator, tightly covered with plastic wrap, for up to 3 days. For longer storage, see "Freezing Yeasted Doughs," page 225.

rich sour cream dough

MAKES 2 POUNDS OF DOUGH, ENOUGH FOR 1 LARGE OR 2 MEDIUM COFFEE CAKES,

OR 2 TO 3 DOZEN INDIVIDUAL COFFEE CAKES

PLAN AHEAD: Refrigerate overnight

4 tablespoons sugar

¼ cup warm water (110° to 115°F)

1 package active dry yeast

3 cups unbleached all-purpose flour, spooned in
and leveled (plus ¼ cup for Hand Method)

1 teaspoon salt

¾ cup (1½ sticks) unsalted butter, cut into
½-inch cubes (see "Two Master Doughs,"
page 163), plus 1 teaspoon soft butter for
brushing top of dough

2 large eggs

½ cup sour cream

1 teaspoon pure vanilla extract

1. Rinse a small bowl in hot water to warm it. Add 1 tablespoon of the sugar and the warm water to the bowl. Sprinkle the yeast over the water. Do *not* stir. Cover the bowl with a saucer and let the mixture stand for 5 minutes. Stir it briefly with a fork, cover again, and let it stand for 2 to 3 minutes, or until bubbly. (See "Working with Yeast," page 186.)

MAKE THE DOUGH

Stand Mixer Method

2. In the bowl of an electric mixer fitted with the paddle attachment, mix on low speed the 3 cups of flour, remaining 3 tablespoons of sugar, and the salt. Add the *slightly* firm butter and continue to mix until meal-size crumbs form, 2 to 4 minutes, depending upon the temperature of the butter. Stop the mixer.

3. Using a fork, in a large bowl, mix the eggs, sour cream, and vanilla. Add the sour cream mixture to the flour, along with the dissolved yeast, and mix on low speed until a rough dough is formed. *Note:* This is a soft dough.

Hand Method

2. In a large mixing bowl, whisk together the 3 cups of flour, remaining 3 tablespoons of sugar, and the salt. Add the *soft* cubed butter, and using a pastry blender or your fingertips, work in the butter until the mixture resembles fine meal.

3. Make a well in the center. Using a fork, blend together in a small bowl the eggs, sour cream, and vanilla. Pour the sour cream mixture into the well and add the dissolved yeast. With a wooden spoon, gradually work the crumbs into the liquids, mixing until all the crumbs are incorporated and a rough dough is formed. Sprinkle the work surface with about 2 tablespoons of the remaining flour. Turn the dough onto the floured surface, add the remaining 2 tablespoons of flour, and knead until smooth. *Note:* This is a soft dough

4. Lightly butter a medium bowl for storing the dough. Turn the dough into the prepared bowl, smoothing the top with lightly floured hands. Brush the top lightly with the soft butter. Cover tightly with plastic wrap and refrigerate overnight.

STORAGE: This dough may be kept in the refrigerator, tightly covered with plastic wrap, for up to 3 days. For longer storage, see "Freezing Yeasted Doughs," page 225.

crumb buns

MAKES 9 CRUMB BUNS

If you are addicted to streusel toppings as much as I am, try your hand at these irresistible crumb buns. These classic buns, with their thick crown of melt-in-your-mouth crumbs, are always a crowd pleaser. I have yet to see anyone resist plucking away at the crunchy crumbs.

AT A GLANCE
PAN: 9 x 9 x 2-inch square pan
PAN PREP: Butter generously
RISING TIME: 45 minutes
OVEN TEMP: 350°F
BAKING TIME: 30 to 35 minutes
DIFFICULTY: 🍵

½ recipe (about 1 pound) Simple Sweet Dough (page 164) or Rich Sour Cream Dough (page 166)

1 small recipe Carole's Favorite Streusel (page 350)

1 large egg lightly beaten with 1 teaspoon water, for egg wash

Powdered sugar, for dusting

1. Remove the dough from the refrigerator 1 to 1½ hours before shaping.

2. Generously butter a 9 × 9 × 2-inch square pan. On a lightly floured surface, knead the dough gently six to eight times, or until smooth, then pat it into a square. Using a dough scraper or a sharp knife, divide the dough evenly into nine pieces. Cupping your hand over each piece, roll the dough on a barely floured surface, continuously rotating it until it forms a ball.

3. Arrange the balls in the pan, placing three pieces across and three pieces down. Be sure to space them evenly. Flatten the balls slightly until they are about ¾ inch apart; they do not have to touch. Cover the pan with a tea towel and set in a warmish place to rise for 45 minutes, or until the balls begin to touch each other. While the buns are rising, prepare the streusel.

4. Fifteen minutes before baking, position the rack in the lower third of the oven. Heat the oven to 350°F.

5. Gently brush the tops of the buns with the egg wash. Sprinkle the crumb mixture heavily over the dough. Press the streusel slightly into the dough. Bake for 30 to 35 minutes, or until the streusel is lightly browned. Remove from the oven and place on a rack to cool. To remove the pan, place a 12-inch piece of aluminum foil on top of the pan, cupping it around the side to hold the streusel in place. Cover with a cooling

rack, invert, and carefully lift off the pan. Cover with another rack, invert again, remove the aluminum foil, and cool right side up. When the buns are almost cool, dust the tops heavily with powdered sugar. Reheat before serving. Break apart when ready to serve.

STORAGE: Store at room temperature, tightly wrapped in aluminum foil, for up to 3 days. These buns may be frozen (see "Refreshing Yeasted Coffee Cakes," page 213).

"All happiness depends upon a leisurely breakfast."

JOHN GUNTHER

cinnamon buns

Get ready for Sunday morning breakfast with these scrumptious cinnamon buns. With the sweet scent of cinnamon swirling through the house, these buns are sure to awaken even the deepest of sleepers. Children and adults alike will dash to the kitchen to devour the buns.

AT A GLANCE

PAN: 8 x 8 x 2-inch square baking pan
PAN PREP: Butter generously/line with parchment
RISING TIME: 45 to 60 minutes
OVEN TEMP: 350°F
BAKING TIME: 30 to 35 minutes
DIFFICULTY: ☕

½ recipe (about 1 pound) **Simple Sweet Dough (page 164)** or **Rich Sour Cream Dough (page 166)**

3 tablespoons unsalted butter, softened

3 tablespoons granulated sugar

3 tablespoons (firmly packed) dark brown sugar

2 tablespoons **Lyle's Golden Syrup (see page 379)** or light corn syrup

1 tablespoon ground cinnamon

⅛ teaspoon salt

1 large egg lightly beaten with 1 teaspoon water, for egg wash

1 small recipe **Vanilla Glaze (page 359)**, optional

1. Remove the dough from the refrigerator 1 to 1½ hours before using.

2. Generously butter an 8 × 8 × 2-inch square pan. Line the bottom with parchment. Set aside.

3. In a medium bowl, using a wooden spoon, mix the butter, sugars, syrup, cinnamon, and salt until smooth.

4. Place the dough on a lightly floured surface. Gently knead six or eight times to coat with flour. Pat or shape the dough into a rectangle. Roll the dough into a 9 × 12-inch rectangle with the 9-inch side parallel to the edge of the counter.

5. Spoon dollops of the cinnamon filling evenly across the dough, making three rows across and three rows down. Using a small offset metal spatula, spread the filling evenly across the dough, leaving a 1½-inch border on the far edge. Lightly brush the border with the egg wash. Starting at the side of the rectangle closest to you, roll the dough tightly. Pinch the seam well to seal the flap. Roll the log back and forth a few times to seal the layers. With your hands, gently stretch the log until it measures about 12 inches.

6. Cut the log into nine 1¼-inch pieces (see "About Yeasted Coffee Cakes," page 159), and place them cut side up in the baking pan, spacing them evenly, three rows across and three rows down. Press the tops of the buns gently to even the surface.

7. Cover the pan with a tea towel and set it in a warmish place to allow the buns to rise until puffy and almost doubled, 45 to 60 minutes.

8. Fifteen minutes before baking, position the rack in the middle of the oven. Heat the oven to 350°F.

9. Gently brush the tops of the buns with egg wash. Bake for 30 to 35 minutes, or until golden brown. If the buns are browning too quickly, lay a sheet of aluminum foil over the top to allow the center of the buns to bake through. Remove the buns from the oven and allow them to sit for 15 minutes. While the buns are cooling, make the glaze.

10. To remove the pan, cover it with a cooling rack, invert the buns and carefully lift off the pan. Remove the parchment, then cover the buns with another rack and turn the buns top side up. If the buns have risen unevenly while baking, gently press the tops to level them. While the buns are still warm, drizzle the glaze over the top by dipping a small whisk or fork into the icing and waving it rapidly back and forth over the surface of the buns.

STORAGE: Store at room temperature, tightly wrapped in aluminum foil, for up to 3 days. Heat before serving. These buns may be frozen (see "Refreshing Yeasted Coffee Cakes," page 213).

swedish tea ring

MAKES ONE 11- TO 12-INCH TEA RING, 8 TO 10 SERVINGS

When I made this tea ring during my teenage years, this was my favorite way to shape the dough. The cake, filled with brown and white sugars, cinnamon, nuts, and sometimes raisins, was rolled into a log and then shaped into a ring on a cookie sheet. With a simple snip of the scissors, the ring was cut at intervals. The slices were turned on their side to form a ring of "petals." After baking, a drizzle of vanilla glaze gives just the right finishing touch. This beautiful coffee cake promises to be a hit every time you serve it.

AT A GLANCE
PAN: Large cookie sheet
PAN PREP: Line with parchment
RISING TIME: 45 to 60 minutes
OVEN TEMP: 350°F
BAKING TIME: 25 to 28 minutes
DIFFICULTY: ☕

¼ cup granulated sugar

¼ cup light brown sugar

1 teaspoon ground cinnamon

½ recipe (about 1 pound) Simple Sweet Dough (page 164) or Rich Sour Cream Dough (page 166), cold

1 large egg white lightly beaten with 1 teaspoon water, for egg wash

¾ cup medium-finely chopped toasted pecans (see pages 391–392)

½ cup golden raisins, plumped (see page 389), optional

1 small recipe Vanilla Glaze (page 359)

1. In a small bowl, combine the granulated and brown sugars and cinnamon. Set aside.

2. Butter the corners of a large cookie sheet to secure the baking parchment, then line the pan with the parchment.

3. On a lightly floured surface, knead the *cold* dough gently six to eight times. Roll the dough into a 9 × 16-inch rectangle with the 16-inch side parallel to the edge of the counter. Brush the dough with the egg wash. Sprinkle the top with the sugar/cinnamon mixture, leaving a 1-inch border on the far side. Scatter the chopped nuts and raisins, if using, over the dough and gently pat them into the surface.

4. Beginning at the side of the rectangle closest to you, roll the dough tightly, jelly roll style, to form a log. As you roll, be sure to square the ends of the log with a dough scraper to even the thickness of the log. Pinch the seam, sealing it well and gently roll the log back and forth, elongating the log until it measures 16 to18 inches.

5. Place the log *seam side down* on the prepared cookie sheet and form it into a circle, 7 to 8 inches round. To make the ring, brush one of the ends with the egg wash and seal it to the opposite end by pinching them together. Invert a 4½-inch (8-ounce) heat-proof custard cup, with 1 inch of the outer rim buttered, into the center of the ring. This will help to keep the shape of the circle. Adjust the shape and flatten the circle slightly with the palm of your hand.

6. Using sharp scissors, cut sixteen to eighteen slits about three-quarters of the way through the dough, spacing them about 1 inch apart. Turn the slices out so the cut portions lay flat against the pan (see illustrations). Cover the ring with a tea towel and set in a warmish place to rise for 45 to 60 minutes, or until puffy and almost doubled.

7. Fifteen minutes before baking, position the rack in the lower third of the oven. Heat the oven to 350°F.

8. Brush the top of the ring with the egg wash and bake for 25 to 28 minutes, or just until golden brown. *Do not overbake.*

9. While the ring is baking, prepare the glaze. Drizzle the glaze over the top of the warm cake by dipping a small whisk or fork into the icing and waving it rapidly back and forth over the surface of the cake.

STORAGE: Store at room temperature, tightly wrapped in aluminum foil, for up to 3 days. This cake may be frozen (see "Refreshing Yeasted Coffee Cakes," page 213).

"Life, within doors, has few pleasanter prospects than a neatly arranged and well-provisioned breakfast table."
NATHANIEL HAWTHORNE

dried plum tea ring

MAKES TWO 11- TO 12-INCH TEA RINGS, 8 TO 10 SERVINGS

Dried plums, commonly referred to as prunes, enjoy a long
history in the United States. The first La Petite d'Agen plum
tree was brought from France to California in 1856. Today,
Yuba and Sutter counties in California have the reputation for
being the dried plum capitals of the world! Dried plums make
a marvelous filling for sweet yeast-raised cakes. While pre-
made dried plum fillings are available, I much prefer making
mine from scratch. You will find this filling simple to make, and whether it wears the guise of dried plums or
prunes, it promises to please.

AT A GLANCE
PANS: Two large cookie sheets
PAN PREP: Line with parchment
RISING TIME: 45 to 60 minutes
OVEN TEMP: 350°F
BAKING TIME: 25 to 28 minutes
DIFFICULTY: ☕

1 generous packed cup pitted prunes (not
    organic; about 8 ounces)

²/₃ cup water

¹/₃ cup orange juice

¹/₄ cup sugar

¹/₂ ounce bittersweet chocolate, chopped

¹/₂ teaspoon freshly grated navel orange zest

¹/₂ teaspoon pure vanilla extract

¹/₈ teaspoon salt

2 tablespoons unsalted butter

1 tablespoon Grand Marnier liqueur

1 recipe Simple Sweet Dough (page 164) or
    Rich Sour Cream Dough (page 166), cold

1 large egg lightly beaten with 2 teaspoons
    water, for egg wash

1 large recipe Vanilla Glaze (page 359)

1. In a medium saucepan, combine the prunes, water, orange juice, and sugar. Bring
to a boil, lower the heat, and simmer, covered, for 30 minutes, or until very soft.

2. Remove from the heat and whip with a fork to form a puree. Add the chocolate,
orange zest, vanilla, salt, butter, and liqueur, and stir to combine. Set aside to cool to
room temperature.

3. Butter the corners of two large cookie sheets to secure the baking parchment,
then line the pans with the parchment.

4. Remove the dough from the bowl, and using a dough scraper, divide it in half.
Working with one piece at a time (return the unused piece to the refrigerator), place
the cold dough on a lightly floured work surface and knead gently six to eight times.
Roll the dough into a 9 × 16-inch rectangle, with the 16-inch side parallel to the edge
of the counter.

5. Using a small offset spatula, spread half of the filling over the dough, leaving a 1-inch border at the far edge. Brush the far edge with some of the egg wash. Beginning at the side of the rectangle closest to you, roll the dough tightly, jelly roll style, to form a log. As you roll, be sure to square the ends of the log with a dough scraper to even the thickness of the log. Pinch the seam, sealing it well, and gently roll the log back and forth, elongating it until it measures 16 to 18 inches.

6. Place the log *seam side down* on the parchment-lined cookie sheet and form it into a ring 7 to 8 inches round. To make the ring, brush one of the ends with the egg wash and seal it to the opposite end by pinching them together. Invert a $4\frac{1}{2}$-inch (8-ounce) heatproof custard cup, with 1 inch of the outer rim buttered, into the center of the ring. This will help to keep the shape of the circle. Adjust the shape and flatten the circle slightly with the palm of your hand.

7. Using sharp scissors, cut sixteen to eighteen slits about three-quarters of the way through the dough, spacing them about 1 inch apart. Turn the slices out so that the cut portions lay flat against the pan (see illustrations, page 173). Cover the ring with a tea towel and set in a warmish place to rise for 45 to 60 minutes, or until puffy and almost doubled. Repeat with the other half of the dough.

8. Fifteen minutes before baking, position the racks in the upper and lower thirds of the oven. Heat to 350°F.

9. Brush the top of the rings with the egg wash and bake for 25 to 28 minutes, or just until golden brown. To ensure even browning, toward the end of baking time, rotate the pans top to bottom and front to back. *Do not overbake.*

10. While the cakes are baking, make the glaze. Drizzle the glaze over the top of the *warm* cakes by dipping a small whisk or fork into the icing and waving it rapidly back and forth over the surface of the cakes.

STORAGE: Store at room temperature, tightly wrapped in aluminum foil, for up to 3 days. These cakes may be frozen (see "Refreshing Yeasted Coffee Cakes," page 213).

holiday stollen

Stollen, the classic German sweet bread of Dresden, is traditionally served at Christmas and has more than 500 years of history. This breadlike yeast cake is characteristically made with citron and other dried fruits, almonds, and spices. It has a crescent shape with tapered ends; the dough is folded over itself, resembling a giant Parker House roll. A classic stollen is not sweet and the texture is somewhat dry.

> **AT A GLANCE**
> **PANS:** Two 14 x 17-inch cookie sheets
> **PAN PREP:** Line with parchment
> **RISING TIME:** 1 hour
> **OVEN TEMP:** 375°F
> **BAKING TIME:** 20 to 25 minutes
> **DIFFICULTY:** 🍵 🍵

My adaptation is a lighter version of this classic pastry. It is made with candied orange and lemon peel along with dried apricots and raisins. While this recipe is not a traditional stollen, the final result is a delicious cake.

1 recipe **Simple Sweet Dough** (page 164) or
  Rich Sour Cream Dough (page 166)

½ cup **golden raisins, plumped** (see page 389)

½ cup **dark raisins, plumped** (see page 389)

¼ cup **dried apricots (not organic), diced into**
  ¼-inch pieces, plumped (see page 389)

¼ cup **candied orange peel**

¼ cup **candied lemon peel**

½ cup **brandy, such as Courvoisier, Hennessy,**
  St. Remy Napoleon, or applejack

¾ cup **sliced blanched almonds, lightly toasted**
  (see page 391)

6 tablespoons **unsalted butter, melted**

¼ cup **powdered sugar, for dusting**

1. Remove the dough from the refrigerator 1½ hours before using.

2. Place the plumped raisins and apricots in a 1-quart bowl. Add the candied orange and lemon peels and the brandy, then mix well to distribute the brandy through the fruit. Let macerate for at least 1 hour, mixing occasionally.

3. Drain the excess brandy from the fruit. Transfer the fruit to a double thickness of paper towels. Blot the top of the fruit with more paper towels. Empty into a bowl and set aside.

4. Butter the corners of two 14 × 17-inch cookie sheets to secure the baking parchment, then line the pans with the parchment.

5. Divide the dough in half. On a lightly floured surface, working with half at a time, gently knead in half of the macerated fruits and half of the toasted almonds. Pat the dough into an oval. With a floured rolling pin, roll the dough into a larger 8 × 12-

inch oval, keeping the 12-inch side parallel to the edge of the counter. Make a slight depression lengthwise in the center of the 12-inch side with the rolling pin. Fold the dough over, leaving 1 inch of the bottom half exposed, like a huge Parker House roll, patting the top gently.

6. Place the stollen on a cookie sheet and reshape it. Repeat with the second half of dough. Cover the stollen with tea towels and let them rise in a warmish place until puffy and almost doubled, about 1 hour.

7. Fifteen minutes before baking, position the racks in the upper and lower thirds of the oven. Heat the oven to 375°F.

8. Gently brush each stollen with 2 tablespoons of the melted butter. Bake for 20 to 25 minutes, or until golden brown. To ensure even browning, toward the end of baking time, rotate the pans top to bottom and front to back. Remove from the oven and brush the tops with the remaining melted butter. Place the powdered sugar in a strainer or sugar shaker and coat the tops of the stollen with half of the sugar. When the stollen are cool, dust again with the remaining sugar.

STORAGE: Store at room temperature, tightly covered with aluminum foil, for up to 3 days. These cakes may be frozen (see "Refreshing Yeasted Coffee Cakes," page 213).

"Nothing tastes better than homemade bread."

JULIA CHILD

rustic cinnamon walnut horns

MAKES TWENTY 3½- TO 4-INCH HORNS

These rustic crescents differ from a typical yeasted pastry in that they have a somewhat crispy texture. The dough is rolled in a mixture of coarsely chopped walnuts, sugar, and cinnamon. During baking, the sugar caramelizes, leaving an enticing crust. When I tested this recipe, the only difficulty my assistant and I had was that it was impossible to stop eating these. As we broke off a piece or two to sample, before we knew it they were devoured.

AT A GLANCE
PANS: Two rimmed cookie sheets
PAN PREP: Line with parchment
RISING TIME: 45 to 60 minutes
OVEN TEMP: 350°F
BAKING TIME: 18 to 20 minutes
DIFFICULTY: ♨ ♨ ♨

Take note that the walnuts are chopped into two different consistencies. First, the dough is rolled in coarsely chopped walnuts, then it is sprinkled with medium chopped nuts. It's okay if the dough tears when it is rolled in the larger nuts. This adds to the rustic charm of the horns.

1⅔ cups walnuts

5 tablespoons granulated sugar

3 tablespoons light brown sugar

1¼ teaspoons ground cinnamon

½ recipe (about 1 pound) of Simple Sweet Dough (page 164) or Rich Sour Cream Dough (page 166), cold

1 large egg, lightly beaten with 2 teaspoons water, for egg wash

Powdered sugar, for dusting

1. Place the walnuts in the bowl of a food processor fitted with a steel blade. Pulse 5 to 6 times, or until the nuts are coarsely chopped. Remove 1 cup of the walnuts and set aside for rolling. Add 3 tablespoons of the granulated sugar, the brown sugar, and ¾ teaspoon of the cinnamon to the processor bowl, and pulse with the remaining nuts 6 to 8 times, or until the nuts are medium chopped. Empty the filling into a bowl.

2. In a small bowl, combine the remaining 2 tablespoons granulated sugar and remaining ½ teaspoon cinnamon for rolling.

3. Dab the corners of two rimmed cookie sheets with butter and line with baking parchment.

4. Divide the dough in half and shape each piece into a log. Return one log to the refrigerator. Sprinkle the work surface with one-fourth of the coarsely chopped walnuts and one-fourth of the cinnamon/sugar mixture for rolling. Working with one log

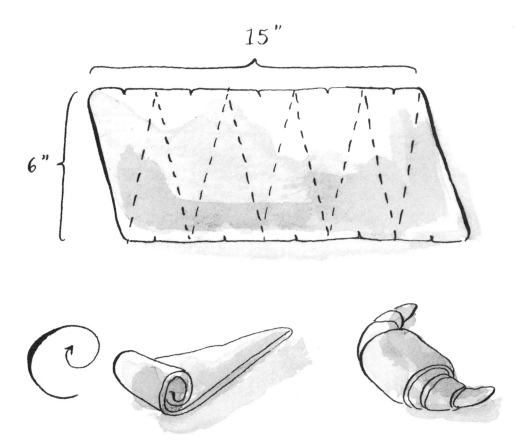

at a time and using your hands, roll the log in this mixture. As you roll, sprinkle the work surface with another one-fourth of the walnuts and one-fourth of the cinnamon/sugar mixture. After the dough is coated on both sides, roll it into a 6 × 15-inch parallelogram, with the 15-inch side parallel to the edge of the counter. To do this, as you roll, angle the bottom right-hand corner outwards and the upper left-hand corner outwards until the parallelogram measures about 6 × 15 inches. This will enable you to shape the horns without wasting the ends.

5. Brush the surface of the dough with the egg wash. Sprinkle with half of the nut filling, and lightly press it into the dough. Lay a ruler against the long side of the dough closest to you. With a dough scraper or a pizza cutter, make a small (¼-inch) indentation in the dough every 3 inches. You will have four indentations. Turn the ruler upside down and lay it along the top of the dough. Make four (¼-inch) indentations, spacing them 3 inches apart. With the indentations as a guide, cut the dough into

recipe continues

continued from previous page

10 triangles. Using the dough scraper or a paring knife, make a ½-inch knick in the center of the 3-inch side of each triangle. This will enable you to stretch the triangles as they are rolled (see illustrations, page 179).

6. Starting at the 3-inch side of the triangle, tightly roll the dough, stretching the crescent to elongate it as you roll. When you reach the end of the triangle, continue to roll the horn two or three times toward the narrow end to seal the layers. To prevent the dough from unraveling, *do not roll the dough back and forth*—only roll in one direction. Place the horn on the prepared pan and bend the ends to form a crescent. Repeat with the remaining dough.

7. Cover the pans with tea towels and set in a warmish place to rise for 45 to 60 minutes. The horns should feel puffy when lightly touched with your fingertip.

8. Fifteen minutes before baking, position the racks in the upper and lower thirds of the oven. Heat the oven to 350°F.

9. Bake the horns for 18 to 20 minutes, or until golden brown. To ensure even browning, toward the end of baking time, rotate the pans top to bottom and front to back. Remove from the oven and place on cooling racks. While the horns are still warm, dust them with powdered sugar. When ready to serve, dust again with powdered sugar.

STORAGE: Store at room temperature, tightly wrapped in aluminum foil, for up to 3 days. These horns may be frozen (see "Refreshing Yeasted Coffee Cakes," page 213).

scalloped chocolate pecan strip

MAKES ONE 15- TO 16-INCH STRIP, 8 TO 10 SERVINGS

If you've never tasted a yeasted cake made with a chocolate filling, you are in for a pleasant surprise. This sweet dough, spread with bittersweet chocolate filling and toasted pecans, is rolled into a log and cut into scallops. The top of the cake is finished with a sprinkling of pearl sugar. Take the time to seek this sugar out: it adds crunch and eye appeal. This gorgeous coffee cake will surely impress even the most discriminating audience.

AT A GLANCE
PAN: Large cookie sheet
PAN PREP: Line with parchment
RISING TIME: 45 to 60 minutes
OVEN TEMP: 350°F
BAKING TIME: 30 minutes
DIFFICULTY: 🥄 🥄

¼ cup water

2 tablespoons granulated sugar

½ teaspoon espresso powder

2½ ounces fine-quality bittersweet chocolate, such as Lindt, chopped (see pages 387–388)

¼ teaspoon lemon juice

¼ teaspoon pure vanilla extract

1 tablespoon unsalted butter, softened

½ recipe (about 1 pound) Simple Sweet Dough (page 164) or Rich Sour Cream Dough (page 166), cold

½ cup pecans, toasted and coarsely chopped (see pages 391–392)

1 large egg lightly beaten with 2 teaspoons water, for egg wash

2 teaspoons opaque pearl sugar (see page 380), optional

1 small recipe Vanilla Glaze (page 359)

1. In a small, heavy saucepan, combine the water, granulated sugar, espresso powder, and chocolate. Cook over low heat, stirring occasionally, for 8 to 10 minutes, or until large bubbles form. Remove from the heat and stir in the lemon juice, vanilla, and butter. Set aside to cool completely. The mixture should have the consistency of soft fudge.

2. Butter the corners of a large cookie sheet to secure the baking parchment, then line the pan with the parchment.

3. Place the dough on a lightly floured work surface and gently knead it six to eight times, or until smooth. Roll it into an 9 × 14-inch rectangle with the 14-inch side parallel to the edge of the counter. Using a small offset spatula, spread the cooled chocolate filling over the surface of the dough, leaving a 1-inch border on all sides. Sprinkle

recipe continues

continued from previous page

the chopped pecans on the chocolate, and using your hand, press the nuts gently into the chocolate. Lightly brush the far edge of the dough with egg wash.

4. Starting at the bottom edge, roll the dough tightly into a log, pinching the seam to seal. Place the log *seam side down*, on the prepared cookie sheet and square the ends with a dough scraper or metal spatula. Flatten the log slightly with the palm of your hand.

5. Using scissors, cut about twelve slits at approximately 1-inch intervals on the right side of the dough, cutting about three-fourths of the way through. For the left side, also cut about twelve slits; however, space the slits so that you are cutting in between the slits on the opposite side. Gently turn the slices to expose the filling, and pull them slightly downward, starting with the right side first. After the right side is done, turn the left side. Flatten the top of the cake gently with your hand, and then lightly press the slices so they lay flat against the pan. Cover the cake with a tea towel and set in a warmish place to rise for 45 to 60 minutes, or until puffy and almost doubled.

6. Fifteen minutes before baking, position the rack in the lower third of the oven. Heat the oven to 350°F.

7. Lightly brush the strip with the egg wash and sprinkle the top with pearl sugar. Bake for 30 minutes, or just until golden brown.

8. While the cake is baking, make the glaze. Remove the cake from the oven and place on a rack to cool. While the strip is still warm, loosen it from the parchment with a long, thin spatula. Drizzle the warm cake with the glaze.

STORAGE: Store at room temperature, tightly wrapped in aluminum foil, for up to 3 days. This cake may be frozen (see "Refreshing Yeasted Coffee Cakes," page 213).

sticky buns

MAKES 15 BUNS

Sticky buns! Everyone, including my son-in-law, Andy, loves them. And no surprise, Andy was raised in Pennsylvania, which is sticky bun country. These honey-glazed rolls are sweet with sugar, cinnamon, and often lots of crunchy pecans.

Sticky buns have a long history dating back to the Middle Ages, with the advent of cinnamon. These sweet little buns are believed to have traveled from Europe to the United States. The Pennsylvania Dutch, whose cuisine was influenced by their German ancestry, introduced us to schnecken, now known as sticky buns. Their popularity has been steadfast over many generations, and I suspect that this will continue for many more. When preparing the pans, do not use nonstick spray, as the topping will not adhere to the sides of the tins. These sticky buns are topped with a generous amount of pecans and finished with a caramelized honey glaze.

> **AT A GLANCE**
> **PAN:** Two standard muffin pans
> **PAN PREP:** Butter generously
> **RISING TIME:** 45 minutes
> **OVEN TEMP:** 350°F
> **BAKING TIME:** 18 to 20 minutes
> **DIFFICULTY:** 🍵 🍵

PECAN TOPPING

¼ cup unsalted butter, softened

¾ cup *very fresh* light brown sugar, packed

2 tablespoons honey

2 tablespoons light corn syrup

⅔ cup broken pecans (see page 392)

½ recipe (about 1 pound) Simple Sweet Dough (page 164) or Rich Sour Cream Dough (page 166), cold

FILLING

2 tablespoons unsalted butter, very soft

2 tablespoons granulated sugar

2 tablespoons light brown sugar, packed

½ teaspoon ground cinnamon

½ cup medium-chopped pecans (see page 392)

2 to 3 tablespoons golden raisins, plumped (see page 389)

1 large egg lightly beaten with 2 teaspoons water, for egg wash

MAKE THE TOPPING

1. Generously butter fifteen muffin tin cavities. Place the softened butter in a medium bowl and gradually add the brown sugar, honey, and corn syrup, mixing until a smooth paste is formed. Divide the mixture evenly into the cavities, using about 2 teaspoons for each. Using the back of a teaspoon, spread the topping as best you can around the bottom and three-fourths of the way up the sides. Sprinkle the bottom of the cavities with the broken pecans.

recipe continues

continued from previous page

SHAPE THE BUNS

2. Remove the dough from the refrigerator, place it onto a lightly floured rolling surface, and press it into a 4 × 6-inch rectangle. Roll the dough into a 10 × 15-inch rectangle with the 15-inch side parallel to the edge of the counter.

3. Using a small offset spatula, spread the dough with the softened butter, leaving a 1½-inch border at the top. In a small bowl, combine the sugars with the cinnamon. Sprinkle the mixture over the dough along with the nuts and raisins, again leaving a 1½-inch border at the top. Brush the border with the egg wash.

4. Roll the dough tightly, starting with the edge closest to you. Pinch the seam well with your fingertips to seal it. Then roll the cylinder back and forth a few times to compress the layers. The finished roll should measure about 15 inches. Using a dough scraper or a thin-bladed sharp knife, cut the dough into 15 even slices (see "About Yeasted Coffee Cakes," page 159). Place the slices into the prepared muffin tins cut side down and press the tops gently with your fingertips to even the surface. Cover with a tea towel and set aside in a warmish place to rise for about 45 minutes, or until puffy and almost doubled.

BAKE AND FINISH THE BUNS

5. Fifteen minutes before baking, position the racks in the upper and lower thirds of the oven. Heat the oven to 350°F. Bake the buns for 18 to 20 minutes, or until they just begin to turn golden brown. To ensure even browning, toward the end of the baking time, rotate the pans top to bottom and front to back. Watch carefully; these should not be overbaked.

6. While the buns are baking, place two cooling racks over sheets of wax paper. Remove the buns from the oven, let stand for 2 to 3 minutes, then invert onto the cooling racks. *Do not remove the pans for 10 minutes to allow the honey syrup to coat the buns.* Carefully remove the pans. If any of the nut topping remains in the pans, spoon it onto the appropriate bun, handling the mixture carefully as it may be hot.

STORAGE: Store at room temperature, tightly wrapped in aluminum foil, for up to 3 days. Heat before serving. These sticky buns may be frozen (see "Refreshing Yeasted Coffee Cakes," page 213).

sticky bun cake

MAKES ONE 9-INCH CAKE, 8 TO 10 SERVINGS

If you want to have your cake and eat it too, try this quick version of sticky buns. Instead of baking the dough in muffin tins, the rounds of dough are arranged in a layer pan. After baking, the pan is inverted to allow the sweet syrup to permeate the cake. This cake can be broken apart or sliced into wedges. Either way, it is quite a treat!

Prepare the Sticky Bun recipe making the following changes: Generously butter a 9-inch round layer pan. Using a small offset spatula or the back of a teaspoon, spread the topping across the bottom of the pan and about ½ inch up the side. Then sprinkle it with the broken pecans.

Proceed with the master recipe, rolling the dough into a 13 × 9-inch rectangle. Fill the dough as directed, and roll it into a 13-inch log. Cut the log into thirteen 1-inch pieces and arrange them in a circle in the pan, using nine pieces on the outer circle and four on the inside. They do not have to touch; they will join during baking. Let rise for about 45 minutes, or until almost doubled. Bake in a 350°F oven for 35 to 40 minutes. Follow the directions in the master recipe for removing the pan, using only one cooling rack.

STORAGE: Store at room temperature, tightly wrapped in aluminum foil, for up to 3 days. Heat before serving. This cake may be frozen (see "Refreshing Yeasted Coffee Cakes," page 213).

WORKING WITH YEAST

THE KIND OF YEAST I like to use is active dry yeast (see page 379). Some people shy away from recipes that use this product because they have poor success with reconstituting it. Begin by ignoring the package directions.

Yeast loves to live in a warm environment, and it thrives on sweeteners such as sugar or honey. Dissolving a bit of sugar in the warm liquid causes the yeast mixture to bubble or foam, a process that is known as proofing. These bubbles tell you that the yeast is activated and ready to go to work.

HERE ARE A FEW SIMPLE STEPS TO FOLLOW

• Start with a small bowl, preferably stainless steel, that is at least 3 inches across the bottom to give enough surface area for the yeast to proof. Warm the bowl by rinsing it with hot water.

• Measure the liquid, taking care that the temperature is correct. It should fall between 110° and 115°F. Use an instant-read thermometer to determine this. The thermometer should not register below 110°F because as the liquid is poured into the bowl, the temperature will drop several degrees and be too cool.

• Add the sugar to the bowl and pour in the warm liquid. Sprinkle the yeast over the top, and without stirring, cover the bowl with a saucer and let it stand for 5 minutes.

• After 5 minutes, stir the mixture with a small whisk or fork. Cover the bowl again, and let it stand for an additional 2 to 3 minutes or until bubbly. Now the yeast is proofed and ready to use. Note: Yeast dissolved in warm milk may take longer to proof.

• At times, the dissolved yeast will multiply five or six times its original volume. This will depend on the amount of liquid called for in the recipe. If the yeast begins to overflow the bowl, stir it down and let it rise again. It's okay for the yeast mixture to wait for you.

sour cherry cream kuchen

MAKES ONE 9-INCH CAKE, 8 TO 10 SERVINGS

In this recipe, streusel-topped cherries crown a layer of pastry cream spread over a sweet yeasted dough. I fell in love with the idea of using a baked pastry cream with fruit when I studied pastry-making in Vienna.

   Morello cherries, tart in flavor and deep red in color, are widely used throughout Europe primarily for pastries and desserts. They can be found in many supermarkets and stores, such as Trader Joe's. They are sold in large jars either in light syrup or water-packed. If you can't find the Morello variety, look for a water-packed dark, sour cherry sometimes packed in cans, but do not use cherry pie filling. This kuchen is a special treat and well worth the effort.

AT A GLANCE

PAN: 9-inch springform or 8 x 8 x 2-inch square pan
PAN PREP: Butter generously
RISING TIME: 25 to 30 minutes
OVEN TEMP: 350°F
BAKING TIME: 45 to 50 minutes
DIFFICULTY: 🍵 🍵

½ recipe (about I pound) Simple Sweet Dough (page 164) or Rich Sour Cream Dough (page 166)

I small recipe Carole's Favorite Streusel (page 350)

CHERRY FILLING

I (24-ounce) jar pitted dark Morello cherries in light syrup (about 2½ cups), well drained, juice reserved

2 tablespoons cornstarch

¼ cup sugar

½ teaspoon fresh lemon juice

¼ teaspoon almond extract

3 or 4 drops red food coloring (optional)

I tablespoon unsalted butter, softened

PASTRY CREAM

2 tablespoons cornstarch

I cup milk

4 tablespoons sugar

2 large egg yolks

I tablespoon plus I teaspoon unsalted butter

¾ teaspoon pure vanilla extract

1. Remove the dough from the refrigerator 1 to 1½ hours before shaping.

MAKE THE CHERRY FILLING

2. In a medium saucepan, combine ⅔ cup of the reserved cherry juice, the cornstarch, and sugar, stirring until no lumps remain. Place the pan over medium-low heat. Allow the liquid to come to a boil, stirring gently until the mixture is very thick.

recipe continues

continued from previous page

Remove the pan from the heat and stir in the lemon juice, almond extract, food coloring (if using), and butter. Using a rubber spatula, gently stir in the drained cherries. Set aside until ready to use.

MAKE THE PASTRY CREAM

3. Place the cornstarch in a medium mixing bowl. Stir in ¼ cup of the milk and mix until smooth. Whisk in 2 tablespoons of the sugar and the egg yolks. Set aside.

4. In a two-quart saucepan, heat the remaining ¾ cup milk and remaining 2 tablespoons sugar. Stir until blended. On low heat, bring the mixture to a slow boil. Stir one-third of the hot milk/sugar mixture into the egg mixture. Pour the egg mixture into the saucepan and stir with a whisk to combine. Return the pan to medium-low heat and bring it to a full boil, *whisking rapidly and constantly* until the pastry cream is thick and smooth. Remove the pan from the heat and stir in the softened butter and vanilla. *Do not overmix.* Cover the pastry cream with buttered plastic wrap and set aside until ready to use.

SHAPE THE DOUGH

5. Generously butter a 9-inch springform pan and set aside. On a lightly floured work surface, knead the dough a few times and shape it into a flat disk. With lightly floured hands, press the dough into the prepared pan, stretching it to completely cover the bottom. Push the dough up against the side of the pan, forcing it up to form a wall ¼ inch thick and ¾ inch high. Be sure to press it well into the crease of the pan. If the dough becomes too elastic, let it rest for a few minutes. Prick the surface of the dough ten to twelve times with a fork. Cover the pan with a tea towel and set it in a warmish place to rise until puffy but *not doubled*, 25 to 30 minutes. While the dough is rising, prepare the streusel.

FINISH THE KUCHEN

6. Fifteen minutes before baking, position the rack in the lower third of the oven. Heat the oven to 350°F. Redefine the lip of the dough with your thumb and gently depress the center with your hand.

7. Leaving a ¾-inch rim of dough exposed, drop dollops of the *tepid* pastry cream around the edge of the pan. Using an offset spatula, bring the pastry cream into the center, smoothing the surface, as best you can.

8. Top the pastry cream with the cherry filling in one layer. Sprinkle the streusel over the cherries, pressing it gently into the surface. Place the pan on a sheet of heavy-duty aluminum foil and wrap the pan with the foil to catch any spills.

9. Bake the kuchen for 45 to 50 minutes, or until it begins to release from the side of the pan and the streusel is golden brown. If the streusel is browning too quickly, lay a sheet of aluminum foil loosely over the top.

10. Remove the kuchen from the oven and let stand on a cooling rack for 20 minutes. Release and remove the side of the pan and let cool for 30 minutes longer. To remove the bottom of the pan, place a 12-inch strip of aluminum foil directly onto the top of the cake, cupping the foil around the side to hold the topping in place. Cover with a cooling rack, invert the cake, and carefully lift off the bottom of the pan. *Immediately* cover with another rack, turn the cake top side up, and remove the foil.

STORAGE: Store in the refrigerator, tightly wrapped with aluminum foil, for up to 3 days. Reheat before serving in a 325°F oven for 20 to 25 minutes, or until slightly warm. This cake is best served the day it is made and cannot be frozen.

VARIATION

prune plum cream kuchen

This plum kuchen is made with Italian prune plums—the little oval plums that are
in season from mid-August to mid-September. During baking, the plums turn a deep rosy hue.

Follow the recipe for Sour Cherry Cream Kuchen, making the following change: Use ¾ pound ripe prune plums of uniform size, pitted and cut into quarters. Arrange the plums in concentric circles over the pastry cream. Sprinkle the streusel generously over the plums, pressing the crumbs gently into the surface. Place the pan on a sheet of heavy-duty aluminum foil and wrap the pan with the foil to catch any leakage.

cheese kuchen

MAKES ONE 9-INCH CAKE, 8 TO 10 SERVINGS

Kuchen, the German word for "cake," is used to describe various types of coffee cakes made with either sweet yeasted doughs or leavened cake batters. These cakes can be made with a custard or cheese filling, fresh or dried fruit, or fragrant spices and nuts.

For this recipe, a sweet yeasted dough is pressed into a springform pan. The center holds a flavorful cream cheese filling accented with sweet golden raisins, orange juice, and lemon zest, then topped with slivered almonds and a sprinkling of cinnamon and sugar. When the kuchen is baked, the top turns a light golden brown.

> **AT A GLANCE**
> **PAN:** 9-inch springform pan
> **PAN PREP:** Butter generously
> **RISING TIME:** 25 to 30 minutes
> **OVEN TEMP:** 350°F
> **BAKING TIME:** 35 to 40 minutes
> **DIFFICULTY:** 🥄

½ recipe (about 1 pound) Simple Sweet Dough (page 164) or Rich Sour Cream Dough (page 166)

3 tablespoons golden raisins, plumped (see page 389)

3 tablespoons fresh navel orange juice

1 (8-ounce) package cream cheese, at room temperature

¼ cup sugar

1 large egg yolk

1 tablespoon all-purpose flour

1 tablespoon sour cream

2 teaspoons melted butter

1 teaspoon fresh lemon juice

½ teaspoon freshly grated lemon zest

½ teaspoon pure vanilla extract

TOPPING

3 tablespoons slivered almonds

2 teaspoons sugar

¼ teaspoon ground cinnamon

1. Remove the dough from the refrigerator 1 to 1½ hours before shaping.

2. In a small bowl, soak the raisins in the orange juice for 30 minutes. Drain well and place on paper towels to dry. Set aside.

3. Generously butter a 9-inch springform pan and set aside. On a lightly floured work surface, gently knead the dough six to eight times, and shape it into a disk. With lightly floured hands, press the dough into the prepared pan stretching it to completely cover the bottom. Using the outer part of your thumb (where it meets the wrist), push the dough against the side of the pan, forcing it up to form a wall about ¾ inch high and ¼ inch thick. Be sure to press the dough well into the crease of the pan. If the dough becomes too elastic, let it rest for a few minutes. Pierce the dough

ten to twelve times with a fork. Cover the pan and let it rise in a warmish place for 25 to 30 minutes, or until puffy but not doubled.

4. While the dough is rising, prepare the cheese filling. In a medium bowl, mix the cream cheese with a wooden spoon until no lumps remain. Gradually blend in the sugar, mixing until very smooth. Stir in the egg yolk, then blend in the flour, sour cream, melted butter, lemon juice, lemon zest, and vanilla. Stir in the raisins.

5. Position the rack in the lower third of the oven. Heat the oven to 350°F.

6. When the dough is puffy, gently drop spoonfuls of the cheese filling over the top of the dough. Start with an outside circle of cheese, then fill in the middle, leaving a 1-inch border of dough around the edge. *Do not press on the dough.* Using a small offset spatula, gently smooth the filling across the top.

7. Combine the almonds, sugar, and cinnamon and sprinkle the mixture evenly over the cheese filling.

8. Place the pan on a sheet of aluminum foil and wrap it up the side of the pan to catch any leakage. Bake the kuchen for 35 to 40 minutes, or until the top is golden brown. Transfer to a cooling rack for 30 minutes.

9. Run a thin knife around the edge of the cake, and remove the side of the pan. Place a 12-inch strip of aluminum foil directly on top of the cake, cupping it around the side to hold the topping in place. Cover with a cooling rack, invert the cake, and carefully lift off the bottom of the pan. Using another rack, turn the cake top side up and remove the foil. Cool completely.

STORAGE: Store at room temperature, loosely wrapped with aluminum foil, for up to 12 hours. For longer storage, refrigerate for up to 3 days. Reheat before serving. This cake may be frozen (see "Refreshing Yeasted Coffee Cakes," page 213).

> *"Cheese is probably the friendliest of foods. It endears itself to everything and never tires of showing off to great advantage."*
> JAMES BEARD

blueberry pizza

MAKES TWO 8-INCH PIZZAS, 4 TO 6 SERVINGS PER PIZZA

Try this contemporary adaptation of the Sour Cherry Cream Kuchen (page 187). Thinly rolled sweet yeasted dough is placed on a cookie sheet and baked free-form. The dough is spread with pastry cream and topped with plump blueberries and lots of crunchy streusel. This tasty pizza is cut into wedges just like the savory style, making it an unusual coffee cake treat.

AT A GLANCE
PANS: Two cookie sheets
PAN PREP: Butter generously
RISING TIME: 25 to 30 minutes
OVEN TEMP: 375°F
BAKING TIME: 22 to 25 minutes
DIFFICULTY: ☕

½ recipe (about 1 pound) Simple Sweet Dough (page 164) or Rich Sour Cream Dough (page 166)

1 large recipe Carole's Favorite Streusel (page 350)

PASTRY CREAM

2 tablespoons cornstarch

1 cup milk

4 tablespoons sugar

2 large egg yolks

1 tablespoon plus 1 teaspoon unsalted butter, softened

¾ teaspoon pure vanilla extract

2½ to 3 cups fresh blueberries, washed and well dried (see page 390)

Powdered sugar, for dusting

1. Remove the dough from the refrigerator 1 to 1½ hours before shaping.

2. Place the dough on a lightly floured work surface and divide the dough in half. Dust each piece lightly with flour and shape into disks. Place the disks directly onto two buttered cookie sheets, and reshape them into circles with your fingertips. Roll each piece of dough into a 7- to 8-inch circle. The circles should be very thin. Pinch the dough to form a ½-inch lip around the edge. Prick the surface of the dough several times with a fork.

3. Cover the pans with tea towels and set in a warmish place to rise for 25 to 30 minutes, or until puffy.

4. While the dough is rising, prepare the pastry cream. Place the cornstarch in a medium mixing bowl. Stir in ¼ cup of the milk and mix until smooth. Whisk in 2 tablespoons of the sugar and the egg yolks. Set aside.

5. In a 2-quart saucepan, heat the remaining ¾ cup milk and 2 tablespoons sugar, stirring until blended. On low heat, bring the mixture to a slow boil. Stir one-third of

the hot milk/sugar mixture into the egg mixture. Pour the egg mixture into the saucepan and stir with a whisk to combine. Return the pan to medium-low heat and bring it to a full boil, *whisking rapidly and constantly* until the pastry cream is thick and smooth. Remove from the heat and stir in the softened butter and vanilla. *Do not overmix.* Cover the pastry cream with buttered plastic wrap and set aside until ready to use.

6. Fifteen minutes before baking, position the racks in the upper and lower thirds of the oven. Heat the oven to 375°F. Redefine the lip of the dough with your thumb and depress the center with your hand.

7. Using half of the *tepid* pastry cream for each pizza, drop dollops around the edge of the dough. Leaving a ¾-inch rim of dough exposed, gently spread the pastry cream to the center with an offset spatula, smoothing the surface as best you can. Arrange the blueberries in one layer over the pastry cream, pressing them slightly into the cream. Sprinkle the streusel evenly over the berries.

8. Bake the pizzas for 22 to 25 minutes, or until the streusel begins to turn golden brown. To ensure even browning, toward the end of baking time, rotate the pans top to bottom and front to back. Remove the pizzas from the oven and let stand on a cooling rack for 15 to 20 minutes. Use a large, straight spatula to loosen the pizzas from the pans while they are still warm. When cool, dust with powdered sugar.

STORAGE: Store in the refrigerator, tightly wrapped with aluminum foil, for up to 3 days. Reheat before serving in a 325°F oven for 10 to 15 minutes, or until slightly warm. These pizzas are best served the day they are made and cannot be frozen.

"However you put berries in a dessert, do not disguise their inherent flavor."
EMILY LUCHETTI

apple and dried cranberry coffee cake

MAKES ONE 9-INCH CAKE, 8 TO 10 SERVINGS

Sautéed apples and dried cranberries, delicately spiced, are nestled in a sweet yeasted dough that is pressed into a springform pan. After baking, the fruit that adorns the top is glazed with apricot preserves. This is a pretty cake and one that highlights autumn's best flavors.

AT A GLANCE
PAN: 9-inch springform pan
PAN PREP: Butter/line with parchment
RISING TIME: 25 to 30 minutes
OVEN TEMP: 375°/350°F
BAKING TIME: 50 to 55 minutes
DIFFICULTY: 🥄

½ recipe (about I pound) **Simple Sweet Dough** (page 164) or **Rich Sour Cream Dough** (page 166)

2 tablespoons unsalted butter

I pound **Golden Delicious apples (2 large),** peeled, halved, cored, and sliced ¼ inch thick

¼ cup dried cranberries (not organic)

3 tablespoons sugar

½ teaspoon ground cinnamon

Pinch of ground allspice

2 teaspoons fresh lemon juice

GLAZE

¼ cup apricot preserves

2 teaspoons water

1. Remove the dough from the refrigerator 1 to 1½ hours before using.

2. In a heavy 10-inch sauté pan, melt the butter over low heat. Add the apples, cranberries, sugar, cinnamon, and allspice. Sauté the mixture until the apples are soft, translucent, and caramelized, 20 to 25 minutes. Remove from the heat and add the lemon juice. Set aside to cool completely.

3. Butter a 9-inch springform pan and line the bottom with parchment. Set aside. On a lightly floured work surface, gently knead the dough six to eight times, and shape it into a disk. With lightly floured hands, press the dough into the prepared pan, stretching it to completely cover the bottom. Push the dough up against the side of the pan, forcing it up to form a wall ¼ inch thick and ¾ inch high. Be sure to press it well into the crease of the pan. If the dough becomes too elastic, let it rest for a few minutes. Prick the surface of the dough ten to twelve times with a fork. Cover the pan with a tea towel and set it in a warmish place to rise until puffy but *not doubled*, 25 to 30 minutes.

4. Fifteen minutes before baking, position the rack in the lower third of the oven. Heat the oven to 375°F. Redefine the lip of the dough with your thumb and gently depress the center with your hand.

5. Carefully spoon the *cooled* filling over the dough, leaving a ¾-inch border around the edge and then filling in the center. Place the pan on a sheet of heavy-duty aluminum foil and wrap the pan with the foil to catch any leakage. Cover the pan loosely with aluminum foil and bake for 10 minutes. Remove the top foil and *reduce* the oven temperature to 350°F. Bake for an additional 40 to 45 minutes, or until the top is golden brown and the sides begin to release.

6. While the cake is baking, make the apricot glaze. Place the apricot preserves and water in a microwave-safe bowl. Stir to combine. Heat on medium-power until the mixture is bubbly, then pass it through a medium-gauge strainer.

7. Remove the cake from the oven and let it stand on a cooling rack for 20 minutes. Release and remove the side of the pan and cool for 30 minutes longer. To remove the bottom of the pan and the parchment, place a 12-inch strip of aluminum foil directly onto the top of the cake, cupping the foil around the side to hold the topping in place. Cover with a cooling rack, invert the cake, and carefully lift off the bottom of the pan and remove the parchment. *Immediately* cover with another rack, turn the cake top side up, and remove the foil. While the cake is still warm, brush the fruit with the apricot glaze. This cake is best served slightly warm.

STORAGE: Store in the refrigerator, lightly wrapped in aluminum foil, for up to 3 days. Reheat before serving in a 325°F oven for 10 to 15 minutes, or until slightly warm. This cake may be frozen (see "Refreshing Yeasted Coffee Cakes," page 213).

"The apples on the other side of the wall are always the sweetest."

W. G. BENHAM

fig and walnut loaf

MAKES 3 LOAVES, 6 TO 8 SERVINGS PER LOAF

Marsala-steeped Calimyrna figs, toasted walnuts, cinnamon, and sugar are the flavor elements that make this coffee cake so special. Be careful not to overwork the dough as you knead it because you want to create a marbled effect with the cinnamon and sugar mixture. When these ingredients are properly kneaded throughout the dough, the look and the taste of the finished result will dazzle even the most the sophisticated of palates.

AT A GLANCE
PANS: Three 8 x 3¾ x 2½-inch aluminum foil loaf pans/rimmed cookie sheet
PAN PREP: Butter generously/line with parchment
RISING TIME: 1½ to 2 hours
OVEN TEMP: 325°/350°F
BAKING TIME: 30 minutes, 10 minutes
DIFFICULTY: 🥄

While dried Calimyrna figs are available year-round, they are freshest during late fall, as the holiday season approaches. Because the figs are imbibed in Marsala, be sure to choose fruit that is soft and plump.

I recipe Simple Sweet Dough (page 164) or Rich Sour Cream Dough (page 166)

6 ounces soft dried Calimyrna figs (not organic), cut into sixths

½ cup sweet Marsala wine

½ cup sugar

2 teaspoons ground cinnamon

1½ cups toasted walnuts, broken (see pages 391–392)

I large egg lightly beaten with 2 teaspoons water, for egg wash

⅓ cup sugar

⅓ cup water

⅓ cup walnut pieces, for garnish

1. Remove the dough from the refrigerator 1 to 1½ hours before using.

2. In a small microwave-proof bowl, combine the figs and Marsala. Heat on the defrost setting for 1 minute, or until warm. Do not allow the Marsala to become too hot. Let stand for 5 minutes. Drain the figs, discarding the liquid. Place the figs on a double layer of paper towels and blot dry with another double layer of paper towels.

3. Using a pastry brush, generously butter three 8 × 3¾ × 2½-inch aluminum foil loaf pans. Place a 12 × 8-inch strip of baking parchment in each pan, positioning it to allow about 1½ inches of the parchment to extend over each wide side.

4. Divide the dough into thirds. In a small bowl, mix the ½ cup sugar and the cinnamon. Sprinkle 1 teaspoon of the sugar/cinnamon mixture on a pastry board or other rolling surface. Working with one-third of the dough at a time, knead in one-third of the toasted walnuts and one-third of the figs. As you knead, gradually sprinkle

4 to 5 teaspoons of the sugar/cinnamon mixture over the dough, working the ingredients just until incorporated. The sugar/cinnamon should have a marbled effect.

5. Divide each ball of dough into three equal pieces. Sprinkle the work surface lightly with sugar/cinnamon. Cupping your hand over the dough, roll each piece on the prepared surface, continuously rotating the dough until it forms a ball. Place the ball into the prepared pan, positioning it on the far right side of the pan. Repeat with the remaining two pieces of dough, sugaring the board as needed. Place them side by side in the pan next to the first ball of dough, brushing the side of the first ball with egg wash and then the side of the second ball with egg wash. Flatten the balls slightly until they touch. This will keep the loaf intact after baking. Repeat the procedure, making two more loaves with the remaining dough.

6. Place the pans on a rimmed cookie sheet and cover them with a tea towel. Let rise in a warmish spot until puffy and almost doubled, 1½ to 2 hours.

7. Fifteen minutes before baking, position the rack in the lower third of the oven. Heat the oven to 325°F. Bake the loaves for 30 minutes.

8. A few minutes before the end of the baking time, combine the ⅓ cup sugar and the water in a heavy 1-quart saucepan and bring to a boil over low heat stirring occasionally. After the sugar is dissolved, continue to cook for 1 minute longer. Watch carefully.

9. Remove the loaves from the oven and *increase* the temperature to 350°F. Using a pastry brush, brush about half of the hot syrup over the tops of the loaves. Brush each loaf again with the hot syrup. As each is brushed, immediately press a few large pieces of walnuts on top, then brush the nuts with enough syrup to make them adhere.

10. Return the loaves to the oven and bake for an additional 10 minutes, or until the tops are shiny and golden brown. Remove the loaves from the oven and place on a cooling rack. When the loaves are cool, grasp the parchment on either side of each pan and lift the loaf from the pan. Carefully slide the parchment from under the loaf, and return the loaf to the pan for storage.

STORAGE: Store at room temperature, tightly wrapped in aluminum foil, for up to 3 days. Reheat before serving. These loaves may be frozen (see "Refreshing Yeasted Coffee Cakes," page 213).

"To eat figs off the tree in the very early morning, when they have been barely touched by the sun, is one of the exquisite pleasures of the Mediterranean."

ELIZABETH DAVID

woven apricot-almond strip

MAKES ONE 14- TO 15-INCH STRIP, 8 TO 10 SERVINGS

Your friends will marvel at this beautiful cake. Sweet-tart dried apricots are cooked until soft and then whipped with a fork to form a rustic filling with a subtle almond flavor. The pureed fruit is spread in a strip down the center of the dough. The dough is slashed diagonally on either side of the apricots, and then woven to create a braidlike effect. This eye-catching cake looks harder to make than it actually is.

AT A GLANCE

PAN: Large cookie sheet
PAN PREP: Butter
RISING TIME: 45 to 60 minutes
OVEN TEMP: 350°F
BAKING TIME: 30 to 35 minutes
DIFFICULTY: 🥄 🥄

APRICOT PUREE

4 ounces dried apricots (not organic)

½ cup (lightly packed) light brown sugar

1 tablespoon unsalted butter

¼ teaspoon almond extract

SUGAR CINNAMON SPRINKLE

2 tablespoons granulated sugar

2 tablespoons light brown sugar

¼ teaspoon ground cinnamon

2 tablespoons chopped almonds, toasted (see pages 391–392)

½ recipe (about 1 pound) Simple Sweet Dough (page 164) or Rich Sour Cream Dough (page 166), cold

2 tablespoons unsalted butter, *very soft*

1 large egg white lightly beaten with 1 tablespoon cool water, for egg wash

2 tablespoons slivered almonds

2 tablespoons granulated sugar

MAKE THE APRICOT PUREE

1. In a heavy 1-quart saucepan, combine the apricots and ½ cup water. Cover and bring to a boil, then reduce the heat and simmer for 15 to 18 minutes, or until the apricots are very soft. If too much of the water evaporates, add 1 to 2 tablespoons, or more as needed to prevent the apricots from burning. Stir in the brown sugar, then simmer for another minute or two. Remove the pan from the heat. Using a fork, whip in the butter and almond extract, mixing until the consistency is fairly smooth. Let cool. (You should have about ¾ cup.)

recipe continues

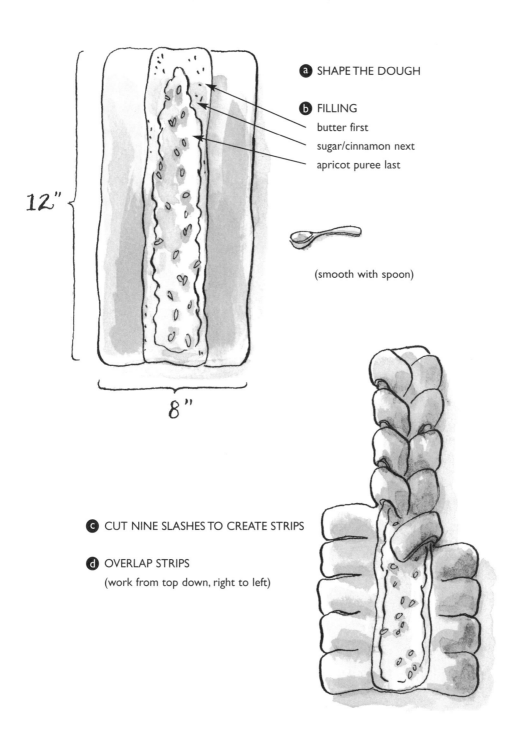

a SHAPE THE DOUGH

b FILLING

butter first

sugar/cinnamon next

apricot puree last

(smooth with spoon)

c CUT NINE SLASHES TO CREATE STRIPS

d OVERLAP STRIPS

(work from top down, right to left)

12"

8"

continued from *page 198*

MAKE THE SPRINKLE

2. In a small bowl, combine the granulated and brown sugars, cinnamon, and almonds. Set aside.

SHAPE THE DOUGH

3. Butter a large cookie sheet and set aside. Place the chilled dough on a lightly floured work surface. Knead five or six times, then let rest for 5 minutes. Using a lightly floured rolling pin, shape the dough into an 8 × 12-inch rectangle. Roll the dough onto the rolling pin and place it on the prepared cookie sheet, stretching the dough back into shape.

4. Using an offset spatula, spread a 3-inch strip of soft butter down the length of the dough. Sprinkle the sugar/cinnamon mixture over the butter. Spoon the apricot puree over the sugar mixture. With the back of the spoon, smooth the puree over the sugar/cinnamon as best you can. Brush both sides of the dough with a 1-inch strip of egg wash.

5. With a dough scraper or a sharp knife, cut nine slashes, about 1¼ inches apart, on both sides of the dough, being careful not to cut into the strip of filling. Starting from the top, overlap the strips from right to left, pulling down slightly to cover the filling. Pinch the seams on the top and bottom so the filling will not seep out (see illustrations, page 199). Cover the strip with a tea towel and set in a warm place to rise for 45 to 60 minutes, or until puffy and *almost* doubled.

BAKE THE STRIP

6. Fifteen minutes before baking, position the rack in the lower third of the oven. Heat the oven to 350°F. Brush the top of the strip with the egg wash and sprinkle with the almonds and sugar. Bake for 30 to 35 minutes, or until golden brown. *Do not overbake.*

7. Remove from the oven and let stand on the cookie sheet for 10 minutes, then loosen with a large metal spatula. When firm enough to handle, transfer to a cooling rack.

STORAGE: Stored at room temperature, well wrapped in heavy-duty aluminum foil, for up to 3 days. Heat before serving. This cake may be frozen (see "Refreshing Yeasted Coffee Cakes," page 213).

APPLE WALNUT CARAMEL KUCHEN, PAGE 50

SOUR CREAM MARBLE CAKE, PAGE 46

BROWN BUTTER ALMOND CAKE, PAGE 56, WITH STEWED FRUIT, PAGE 306

IRISH WHISKEY CAKE, PAGE 68, WITH MIDNIGHT CHOCOLATE GLAZE, PAGE 363

CHOCOLATE CHOCOLATE STREUSEL SQUARES, PAGE 44

CLASSIC SOUR CREAM CINNAMON AND NUT COFFEE CAKE, PAGE 36

PLUM-TOPPED POUND CAKE SQUARES, PAGE 30

RHUBARB UPSIDE-DOWN MUFFINS, PAGE 108

ORANGE CREAM CHEESE MUFFINS WITH PEPITA CRUNCH, PAGE 106

JEFF'S CHOCOLATE-GLAZED MIDNIGHT MUFFINS, PAGE 88

FAVORITE VANILLA MUFFINS, PAGE 86

ZACH'S BLUEBERRY BUTTERMILK MUFFINS WITH STREUSEL TOPPING, PAGE 98

ULTRA-RICH CORN MUFFINS, PAGE 82

ZUCCHINI LOAF WITH APRICOTS
AND DATES, PAGE 124

GRANDMA JENNIE'S DATE
AND NUT BREAD, PAGE 120

COUNTRY CHERRY HONEY SCONES, PAGE 152

**OLD-FASHIONED BUTTERMILK BISCUITS, PAGE 132,
WITH APPLE CIDER CARAMEL, PAGE 365**

SWEET POTATO DROP BISCUITS, PAGE 142, AND
CRANBERRY PECAN CREAM SCONES, PAGE 154, WITH
CRANBERRY ORANGE SPREAD, PAGE 366

pineapple cheese braid

MAKES TWO 15- TO 16-INCH BRAIDS, 10 TO 12 SERVINGS

PLAN AHEAD: *Chill cheese filling several hours or overnight*

*Here is a perfect cheese filling (that promises not to run),
woven throughout a tender cake. A strip of pineapple preserves
nestled in the center, along with a sprinkling of dried
pineapple, enhances the flavor of the cheese. If you don't have
a dough scraper to cut the logs, use a thin-bladed sharp knife.
While braiding the dough may seem daunting, don't despair;
it's easier than you think. And the end result is fantastic!*

> **AT A GLANCE**
> **PANS:** Two cookie sheets
> **PAN PREP:** Butter generously
> **RISING TIME:** 45 to 60 minutes
> **OVEN TEMP:** 350°F
> **BAKING TIME:** 30 to 35 minutes
> **DIFFICULTY:** 🥄 🥄

1 (7.5-ounce) package farmer cheese, at room temperature, cut into 1-inch pieces

12 ounces cream cheese, at room temperature, cut into 1-inch pieces

⅓ cup sugar

2 tablespoons all-purpose flour

Pinch of salt

2 large egg yolks

1 teaspoon freshly grated navel or Valencia orange zest, or to taste

1 teaspoon freshly grated lemon zest, or to taste

¾ teaspoon pure vanilla extract

1 recipe (about 2 pounds) Simple Sweet Dough (page 164) or Rich Sour Cream Dough (page 166), cold

½ cup all-fruit pineapple preserves

½ cup finely diced dried pineapple

1 large egg white beaten with 2 teaspoons water, for egg wash

Clear Shiny Glaze (page 360)

1. Generously butter two large cookie sheets.

2. Place a food mill or a potato ricer over a medium bowl. Sieve the farmer cheese through the mill, then sieve the cream cheese. Using a wooden spoon, blend in the sugar, mixing until smooth. Stir in the flour and salt, then blend in the yolks, zests, and vanilla. Chill for several hours or overnight.

3. Divide the dough into two equal pieces. Working with one piece at a time, place the dough on a lightly floured work surface and shape into a log. Roll the dough into a 10 × 15-inch rectangle with the 15-inch side parallel to the edge of the counter.

recipe continues

continued from *previous page*

4. Spread half of the cheese filling centered in a 4-inch-wide strip, spreading it from right to left across the 15-inch side of the dough. Using the back of a teaspoon, make a well down the center of the cheese strip and fill it with half of the preserves. Sprinkle 3 tablespoons of the diced pineapple over the surface of the filling.

5. Brush the far edge of the dough with some of the egg wash. Roll the dough up jelly roll style. Pinch the seam to seal, then roll the log back and forth two or three times. Carefully lift the roll onto a prepared cookie sheet, placing it seam side down, angling it as necessary. Using a rolling pin or the palm of your hand, slightly flatten the log until it measures about $3\frac{1}{2} \times 15$ inches.

6. Using a dough scraper or a thin-bladed sharp knife, score the dough lengthwise into three equal strips, then cut through the log. Starting in the center, braid the strips as best you can. Don't worry if it is a little messy. Then braid to the opposite end. Pinch the ends together well and tuck under (see illustrations). Sprinkle the braid with 1 tablespoon of diced pineapple. Repeat, shaping the second piece of dough.

7. Cover each braid with a tea towel and set in a warmish place to rise for 45 to 60 minutes, or until puffy and almost doubled.

8. Fifteen minutes before baking, position the racks in the upper and lower thirds of the oven. Heat the oven to 350°F. Bake for 30 to 35 minutes, or until golden brown. To ensure even browning, toward the end of baking time, rotate the pans top to bottom and front to back.

9. About 15 minutes before the braids are done, prepare the glaze.

10. Remove the braids from the oven and *immediately* brush the surfaces with the *hot* glaze. After 10 minutes, loosen with a large metal spatula. When firm enough to handle, transfer to cooling racks.

STORAGE: Store at room temperature, wrapped in aluminum foil, for up to 12 hours. For longer storage, refrigerate for up to 3 days. Reheat before serving. These cakes may be frozen (see "Refreshing Yeasted Coffee Cakes," page 213).

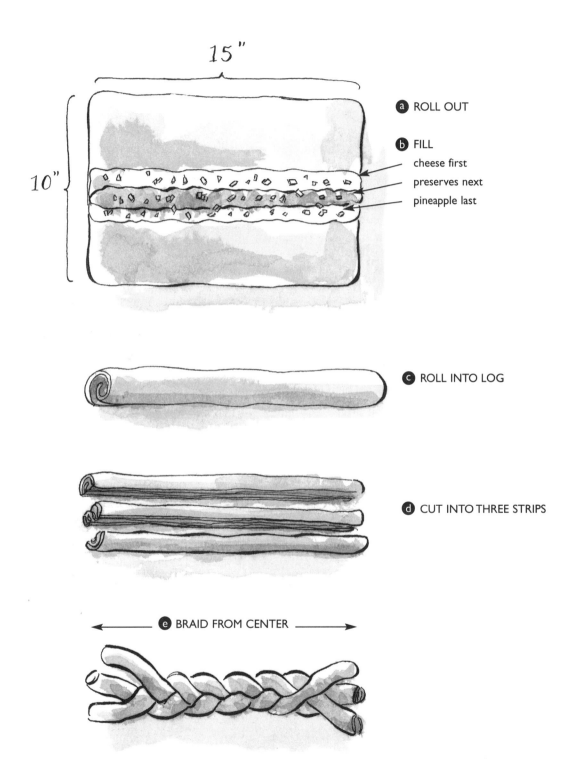

15"

10"

a ROLL OUT

b FILL

cheese first

preserves next

pineapple last

c ROLL INTO LOG

d CUT INTO THREE STRIPS

e BRAID FROM CENTER

golden raisin poppy seed twist

MAKES ONE 15- TO 16-INCH TWIST, 10 TO 12 SERVINGS

Poppy seeds and raisins are an Old World combination. The whole seeds are commonly ground for these types of pastries. Since most kitchens do not have a poppy seed grinder, for this recipe I omitted the grinding and cooked the whole seeds with raisins, along with sweet and fragrant ingredients like honey and orange. The tasty filling is braided through the pastry, making a striking finish. If you like poppy seeds as much as I do, you must try this wonderful recipe.

AT A GLANCE

PAN: Large cookie sheet
PAN PREP: Line with parchment
RISING TIME: 45 to 60 minutes
OVEN TEMP: 350°F
BAKING TIME: 30 to 35 minutes
DIFFICULTY: 🍵 🍵

1 ¼ cups golden raisins

¼ cup (1 ounce) poppy seeds

¼ cup toasted almonds, finely chopped (see pages 391–392)

2 tablespoons sugar

2 tablespoons honey

2 tablespoons unsalted butter

½ teaspoon freshly grated navel orange zest

½ teaspoon pure vanilla extract

1 large egg white

½ recipe (about 1 pound) Simple Sweet Dough (page 164) or Rich Sour Cream Dough (page 166), cold

2 to 3 tablespoons fresh navel orange juice, for thinning

1 large egg white lightly beaten with 1 teaspoon water, for egg wash

Clear Shiny Glaze (page 360)

1. Dab each corner of a large cookie sheet lightly with butter and line with baking parchment.

2. Place the raisins in a food processor fitted with the steel blade, and pulse until coarsely chopped. Empty them into a heavy-duty medium saucepan and add the poppy seeds, almonds, sugar, honey, butter, orange zest, vanilla, and egg white. Over medium-low heat, stir the mixture until the sugar dissolves, 3 to 4 minutes. Watch carefully to prevent scorching. Set aside to cool.

3. Place the dough on a lightly floured work surface and shape it into a log. Roll the dough into a 10 × 15-inch rectangle, with the 15-inch side parallel to the edge of the counter.

4. Add enough orange juice to the poppy seed filling to achieve a spreading consistency. Spread a 3-inch-wide strip of filling in the center of the dough, spreading it

from right to left across the 15-inch side of the dough. Smooth the filling with a small offset spatula or moistened fingertips. Lightly brush the far edge of the dough with egg wash. Roll the dough up jelly roll style. Pinch the seam to seal, then roll the log back and forth two or three times. Carefully lift the roll onto the parchment-lined cookie sheet, placing it seam side down, angling it as necessary. Using a rolling pin or the palm of your hand, flatten the log until it measures about $3\frac{1}{2} \times 15$ inches.

5. Using a dough scraper or thin-bladed sharp knife, score the log lengthwise into three equal strips, then cut through. Starting in the center, braid the strips, then repeat with the opposite side (see illustrations, page 203). Pinch the ends together well and tuck under. Cover the pan with a tea towel and set in a warmish place to rise for 45 to 60 minutes, until puffy and *almost* doubled.

6. Fifteen minutes before baking, position the rack in the lower third of the oven. Heat the oven to 350°F. Bake for 30 to 35 minutes, or until golden brown.

7. About 15 minutes before the twist is done, prepare the glaze. Remove the braid from the oven and *immediately* brush the surface with the *hot* glaze. After 10 minutes, loosen with a large metal spatula. When firm enough to handle, transfer to a cooling rack.

STORAGE: Store at room temperature, tightly wrapped in aluminum foil, for up to 3 days. This cake may be frozen (see "Refreshing Yeasted Coffee Cakes," page 213).

golden cinnamon loaf

MAKES TWO 8-INCH LOAVES, 8 TO 10 SERVINGS PER LOAF

This recipe has been in my repertoire for years. When my children, Pam and Frank, were growing up, this was their favorite breakfast sweet. Rich and buttery with a cinnamon-sugar swirl, this bread makes wonderful cinnamon toast. For a decadent breakfast treat, use this bread to make French toast.

AT A GLANCE
PANS: Two 8 x 3¾ x 2½-inch aluminum foil loaf pans/rimmed cookie sheet
PAN PREP: Butter generously/line with parchment
RISING TIME: First rise, 1¼ hours; second rise, after shaping, 45 to 60 minutes
OVEN TEMP: 350°F
BAKING TIME: 35 minutes
DIFFICULTY: 🍵

DOUGH

¼ cup warm water (110° to 115°F)

⅓ cup plus 1 tablespoon sugar

1 package active dry yeast

3¼ cups all-purpose flour, spooned in and leveled

½ teaspoon salt

⅓ cup (⅔ stick) unsalted butter, diced (softened for Hand Method)

½ cup milk

1 large egg

2 large egg yolks (reserve 1 egg white for egg wash)

1 teaspoon pure vanilla extract

1 large egg white plus 2 teaspoons water, lightly beaten, for egg wash

⅓ cup sugar mixed with 2½ teaspoons ground cinnamon, for filling

1 tablespoon unsalted butter, melted

1. Rinse a small bowl in hot water to warm it. Add the warm water and 1 *tablespoon* of the sugar to the bowl. Sprinkle the yeast on top of the water. *Do not stir.* Cover with a saucer and let stand for 5 minutes, swirling the bowl every so often. Stir with a small whisk or a fork and cover again for about 3 minutes, or until the yeast is bubbly and dissolved.

MAKE THE DOUGH
Stand Mixer Method

2. In the bowl of an electric mixer fitted with the paddle attachment, mix the flour, remaining ⅓ cup sugar, and salt on low speed. Add the butter and continue to mix until meal-size crumbs form.

3. In a small bowl, whisk together the dissolved yeast, milk, whole egg, yolks, and vanilla. On low speed, add the liquids to the dry ingredients and mix for 1 minute longer, or until a soft dough forms.

Hand Method

2. In a large mixing bowl, whisk together 3 cups of the flour, the remaining ⅓ cup sugar, and the salt. Add the *softened* butter, and using a pastry blender or your fingertips, work in the butter until the mixture resembles fine meal.

3. Make a well in the center. In a small bowl, whisk together the dissolved yeast, milk, whole egg, yolks, and vanilla. Empty the mixture into the well. With a wooden spoon, gradually work the crumbs into the liquid, mixing until all the crumbs are incorporated and a rough dough is formed. Dust the work surface with half of the remaining ¼ cup flour. Turn the dough onto the floured surface, and incorporate the remainder of the flour, kneading the dough lightly until it is smooth.

SHAPE THE DOUGH

4. Shape the dough into a ball, then place it in a buttered bowl large enough for the dough to double. Turn the dough a few times to coat it with butter. Cover the bowl with plastic wrap and place it in a warm spot to rise until doubled, about 1¼ hours.

5. Generously butter two 8 × 3¾ × 2½-inch aluminum foil loaf pans and line the bottoms with baking parchment. Line a rimmed cookie sheet with parchment.

6. Working with one piece of dough at a time, roll it into a 6 × 13-inch rectangle with the 6-inch side parallel to the counter. Brush with some of the egg wash. Remove 1 tablespoon of the cinnamon/sugar mixture and set aside for garnish. Sprinkle the dough evenly with half of the remaining cinnamon/sugar mixture, leaving a 1-inch border on the top. Starting with the 6-inch side closest to you, roll *very tightly* to form a cylinder. Pinch the seam together very well and roll the cylinder back and forth three or four times to seal the layers. Place the roll in the prepared loaf pan, making sure the seam is on the bottom. The dough does not have to touch the sides of the pan. Repeat with the remaining dough. Place the loaves on the prepared cookie sheet. Cover the loaves with a tea towel and place in a warmish spot to rise until puffy and almost doubled, 45 to 60 minutes.

recipe continues

continued from previous page

BAKE THE LOAVES

7. Fifteen minutes before baking, position the rack in the lower third of the oven. Heat the oven to 350°F. Bake the loaves for 25 minutes, remove from the oven, and then brush the tops with melted butter and sprinkle with the remaining cinnamon/sugar mixture. Bake for 10 to 15 minutes longer, until golden.

8. Remove loaves from the oven and let rest for 5 minutes. *Reduce the oven temperature to 300°F.* Turn the breads on their side and carefully remove them from the pans. Peel off the baking parchment if it adheres to the loaves. Place the loaves on the oven rack for 1 to 2 minutes to crisp, turning them to the opposite side halfway through. Remove from the oven and place onto a rack to cool.

STORAGE: Store at room temperature, tightly wrapped in aluminum foil, for up to 3 days. These loaves may be frozen (see "Refreshing Yeasted Coffee Cakes," page 213).

"The smell of that buttered toast simply talked to Toad . . . of warm kitchens, of breakfasts on bright frosty mornings, of cozy parlour firesides on winter evenings. . . ."

KENNETH GRAHAME, *THE WIND IN THE WILLOWS*

dimpled sugar cake

MAKES ONE 8-INCH CAKE, SIXTEEN 2-INCH SQUARES

If you want to make a quick yeasted coffee cake, this recipe is for you. The dough is pressed into the pan and dimpled much like a focaccia. The holes are filled with brown sugar and butter, and the top is sprinkled generously with granulated sugar and cinnamon. When the sugars melt during baking, the top develops a sweet, crusty surface. This cake is perfect not only as a mid-morning snack, but any time of day.

> **AT A GLANCE**
> **PAN:** 8 x 8 x 2-inch baking pan
> **PAN PREP:** Butter generously/line with parchment
> **RISING TIME:** 60 minutes
> **OVEN TEMP:** 375°F
> **BAKING TIME:** 25 to 28 minutes
> **DIFFICULTY:** 🍵

½ recipe (about 1 pound) Simple Sweet Dough (page 164) or Rich Sour Cream Dough (page 166)

⅓ cup golden raisins, plumped (see page 389)

6 tablespoons dark brown sugar

¼ cup (½ stick) cold unsalted butter, cut into 32 cubes

2 tablespoons granulated sugar mixed with ½ teaspoon ground cinnamon

1. Remove the dough from the refrigerator 1 to 1½ hours before using.

2. Butter an 8 × 8 × 2-inch pan and line the bottom with parchment. On a lightly floured work surface, knead the raisins into the dough. Let the dough rest for a few minutes and then shape it into a 7- to 8-inch rectangle. Place the dough in the prepared pan and press it with your hand until the entire bottom is evenly covered. Place a tea towel over the top and set it in a warmish place to rise for about 1 hour, or until puffy and almost doubled.

3. Fifteen minutes before baking, position the rack in the middle of the oven. Heat the oven to 375°F.

4. Using two fingers, make depressions randomly in the dough about every 1½ to 2 inches. You should make thirty-two holes. Drop about ½ teaspoon of brown sugar into each hole as best you can. Press a cube of butter deeply into the sugar. It's okay if some of the sugar spreads onto the top of the dough. Sprinkle the top of the cake heavily with the cinnamon/sugar mixture.

5. Bake the cake for 25 to 28 minutes. Remove from the oven and place on a cooling rack for 20 minutes. To remove the baking parchment, cover the pan with a square

recipe continues

continued from previous page

of aluminum foil, cupping it around the side to hold it in place. Place the cooling rack on top of the cake, invert it, and lift off the pan. Remove the parchment, then cover the cake with another rack and turn the cake top side up.

STORAGE: Store at room temperature, tightly wrapped in aluminum foil, for up to 3 days. This cake may be frozen (see "Refreshing Yeasted Coffee Cakes," page 213).

VARIATION

strawberry dimpled sugar cake

Here is a play on the Dimpled Sugar Cake. Instead of brown sugar, fill the dimples with strawberry preserves. During baking, the melted preserves and sugary top coating form an appealing pink-and-white marbled surface. In Step 4 of the recipe, substitute ¼ cup strawberry preserves for the brown sugar. Place ½ teaspoon of preserves in each hole, as best you can. Press a cube of butter deeply into the preserves and sprinkle the top of the cake heavily with the cinnamon/sugar mixture. Proceed with Step 5 of the recipe.

"The only stumbling block is fear of failure. In cooking, you've got to have a what-the-hell attitude."

JULIA CHILD

kugelhopf

MAKES ONE 8-INCH CAKE, 8 TO 10 SERVINGS

Here is a twist on a kugelhopf, the sweet bread that is commonly eaten in Middle European countries, such as Germany and Austria, whose pan, a fluted ring mold, inspired the design of the Bundt and other fluted ring molds that we use today. A traditional kugelhopf is made from yeasted dough enriched with butter, eggs, dried fruits, nuts, and brandy. The texture is often dry and requires dunking in a cup of hot coffee or tea.

My recipe for kugelhopf is a lighter version of the classic coffee cake. The texture is a cross between a leavened cake and one made with yeast. Bits of dried apricots, golden raisins, and dried cherries, along with walnuts, are kneaded into an orange-scented soft dough. It is important to mix the dough for the time given in the recipe, about 10 minutes, adding the flour slowly as directed. This contributes to the cake's marvelous texture. Therefore, using a stand mixer is highly recommended. However, don't be tempted to add the dried fruits and nuts in the mixer because they will darken the dough. Is all this work worth the effort? You bet it is!

> **AT A GLANCE**
> **PAN:** 8-cup fluted tube or Kugelhopf pan
> **PAN PREP:** Butter generously
> **RISING TIME:** First rise, 1 to 1½ hours; optional second rise, 45 to 60 minutes; rise after shaping, 45 to 60 minutes.
> **OVEN TEMP:** 350°F
> **BAKING TIME:** 30 to 35 minutes
> **DIFFICULTY:** ♨ ♨

FRUIT

¼ cup dried apricots (not organic), plumped (see page 389)

¼ cup golden raisins (not organic), plumped (see page 389)

¼ cup dried cherries (not organic), plumped (see page 389)

½ cup **Grand Marnier liqueur**

DOUGH

½ cup milk

2 tablespoons water

⅓ cup plus 1 teaspoon sugar

1 package active dry yeast

2¼ cups unbleached all-purpose flour, spooned in and leveled

⅓ cup (⅔ stick) unsalted butter, plus 1 teaspoon for brushing dough, softened

2 large eggs

½ teaspoon pure vanilla extract

1 teaspoon freshly grated orange zest

1 teaspoon ground cardamom

1 teaspoon salt

¾ cup broken walnuts (see page 392)

Orange Glaze (page 362)

1. In a medium bowl, macerate the plumped dried fruits in the Grand Marnier for 30 minutes. Drain the fruits and let dry on a double layer of paper towels. Set aside.

recipe continues

continued from previous page

MAKE THE DOUGH

2. In a small saucepan, heat the milk and water to 110° to 115°F. Stir in 1 teaspoon of the sugar and sprinkle the yeast over the warm liquid. Cover and let stand 5 minutes. Stir gently with a small whisk and add ½ cup of the flour. Whisk until smooth, cover, and let stand for 10 minutes, or until bubbly.

Stand Mixer Method

3. In the bowl of an electric mixer fitted with the paddle attachment, on medium speed, mix the butter with the remaining ⅓ cup sugar, the eggs, vanilla, and orange zest. Add the yeast mixture and mix thoroughly.

4. Remove 1 teaspoon of the flour, and combine it in a small bowl with the cardamom and salt. Reduce the mixer speed to low and add about 1¼ cups flour, along with the cardamom mixture, and mix well. Add the remaining ½ cup flour, 1 tablespoon at a time, over the course of 10 minutes. Continue to beat for 10 minutes longer.

Hand Method

3. In a large bowl, using a wooden spoon, blend together the butter and the remaining ⅓ cup sugar. Add the eggs one at a time, then the vanilla, and orange zest. Blend in the yeast mixture and mix thoroughly to combine.

4. Remove 1 teaspoon of the flour, and combine it in a small bowl with the cardamom and salt. Add 1¼ cups flour, along with the cardamom mixture, and mix until a soft dough is formed. Empty the dough onto a lightly floured work surface and knead in the remaining ½ cup flour, 1 tablespoon at a time, over 10 minutes. If the dough becomes too elastic, it's okay to rest it for a few minutes. Continue to knead for another 10 minutes, until a smooth dough is formed, again resting it as needed.

SHAPE THE KUGELHOPF

5. On a lightly floured work surface, knead in the dried fruits and nuts, working the dough just until incorporated. Turn the dough into a medium buttered bowl and brush the top lightly with soft butter. Cover the bowl with a tea towel and let rise in a warmish place for 1 to 1½ hours, or until doubled.

6. Punch down the dough and cover with a tea towel and let rise again in a warmish place, about 45 minutes. While the second rise improves texture and takes less time, this rise is optional.

7. Generously butter an 8-cup fluted tube or Kugelhopf pan. After the final rise, punch down the dough and, using a large spoon or dough scraper, distribute equal mounds of dough around the pan. Smooth the top of the dough with your fingers as best you can. Cover with a tea towel and set in a warmish place to rise until almost doubled, 45 to 60 minutes.

BAKE THE KUGELHOPF

8. Fifteen minutes before baking, position the rack in the lower third of the oven. Heat the oven to 350°F. Bake for 30 to 35 minutes, or until golden brown. Remove from the oven and let stand on a cooling rack for 10 minutes, and then invert the cake and remove the pan. While the cake is cooling, prepare the glaze. While the cake is still warm, drizzle it with the glaze.

STORAGE: Store at room temperature, tightly wrapped in aluminum foil, for up to 3 days. This cake may be frozen before glazing (see "Refreshing Yeasted Coffee Cakes," below).

REFRESHING YEASTED COFFEE CAKES

NOTHING IS as irresistible as the taste of homemade yeasted pastries, warm from the oven with their freshly baked fragrance swirling through the air. Surely these treats are at their best soon after baking. However, because they do not contain preservatives, they will lose their freshness much sooner than store-bought.

To restore their fresh-baked goodness, these types of pastries should be reheated before serving. Whether a whole cake or bread, or an individual serving, it should be *loosely* wrapped in aluminum foil and reheated in a low oven, about 300°F. The amount of time depends upon the size of the pastry; individual pastries should be ready in 6 to 8 minutes, while larger ones can take up to 20 or more minutes. If the pastry was heated while still frozen, allow some extra time (see "Freezing Yeasted Doughs," page 225).

To determine when the pastry is ready, lightly press the aluminum foil with your fingertip to test the softness of the pastry. Tear open the foil and bake the pastry for 1 to 2 minutes longer. If it yields easily, the pastry is ready. After removing it from the oven, let the pastry cool, because if eaten too hot, it will be doughy and unpleasant. When tepid, it is ready to be enjoyed—and when it was made will be your best kept secret.

old-fashioned babka dough

MAKES ABOUT 2 POUNDS OF DOUGH, ENOUGH FOR 3 LOAVES

PLAN AHEAD: Refrigerate overnight

Babka, a coffee cake of Polish origin, has enjoyed great popularity among customers of Jewish-style bakeries and delicatessens, especially in the New York area. It is often made with a rich sour-cream yeasted dough that is filled with any variety of sweet fillings. Sometimes the top is left plain, while at other times it is finished with a sugar glaze, a dusting of powdered sugar, or an irresistible streusel topping.

My recipe for babka is one that I have treasured for years. It comes from a blend of recipes that date back to the 1940s and '50s. When I was growing up, the one I remember best is a buttery dough that was filled with a tasty mixture of white and brown sugars, cinnamon, lots of nuts, and often raisins. The fragrance of the sweet yeasted dough combined with these ingredients was absolutely intoxicating to my young senses.

Over the years, the varieties broadened and the fillings have become more substantial. Cheese, chocolate chip, and dried fruit varieties are now popular. When you make this recipe, with good planning, you can make more than one variety of babka with the same master dough (see "Playing with Dough," page 222).

Although generous amounts of fillings seem to be the current trend, your babka will be better if you don't become overzealous. The weight of the filling can cause the cake to collapse and become too doughy. When the lovely texture of the cake is perfectly balanced with the sweet surprise within, the end result is absolutely divine.

¼ cup plus 1 teaspoon sugar	¾ teaspoon salt
¼ cup warm water (110° to 115°F)	½ cup (1 stick) unsalted butter, slightly firm, cut into ½-inch cubes
1½ packages active dry yeast (1 tablespoon plus 1½ teaspoons)	¾ cup sour cream
3¾ cups unbleached all-purpose flour, spooned in and leveled	3 large eggs
	½ teaspoon pure vanilla extract

1. Rinse a small bowl in hot water to warm it. Add 1 teaspoon of the sugar and the warm water to the bowl. Sprinkle the yeast on top of the water. *Do not stir.* Cover with a saucer and let stand for 5 minutes, swirling the bowl every so often. Stir with a small whisk or a fork and cover again for 2 to 3 minutes, or until the yeast is bubbly and dissolved.

MAKE THE DOUGH

Stand Mixer Method

2. In the bowl of an electric mixer fitted with the paddle attachment, mix on low speed the flour, remaining ¼ cup sugar, and the salt. Add the butter and continue to mix until meal-size crumbs form, 3 to 4 minutes. *Stop the mixer.*

3. In a separate bowl, using a small whisk or a fork, mix the sour cream, eggs, and vanilla. Stir in the dissolved yeast. Pour the liquids into the crumb mixture, and combine on low speed until a rough dough is formed. Scrape down the bowl and continue to mix for 3 to 4 minutes, until smooth.

Hand Method

2. In a large mixing bowl, whisk together 3½ cups of the flour, remaining ¼ cup sugar, and the salt. Add the cubed butter, and using a pastry blender or your fingertips, work in the butter until the mixture resembles meal-size crumbs.

3. Make a well in the center of the crumb mixture. In a separate bowl, using a small whisk or fork, mix the sour cream, eggs, and vanilla. Stir in the dissolved yeast and pour the liquids into the well. With a wooden spoon, gradually work the crumbs into the liquid, mixing until all the crumbs are incorporated and a rough dough is formed. Sprinkle the work surface with half of the remaining ¼ cup flour. Turn the dough onto the floured surface and knead the dough for 6 to 8 minutes, gradually incorporating the remainder of the flour.

FINISH THE DOUGH

4. Turn the dough out onto a lightly floured surface. Knead the dough a few times to cover it with a thin coating of flour, just until it is no longer sticky. Using a dough scraper or large sharp knife, divide the dough into three equal pieces (a kitchen scale is helpful here). Knead each piece of dough two or three times to seal the cut sides of the dough with a light dusting of flour (see "Forming a Skin," page 141).

5. Place each piece of dough in a medium plastic bag, leaving enough space for the dough to expand slightly. Refrigerate overnight or for up to 3 days. This dough may be frozen (see "Freezing Yeasted Doughs," page 225).

"Nothing beats a babka!"

ELAINE BENNES, *SEINFELD*

carole's streusel-topped babka

MAKES THREE 8-INCH LOAVES, 6 TO 8 SERVINGS PER LOAF

This classic babka is filled with a combination of light and dark brown sugars, cinnamon, cocoa powder, chopped untoasted walnuts, and golden raisins, all bound with some dried bread crumbs (store-bought plain bread crumbs will do). Large pieces of toasted pecans are kneaded through the dough to give extra crunch, while a generous coating of streusel crumbs will be a test of will for lovers of these buttery morsels.

AT A GLANCE

PANS: Three 8 x 3¾ x 2½-inch aluminum foil loaf pans/rimmed cookie sheet

PAN PREP: Butter generously/line with parchment

RISING TIME: 1½ to 2 hours

OVEN TEMP: 350°F

BAKING TIME: 30 to 35 minutes

DIFFICULTY: 🍵 🍵

⅓ cup granulated sugar

⅓ cup (lightly packed) dark brown sugar

2 tablespoons fine dry unflavored bread crumbs

2 tablespoons Dutch-process cocoa powder (optional)

1½ teaspoons ground cinnamon

½ cup (1 stick) *very soft* unsalted butter

Old-Fashioned Babka Dough (page 214), cold

¾ cup broken toasted pecans (see page 391)

1 cup medium-chopped walnuts (see page 392)

½ cup golden raisins (optional), plumped (see page 389)

1 large egg lightly beaten with 2 teaspoons water, for egg wash

1 small recipe Carole's Favorite Streusel (page 350)

Powdered sugar, for dusting

1. In a small bowl, combine the granulated and brown sugars, bread crumbs, cocoa (if using), and cinnamon. Set aside.

2. Using a pastry brush, coat three 8 × 3¾ × 2½-inch aluminum foil loaf pans generously with some of the *very soft* butter. If desired, line each loaf pan with a 15 × 3-inch strip of parchment to form a cradle. (This will enable you to lift the babkas from the pan without inverting them.) Have ready a rimmed cookie sheet lined with baking parchment.

3. Working one piece of dough at a time, place the dough on a lightly floured work surface, and with lightly floured hands, knead the dough three or four times, or just until it is manageable and not sticky, working in one-third of the broken pecans as you knead. Let the dough rest for 5 minutes before shaping.

4. *Clean the board with a pastry scraper and flour the board again.* Roll the dough into a rectangle, measuring approximately 9 × 12 inches, with the 12-inch side parallel to the edge of the counter. It's okay if the pecans poke through or tear the dough slightly.

5. Using a small offset spatula or pastry brush, spread the dough with a thin layer of the *very soft* butter (about 1½ tablespoons), leaving a 1½-inch margin on the far edge of the dough. Sprinkle on one-third of the sugar mixture, one-third of the chopped walnuts, and one-third of the raisins (if using), again leaving a 1½-inch margin on the far edge of the dough. Using your hand, gently press the mixture into the dough. *Lightly* brush the far edge of the dough with egg wash.

6. Starting at the bottom edge, roll the dough tightly into a log, pinching the seam to seal. Lightly reflour the board and roll the log back and forth several times to seal the layers. It should measure about 12 inches. With a dough scraper or sharp long-bladed knife, cut the log into eight even pieces.

7. Arrange the pieces cut side down in the prepared pan, making two rows across and four rows down. Select the larger pieces for the center and the smaller pieces for the ends. As you place each piece of dough into the pan, brush the exposed edge with some of the egg wash to adhere the slices to each other. Press the top of the slices to even the surface, then press around the outer edge with your fingertips to mound the slices slightly in the center. Repeat the procedure using the other two pieces of dough. Cover the pans with a tea towel and let rise in a warmish spot until puffy and *almost* doubled, 1½ to 2 hours. While the babkas are rising, prepare the streusel.

8. Fifteen minutes before baking, position the rack in the lower third of the oven. Heat the oven to 350°F. Set the pans on wax paper and gently brush the tops of the babkas with egg wash (handle carefully so as not to jar the cakes or they will fall). Generously cover the tops of the babkas with the streusel crumbs, pressing them *lightly* onto the surface.

9. Place the loaf pans on the prepared cookie sheet. Bake the babkas for 30 to 35 minutes, or until golden brown on top. If the tops of the babkas are browning too quickly, lay a strip of aluminum foil lightly over the surface and continue baking until done. Remove from the oven and place on a cooling rack. When the babkas are cool, if using parchment, grasp the parchment on either side of the pans and lift the babkas from the pans. Carefully slide the parchment from under the cakes, and if desired, return the cakes to the pans for storage. Dust with powdered sugar before serving.

STORAGE: Store at room temperature, tightly wrapped in aluminum foil, for up to 3 days. Reheat before serving in a 325°F oven for 10 to 15 minutes, or until slightly warm. These cakes may be frozen (see "Refreshing Yeasted Coffee Cakes," page 213).

apricot-raisin babka

MAKES THREE 8-INCH LOAVES, 6 TO 8 SERVINGS PER LOAF

This buttery babka is studded with pieces of dried apricots and golden raisins. Marbled throughout the cake are the rich flavors of apricot preserves, brown sugar, cinnamon, and a hint of almond. When you spread the dough with the apricot preserves, be sure to leave the 3-inch margin as the recipe indicates. Because preserves are somewhat runny, when the dough is rolled the preserves have a tendency to spread. Don't be concerned if they begin to ooze when you arrange the pieces in the pan. When the cakes are baked, you are left with a yummy end result.

> **AT A GLANCE**
> **PANS:** Three 8 x 3¾ x 2 ½-inch aluminum foil loaf pans/rimmed cookie sheet
> **PAN PREP:** Butter generously/line with parchment
> **RISING TIME:** 1½ to 2 hours
> **OVEN TEMP:** 350°F
> **BAKING TIME:** 35 to 38 minutes
> **DIFFICULTY:** 🥄 🥄

¾ cup golden raisins (not organic)

¾ cup dried apricots (not organic), cut in ¼-inch dice

⅓ cup (⅔ stick) unsalted butter, *very soft*

⅓ cup granulated sugar

⅓ cup (lightly packed) *very fresh* dark brown sugar

1½ teaspoons ground cinnamon

¾ teaspoon pure almond extract

Old-Fashioned Babka Dough (page 214), cold

1 large egg lightly beaten with 2 teaspoons water, for egg wash

¾ cup thick apricot preserves

1 large recipe Vanilla Glaze (page 359)

1. Place the raisins and apricots in a 1-quart bowl. Pour enough boiling water over the fruit to cover it completely. Let stand for 5 minutes. Empty the fruit into a strainer and rinse with cool water. Place the fruit on a double layer of paper towels and blot it well with another double layer of paper towels.

2. Using a pastry brush, coat three 8 × 3¾ × 2½-inch aluminum foil loaf pans generously with some of the *very soft* butter. If desired, line each loaf pan with a 15 × 3-inch strip of parchment to form a cradle. (This will enable you to lift the babkas from the pan without inverting them). Have ready a rimmed cookie sheet lined with baking parchment.

3. In a small bowl, thoroughly combine the remaining butter with the sugars, cinnamon, and almond extract to form a smooth paste. Set aside.

4. Working with one piece of dough at a time, place it on a lightly floured work surface and flatten with a rolling pin to about a ½-inch thickness. Taking ⅓ cup of the plumped fruit, sprinkle the surface of the dough with about half of it. Fold the dough

and pat the surface with your hands to flatten it again to about ½-inch thickness. Sprinkle the dough with the remaining fruit, fold the dough over again, and knead the dough a few times to incorporate the fruit.

5. *Clean the board with a dough scraper and flour the board again.* Roll the dough into a 9 × 12-inch rectangle, with the 12-inch side parallel to the edge of the counter. It's okay if the fruit pokes through the dough.

6. Using a small offset spatula, spread one-third of the butter mixture smoothly over the dough, leaving a 1½-inch margin on the far edge of the dough. Brush the margin lightly with the egg wash. Spread ¼ cup of the apricot preserves over the butter mixture, *leaving a 3-inch margin* on the far edge (see headnote).

7. Starting at the bottom edge, roll the dough tightly into a log, pinching the seam to seal. Reflour the board lightly and roll the log back and forth to seal the layers. It should measure about 12 inches. With a dough scraper or a sharp long bladed knife, cut the log into eight even pieces. It's okay if the filling oozes.

8. Arrange the pieces cut side down in the prepared pan, making two rows across and four rows down. Select the larger pieces for the center and the smaller pieces for the ends. As you place each piece of dough into the pan, brush the exposed edge with the egg wash to adhere the slices to each other. Press the top of the slices to even the surface, then press around the outer edge with your fingertips to mound the slices slightly in the center. Repeat the procedure using the other two pieces of dough. Cover the pans with a tea towel and let rise in a warmish place until puffy and almost doubled, 1½ to 2 hours.

9. Fifteen minutes before baking, position the rack in the lower third of the oven. Heat the oven to 350°F. Brush the tops of the cakes gently with the egg wash.

10. Place the loaf pans on the prepared cookie sheet. Bake the babkas for 35 to 38 minutes, or until golden brown on top. If the tops of the babkas are browning too quickly, lay a strip of aluminum foil loosely over the surface and continue baking until done. Remove from the oven and place on a rack to cool.

11. While the cakes are cooling, prepare the glaze. Using the back of a tablespoon, apply the glaze to the warm cakes. When the cakes are cool, if using parchment, grasp the parchment on either side of the pans and lift the cakes from the pans. Carefully remove the parchment, and if desired, return the cakes to the pans for storage.

STORAGE: Store at room temperature, tightly wrapped in aluminum foil, for up to 3 days. Reheat before serving. These cakes may be frozen (see "Refreshing Yeasted Coffee Cakes," page 213).

double chocolate walnut babka

MAKES THREE 8-INCH LOAVES, 6 TO 8 SERVINGS PER LOAF

This recipe is perfect for the chocolate-obsessed. The filling contains mini chocolate chips as well as cocoa powder and lots of walnuts. Here, pieces of toasted walnuts are kneaded into the dough along with chopped untoasted walnuts that are added to the filling. Do not substitute regular-size chocolate chips in place of the minis; the weight of the larger pieces of chocolate can affect the rising of the dough.

I like to finish these babkas with a thin layer of chocolate glaze. A dusting of powdered sugar can also be used, but the glaze really dresses them up.

AT A GLANCE
PANS: Three 8 x 3¾ x 2½-inch aluminum foil loaf pans/rimmed cookie sheet
PAN PREP: Butter generously
RISING TIME: 1½ to 2 hours
OVEN TEMP: 350°F
BAKING TIME: 30 to 35 minutes
DIFFICULTY: 🥄 🥄

½ cup (1 stick) unsalted butter, *very soft*

⅓ cup granulated sugar

¼ cup (lightly packed) *very fresh* dark brown sugar

3 tablespoons Dutch-process cocoa powder

¾ teaspoon ground cinnamon

Old-Fashioned Babka Dough (page 214), cold

1 cup broken toasted walnuts (see pages 391–392)

1½ cups semi-sweet mini chocolate chips

¾ cup medium-chopped walnuts (see page 392)

1 large egg lightly beaten with 2 teaspoons water, for egg wash

Midnight Chocolate Glaze (page 363)

1. Using a pastry brush, coat three 8 × 3¾ × 2½-inch aluminum foil loaf pans generously with some of the *very soft* butter. If desired, line each loaf pan with a 15 × 3-inch strip of parchment to form a cradle. (This will enable you to lift the babkas from the pans without inverting them.) Have ready a rimmed cookie sheet lined with baking parchment.

2. In a small bowl, combine the granulated sugar, brown sugar, cocoa powder, and cinnamon. Set aside.

3. Working with one piece of dough at a time, place it on a lightly floured work surface. With lightly floured hands, knead the dough three or four times or just until it is not sticky. Knead in one-third of the walnuts. Let the dough rest for 5 minutes before shaping.

4. Clean the board with a dough scraper and lightly flour the board again. Roll the dough into a rectangle, measuring approximately 9 × 12 inches, with the 12-inch side parallel to the counter. It's okay if the nuts poke through or tear the dough slightly.

5. Using a small offset spatula or pastry brush, spread the dough with a thin layer of *very soft* butter (about 1½ tablespoons), leaving a 1½-inch margin on the far edge. Sprinkle on one-third of the sugar mixture, ½ cup of the mini chocolate chips, and ¼ cup of the chopped, untoasted walnuts, again leaving a 1½-inch margin on the far edge of the dough. Using your hand, gently press the mixture into the dough. *Lightly* brush the far edge of the dough with the egg wash.

6. Starting at the bottom edge, roll the dough tightly into a log, pinching the seam to seal. Reflour the board lightly and roll the log back and forth several times to seal the layers. It should measure about 12 inches. With a dough scraper or sharp long bladed knife, cut the log into eight even pieces.

7. Arrange the pieces cut side down in the prepared pan, making two rows across and four rows down. Select the larger pieces for the center and the smaller pieces for the ends. As you place each piece of dough into the pan, brush the exposed edge with some of the egg wash to adhere the slices to each other. Press the top of the slices to even the surface, then press around the outer edge with your fingertips to mound the slices slightly in the center. Repeat the procedure using the other two pieces of dough. Place the pans on the prepared cookie sheet. Cover the pans with a tea towel and let rise in a warmish spot until puffy and *almost* doubled, 1½ to 2 hours.

8. Fifteen minutes before baking, position the rack in the lower third of the oven. Heat the oven to 350°F. Brush the tops of the cakes with egg wash (handle carefully so as not to jar the cakes or they will fall).

9. Place the loaf pans on the prepared cookie sheet. Bake the babkas for 30 to 35 minutes, or until golden brown on top. If the tops of the babkas are browning too quickly, lay a strip of aluminum foil lightly over the surface and continue baking until done. Remove from the oven and place on a cooling rack.

10. While the cakes are cooling, prepare the glaze. Using the back of a tablespoon, apply the glaze while the cakes are still warm. The glaze will harden as the cakes cool. When the cakes are cool, if using parchment, grasp the parchment on either side of the pans and lift the cakes from the pans. Carefully slide the parchment from under the cakes and, if desired, return the cakes to the pans for storage.

STORAGE: Store at room temperature, tightly wrapped in aluminum foil, for up to 3 days. Reheat before serving. These cakes may be frozen before glazing (see "Refreshing Yeasted Coffee Cakes," page 213).

double chocolate babka

Prepare the recipe for Double Chocolate Walnut Babka, omitting the walnuts in Steps 3 and 5. Then proceed with the recipe.

"Research tells us that fourteen out of any ten individuals like chocolate."

SANDRA BOYNTON

PLAYING WITH DOUGH

ONE OF THE greatest advantages to working with yeasted sweet dough is that there is a lot of flexibility when it comes to changing the finished size. It is so easy to divide master recipes of dough into any size cakes, muffins, or individual pastries that you wish. By playing with your dough, you can come up with many wonderful creations of your own.

The recipes for yeasted sweet dough in this book are calculated by weight, the method used by professional bakers known as scaling. Once you get the hang of scaling dough, dividing it is easy! For example, if the total weight of the dough is one pound (16 ounces), you can divide the dough in half, making two 8-ounce pieces for smaller cakes. For individual pastries, the dough can be cut into yet smaller pieces. You can make eight 2-ounce pieces for muffins or sixteen 1-ounce pieces, depending on the size of your muffin pan. The pieces of dough can also be baked free-form on rimmed cookie sheets.

While the baking times will change, keep the oven temperatures the same. Pastries are usually done when you begin to smell their baked fragrance coming from the oven. At that time, take a peek into the oven and look for a golden brown surface, with a top that feels firm to the touch. When that point has been reached, the pastry is done.

glazed loaded-with-nuts babka

MAKES THREE 8-INCH LOAVES, 6 TO 8 SERVINGS PER LOAF

Here is a babka for anyone who loves nuts. A cooked walnut filling is spread on the dough, while pieces of walnuts are kneaded through. Cinnamon, orange zest, and vanilla accent the rich walnut flavor. Baking with a cooked nut filling is a method used in Eastern European countries. It heightens the flavor of the nuts and makes a superb match for the sweetness of dough.

AT A GLANCE

PANS: Three 8 x 3¾ x 2½-inch aluminum foil loaf pans/rimmed cookie sheet
PAN PREP: Butter generously/line with parchment
RISING TIME: 1½ to 2 hours
OVEN TEMP: 350°F
BAKING TIME: 30 to 35 minutes
DIFFICULTY: 🥄 🥄

FILLING

1 cup walnuts

¼ cup sugar

¼ teaspoon ground cinnamon

1 tablespoon unsalted butter

6 tablespoons milk

½ teaspoon freshly grated navel orange zest

¼ teaspoon pure vanilla extract

3 tablespoons unsalted butter, *very soft*

Old-Fashioned Babka Dough (page 214), cold

1 cup broken walnuts (see page 392)

1 large egg lightly beaten with 2 teaspoons water, for egg wash

Clear Shiny Glaze (page 360)

MAKE THE FILLING

1. In the work bowl of a food processor fitted with the steel blade, finely chop the walnuts with the sugar and cinnamon.

2. Melt the butter in a heavy 2-quart saucepan. Stir in the milk and the nut mixture. Cook over low heat until it is as thick as oatmeal, 8 to 15 minutes, depending on the thickness of the saucepan. Off the heat, add the orange zest and vanilla. Cool thoroughly. (The filling will keep in the refrigerator for up to 1 week. Bring to room temperature before using. If needed, add a small amount of milk to make it spreadable.)

SHAPE THE DOUGH

3. Butter three 8 × 3¾ × 2½-inch aluminum foil loaf pans generously with some of the *very soft* butter. Line each loaf pan with a 15 × 3-inch strip of parchment to form a cradle. Have ready a rimmed cookie sheet lined with baking parchment.

4. Working with one piece of dough at a time, place it on a lightly floured work

recipe continues

surface and, with lightly floured hands, knead three or four times, or just until it is manageable and not sticky, working in ⅓ cup of the broken walnuts as you knead. (See "About Yeasted Coffee Cakes," page 159.)

5. *Clean the board with a dough scraper and lightly flour the board again.* Roll the dough into a rectangle measuring approximately 9 × 12 inches, with the 12-inch side parallel to the counter. It's okay if the nuts poke through or tear the dough slightly.

6. Using a small offset spatula, evenly spread one-third of the nut filling over the dough, leaving a 1½-inch margin on the far edge. Lightly brush the edge of the dough with egg wash.

7. Starting at the bottom edge, roll the dough tightly into a log, pinching the seam to seal. Lightly reflour the board and roll the log back and forth several times to seal the layers. It should measure about 12 inches. With a dough scraper or sharp long-bladed knife, cut the log into eight even pieces.

8. Arrange the pieces cut side down in the prepared pan, making two rows across and four rows down. Use the larger pieces for the center and the smaller ones for the ends. As you place each piece in the pan, brush the exposed edge with some of the egg wash to adhere the slices to each other. Press the top of the slices to even the surface, then press around the outer edge to mound the slices slightly in the center. Repeat the procedure using the other two pieces of dough. Cover the pans with a tea towel and let rise in a warmish spot until puffy and almost doubled, 1½ to 2 hours.

BAKE AND GLAZE THE BABKAS

9. Fifteen minutes before baking, position the rack in the lower third of the oven. Heat the oven to 350°F. Brush the tops of the cakes with egg wash (handle carefully so as not to jar the cakes or they will fall).

10. Place the loaf pans on the prepared cookie sheet. Bake the babkas for 30 to 35 minutes, or until golden brown on top. If the tops of the babkas are browning too quickly, lay a strip of aluminum foil lightly over the surface and continue baking until done. While the cakes are baking, make the glaze. Remove the babkas from the oven and *immediately* brush the tops with the *hot* glaze. Place on a rack to cool.

11. When the cakes are cool, if using parchment, grasp the parchment on either side of the pans and lift the cakes from the pans. Carefully slide the parchment from under the cakes and, if desired, return the cakes to the pans for storage.

STORAGE: Store at room temperature, tightly wrapped in aluminum foil, for up to 3 days. Reheat before serving. These cakes may be frozen (see "Refreshing Yeasted Coffee Cakes," page 213).

FREEZING YEASTED DOUGHS

THE YEASTED DOUGH recipes in this book freeze extremely well because of their richness. This includes the recipes in this chapter, as well as those in the Brioche, Croissants & Danish chapter. This is of great benefit when you wish to prepare dough to be kept on hand for later use. The dough can either be frozen without shaping, or shaped and frozen, ready for baking.

When dough is to be frozen, it is essential that it have its first rise before freezing. Since most of the dough in this book is refrigerated, the first rise, though not always significant, takes place under refrigeration. After the first rise, the dough must be deflated to eliminate the air. Then it is ready for freezing.

To prepare the dough for freezing, always divide it beforehand so you can use smaller pieces as needed. Cut the dough into halves or thirds, or according to the recipe you anticipate making. Cover each piece tightly in plastic wrap, date it, and place in plastic bags. Be sure to squeeze out the excess air, then secure the bag well. The dough can be frozen for at least 3 months, depending upon the temperature of your freezer; zero degrees or below is the optimum.

When ready for use, if the dough has been frozen without shaping, it should be placed in the refrigerator to thaw slowly overnight. If the dough has already been shaped, remove it from the freezer and let it thaw at room temperature. After thawing, refer to the appropriate recipe for the amount of time that the dough should rise.

brioche, croissants & danish

CLASSIC DANISH PASTRIES

Danish Pastry Dough

Pastry Cream for Danish

Sweet Butter Spread

Soft Almond Filling

Firm Almond Filling

Dry Nut Mix

Egg Wash for Danish

Sugar Syrup for Danish

Cheese Filling for Danish

Prune Filling for Danish

Apricot Filling for Danish

Pineapple Filling for Danish

Grandmother's Cake

Danish Almond Cake

Danish Cheese Squares

Danish Nut Squares

Pineapple Cheese Bow Ties

Prune Pinwheels

Chocolate Glazed Cream Buns

Apricot Twists

Bear Claws

ABOUT BRIOCHE, CROISSANTS, AND DANISH

Listed below are my helpful hints to build confidence and guide you along when making these marvelous pastries. With a little practice, working with these doughs can actually be a lot of fun.

• When preparing these European-style doughs, pay close attention to the temperature of the butter. If the butter is too soft, the dough will be difficult to handle; if the butter is too hard, it will not blend properly with the flour.

• Brioche dough should be made in a heavy-duty stand mixer as the mixing process is longer than usual.

• When shaping dough, if it is to be divided, always return the remaining portion to the refrigerator until ready to shape.

• To form a nicely rounded piece of dough, grasp the dough in your hand and rotate it against the work surface, going around and around. As the dough is rotated, a nicely rounded ball will form.

• When shaping doughs for brioche, croissants, and danish, use flour sparingly. It's easier to achieve the desired shape if the dough grabs the rolling surface. Too much flour causes the balls of dough to slide, making them difficult to shape.

• Let the dough rest occasionally when shaping or rolling to prevent it from becoming too elastic.

• Flipping the dough over occasionally will help to roll it thinner. At first it will shrink slightly, but eventually it will thin as you roll.

• Apply the most pressure on the center of the dough, not on the ends.

• Always strive for the width before rolling the length.

• If you have trouble squaring the corners of the dough, try gently pulling them into shape with your fingertips.

• Pricking (docking) the dough with a fork helps to prevent shrinking.

• A sharp pizza wheel (not fluted) makes the cleanest cut when dividing the dough into pieces.

• After shaping, avoid overrising the dough. The pastries should be puffy, but NOT doubled.

• To prevent pastries from unrolling during baking, always place them seam side down on the baking sheet. Applying a thin coat of egg wash to the bottom seam also helps.

• Always use a ruler to measure the dimensions of rolled dough for accuracy. Use a ruler also for dividing the dough into individual pastries.

classic brioche

MAKES ABOUT 3 POUNDS OF DOUGH; ENOUGH FOR TWO ROUND BRIOCHE (8 TO 10 SERVINGS PER ROUND) OR THREE BRIOCHE LOAVES (6 TO 8 SERVINGS PER LOAF)

PLAN AHEAD: Refrigerate overnight

Brioche is a popular French bread that is rich with butter and eggs, which give the crumb a delicate golden color and addictive flavor. When doing a short working stint at Troisgros, the three-star Guide Michelin restaurant in Roanne, France, wasn't I lucky when the pastry chef asked me if I would like to have the recipe for his marvelous brioche?

While the dough is easy to prepare, it requires a longer than usual kneading time, which is essential to achieve the fine quality of this superb bread. This is where a heavy-duty

> **AT A GLANCE**
> **PANS:** Two large (5 cup) brioche pans or three 8 x 3¾ x 2½-inch aluminum foil loaf pans/ rimmed cookie sheet
> **PAN PREP:** Butter lightly
> **RISING TIME:** 1½ to 2 hours for first rise; 1 hour for shaped dough
> **OVEN TEMP:** 375°/325°F
> **BAKING TIME:** 15 minutes/20 to 25 minutes
> **DIFFICULTY:** 🥄 🥄

stand mixer is a blessing. When shaping the dough, it is best to have your work surface barely coated with flour. Too much flour causes the balls of dough to slide making them difficult to shape. To form a nicely rounded piece of dough, grasp the dough in your hand, and rotate it against the work surface, going around and around. As the dough is rotated, a nicely rounded ball will form.

DOUGH

½ cup warm water (110° to 115°F)

6 tablespoons plus 1 teaspoon sugar

2 packages active dry yeast

4½ cups bread flour, spooned in and leveled, sifted if lumpy

2 teaspoons salt

6 large eggs, lightly beaten

1 cup (2 sticks) unsalted butter, at room temperature

EGG WASH

1 large egg

2 teaspoons cool water

½ teaspoon sugar

MAKE THE DOUGH

1. Rinse a small bowl in hot water to warm it. Add the warm water and stir in 1 teaspoon of the sugar. Sprinkle the yeast over the water. Do not stir. Cover the bowl with a saucer and let the mixture stand for 5 minutes. Stir it briefly with a fork, cover again, and let it stand for 2 to 3 minutes more, or until bubbly.

2. Place the flour and salt in the bowl of an electric mixer fitted with a dough hook.

Stir down the yeast mixture, add it to the eggs, and mix well to combine. *With the mixer off*, add the liquid to the flour. *With the mixer on low speed*, blend the ingredients. At first the mixture will be very crumbly, but as it continues to mix, a very stiff dough will form and all of the crumbs will be absorbed. This will take 5 to 7 minutes.

3. In a medium bowl, using a wooden spoon, cream the butter and remaining 6 tablespoons sugar together, mixing until smooth. Do not let the butter become too soft.

4. With the mixer on low speed, add the butter/sugar to the flour mixture, 1 tablespoon at a time. This should take 10 to 12 minutes. *After the first 5 minutes, remove the dough hook and replace it with the paddle attachment.* After the remaining butter is incorporated, continue to mix for another 1 to 2 minutes. The dough should become very smooth and shiny.

5. Empty the dough onto a lightly floured work surface, and knead it briefly just to coat the surface with flour. Place the dough in a large buttered bowl. Turn the dough over to coat the surface with butter, then tightly cover with plastic wrap. Set the bowl in a warm place to rise until doubled, 1½ to 2 hours. Punch the dough down to expel the air, cover with plastic wrap, and refrigerate overnight.

6. Prepare the egg wash: In a small bowl, lightly beat the egg, water, and sugar together with a fork. Refrigerate until ready to use.

SHAPE THE DOUGH

Classic Brioche

7. Using a pastry brush, lightly butter two large brioche pans and set aside. Divide the cold dough in half. Working with half of the dough at a time, remove about one-fifth for the knob of the brioche. Form the larger piece of dough into a ball by rotating it on the work surface (see headnote). Place the ball into a prepared brioche pan. Cut a deep X into the center of the ball using a pair of scissors. Shape the smaller piece of dough into a cone. Moisten two of your fingertips with cool water and form a deep hole by spreading the X apart. Insert the cone point down, deep into the hole. Gently press around the seam, but be sure the knob is well defined. Repeat with the remaining half of the dough.

Brioche Loaves

7. Using a pastry brush, lightly butter three 8 × 3¾ × 2½-inch aluminum foil loaf pans. Divide the cold dough in thirds. Working with one-third of the dough at a time, cut each into three equal pieces. Shape the dough into balls by rotating them on the work surface (see headnote). Place one ball into a prepared loaf pan. Brush the exposed side of

recipe continues

continued from previous page

the ball with egg wash. Place the second ball against the first, and again brush the exposed side with egg wash. Fit the third ball into the pan. Repeat with the remaining dough.

8. Cover the shaped dough loosely with a tea towel. Let rise in a warmish place until puffy and almost doubled, about 1 hour.

9. Fifteen minutes before baking, position the rack in the lower third of the oven. Heat the oven to 375°F.

For Classic Brioche

10. Brush the tops of the risen dough gently with the egg wash. Be careful not to let the egg drip into the area where the ball and cone are joined. Using scissors, cut into the brioche where the knob is joined with the large ball, continuing around the knob of dough. This will allow the knob to rise during baking.

For Brioche Loaves

10. Brush the tops of the risen dough gently with the egg wash. Be careful not to let the egg drip down the side of the pans. For ease of handling, place the aluminum foil pans on a rimmed cookie sheet before baking.

11. Bake the brioche for 15 minutes. *Reduce the heat to 325°F*, and continue baking for 20 to 25 minutes, or until golden brown. (If the top of the bread is browning too fast, cover the pans loosely with aluminum foil.) Remove from the oven and let stand on a rack for 10 minutes. Remove from the pans and place on a rack to cool.

STORAGE: Store at room temperature, tightly covered with plastic wrap or aluminum foil, for up to 3 days. This bread may be frozen (see "Refreshing Yeasted Cakes, page 213).

VARIATION

golden raisin brioche

Golden raisins make a lovely addition to the buttery crumb of brioche. Plumping the raisins brings out their sweetness and tenderizes the fruit, making them a perfect complement to this elegant bread.

Make Classic Brioche dough as directed above. In Step 4, during the last minute of mixing, add 1 cup golden raisins, plumped (see page 389). Proceed with Step 5 of the recipe.

chocolate duet brioche

MAKES THREE 8-INCH LOAVES, 6 TO 8 SERVINGS PER LOAF

This buttery brioche flavored with a hint of orange has small pieces of bittersweet and milk chocolate kneaded into the dough. I always warm my slice of brioche before I eat it because I love the taste sensation of melting chocolate with sweet bread. When preparing the brioche dough, add 2 teaspoons freshly grated orange zest to the batter in step 3. And be sure to use fine-quality chocolate here. It makes a difference.

AT A GLANCE

PANS: Three 8 x 3¾ x 2½-inch aluminum foil loaf pans/rimmed cookie sheet
PAN PREP: Butter generously
RISING TIME: First rise: 1½ to 2 hours; rise after shaping, 2 hours
OVEN TEMP: 375°/325°F
BAKING TIME: 10 minutes/25 to 30 minutes
DIFFICULTY: 🥄 🥄

Classic Brioche dough (page 230), cold (see headnote)

2 ounces fine-quality milk chocolate, such as Lindt, diced into ¼-inch pieces

2 ounces fine-quality bittersweet chocolate, such as Lindt, diced into ¼-inch pieces

2 tablespoons granulated sugar

1 large egg lightly beaten with 2 teaspoons cool water, for egg wash

3 tablespoons sparkling sugar (see page 380)

1. Prepare the recipe for the dough, but in Step 3, blend the orange zest into the butter/sugar mixture, being careful not to let the butter become too soft. Then proceed with the recipe starting with Step 4.

2. Combine the chocolates in a small bowl.

3. On a lightly floured work surface, roll the cold dough into a square approximately 9 inches. Sprinkle the dough with one-third of the chocolates and 2 teaspoons of the granulated sugar. Enclose the chocolates and sugar by folding the corners of the dough inward to meet in the center, forming a smaller square. Pinch the seams and flatten the square. Overlap your hands and press down firmly to spread the dough into a larger square. Sprinkle the top of the dough again, using half of the remaining chocolates and sugar. Enclose the chocolates and sugar again by folding in the corners to meet in the center. Flatten the dough with your hands, as best you can, into another square. Let it rest for 5 minutes to relax the dough.

recipe continues

continued from previous page

4. Lift the dough and sprinkle the work surface with half of the remaining chocolates and sugar. Place the dough on top of these ingredients and sprinkle the top with the remaining chocolates and sugar. Knead the dough briefly, as best you can, to incorporate them. If any pieces of chocolate fall off, press them into the dough.

5. Using a pastry brush, generously butter the loaf pans and set aside. Weigh the dough and divide it into thirds, cutting it with a dough scraper. Working with one piece at a time, divide it evenly into three pieces. Cupping your hand over the dough, roll each piece on a barely floured surface, continuously rotating the dough until it forms a ball (see headnote, page 230). Place one ball into the prepared loaf pan. Brush the exposed side of the ball with egg wash. Place the second ball against the first, and again brush the exposed side with egg wash. Fit the third ball into the pan. Repeat with the remaining dough, forming two more loaves. Set the loaf pans on a rimmed cookie sheet, cover with a tea towel, and set in a warmish place to rise for about 2 hours, or until puffy and almost doubled.

6. Fifteen minutes before baking, position the rack in the lower third of the oven. Heat the oven to 375°F.

7. Gently brush the tops of the loaves with some of the egg wash. Sprinkle 1 tablespoon of the sparkling sugar on each loaf. Bake for 10 minutes, then *reduce the heat to 325°F* and continue to bake for 25 to 30 minutes. If the loaves are browning too quickly, lay a piece of aluminum foil loosely over the top. Remove from the oven and let stand for 10 minutes. Remove from the pans and place on a rack to cool.

STORAGE: Store at room temperature, tightly covered with plastic wrap or aluminum foil, for up to 3 days. This bread may be frozen (see "Refreshing Yeasted Coffee Cakes," page 213).

cinnamon walnut brioche loaf

MAKES THREE 8-INCH LOAVES, 6 TO 8 SERVINGS PER LOAF

If you are an aficionado of French cuisine, you'll take delight in biting into a slice of this sophisticated brioche. The golden dough, with toasted broken walnuts throughout, is marbled with a mixture of brown and white sugar and a generous amount of cinnamon. A cup of fresh brewed coffee and a slice of this flavorful brioche . . . ooh-la-la.

For those of you who prefer raisins over nuts, you can make a cinnamon raisin brioche loaf by substituting 2 cups of golden raisins for the nuts. Be sure to plump the raisins first (see page 389). It makes all the difference.

EGG WASH

I large egg

2 teaspoons cool water

½ teaspoon granulated sugar

½ cup (lightly packed) *very fresh* light brown sugar

¼ cup granulated sugar

I tablespoon plus I teaspoon ground cinnamon

Classic Brioche dough (see page 230), cold

2 cups toasted broken walnuts (see page 392)

3 tablespoons sparkling sugar (see page 380)

1. Prepare the egg wash: In a small bowl, lightly beat the egg, water, and granulated sugar together with a fork. Refrigerate until ready to use.

2. In a medium bowl, combine the sugars and cinnamon. Set aside.

3. On a lightly floured work surface, roll the cold dough into a square approximately 9 inches. Sprinkle the dough with one-third of the nuts and one-third of the sugar/cinnamon mixture. Enclose the nuts and sugar mixture by folding the corners of the dough inward to meet in the center, forming a smaller square. Pinch the seams and flatten the square. Overlap your hands and press down firmly to spread the dough into a larger square. Sprinkle the top of the dough again, using half of the remaining nuts and sugar mixture. Enclose the nuts and sugar mixture again by folding in the corners to meet the center. Flatten the dough with your hands, as best you can, into another square. Let it rest for 5 minutes to relax the dough.

recipe continues

continued from previous page

4. Lift the dough and sprinkle the work surface with half of the remaining nuts and sugar mixture. Place the dough on top of these ingredients and sprinkle the top with the remaining nuts and sugar mixture. Knead the dough briefly until they are well incorporated. Don't be concerned if pieces of nuts fall off. In the end, it will all come together.

5. Using a pastry brush, generouslly butter three 8 × 3¾ × 2½-inch loaf pans and a rimmed cookie sheet and set aside. Weigh the dough and divide it into thirds, cutting it with a dough scraper. Working with one-third of the dough at a time, divide it evenly into three pieces. Cupping your hand over the dough, roll each piece on a barely floured surface, continuously rotating the dough until it forms a ball (see "About Brioche, Croissants, and Danish," page 229). Place one ball into a prepared loaf pan. Brush the exposed side of the ball with egg wash. Place the second ball against the first, and again brush the exposed side with egg wash. Fit the third ball into the pan. Repeat with the rest of the dough, forming two more loaves. Set the loaf pans on the prepared cookie sheet, cover with a tea towel, and set in a warmish place to rise for about 2 hours, or until puffy and almost doubled.

6. Fifteen minutes before baking, position the rack in the lower third of the oven. Heat the oven to 375°F.

7. Gently brush the tops of the loaves with some of the egg wash. Sprinkle 1 tablespoon of the sparkling sugar on each loaf. Bake for 10 minutes, then *reduce the heat to* 325°F and continue to bake for 25 to 30 minutes. If the loaves are browning too quickly, lay a piece of aluminum foil loosely over the top. Remove from the oven and let stand for 10 minutes. Remove from the pans and place on a rack to cool.

STORAGE: Store at room temperature, tightly covered with plastic wrap or aluminum foil, for up to 3 days. This bread may be frozen (see "Refreshing Yeasted Coffee Cakes," page 213).

brioche buns with dried pears and camembert

MAKES EIGHTEEN 2½-INCH BUNS

When I created this recipe, my assistants and I found these buns impossible to resist. Imagine biting into warm, tender brioche with a background of creamy Camembert and toothsome candied pears, topped with the crunch of sugar crystals! Since the recipe uses only half of the brioche dough, the remaining dough can be frozen for later use or baked in a 9 x 5 x 2¾-inch loaf pan.

AT A GLANCE
PANS: Two standard muffin pans
PAN PREP: Butter generously
RISING TIME: 45 minutes
OVEN TEMP: 375°/325°F
BAKING TIME: 10 minutes/6 to 8 minutes
DIFFICULTY: 🥄 🥄

When you purchase a wedge of Camembert, look for a piece with a slight sign of swelling. The interior should be creamy and of thick spreading consistency. Avoid purchasing under-ripe cheese or a piece that is overly soft.

4 ounces dried pears (not organic), cut into ³⁄₄-inch dice

½ cup orange juice

½ cup water

¼ cup granulated sugar

¾ teaspoon whole cardamom seeds (without pods), crushed

4 whole peppercorns

4 ounces ripe Camembert

½ recipe Classic Brioche dough (page 230), cold

½ cup chopped toasted walnuts (see pages 391–392)

1 large egg lightly beaten with 2 teaspoons water, for egg wash

3 tablespoons sparkling sugar (see page 380)

1. Place the dried pears, orange juice, water, granulated sugar, cardamom, and peppercorns in a heavy 2-quart saucepan. Bring to a boil over medium heat, cover the saucepan, and reduce the heat to low. Simmer the pears until they are candied and the liquid is evaporated, about 45 minutes, depending on the weight of the pan and the freshness of the pears. The pears are done when they have a shiny gloss over the surface. (If too much liquid evaporates before the pears are tender, add more water as needed, 2 to 3 tablespoons at a time.) Discard the peppercorns, cool the pears completely, and coarsely chop them.

2. While the fruit is cooking, place the Camembert in the freezer for 15 minutes. When the cheese has firmed, carefully remove the rind with a paring knife, trimming as close to the cheese as possible. While the cheese is still cold, shred it on the large holes of a box grater. Refrigerate until ready to use.

recipe continues

continued from previous page

3. Place the cold dough on a lightly floured work surface. Knead in the shredded cheese and then the nuts. Allow the dough to rest for 5 minutes before working it further.

4. With floured hands, press the dough into a 9-inch square. Sprinkle half of the candied pears over the bottom half of the dough. Fold the top half over the bottom to enclose the pears and press the two layers together. Reshape the dough again as best you can. Sprinkle the bottom half with the remaining pears, fold the dough over, and press the layers together again. Then gently knead the dough to more thoroughly incorporate the pears.

5. Generously butter eighteen muffin cavities and set the pans aside. Weigh the dough and divide it into thirds, cutting it with a dough scraper. Working one piece at a time, divide each third into six equal pieces. Shape each piece into a ball by rotating the dough on the rolling surface, using as little flour as possible (see "About Brioche, Croissants, and Danish," page 229). Place the balls in the muffin pans, cover them with a tea towel, and set in a warmish place to rise for 45 minutes, or until almost doubled and puffy.

6. Fifteen minutes before the buns are ready to be baked, position the racks in the upper and lower thirds of the oven. Heat the oven to 375°F. Brush the tops of the buns gently with the egg wash and sprinkle each with a ½ teaspoon of sparkling sugar.

7. Bake at 375°F for 10 minutes. *Reduce the heat to 325°F* and continue to bake for another 6 to 8 minutes, or until golden brown. To ensure even browning, toward the end of baking time, rotate the pans top to bottom and front to back. Remove from the oven and *immediately* loosen the buns from the pans using the tip of a sharp knife. When the buns are cool enough to handle, place them on a cooling rack. These buns are at their best when served slightly warm.

STORAGE: Store at room temperature, tightly wrapped in aluminum foil, for up to 3 days. These buns may be frozen (see "Refreshing Yeasted Coffee Cakes," page 213).

CROISSANTS

Although many wives' tales exist about the early origins of croissants, the first mention of croissants in historical documents seems to be around the mid-1800s—relatively late compared to early writings in which dough is mentioned. The word *croissant* first appeared in a dictionary in 1683, and the first recipe was published in 1891. The recipe for croissants—the variety that we are familiar with today—was published in 1905. It should come as no surprise that this took place in France. The crescent shape is believed to derive from the symbol on the Turkish flag, and with the history of wars that took place during that era, eventually the shape of the croissant made its way to France.

Homemade croissants have a crisp, flaky crust and a tender, buttery inside crumb, unlike their doughy mass-produced counterparts. As with all butter-layered pastry, patience is a virtue. While a certain amount of skill is required, the key here is *temperature and timing*. When the butter and the dough are of similar consistencies, they can easily be joined and you will have a perfect marriage. After the final shaping of the croissants, avoid the temptation to overrise the pastries. The croissants will rise like magic in the heat of the oven.

flaky croissants

MAKES 3 POUNDS DOUGH, ENOUGH FOR 32 CROISSANTS
PLAN AHEAD: Chill 6 hours or overnight

When it's time to serve these delectable treats, warm them briefly. Won't your family and friends be lucky when you pass your breadbasket filled with something as special as homemade croissants!

Who can resist a freshly baked croissant, hot out of the oven? These simple but elegant crescents are always a special treat anytime they are served. The rave reviews you receive will make your effort worthwhile.

> **AT A GLANCE**
> **PANS:** Rimmed cookie sheets
> **PAN PREP:** Line with parchment
> **RISING TIME:** 45 to 60 minutes
> **OVEN TEMP:** 400°/350°F
> **BAKING TIME:** 10 minutes/10 to 12 minutes
> **DIFFICULTY:** 🍳 🍳 🍳

recipe continues

continued from previous page

SPONGE

2 cups milk

I tablespoon sugar

I package active dry yeast

I cup unbleached all-purpose flour, spooned in and leveled

BUTTER

¼ cup unbleached all-purpose flour

I pound (4 sticks) unsalted butter, slightly firm (see the sidebar on page 245)

DOUGH

4 cups unbleached all-purpose flour, spooned in and leveled

⅓ cup sugar

2 teaspoons salt

2 tablespoons unsalted butter, very soft

⅓ cup milk, for brushing croissants

I large egg lightly beaten with I teaspoon of water, for egg wash

MAKE THE SPONGE

1. In a 2-quart saucepan, warm the milk to 110° to 115°F. Stir in the sugar and sprinkle the yeast over the top. *Do not stir.* Cover the pot and let the mixture stand for 5 minutes. Stir it briefly with a fork, cover again, and let it stand for 5 minutes longer,

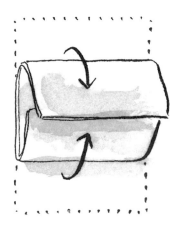

or until the yeast is bubbly and dissolved. Using a small whisk, stir in the flour. It's okay if the mixture is somewhat lumpy. Cover and let stand until the sponge has doubled in size, 25 to 30 minutes or more as needed.

PREPARE THE BUTTER

2. Sprinkle a cool work surface with 1 tablespoon of flour. Unwrap the butter and lay the bars side by side on the work surface. With floured hands, push the bars of butter firmly together to form a solid mass. Sprinkle the top of the butter with one more tablespoon of flour, patting it over the surface with your hand. With a floured rolling pin, roll the butter into an 8-inch square, using the additional 2 tablespoons of flour as needed. Cover the butter with plastic wrap and place it on a cookie sheet. Refrigerate while you prepare the dough.

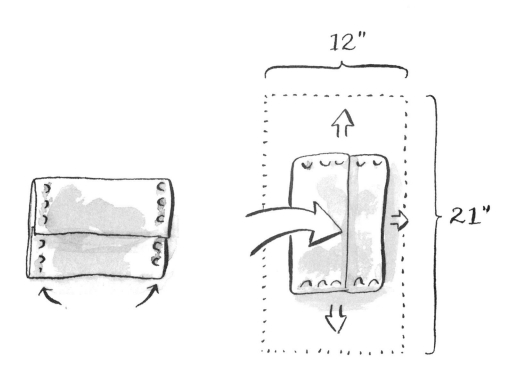

recipe continues

continued from previous page

MAKE THE DOUGH

Stand Mixer Method

3. Place the flour, sugar, and salt in the bowl of a stand mixer fitted with the paddle attachment. On low speed, mix briefly to combine. Add the 2 tablespoons of soft butter and mix for 30 seconds. With the mixer off, add the sponge to the bowl, then mix on low speed, until all of the dry ingredients are incorporated and the mixture is fairly smooth, 1 to 1½ minutes. *Do not overmix.*

Hand Method

3. Place the flour in a large mixing bowl. Using a pastry blender, mix in the sugar and salt. Add the soft butter and work the dry ingredients and butter together until the butter is cut into fine pieces. Make a large well in the center of the flour mixture, stir the sponge, and pour the mixture into the well. Using a wooden spoon, mix the ingredients until well blended. The dough should be fairly smooth. *Do not overmix.*

ENCASE THE BUTTER

4. Place the dough on a lightly floured, cool work surface and gently knead for six to eight turns, or just until smooth. Pat the dough into a 6- to 8-inch rectangle and let it rest for about 2 minutes.

5. With a floured rolling pin, roll the dough into a 12 × 16-inch rectangle with the 12-inch side parallel to the edge of the counter. Center the block of butter on the dough (see illustration, page 241). Bring the lower portion of dough up and over to the middle of the butter, then fold the upper portion over to cover the remaining butter, firmly pinching the seam together. You will have a 1- to 2-inch margin of dough on the right and left side. With your thumb, press these edges thoroughly together to seal them. (See illustrations a, b, c, and d, page 241).

MAKE THE TURNS

6. Give the dough a quarter-turn clockwise. Roll the dough lengthwise into a rectangle measuring about 21 × 12 inches (see illustration d, page 241). Flip the dough over, brushing off the excess flour as needed. If the butter seeps through, seal it by brushing the exposed butter with a light coating of flour. When the desired size is reached, fold the dough into thirds, letter style, making sure all the edges are even. It's

okay to gently stretch the corners to even the block. Enclose the dough in plastic wrap, place it on a cookie sheet, and chill for about 20 minutes. You have now completed the first turn.

7. Remove the dough from the refrigerator and turn it so the open seam is to your right. Roll the dough on a lightly floured surface into a 21 × 12-inch rectangle. Fold into thirds, stretching the corners as needed. You have now completed two turns. Wrap and chill again for 20 minutes.

8. Repeat the procedure two more times, giving the dough a total of four turns. Wrap the dough with plastic wrap, making the package airtight. Chill for at least 6 hours, or up to 3 days. If you wish to freeze the dough, be sure to deflate it first (see "Freezing Yeasted Doughs," page 225).

SHAPE THE CROISSANTS

9. Remove the dough from the refrigerator. Line the baking sheets with parchment.

10. On a cold, lightly floured work surface, divide the dough into quarters using a dough scraper. Working with one-quarter at a time, roll the dough into a 16 × 8-inch strip. Turn the dough so the 16-inch side is parallel to the edge of the counter. (See "About Brioche, Croissants, and Danish," page 229.) Angle the bottom right-hand corner outwards and the upper left-hand corner outwards to form a parallelogram (see illustration, page 241, adjusting measurements). This will enable you to shape the croissants without wasting the ends. Pierce the dough with a fork at 1-inch intervals to prevent it from shrinking.

11. Lay a ruler against the long side of the dough closest to you. Make three light indentations in the dough, spacing them every 4 inches. Lay the ruler against the opposite side and repeat, starting at the left side. With the indentations as a guide, cut the dough into eight triangles, using a pizza cutter or a dough scraper. At the wide end of each triangle, cut a ½-inch knick using the pizza cutter or dough scraper.

12. Stretch the corners of the wide end of the dough outwards slightly and begin to roll the dough. After you roll about one-third of the way up the triangle, begin to stretch the tip outwards with the opposite hand that you are rolling with. Continue to roll the triangle, making three complete turns. Place the croissant on the prepared pan, making sure that the tip of the croissant is on the bottom. Curve the ends of the croissant to form a crescent shape so the widest part of the arch is at the top and the tip is underneath. Continue working with one-quarter of the dough at a time, making thirty-two croissants.

recipe continues

continued from previous page

13. Brush the tops and sides of the croissants lightly with milk, and place in a warmish spot to rise until puffy and almost doubled, 45 to 60 minutes. Brush the croissants again with the milk two or three times during this rising time.

BAKE THE CROISSANTS

14. Fifteen minutes before baking, position the racks in the upper and lower thirds of the oven. Heat the oven to 400°F. Gently brush the tops of the croissants with the egg wash, working from the bottom upward. Do not drip the wash onto the baking sheet. Bake for 10 minutes. *Reduce the oven temperature to 350°F* and bake for 10 to 12 minutes longer, or until golden brown. Place on a rack to cool. To ensure even browning, toward the end of baking time, rotate the pans top to bottom and front to back.

STORAGE: Store at room temperature, tightly wrapped in aluminum foil, for up to 3 days. For longer storage, it is best to freeze them (see "Refreshing Yeasted Coffee Cakes," page 213).

PREPARING BUTTER FOR CROISSANT AND DANISH DOUGH

- For ease of preparation, choose sticks of butter rather than blocks. They are easier to work with.
- Be sure that the butter is slightly firm when you start to prepare it. To determine this, press the bar with your fingertips. You should be able to make a slight impression.
- When the butter is prepared, it is essential that it be the correct temperature. If the butter is too cold, it will be difficult to achieve a smooth consistency when mixed. If the butter is too soft, it will become oily and hard to handle. The soft butter should be returned to the refrigerator until the correct degree of firmness is reached.
- For the butter to be rolled through dough, it is essential that it be pliable. *It is ready when it has reached the same degree of softness as the dough.* Then it will roll smoothly through the dough.

pain au chocolat

MAKES 24 PAINS AU CHOCOLAT

The popularity of yeasted bread with chocolate is growing by leaps and bounds in the United States, making this recipe for pain au chocolat very au courant. Bittersweet chocolate is nestled in a square of croissant dough and formed into a bun. After baking, the flaky golden crust has a center of warm, melted chocolate. This is a favorite breakfast or after-school snack with French children. And let's not forget about the adults!

> **AT A GLANCE**
> **PANS:** Rimmed cookie sheets
> **PAN PREP:** Line with parchment
> **RISING TIME:** 45 to 60 minutes
> **OVEN TEMP:** 400°/350°F
> **BAKING TIME:** 10 minutes/10 to 12 minutes
> **DIFFICULTY:** ♨ ♨ ♨

Be sure to purchase high-quality chocolate. Chocolates such as Lindt, Perugina, and Valrhona are sold in thin candy bars, which are perfect for cutting into strips.

Dough for Flaky Croissants (page 240)

6 (3.5-ounce) bars fine-quality bittersweet chocolate, such as Lindt

1 large egg lightly beaten with 1 teaspoon of water, for egg wash

⅓ cup milk, for brushing croissants

1. Working with half of the dough at a time, roll the dough into a rectangle measuring 20 inches long and 15 inches wide. (See "About Brioche, Croissants, and Danish," page 229.) Pierce the surface of the dough several times with a fork. Divide the dough into 5-inch squares. You should have twelve pieces.

2. Dab the corners of rimmed cookie sheets with butter, line with baking parchment, and set aside. Using 1 ounce of chocolate for each piece of dough, break the chocolate into 1-inch strips so it can be aligned down the center of the square. Brush the edges of the dough with egg wash. Lift the bottom and top of the dough to the center, folding one over the other to enclose the chocolate, and press to seal, then press the ends gently. Place seam side down on parchment-lined pan. Continue shaping the dough until you have twenty-four croissants.

3. Brush the tops and sides of the croissants lightly with milk and place in a warmish spot to rise until almost doubled, 45 to 60 minutes. Brush the croissants again with the milk 1 or 2 times during rising time.

4. Fifteen minutes before baking, position the racks in the upper and lower thirds of the oven. Heat the oven to 400°F. Gently brush the tops of the croissants with the egg wash, working from the bottom of the croissant upward. *Do not drip the egg wash on the baking sheet.* Bake for 10 minutes. *Reduce the oven temperature to 350°F* and bake for 10 to 12 minutes longer, or until golden brown. To ensure even browning, toward the end of baking time, rotate the pans top to bottom and front to back. Remove from the oven and place on a rack to cool.

STORAGE: Store at room temperature, tightly wrapped in aluminum foil, for up to 3 days. Reheat before serving. These croissants may be frozen (see "Refreshing Yeasted Coffee Cakes," page 213).

almond croissants

MAKES 32 CROISSANTS

To make this recipe, you will have to stash away an extra batch of croissants because these almond pastries are traditionally made with the leftovers of the day. Imagine flaky, buttery pastries filled with sweet almond cream, then sandwiched, slathered with more almond cream, and dipped into sliced almonds. During baking, the sliced almonds become golden brown and the almond cream melts into the croissant. If you ever want to taste a little bit of heaven, you can stop right here.

AT A GLANCE

PANS: Rimmed cookie sheets
PAN PREP: Line with parchment
OVEN TEMP: 400°F
BAKING TIME: 10 minutes
DIFFICULTY: ♨ ♨ ♨

ALMOND PASTRY CREAM

1½ cups blanched almonds

1 cup granulated sugar

1 cup (2 sticks) unsalted butter, slightly firm

1 cup (9 ounces) soft almond paste, shredded

3 large eggs

1 teaspoon pure almond extract

1 cup Pastry Cream (page 187)

½ cup sliced almonds

32 baked croissants, preferably day-old

Powdered sugar, for dusting

MAKE THE ALMOND PASTRY CREAM

1. Combine the blanched almonds and ¼ cup of the granulated sugar in the work bowl of a food processor fitted with a steel blade. Pulse for about 20 seconds, or until the almonds are ground extremely fine. Set aside.

2. In the bowl of an electric mixer fitted with the paddle attachment, mix the butter on medium speed until softened and light in color, about 2 minutes. Add the almond paste and continue to mix for 3 minutes. Add the eggs and almond extract, and mix for 30 seconds, or until well combined.

3. Add the pastry cream and mix until blended. Add the ground almonds and remaining ¾ cup sugar. Mix for 30 seconds longer. Set aside. This can be made up to 3 days ahead and refrigerated. Bring to room temperature before using.

ASSEMBLE THE CROISSANTS

4. Position the racks in the upper and lower thirds of the oven. Heat the oven to 400°F. Line rimmed cookie sheets with baking parchment.

5. Place the sliced almonds into a shallow pie pan and set aside.

6. Using a serrated bread knife, carefully slice the baked croissants lengthwise. Spread 2 tablespoons of the almond pastry cream onto the bottom half of the croissant. Replace the top of the croissant and spread 1 tablespoon of the almond pastry cream on the top of the croissant. Dip the tops of the croissants into the sliced almonds and place on parchment-lined baking pans.

7. Bake the filled croissants for 10 minutes. Remove from the oven and place on a cooling rack. Let stand 10 minutes, then dust the croissants with powdered sugar. Serve warm.

STORAGE: No need to store these . . . you'll eat them right away! However, any leftovers should be refrigerated, tightly wrapped in aluminum foil, for up to 1 day (see "Refreshing Yeasted Coffee Cakes," page 213).

chocolate pecan sugar-crusted snails

MAKES 16 SNAILS

These irresistible pastries are made with triangles of croissant dough spread with a layer of chocolate pastry cream and chopped pecans. After the snails are formed, they are brushed with egg wash and finished with crunchy sparkling white sugar and more pecans. Bring out a cup of java and enjoy!

AT A GLANCE
PANS: Rimmed cookie sheets
PAN PREP: Line with parchment
RISING TIME: 1 to 1½ hours
OVEN TEMP: 350°F
BAKING TIME: 28 to 30 minutes
DIFFICULTY: ♨ ♨ ♨

CHOCOLATE PASTRY CREAM

½ cup milk

¼ cup granulated sugar

¾ teaspoon freshly grated navel orange zest
2 large egg yolks

1 tablespoon cornstarch

Pinch of salt

1 (3.5-ounce) bar fine-quality bittersweet chocolate, such as Lindt, finely chopped

½ teaspoon pure vanilla extract

½ recipe Dough for Flaky Croissants (page 240)

1 large egg lightly beaten with 1 teaspoon water, for egg wash

1 cup medium-chopped toasted pecans (see pages 391–392)

¼ cup milk, for brushing snails

3 tablespoons sparkling sugar (see page 380), for finishing

MAKE THE PASTRY CREAM

1. Place the milk, 1 tablespoon of the granulated sugar, and the orange zest in a small saucepan and stir to combine.

2. In a small bowl, whisk the egg yolks until light in color. Add the remaining sugar, 1 tablespoon at a time, and whisk until incorporated. Blend in the cornstarch and salt.

3. Heat the milk to just below the boil. Stir one-third of the hot milk into the egg/sugar mixture and stir with a whisk to combine. Pour the egg mixture back into the saucepan and stir with a whisk. Return the pan to medium-low heat and bring to a slow boil, whisking *rapidly and constantly*, until the pastry cream is thick and smooth. Scrape the crease of the pan to incorporate any unblended pastry cream and whisk again. Remove from the heat and sprinkle the chopped chocolate over the top. Gently press the chocolate into the pastry cream and let it stand a few minutes. Stir gently with a whisk until the chocolate is melted and the mixture is smooth. Add the vanilla. Butter a strip of plastic wrap and place it directly on top of the pastry cream. Set aside to cool.

SHAPE THE DOUGH

4. Dab the corners of rimmed cookie sheets with butter, line with baking parchment, and set aside. On a cold, lightly floured work surface, divide the dough in half using a dough scraper. Working with half at a time, roll the dough into a long strip. (See "About Brioche, Croissants, and Danish," page 229.) Angle the bottom right-hand corner outwards and the upper left-hand corner outwards to form a parallelogram measuring 16 × 8 inches, with the 16-inch side parallel to the counter (see illustration, page 241). This will enable you to shape the snails without wasting the ends. Pierce the dough with a fork at 1-inch intervals to prevent it from shrinking.

5. Spread half of the chocolate pastry cream evenly over the dough, leaving a ½-inch border at the top and bottom. Brush the top and bottom edges with egg wash. Sprinkle with 6 tablespoons of the pecans, and press them lightly into the pastry cream.

6. Lay a ruler against the long side of the dough closest to you. Make a slight cut in the dough every 4 inches. You will have three indentations. Lay the ruler against the opposite side and repeat, starting at the left side. With the indentations as a guide, cut the dough into eight triangles, using a pizza cutter or a dough scraper. Starting at the wide end of the triangle, roll the dough, making three complete turns. Place the snail on a prepared pan, *making sure that the tip of the pastry is on the bottom.* Gently press the ends of the pastry toward the center to "plump" the shape. Do not curl the ends to form a crescent shape. Repeat with the remaining half of the dough.

7. Brush the tops and sides of the snails lightly with milk and place in a warmish spot to rise until puffy and almost doubled, 1 to 1½ hours. Brush the snails again with the milk 2 or 3 times during the rising time.

BAKE THE SNAILS

8. Fifteen minutes before baking, position the racks in the upper and lower third of the oven. Heat the oven to 350°F. Gently brush the tops of the snails with the egg wash, working from the bottom of the pastry upward. *Do not drip the wash onto the baking sheets.* Sprinkle with the remaining nuts and sparkling sugar, and bake for 28 to 30 minutes. Remove from the oven and place on racks to cool.

STORAGE: Store at room temperature, tightly wrapped in aluminum foil, for up to 3 days. Reheat before serving. These pastries may be frozen (see "Refreshing Yeasted Coffee Cakes," page 213).

flaky apple and cherry puffs

MAKES 16 PUFFS

Here we have a filling made with fresh Golden Delicious apples, dried cherries, and sugar sautéed in butter until the apples are caramelized. A medley of spices and a few splashes of Calvados liqueur enhance the flavor. This sophisticated combo is spread in a strip on a rectangle of buttery croissant dough. If you want a memorable ending for your next New Year's Day brunch, these are the pastries to serve.

AT A GLANCE
PANS: Rimmed cookie sheets
PAN PREP: Line with parchment
RISING TIME: 45 to 60 minutes
OVEN TEMP: 400°/350°F
BAKING TIME: 10 minutes/10 to 12 minutes
DIFFICULTY: 🍶 🍶 🍶

APPLE FILLING

3 tablespoons unsalted butter

2 pounds (about 4 large) Golden Delicious apples, peeled, halved, cored, and sliced across the stem end into ¼-inch-thick slices

½ cup dried cherries (not organic)

½ cup granulated sugar

1 teaspoon ground cinnamon

½ teaspoon ground ginger

¼ teaspoon ground nutmeg

⅛ teaspoon ground allspice

3 to 4 grindings fresh black pepper

1 tablespoon fresh lemon juice

2 tablespoons Calvados, applejack, or Kirsch

½ recipe dough for Flaky Croissants (page 240)

¼ cup milk, for brushing puffs

1 large egg lightly beaten with 1 teaspoon water, for egg wash

Powdered sugar, for dusting

MAKE THE APPLE FILLING

1. In a heavy 10-inch sauté pan, melt the butter over low heat. Add the apples, cherries, granulated sugar, cinnamon, ginger, nutmeg, allspice, and black pepper. Sauté the mixture on medium-low heat until the apples are soft, translucent, and caramelized, 20 to 25 minutes. Remove from the heat and add the lemon juice and liqueur. Set aside to cool completely.

SHAPE THE DOUGH

2. Dab the corners of rimmed cookie sheets with butter and line with baking parchment. Set aside. On a lightly floured, cold work surface, using a dough scraper, cut the block of dough in half. Working with one piece at a time, roll the dough into a

10×12-inch rectangle, keeping the 12-inch side parallel to the edge of the work surface. (See "About Brioche, Croissants, and Danish," page 229.) Pierce the dough several times with a fork at 1-inch intervals to prevent it from shrinking. Using a pizza cutter, cut the dough into eight 3×5-inch rectangles. Working with one piece of dough at a time, stretch each piece back to a 3×5-inch rectangle.

3. Working with one piece at a time, spoon 2 tablespoons of the filling in a strip, centering it across the 3-inch side of dough. Brush the far edge with the egg wash. Bring the opposite edge over the filling, then overlap it with the egg-washed edge. Pinch the seam well and place the pastry, *seam side down* on a prepared pan. Repeat with the remaining half of the dough.

4. Brush the tops and sides of the croissants lightly with milk and place in a warmish spot to rise until almost doubled, 45 to 60 minutes. Brush the croissants again with the milk 1 or 2 times during rising time.

BAKE THE PUFFS

5. Fifteen minutes before baking, position the racks in the upper and lower third of the oven. Heat the oven to 400°F. Gently brush the tops of the croissants with the egg wash, working from the bottom of the croissant upward. *Do not drip the wash onto the baking sheets.* Bake the croissants for 10 minutes, then *reduce the oven temperature to 350°F and* continue to bake for 10 to 12 minutes, or until golden brown. To ensure even browning, toward the end of baking time, rotate the pans top to bottom and front to back.

6. Remove from the oven and place on racks to cool. Loosen the pastries on the pan and cool for 20 minutes. *Note:* If any of the filling has run out of the ends of the pastries, take a small spatula and slide it back into the puffs. Dust with powdered sugar before serving.

STORAGE: Store at room temperature, tightly wrapped in aluminum foil, for up to 3 days. Reheat before serving. These croissants may be frozen (see "Refreshing Yeasted Coffee Cakes," page 213).

croissant pockets with apricots and brie

MAKES 16 POCKETS

Here we have rectangles of dough that have a spread of brown sugar, butter, and walnuts, applied in a strip down the center. On top of the spread is a spoonful of brandied apricots and a slice of Brie. At this point, these pastries can be made ahead and refrigerated overnight, or frozen unbaked (see "Freezing Yeasted Doughs," page 225) for later use. When the pockets are baked, the melted cheese blends with the apricots, brown sugar, and buttery pastry.

AT A GLANCE
PANS: Rimmed cookie sheets
PAN PREP: Line with parchment
RISING TIME: 45 to 60 minutes
OVEN TEMP: 400°/350°F
BAKING TIME: 10 minutes/10 to 12 minutes
DIFFICULTY: 🍶 🍶

FILLING

**9 ounces dried apricots (not organic; 1 full cup),
 cut into quarters**

1 cup water

2 tablespoons granulated sugar

1 to 2 tablespoons brandy

**½ cup toasted broken walnuts (see pages
 391–392)**

**4 tablespoons (½ stick) unsalted butter,
 softened**

6 tablespoons light brown sugar

½ recipe dough for Flaky Croissants (page 240)

**8 ounces *ripe* Brie cheese, cold, cut into
 ¼-inch-thick slices, 3 inches long**

**1 large egg lightly beaten with 1 teaspoon
 water, for egg wash**

¼ cup milk, for brushing pockets

Powdered sugar, for dusting

MAKE THE FILLING

1. In a small saucepan, combine the apricots and water. Bring to a simmer and cover. Cook for 20 to 25 minutes, or until a little liquid remains. The fruit should be soft. Drain the apricots, reserving the liquid that remains.

2. Return the liquid to the pan and add the granulated sugar and 1 to 2 tablespoons of brandy. Over medium-low heat, cook the liquid until the sugar is melted and the alcohol is evaporated. Remove from the heat and add the apricots to the pan. Stir gently to coat the fruit with the syrup. Set aside to cool. Combine the walnuts with the cooled apricot mixture.

3. In a medium bowl, combine the soft butter and brown sugar with a wooden spoon, stirring until a smooth paste is formed. Set aside.

SHAPE THE DOUGH

4. On a lightly floured, cold work surface, using a dough scraper, cut the dough in half. Working with one piece at a time, roll the dough into a 10 × 12-inch rectangle, keeping the 12-inch side parallel to the edge of the work surface. (See "About Brioche,

recipe continues

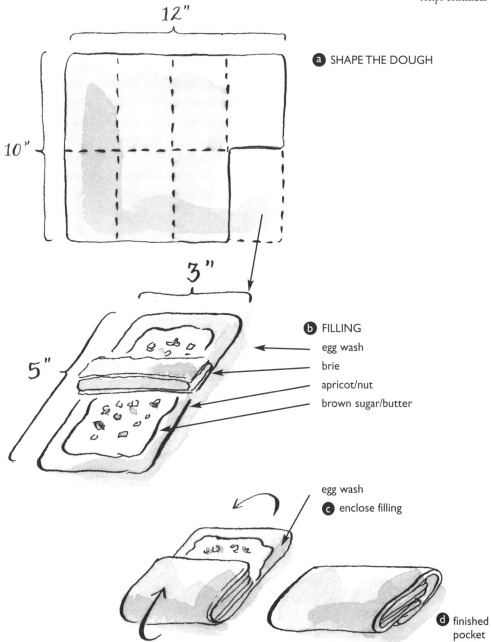

12"

10"

a SHAPE THE DOUGH

3"

5"

b FILLING
egg wash
brie
apricot/nut
brown sugar/butter

egg wash
c enclose filling

d finished pocket

continued from previous page

Croissants, and Danish," page 229.) Pierce the surface of the dough several times with a fork to prevent shrinkage. Using a pastry cutter or a pizza wheel, cut the dough into eight pieces.

5. Working with one piece of dough at a time, gently reshape the dough into a 3 × 5-inch rectangle. Spread a generous teaspoon of the brown sugar/butter mixture in a strip down the center of the 3-inch side of the rectangle. Place a slightly full tablespoon of the apricot/nut mixture over the brown sugar/butter strip. Place a slice of cheese over the apricot mixture. *Do not overfill.* (See illustration b, page 255.)

6. Brush the far edge of the dough with egg wash. Bring the opposite edge over the filling to enclose it, then overlap it with the egg-washed edge. Gently pinch the seam, leaving the sides open, and place the pocket seam side down on a parchment-lined baking pan. Repeat with the remaining dough. Brush the tops and sides of the croissants lightly with milk and place in a warmish spot to rise until almost doubled, 45 to 60 minutes. Brush the croissants again with the milk 2 or 3 times during rising time.

BAKE THE POCKETS

7. Fifteen minutes before baking, position the racks in the upper and lower third of the oven. Heat the oven to 400°F. Gently brush the tops of the pastries with the egg wash, working from the bottom of the pocket upward. *Do not drip the egg wash onto the baking sheets.* Bake for 10 minutes, then *reduce the oven temperature to 350°F* and continue to bake for 10 to 12 minutes, or until golden brown. To ensure even browning, toward the end of baking time, rotate the pans top to bottom and front to back.

8. Remove from the oven and place on racks to cool. Loosen the pastries on the pan and cool for 20 minutes. *Note:* If any of the filling has run out of the ends of the pockets, take a small spatula and slide it back into the pockets. Dust with powdered sugar before serving.

STORAGE: Store in the refrigerator, tightly wrapped in aluminum foil, for up to 3 days. Reheat before serving. These pastries may be frozen (see "Refreshing Yeasted Coffee Cakes," page 213).

CLASSIC DANISH PASTRIES

I was introduced to real Danish pastry when I accompanied my husband on numerous business trips to Denmark. This was not the same type of Danish as we see in the United States. When I tasted my first piece, the layers of buttery dough with its subtle background of almonds left me needing to find out how to prepare this extraordinary treat.

Through the contacts of culinary friends several years ago, I was led to Gunner Pedersen's Patisserie in the suburbs of Copenhagen, where I spent a week in the kitchen of the pastry shop. Mr. Pedersen and all of the bakers were elderly gentlemen whom I am sure are no longer with us. They took me under their wing, and in this intimate atmosphere allowed me to learn. On Friday afternoon, when I was ready to depart, Mr. Pedersen handed me an envelope and warmly smiled. He told me that in the envelope was the formula for his Danish. I took a deep breath and felt that I had just found the combination to Fort Knox.

The following recipes are my adaptation of the many varieties of Danish that were prepared in the pastry shop. When it's Danish time, I put aside two days for preparation. The first day, I make my dough along with the spreads and fillings. The second day is put aside for shaping, baking, and the best part—eating.

When preparing Danish dough, as well as all butter-layered (laminated) pastry dough, you shape the mixture into a large block. Calculate the quantity of dough you need to make a recipe by determining how the block is divided. For example, a half of a block of dough (½ recipe) is needed for the Grandmother's Cake (page 267), while at times only a quarter of a block of dough (¼ recipe) is used for individual pastries like Apricot Twists (page 281). I determine ahead of time what kind of pastries I want to make using the full block, and prepare my spreads and fillings accordingly.

Another advantage in making Danish pastries is that the dough and many of the spreads and fillings freeze extremely well; therefore, unshaped dough and leftover preparations can easily be stored for later use. The only two fillings that cannot be frozen are the Pastry Cream for Danish (page 261) and the Sweet Butter Spread (page 262).

When I make Danish, I find it easier to bake the entire block of dough. From this, I can make a variety of pastries and freeze some for later use. It's a terrific feeling to know that I can go to my freezer and choose one of these fabulous pastries, completely baked and ready for serving. After thawing in the oven, the warmed Danish is ready to eat.

danish pastry dough

MAKES ABOUT 3¾ POUNDS OF DOUGH

PLAN AHEAD: Refrigerate overnight

BUTTER

1¼ pounds (5 sticks) unsalted butter, slightly
firm (see the sidebar on page 245)

¼ cup unbleached all-purpose flour

DOUGH

⅓ cup warm water (110° to 115°F)

⅓ cup plus 1 teaspoon sugar

2 packages active dry yeast

5 cups unbleached all-purpose flour, spooned in
and leveled

1½ teaspoons salt

2 tablespoons unsalted butter, very soft

3 large eggs, cold, lightly beaten

1 cup ice water

PREPARE THE BLOCK OF BUTTER

1. Criss-cross two 18-inch strips of plastic wrap in an 8 × 8 × 2-inch metal or aluminum foil baking pan and set aside.

Stand Mixer Method

2. Place the butter and flour in the bowl of an electric mixer fitted with the paddle attachment. Mix on medium speed for 10 to 15 seconds, or just until the butter is smooth. If the butter accumulates around the paddle, increase the speed to medium-high for the last few seconds to release it. Do not overmix or the butter will become too soft.

Hand Method

2. Place the butter in a large stainless steel mixing bowl. Sprinkle the flour over the butter. Using one hand for kneading and one to hold the bowl, work the flour into the butter by raking your fingers through the mixture. Continue working the flour and butter together until the mixture is smooth and malleable. At first the butter may stick to your hand, but as it is worked, eventually it will release almost cleanly.

3. Empty the mixture into the prepared baking pan, first spooning a mound of butter into each corner. Enclose the mixture in the plastic wrap and press it until the entire pan is covered. Smooth the top as best you can with the palm of your hand or the bottom of a glass. Be sure the block is even thickness. Refrigerate while you prepare the dough.

MAKE THE DOUGH

4. Rinse a small bowl in hot water to warm it. Add the warm water and stir in 1 teaspoon of the sugar. Sprinkle the yeast over the water. *Do not stir.* Cover the bowl with a saucer and let the mixture stand for 5 minutes. Stir it briefly with a fork, cover again, and let it stand for 2 to 3 minutes more, or until bubbly.

Stand Mixer Method

5. In the bowl of an electric mixer fitted with the paddle attachment, mix on low speed the 5 cups of flour, remaining ⅓ cup sugar, and the salt. Add the 2 tablespoons soft butter and continue to mix for 30 seconds, or until the butter forms meal-size pieces. In a medium bowl, combine the eggs and ice water. With the mixer off, add the liquids to the flour. Stir down the yeast and add it to the bowl as well. On medium speed, mix the ingredients for 45 to 60 seconds, scraping down the side of the bowl frequently. Mix just until a rough dough is formed. *Do not overmix.*

Hand Method

5. Place the 5 cups of flour, remaining ⅓ cup sugar, and the salt in a large bowl. Stir with a whisk to blend. Work in the 2 tablespoons of soft butter with a pastry blender until meal-size pieces are formed. In a medium bowl, combine the eggs and ice water. Make a well in the center of the flour and pour in the liquids. Stir down the yeast and pour it into the well. Using a large wooden spoon, combine the liquids and gradually incorporate the dry ingredients, working the mixture just until a rough dough is formed.

6. Place the dough on a lightly floured work surface and knead it briefly five or six times, or just until smooth.

ENCASE THE BUTTER IN THE DOUGH

7. Have ready a rimmed cookie sheet lined with baking parchment. Remove the butter from the refrigerator and check the firmness. *It must be the same consistency as the*

recipe continues

continued from previous page

dough. (See "Preparing Butter for Croissant and Danish Dough," page 245.) Place the dough on a lightly floured, cool work surface and with a floured rolling pin, roll it into a 10 × 18-inch rectangle, with the 10-inch side parallel to the edge of the counter.

8. Center the block of butter on the dough. Bring the lower portion of dough up and over to the middle of the butter, then fold the upper portion over to cover the remaining butter, firmly pinching the seam together. You will have a 1- to 2-inch margin of dough on the right and left side. With your thumb, press these edges thoroughly together to seal them. Flour the rolling surface. Give the dough a quarter-turn to your right. With crossed hands, press the top to flatten it and even the edges with a dough scraper as best you can. Roll the dough into a 12 × 22-inch rectangle. As the dough is rolled, flip it over once or twice. Remove any excess flour with a soft brush. Fold the dough into thirds, letter style, pressing it with your hand. Stretch the edges to square them. With crossed hands, press the rectangle of dough to seal the layers. Place the dough on the prepared pan and reshape it into a rectangle. Cover it with another piece of parchment. Refrigerate for 15 to 20 minutes. You have now completed the first turn.

9. Remove the dough from the refrigerator, reflour the rolling surface, and turn the dough so the open seam is to your right. Roll the dough into a strip measuring 12 × 22 inches, flipping it over as needed. Remove any excess flour with a soft brush. Fold the dough again, letter style as directed above. Be sure to even the edges with a dough scraper. With one hand on top of the other, press the block of dough six or eight times to slightly flatten it. You have now completed your second turn. Cover with parchment and refrigerate for another 15 to 20 minutes.

10. For the third and final turn, remove the dough from the refrigerator, reflour the rolling surface, and place dough with the open seam to your right. Roll the dough into a 12 × 22-inch strip, flipping it over as needed. Fold the dough letter style as indicated above, brushing away any excess flour and evening the edges. Cut two long strips of plastic wrap and lay them side by side to form a large rectangle. Place the dough in the center and wrap it well to ensure that it is entirely covered. Set the dough on a cookie sheet and refrigerate it overnight. (If you wish to freeze the dough, be sure to deflate it first [see "Freezing Yeasted Doughs," page 225]. Thaw in the refrigerator for 24 hours before shaping.)

STORAGE: This dough will keep for up to 3 days in the refrigerator. The dough may be frozen (see "Refreshing Yeasted Coffee Cakes," page 213).

pastry cream for danish

Here is a versatile pastry cream that is used in many ways in the preparation of classic Danish pastries. A small amount is necessary in the preparation of the Sweet Butter Spread (page 262), and additional amounts are used in some of the recipes. Refer to the individual recipes to determine the amount you need. Note that the amount of pastry cream called for will always take into account the amount needed to make the Sweet Butter Spread.

If any pastry cream is left over, it is fabulous as a filling for cake layers, ready-made sponge shortcake cups, or simply as a vanilla pudding topped with fresh fruit.

SMALL RECIPE	LARGE RECIPE
MAKES 1 GENEROUS CUP	MAKES 2 GENEROUS CUPS
1 cup light cream	**2 cups light cream**
2 large egg yolks	**4 large egg yolks**
2 tablespoons sugar	**¼ cup sugar**
2 tablespoons cornstarch	**¼ cup cornstarch**
¾ teaspoon pure vanilla extract	**1½ teaspoons pure vanilla extract**

1. Place the cream in a heavy 3-quart saucepan and heat on medium-low to just below a simmer. Whisk the yolks together in a large bowl. Gradually whisk in the sugar, beating until well blended and the mixture lightens in color. Blend in the cornstarch.

2. Stir one-third of the hot cream into the egg mixture, stirring constantly with a whisk to blend the mixtures. Pour the egg/cream mixture into the saucepan and combine with the remaining hot cream, blending well.

3. Cook the mixture over low heat, stirring constantly with the whisk until it comes to a boil and is thick and smooth. Simmer for about 30 seconds, moving the mixture gently around the edge of the pan with a heatproof spatula to prevent scorching. Remove the pan from the heat and gently stir in the vanilla.

4. Strain the pastry cream through a fine sieve into a clean bowl and place a piece of buttered plastic wrap on the surface to keep a skin from forming. Chill completely until ready to use.

STORAGE: Leftover pastry cream will keep for up to 3 days in the refrigerator. This filling may not be frozen.

sweet butter spread

<table>
<tr><td>

SMALL RECIPE

MAKES ½ CUP

¼ cup (½ stick) unsalted butter, at room
   temperature

2 tablespoons sugar

¼ cup chilled Pastry Cream for Danish
   (page 261)

⅛ teaspoon pure almond extract

</td><td>

LARGE RECIPE

MAKES 1 CUP

½ cup (1 stick) unsalted butter, at room
   temperature

¼ cup sugar

½ cup chilled Pastry Cream for Danish
   (page 261)

¼ teaspoon pure almond extract

</td></tr>
</table>

In a small bowl, using a wooden spoon, mix the butter and sugar until smooth. Blend in the pastry cream and almond extract. Set aside or refrigerate for up to 3 days. (This filling may not be frozen.)

soft almond filling

MAKES ABOUT 1¼ CUPS

<table>
<tr><td>

½ cup (1 stick) unsalted butter, at room
   temperature

6 tablespoons sugar

</td><td>

½ cup (5 ounces) grated *soft* almond paste

½ teaspoon pure almond extract

</td></tr>
</table>

In a small bowl, using a wooden spoon, mix the butter and sugar until the mixture is smooth. Gradually add the grated almond paste, blending the mixtures until thoroughly smooth. Blend in the almond extract. Set aside or refrigerate for up to 2 weeks, or freeze for up to 3 months.

"American Danish can be doughy, heavy, sticky . . . and is usually wrapped in cellophane.
Danish Danish is light, crisp, buttery . . . it is seldom wrapped in anything but loving care."

R. W. APPLE, JR.

firm almond filling

MAKES ABOUT 1 ¼ CUPS

⅓ cup sugar

1 ¼ cups whole unblanched almonds, toasted
   (see page 391) and cooled

1 large egg

½ teaspoon pure almond extract

Place the sugar and nuts in the bowl of a food processor fitted with the steel blade. Pulse until the nuts are finely chopped. Add the egg and almond extract, and process until the mixture forms a mass. *Do not overprocess*, or the paste will become too soft. Set aside or refrigerate for up to 3 days, or freeze for up to 3 months.

dry nut mix

MAKES ½ CUP

½ cup sliced unblanched almonds

1 tablespoon sugar

¼ teaspoon pure vanilla extract

Place the ingredients in the bowl of a food processor fitted with the steel blade. Pulse the mixture 4 to 5 times, or until the nuts are finely chopped. Set aside or refrigerate for up to 1 month, or freeze for up to 3 months.

egg wash for danish

1 large egg

⅛ teaspoon salt

In a small bowl, lightly beat the egg and salt together with a fork. Refrigerate until needed. To apply, lightly brush on dough as recipe directs. Leftover egg wash should be discarded.

sugar syrup for danish

MAKES ABOUT ½ CUP

Sugar syrup is applied to Danish immediately after the pastry is removed from the oven. A brushing of the hot syrup should sizzle and caramelize as it touches the top of the pastry, leaving a beautiful professional shine.

½ cup water

¼ cup granulated sugar

Combine the water and sugar in a small saucepan. Bring to a slow boil, then lower the heat and simmer for 2 to 3 minutes, stirring as needed to dissolve the sugar on the bottom of the pot. Set aside. Use as recipe directs. This syrup should be applied when it is hot with a pastry brush. Discard remaining syrup.

cheese filling for danish

MAKES ABOUT 1½ CUPS

8 ounces cream cheese, at room temperature

4 ounces farmer cheese, at room temperature

⅓ cup sugar

1 large egg yolk

1½ tablespoons all-purpose flour

1 tablespoon sour cream

1 teaspoon fresh lemon juice

½ teaspoon greshly grated lemon zest

½ teaspoon pure vanilla extract

⅛ teaspoon pure almond extract

Place a food mill over a large bowl and sieve the cream cheese and farmer cheese through the mill. (Alternatively, the cheese may be pressed through a potato ricer or a large gauge strainer.) This ensures a smooth and creamy filling. Add the remaining ingredients and mix until smooth. Chill for at least 1 hour before using.

STORAGE: Leftover filling should be refrigerated in a tightly covered container for up to 3 days, or frozen for up to 3 months. It can be used as a filling for cheese blintzes.

prune filling for danish

MAKES ABOUT 1 CUP

¾ cup pitted prunes, lightly packed

½ cup water

¼ cup navel orange juice

3 tablespoons sugar

½ ounce bittersweet chocolate, finely chopped

½ teaspoon grated navel orange zest

½ teaspoon vanilla extract

Pinch of salt

1½ tablespoons unsalted butter, at room temperature

2 teaspoons Grand Marnier liqueur

1. Combine the prunes, water, orange juice, and sugar in a small, heavy pan. Bring the mixture to a boil, lower the heat, and simmer, covered, for about 30 minutes, or until the prunes are very soft. If the prunes are still not tender, if needed, add a bit more water and continue to cook until they are very soft. Remove the pan from the heat and whip with a fork until the mixture is fairly smooth.

2. Add the chocolate, orange zest, vanilla, salt, butter, and Grand Marnier, stirring with a fork to combine. Set aside to cool to room temperature.

STORAGE: This filling will keep in the refrigerator for several months, stored in a tightly covered container.

apricot filling for danish

MAKES ⅔ CUP

4 ounces dried apricots (not organic)

⅓ cup water

2 tablespoons apricot preserves

¼ to ⅓ cup (lightly packed) light brown sugar

¼ teaspoon almond extract

Place the apricots, water, and preserves in a small, heavy saucepan. Cover and bring to a slow boil on medium-low heat. Simmer for 18 to 20 minutes, or until the apricots are very soft. If the liquid evaporates and the apricots are not ready, add a small amount of water as needed. Stir in the brown sugar and almond extract. Using a fork, mix until the sugar is melted and the mixture is fairly smooth. Set aside to cool before using.

pineapple filling for danish

MAKES 1⅓ CUPS

2 (8-ounce) cans crushed pineapple, packed in natural juice

¼ cup sugar

2 tablespoons cornstarch

Pinch of salt

2 tablespoons unsalted butter

1 teaspoon freshly grated lemon zest

1 teaspoon freshly grated orange zest

1 teaspoon lemon juice

1. Drain the pineapple well in a strainer placed over a bowl. Reserve the pineapple juice.

2. In a 3-quart saucepan, whisk together the sugar, cornstarch, and salt. Slowly whisk in the reserved pineapple juice, mixing until smooth. Over medium-low heat, bring the mixture to a slow boil, stirring constantly with a wooden spoon until it is smooth and thickened. Simmer for 1 minute longer.

3. Remove from the heat and add the crushed pineapple, butter, lemon and orange zests, and lemon juice. Stir gently until the butter is melted. *Do not overmix.* Let cool before using.

STORAGE: Remaining filling can be refrigerated in a tightly covered container for up to 1 week. It can be used as a topping for ice cream.

grandmother's cake

MAKES FOUR 14-INCH STRIPS, 6 TO 8 SERVINGS PER STRIP, OR TWO 10½-INCH RINGS, 10 TO 12 SERVINGS
PER RING

This cake, known as Oldemorstang in Denmark, is one of
the most popular of all Danish pastries. For this classic cake,
a long strip of Danish dough filled with pastry cream and a
tasty soft almond filling is shaped into a large rectangle and
placed on a rimmed cookie sheet. After baking, the cake is cut
into pieces in the middle rather than at the corners. This gives
four elbow-shaped cakes similar to the letter L.

AT A GLANCE
PANS: Two 12 x 18-inch rimmed cookie sheets *or*
two 11-inch tart pans with removable bottoms
PAN PREP: Line cookie sheets with parchment or
generously butter tart pans
RISING TIME: 20 minutes
OVEN TEMP: 425°/375°F
BAKING TIME: 10 minutes/15 to 18 minutes
DIFFICULTY: 🥄 🥄 🥄

For my American version, I form the dough into strips
and bake them free-form on rimmed cookie sheets. I also like to bake the pastry in a tart pan. When
unmolded, the pastry looks beautiful. Whether you form strips or a ring, this recipe is perfect to make for
buffet service. It slices easily and will make you look like a pro. Wouldn't Grandma be proud?

½ recipe Danish Pastry Dough (page 258)

1 small recipe Pastry Cream for Danish (page
261); use ¼ cup to make the Sweet Butter
Spread

1 small recipe Sweet Butter Spread (page 262)

Soft Almond Filling (page 262)

Dry Nut Mix (page 263)

3 tablespoons currants, plumped (see page 389)

Egg Wash for Danish (page 263)

¼ cup sliced unblanched almonds, lightly
crushed

1 tablespoon sparkling sugar (see page 380)

Sugar Syrup for Danish (page 264)

1 large recipe Vanilla Glaze (page 359)

1. Line two 12 × 18-inch rimmed cookie sheets with baking parchment or generously butter two 11-inch tart pans with removable bottoms and set aside. Divide the
dough in half. On a lightly floured work surface, working with one piece at a time, roll
the dough into a long strip approximately 24 × 8 inches. Prick the dough at 1-inch
intervals with a fork to prevent it from shrinking.

2. Using a small offset spatula, spread half of the butter spread in a 3-inch strip
down the center of the dough.

3. Fit a 14-inch pastry bag with a large no. 805 plain round decorating tube. Empty
the pastry cream into the bag and pipe a strip of the cream slightly off center down
the length of the dough. *recipe continues*

continued from previous page

4. Fit another 14-inch pastry bag with a large no. 805 plain round decorating tube and fill with almond filling. Pipe a strip of the filling down the length of the dough, placing it next to the pastry cream (they should touch). Sprinkle the strip with half of the nut mixture and half of the currants.

5. Using a dough scraper or a pizza wheel, slash or cut each side of the strip on the diagonal at 1½-inch intervals, cutting almost to the butter spread. Lightly brush the edges of the strip with egg wash. Enclose the filling by alternating the pieces of slashed dough, overlapping them loosely over the filling. It's okay for some of the filling to show. (Refer to the illustration for Woven Apricot-Almond Strip, page 199, noting that your strip will be 24 inches long instead of 12 inches long and you will make eighteen slashes, not nine.)

To Make Strips

6. With a dough scraper, divide the long strip in half, reshaping the cut ends as best you can. Carefully lift the strips onto the sheet pan and tuck the ends under. Cover the pan with a tea towel and set in a warmish place to rise for 20 minutes, or just until puffy. It should not double in size. Prepare the second half of dough while the cake is rising.

To Make a Ring

7. Place the entire strip of dough in the tart pan, carefully lifting the pastry with the palms of your hands. It is best to ease your hands toward the center of the strip, allowing the remainder to rest on each arm. Transfer the strip to the pan, stretching it until the ends meet, leaving a 4½-inch space in the center of the ring. Join the ends by overlapping them and lightly press the seam with the side of your hand to seal it. Butter a 1-inch strip around the outer rim of an 8-ounce custard cup, and place it inverted into the space to help the ring keep its shape during baking. (See illustration for Swedish Tea Ring, page 173.) Reshape the dough around the custard cup, pressing it with your fingers. Cover the pan with a tea towel and set in a warmish place to rise for 20 minutes, or just until puffy. It should not double in size. Prepare the second half of the dough while the cake is rising.

8. Position the rack in the middle of the oven. Heat the oven to 425°F. Brush the tops of the cakes with egg wash and sprinkle with half of the sliced almonds and half of the sparkling sugar. If using tart pans, before baking place them on pieces of heavy-

duty foil, bringing the sides up to catch any leakage. Bake for 10 minutes, then *reduce the heat* to 375°F. Continue baking for 15 to 18 minutes, or until golden brown. *Note: All of the cakes will not be baked at the same time due to the difference in preparation and rising times.* While the cakes are baking, prepare the sugar syrup and glaze.

9. Remove the cakes from the oven and *immediately* brush the surface with hot sugar syrup. The syrup should sizzle as the tops of the cakes are brushed. While still warm, spread the edges of the cakes lightly with the Vanilla Glaze, applying it with the back of a tablespoon. The glaze will harden as it dries.

STORAGE: Store at room temperature, tightly wrapped in aluminum foil, for up to 3 days. These cakes may be frozen (see "Refreshing Yeasted Coffee Cakes," page 213).

danish almond cake

While working at Gunner Pedersen's pastry shop in Copenhagen, I realized that this coffee cake was one of the more unusual being made. A disk of dough placed in an aluminum foil pie plate has a ring of pastry cream piped over the surface. Filled spirals of dough are arranged over the cream, and the edge of the pastry disk is lifted to partially cover the spirals. After baking, the centers of the risen spirals

> **AT A GLANCE**
> **PANS:** Two 8-inch aluminum foil pie pans/1 medium muffin tin/1 rimmed baking sheet
> **PAN PREP:** Line ungreased muffin tin with paper cupcake liners
> **RISING TIME:** 30 minutes
> **OVEN TEMP:** 425°/375°F
> **BAKING TIME:** 10 minutes/15 to 20 minutes
> **DIFFICULTY:** 🥣 🥣 🥣

are topped with a spoonful of vanilla glaze. I usually have three extra spirals from each log, so keep a muffin tin handy. I like to use the end pieces for the muffins because they are not as plump. You will find the disposable pie plate is especially convenient for gift giving or traveling. Here is my adaptation of Mr. Pedersen's delicious creation. I hope you like this cake as much as I do.

½ **recipe Danish Pastry Dough (page 258)**

1 **small recipe Pastry Cream for Danish (page 261); use** ¼ **cup to make the Sweet Butter Spread**

1 **small recipe Sweet Butter Spread (page 262)**

Firm Almond Filling (page 263)

Dry Nut Mix (page 263)

Egg Wash for Danish (page 263)

2 **tablespoons sliced unblanched almonds, lightly crushed**

2 **teaspoons sparkling sugar (see page 380)**

Sugar Syrup for Danish (page 264)

1 **small recipe Vanilla Glaze (page 359)**

1. On a lightly floured work surface, divide the dough into quarters. Roll two pieces of the dough into 10-inch circles. Pierce the circles at 1-inch intervals with a fork to prevent the dough from shrinking. Invert a foil pie pan on top of each piece of dough. Using a paring knife, cut a circle of dough ½ inch larger than the edge of the pie pan.

2. Turn two 8-inch aluminum foil pie pans right side up and center the dough in the pans. Using a small offset spatula, spread a scant 2 tablespoons of butter spread across the bottom of each piece of dough. Fit a 14-inch pastry bag with a large no. 805 plain round decorating tube, and empty the pastry cream into the bag. Pipe a circle of the cream around the perimeter of each disk, starting 1 inch from the crease of the pan.

3. On a lightly floured work surface, roll the third piece of dough into a 10 × 9-inch rectangle, with the 10-inch side parallel to the edge of the counter. Pierce the dough lightly with a fork at 1-inch intervals to prevent it from shrinking. Spread 2 *level* table-

spoons of butter spread across the dough, leaving a 1-inch margin at the far end. On a lightly floured work surface, roll half of the firm almond filling into a log about 10 inches long and 1 inch wide.

4. Arrange the log on the 10-inch side of the dough, placing it 1 inch from the bottom edge. Sprinkle the dough with half of the nut mixture. Starting at the side closest to you, roll the dough into a tight cylinder, pinching the seam well. Roll the dough back and forth to smooth the shape. The cylinder should measure about 11 inches.

5. Using a dough scraper or a sharp knife, cut the cylinder into eleven 1-inch slices. Remove three of the end pieces and place them in a muffin tin lined with cupcake liners (see headnote). Arrange seven slices evenly spaced on top of the pastry cream and place one piece in the center. Press all of the slices gently with your fingers until they almost meet. It's okay to have open spaces. Place the remaining three spirals in muffin tins lined with paper cupcake liners, pressing their tops to spread them slightly. Refrigerate the spirals while you prepare the remaining piece of dough.

6. With your fingertips, lift the edge of the pastry circle up and over the spirals to partially cover them. Do not pull the dough too tightly because it will need room to rise. Press around the edge gently with your fingertips to adhere the pastry to the spirals. Cover the pan with a tea towel and set it in a warmish place to rise for 30 minutes or until puffy. The cake will not double in size. While the cake is rising, make the second cake with the remaining dough. After the second cake is shaped, let it rise along with the spirals for 30 minutes or until puffy.

7. Fifteen minutes before baking, position the rack in the middle of the oven. Heat the oven to 425°F. Brush the tops of the cakes and spirals lightly with egg wash and sprinkle them with the sliced almonds and the sparkling sugar. Place the cakes on a rimmed baking sheet and bake for 10 minutes. *Reduce the oven temperature to 375°F and bake for 15 to 20 minutes longer, or until golden brown.* While the cakes are baking, prepare the sugar syrup and glaze. *Note:* After the cakes have baked for 5 minutes, place the spirals in the oven. Bake for 10 to 12 minutes. Refer to Step 8 for finishing.

8. Remove the cakes from the oven and *immediately* brush the tops with *hot* sugar syrup. The syrup should sizzle as the tops of the cakes are brushed. While the cakes are slightly warm, spoon a scant teaspoon of Vanilla Glaze in the center of each spiral, then spread a thin layer of glaze around the edge of the cakes using the back of the spoon.

STORAGE: Store at room temperature, tightly wrapped in aluminum foil, for up to 3 days. This cake may be frozen (see "Refreshing Yeasted Coffee Cakes," page 213).

danish cheese squares

MAKES 24 SQUARES

Cheese and Danish is a combination that can't be beat. Here we have a layer of butter spread beneath a mound of flavorful cheese filling. The mixture is encased in the dough and finished with a center piped with pastry cream. Sliced almonds and large crystals of sugar crown the tops of these irresistible pastries.

> **AT A GLANCE**
> **PANS:** Rimmed cookie sheets
> **PAN PREP:** Line with parchment
> **RISING TIME:** 20 minutes
> **OVEN TEMP:** 425°/375°F
> **BAKING TIME:** 8 minutes/6 to 8 minutes
> **DIFFICULTY:** 🥄 🥄 🥄

½ **recipe Danish Pastry Dough (page 258)**

I small recipe Pastry Cream for Danish (page 261); use ¼ cup to make the Sweet Butter Spread

I small recipe Sweet Butter Spread (page 262)

Cheese Filling for Danish (page 264)

Dry Nut Mix (page 263)

Egg Wash for Danish (page 263)

⅓ **cup sliced unblanched almonds, lightly crushed**

2 tablespoons sparkling sugar (see page 380)

Sugar Syrup for Danish (page 264)

I large recipe Vanilla Glaze

1. Dab the corners of rimmed cookie sheets with butter, line with baking parchment, and set aside. On a lightly floured work surface, divide the dough in half. Working with one piece at a time, roll the pastry into a 12 × 16-inch rectangle. Pierce the dough with a fork at 1-inch intervals to prevent it from shrinking. Using a ruler as a guide, nick the dough at 4-inch intervals along the width and length of the rectangle. Align the ruler on opposite ends of the marks, and cut into squares using a pizza wheel or a sharp knife. Reshape the dough by stretching each piece with your hands until it measures about 4 inches across.

2. Using a small offset spatula, spread the center of each square of dough with 1 teaspoon of butter spread. Place a scant tablespoon of the cheese filling in the center of each square. Sprinkle 1 teaspoon of the nut mixture over the cheese. Dab the corners of the square with egg wash. Bring the corners of the dough to the center, and lightly depress the middle with your thumb to seal the tips. Gently spread the open spaces of the dough apart with your fingertips to expose the filling.

3. Carefully transfer the squares to a prepared pan, reshaping them as needed.

Repeat with the remaining dough. Cover the pans with a tea towel and set in a warmish place to rise for 20 minutes, or just until puffy.

4. Fifteen minutes before baking, position the racks in the upper and lower thirds of the oven. Heat the oven to 425°F. *Gently depress the pastry again in the center with your thumb.* Using a disposable quart-size zip-top bag, make a ½-inch cut across one of the bottom corners. Fill the bag with the pastry cream. Pipe a 1-inch dollop of cream into the center of each square. Lightly brush the tops of the pastries with egg wash and sprinkle each with a few crushed almonds and ¼ teaspoon of sparkling sugar. Bake at 425°F for 8 minutes, then *reduce the oven temperature to 375°F.* Continue baking for 6 to 8 minutes, or until golden brown. While the squares are baking, prepare the sugar syrup and glaze.

5. Remove from the oven and *immediately* brush with *hot* sugar syrup. The syrup should sizzle when the tops of the pastries are brushed. While they are slightly warm, garnish the tops with a small amount of glaze by dipping a fork into the glaze and squiggling it a few times over the pastries.

STORAGE: Cheese squares are best eaten the day they are made. They may be frozen (see "Refreshing Yeasted Coffee Cakes," page 213).

"In busy times, few things make us feel as pampered as a leisurely breakfast with homemade pastries."
JULIA CHILD

danish nut squares

MAKES 24 SQUARES

Danish nut squares, also called spandauers, are one of my personal favorites. Squares of Danish dough are coated with tasty butter spread and then topped with a nugget of chewy almond filling. The nut filling is encased in the dough and topped with a dollop of pastry cream. The Danes often finish these pastries with a touch of currant jelly, which adds just the right amount of color. Crisp on the outside, soft and chewy on the inside, this special pastry is not to be missed.

> **AT A GLANCE**
> **PANS:** Rimmed cookie sheets
> **PAN PREP:** Line with parchment
> **RISING TIME:** 20 minutes
> **OVEN TEMP:** 425°/375°F
> **BAKING TIME:** 8 minutes/6 to 8 minutes
> **DIFFICULTY:** ♨ ♨ ♨

Firm Almond Filling (page 263)

½ recipe Danish Pastry Dough (page 258)

1 small recipe Pastry Cream for Danish (page 261); use ¼ cup to make the Sweet Butter Spread

1 small recipe Sweet Butter Spread (page 262)

Egg Wash for Danish (page 263)

¼ cup currant jelly

⅓ cup sliced unblanched almonds, lightly crushed

Sugar Syrup for Danish (page 264)

1 large recipe Vanilla Glaze (page 359)

1. On a lightly floured work surface, roll half of the almond filling into a log about 12 inches long. Cut the log into twelve 1-inch pieces, and roll them into balls. Cut and shape twelve more pieces with the remaining filling. Cover the balls with plastic wrap while shaping the dough.

2. Dab the corners of rimmed cookie sheets with butter, line with baking parchment, and set aside. On a lightly floured work surface, divide the dough in half. Working with one piece at a time, roll the pastry into a 12 × 16-inch rectangle. Pierce the dough with a fork at 1-inch intervals to prevent it from shrinking. Using a ruler as a guide, nick the dough at 4-inch intervals along the width and length of the rectangle. Align the ruler on opposite ends of the marks, and cut into squares using a pizza wheel or a sharp knife. Reshape the dough by stretching each piece with your hands until it measures about 4 inches across.

3. Using a small offset spatula, spread the center of each square of dough with 1 teaspoon of butter spread. Place a ball of almond filling in the center of each square. Dab the corners of the square with egg wash. Bring the corners of the dough to the center,

and depress the middle with your thumb to seal the tips. Gently spread the open spaces of the dough apart with your fingertips to expose the filling.

4. Carefully transfer the squares to the prepared pans, reshaping them as needed. Repeat with the remaining dough. Cover the pans with tea towels and set in a warmish place to rise for 20 minutes, or just until puffy.

5. Fifteen minutes before baking, position the racks in the upper and lower thirds of the oven. Heat the oven to 425°F. Gently depress the pastry again in the center with your thumb. Using a disposable quart-size zip-top bag, make a ½-inch cut across one of the bottom corners. Fill the bag with the pastry cream. Pipe a 1-inch dollop of cream into the center of each square. Drop a scant ½ teaspoon of currant jelly next to the pastry cream. Lightly brush the tops of the pastries with egg wash and sprinkle with a few crushed almonds. Bake at 425°F for 8 minutes, then *reduce the oven temperature* to 375°F. Continue baking for 6 to 8 minutes, or until golden brown. To ensure even browning, toward the end of baking time, rotate the pans top to bottom and front to back. While baking, prepare the sugar syrup and glaze.

6. Remove from the oven and *immediately* brush with *hot* sugar syrup. The syrup should sizzle when the tops of the pastries are brushed. Lightly frost the edges with the glaze while still warm, using the back of a tablespoon.

STORAGE: Store at room temperature, tightly wrapped in aluminum foil, for up to 3 days. These pastries may be frozen (see "Refreshing Yeasted Coffee Cakes," page 213).

> *"All cooking is a matter of time. In general, the more time, the better."*
>
> JOHN ERSKINE

pineapple cheese bow ties

MAKES 24 PASTRIES

A piquant pineapple filling paired with creamy cheeses rests on layers of Danish dough that are folded into eye-catching bow ties. There is something marvelous about this combination that makes this pastry a timeless classic.

AT A GLANCE
PANS: Rimmed cookie sheets
PAN PREP: Line with parchment
RISING TIME: 20 minutes
OVEN TEMP: 425°/375°F
BAKING TIME: 8 minutes/6 to 8 minutes
DIFFICULTY: ♨ ♨ ♨

½ **recipe Danish Pastry Dough (page 258)**
I small recipe Sweet Butter Spread (page 262)
Cheese Filling for Danish (page 264)
Pineapple Filling for Danish (page 266)

Egg Wash for Danish (page 263)
2 tablespoons sparkling sugar (see page 380)
Sugar Syrup for Danish (page 264)
I large recipe Vanilla Glaze (page 359)

1. Dab the corners of rimmed cookie sheets with butter, line with baking parchment, and set aside. On a lightly floured work surface, divide the dough in half. Working with one piece at a time, roll the pastry into a 12 × 16-inch rectangle. Pierce the dough with a fork at 1-inch intervals to prevent the dough from shrinking. Using a ruler as a guide, nick the dough at 4-inch intervals along the width and length of the rectangle. Align the ruler on opposite ends of the marks, and cut into squares using a pizza wheel or a sharp knife. Reshape the dough by stretching each piece with your hands until it measures about 4 inches across.

2. Using a small offset spatula, spread the center of each square with 1 teaspoon butter spread. Spoon a generous teaspoon of cheese filling on the spread, placing it off center (see illustration, point a). Then spoon a generous teaspoon of pineapple filling opposite the cheese (see illustration, point d), leaving ¼ inch between the fillings. Pull point b two-thirds of the way over the fillings to partially cover them. Brush point c with egg wash, then pull the corner to the opposite side, stretching the pastry as needed to tuck it underneath the bowtie. Place the pastries on the prepared pan. Cover with a tea towel and let rise in a warmish place until puffy, about 20 minutes. Repeat with the second half of dough.

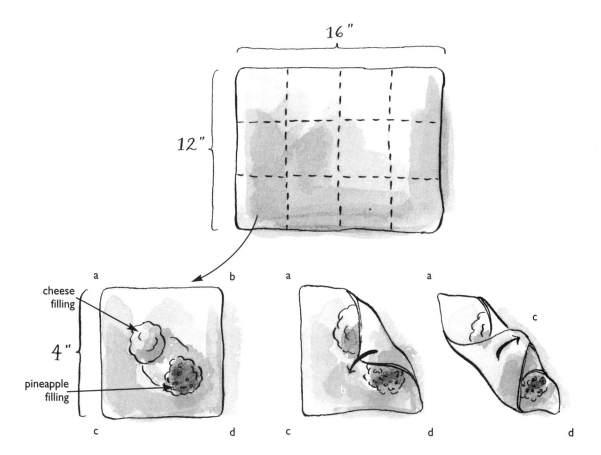

3. Fifteen minutes before baking, position the racks in the upper and lower thirds of the oven. Heat the oven to 425°F. Lightly brush the tops of the pastries with egg wash and sprinkle each with ¼ teaspoon of sparkling sugar. Bake at 425°F for 8 minutes, then *reduce the oven temperature to* 375°F. Continue baking for 6 to 8 minutes, or until golden brown. To ensure even browning, toward the end of baking time, rotate the pans top to bottom and front to back. While the pastries are baking, prepare the sugar syrup and glaze.

4. Remove from the oven and *immediately* brush with *hot* sugar syrup. The syrup should sizzle when the tops of the pastries are brushed. While they are slightly warm, garnish the tops with a small amount of glaze by dipping a fork into the glaze and squiggling it a few times over the pastries.

STORAGE: Pineapple cheese bow ties are best eaten the day they are made. These pastries may be frozen (see "Refreshing Yeasted Coffee Cakes," page 213).

prune pinwheels

MAKES 18 PASTRIES

Prune pinwheels are real eye-catchers. The centers of these pastries are spread with a delectable prune filling made with a hint of chocolate. After the filling is enclosed, a dollop of pastry cream is piped in the center. When baking the pinwheels, watch them carefully, as the tips can quickly overbrown.

AT A GLANCE
PANS: Rimmed cookie sheets
PAN PREP: Line with parchment
RISING TIME: 20 minutes
OVEN TEMP: 375°F
BAKING TIME: 14 to 16 minutes
DIFFICULTY: 🥄 🥄 🥄

½ **recipe Danish Pastry Dough (page 258)**

I small recipe Pastry Cream for Danish (page 261); use ¼ cup to make the Sweet Butter Spread

I small recipe Sweet Butter Spread (page 262)

Prune Filling for Danish (page 265)

Dry Nut Mix (page 263)

Egg Wash for Danish (page 263)

¼ **cup sliced almonds, slightly crushed**

2 tablespoons sparkling sugar (see page 380)

Sugar Syrup for Danish (page 264)

1. Dab the corners of rimmed cookie sheets with butter, line with baking parchment, and set aside. On a lightly floured work surface, divide the dough in half. Working with one piece at a time, roll the pastry into a 14-inch square. Pierce the dough with a fork at 1-inch intervals to prevent the dough from shrinking. Divide the dough into nine squares, each measuring slightly more than 4½ inches. To do this evenly, nick the dough at the approximate spot. Align a ruler on opposite ends of the marks, and using a pizza wheel or a sharp knife, cut into squares (see illustrations).

2. Place the squares on the prepared pans, restretching them as needed to the appropriate size. Spread the center of each square with 1 teaspoon of butter spread. Drop a scant tablespoon of prune filling on top, and spread it into a 2-inch circle. Sprinkle with 1 teaspoon of nut mix.

3. Brush the edges of the square with egg wash and cut the corners with a dough scraper, slashing it from the edge of the filling to the point (see illustration b). Bring the alternating points to the center and seal the tips by pressing them with your thumb (see illustrations c and d). Repeat with the second half of the dough. Cover the pans with a tea towel and set in a warmish place to rise for 20 minutes, or just until puffy.

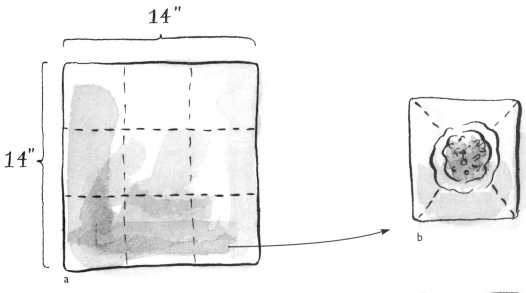

a

b

c

d

4. Fifteen minutes before baking, position the racks in the upper and lower thirds of the oven. Heat the oven to 375°F. Gently depress the pastry again in the center with your thumb. Using a disposable quart-size zip-top bag, make a ½-inch cut across one of the bottom corners. Fill the bag with the pastry cream. Pipe a 1-inch dollop of cream into the center of each pinwheel. Gently brush the tops with egg wash, and sprinkle each with a few almonds and sparkling sugar. Bake for 14 to 16 minutes, or until golden brown, reversing the pans during the last few minutes of baking. Watch carefully; these can quickly overbrown. While baking, prepare the sugar syrup.

5. Remove from the oven and *immediately* brush with *hot* sugar syrup. The syrup should sizzle when the tops of the pastries are brushed.

STORAGE: Store at room temperature, tightly wrapped in aluminum foil, for up to 3 days. These pastries may be frozen (see "Refreshing Yeasted Coffee Cakes," page 213).

chocolate glazed cream buns

MAKES 16 BUNS

Imagine a delicate yeasted bun filled with pastry cream. As the bun bakes, the cream melts, making a divine soft center. The top is finished with a coating of chocolate icing and garnished with crunchy toasted almonds. Because these buns should be eaten the day they are baked, you can shape them ahead and refrigerate them up to three days before baking.

AT A GLANCE
PANS: Two standard muffin pans
PAN PREP: Line with foil cupcake liners
RISING TIME: 15 minutes
OVEN TEMP: 425°/375°F
BAKING TIME: 5 minutes/12 to 14 minutes
DIFFICULTY: 👜 👜 👜

¼ recipe Danish Pastry Dough (page 258)

1 small recipe Pastry Cream for Danish (page 261); use ¼ cup to make the Sweet Butter Spread

1 small recipe Sweet Butter Spread (page 262)

Egg Wash for Danish (page 263)

Midnight Chocolate Glaze (page 363)

3 tablespoons sliced unblanched toasted almonds, slightly crushed

1. On a lightly floured work surface, roll the dough into a 14-inch square. Pierce the dough with a fork at 1-inch intervals to prevent it from shrinking. Divide the dough into 16 squares, stretching each piece of dough to measure 3½ inches as you work with it. Spread each piece with ½ teaspoon butter spread.

2. Line sixteen muffin cavities with foil cupcake liners. Fit a 14-inch pastry bag with a large no. 5 tube and fill it with the pastry cream. Pipe about 1 tablespoon of pastry cream in the center of each square. Brush the edges of the square lightly with egg wash. Bring the opposite corners of the dough together, gently pulling the four points of the dough upward. Pinch the seams well to seal. Invert the buns and place seam down in the cupcake liners. Cover the pans with a tea towel and set in a warmish place to rise until puffy, about 15 minutes.

3. Position the racks in the upper and lower thirds of the oven. Heat the oven to 425°F. Brush the buns with egg wash. Bake for 5 minutes, then *reduce the oven temperature to 375°F* and bake for 12 to 14 minutes longer, or until golden brown. While the buns are baking, prepare the glaze.

4. While the buns are slightly warm, using the back of a tablespoon, spread with the glaze and garnish with the almonds. The glaze will harden as it cools.

STORAGE: These buns are best eaten the day they are made. Freezing is not recommended.

CAROLE'S STREUSEL-TOPPED
BABKA, PAGE 216

CRUMB BUNS, PAGE 168

FIG AND WALNUT LOAF, PAGE 196

PINEAPPLE CHEESE BRAID, PAGE 201

ALMOND CROISSANTS, PAGE 248

SCALLOPED CHOCOLATE PECAN STRIP, PAGE 181

OLD-FASHIONED APPLE WALNUT STRUDEL, PAGE 230

**BRIOCHE BUNS WITH DRIED PEARS
AND CAMEMBERT, PAGE 237**

CHERRY PHYLLO TRIANGLES, PAGE 304

**NUT-CRUSTED
RUGELACH,
PAGE 334**

CHOCOLATE PISTACHIO
THUMBPRINTS, PAGE 324

KIRSCH KRISPS, PAGE 344

MACADAMIA FUDGE SQUARES, PAGE 314

POWDERED SUGAR ITALIAN SLICES, PAGE 332

apricot twists

MAKES 18 TWISTS

Apricot twists are one of the easiest and prettiest shapes to make. Strips of dough are twisted to show a brightly colored apricot filling that weaves through the dough. The tops of the twists are sprinkled with large crystals of sugar that form a crunchy topping to complement the chewy apricots and rich pastry.

AT A GLANCE

PANS: Two rimmed cookie sheets
PAN PREP: Line with parchment
RISING TIME: 15 minutes
OVEN TEMP: 425°/375°F
BAKING TIME: 5 minutes/10 to 12 minutes
DIFFICULTY: ♨ ♨ ♨

¼ **recipe Danish Pastry Dough (page 258)**
Apricot Filling for Danish (page 265)
Egg Wash for Danish (page 263)

2 tablespoons sparkling sugar (see page 380)
Sugar Syrup for Danish (page 264)

1. Line two rimmed cookie sheets with baking parchment. On a lightly floured work surface, divide the dough in half. Working with one half at a time, roll the pastry into an 18 × 7-inch strip. Prick the dough at 1-inch intervals with a fork.

2. Spread half of the apricot filling lengthwise over half of the dough, leaving a ½-inch margin around the edge. Brush the far edge lightly with egg wash. Fold the dough over the filling, then press the edges to seal.

3. Cut the strip of dough into nine 2-inch pieces. Make a 2-inch slash, like a button hole, down the center of each piece. Working one piece at a time, hold the dough up, then loop the top of the dough through the slash to form a twist. Place each twist on the pan, and bring the sides toward the center. Repeat with the second half of dough. Cover with tea towels and set in a warm place to rise for 15 minutes, or just until puffy.

4. Position the rack in the middle of the oven. Heat the oven to 425°F. Brush the twists with egg wash, and sprinkle each with a scant ½ teaspoon of sparkling sugar. Bake for 5 minutes, then *reduce the oven temperature to 375°F* and bake for 10 to 12 minutes longer or until golden brown. To ensure even browning, toward the end of baking time, rotate the pans top to bottom and front to back. While the twists are baking, prepare the sugar syrup.

5. Remove from the oven and *immediately* brush with *hot* sugar syrup.

STORAGE: Store at room temperature, tightly wrapped in aluminum foil, for up to 3 days. These twists may be frozen (see "Refreshing Yeasted Coffee Cakes," page 213).

bear claws

Bear claws are shaped in a manner that simulates the stubby claws of a bear. They are filled with a thin layer of butter spread and sprinkled with sweetened chopped toasted almonds. During baking, the tips of the claws become crisp—perfect for those of you who like your pastries with a little crunch.

Because bear claws require a lot of space, you will need three or four large rimmed cookie sheets for this recipe. If you are limited in the amount of this type of pan, prepare all of the pastry up to cutting and spreading the fingers. The filled strips of dough can be refrigerated until needed. When you are ready to bake them, remove the appropriate amount from the refrigerator, place the pieces on the pans, and form the claws as directed. Allow a few extra minutes for rising because of refrigeration.

> **AT A GLANCE**
> **PANS:** Three to four rimmed cookie sheets
> **PAN PREP:** Line with parchment
> **RISING TIME:** 15 minutes
> **OVEN TEMP:** 375°F
> **BAKING TIME:** 13 to 15 minutes
> **DIFFICULTY:** 🍵 🍵 🍵

½ recipe Danish Pastry Dough (page 258)

¾ cup Sweet Butter Spread (page 262)

1½ recipes Dry Nut Mix (page 263)

Egg Wash for Danish (page 263)

Sugar Syrup for Danish (page 264)

1 tablespoon sparkling sugar (see page 380)

1. Dab the corners of three or four rimmed cookie sheets with butter, line with baking parchment, and set aside. On a lightly floured surface, divide the dough into quarters. Working with one quarter at a time, roll the pastry into a strip measuring 15 × 7 inches. The strip of dough will be very thin. Prick the dough at 1-inch intervals with the tines of a fork to prevent it from shrinking.

2. Using a small offset spatula, spread 3 tablespoons of butter spread evenly over the strip, leaving a ½-inch border at the top and bottom. Sprinkle the surface of the dough with 3 tablespoons of nut mix. Brush the top and bottom borders with egg wash.

3. Starting at the bottom, fold the strip lengthwise into thirds. Press the right and left seams with fingers to seal. Roll the top of the strip lightly with the rolling pin to lengthen the strip to 16 inches. Score the strip at 4-inch intervals, then cut the dough with a straight-bladed pizza wheel or a pastry scraper to make four 4-inch strips (see illustration a).

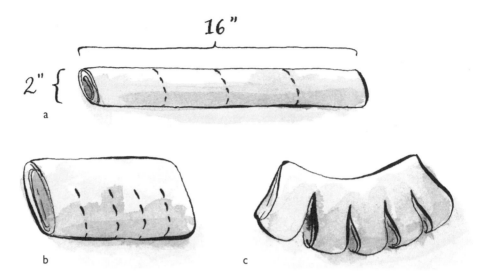

4. Working with one piece at a time, place the strip on the baking sheet, leaving ample room on all sides. Cut four evenly spaced slits three-fourths of the way through with the pizza wheel or pastry scraper. This will give you five fingers (see illustration b). Carefully spread the fingers apart curving the uncut opposite side (see illustration c). Form three more bear claws with the cut pieces of dough. Continue making additional bear claws with the remainder of the dough (see headnote). Cover the pans with tea towels and set them in a warmish place to rise for 15 minutes, or just until puffy.

5. Fifteen minutes before baking, position the racks in the upper and lower thirds of the oven. Heat the oven to 375°F. Lightly brush the tops of the bear claws with the egg wash. Sprinkle each with $1/2$ teaspoon of the nut mixture and $1/4$ teaspoon of the sparkling sugar. Bake for 13 to 15 minutes, or until golden brown, reversing the pans during the last few minutes of baking. Watch carefully as these pastries can easily over-brown. While baking, prepare the sugar syrup.

6. Remove from the oven and *immediately* brush with *hot* sugar syrup. The syrup should sizzle when the tops of the pastries are brushed.

STORAGE: Store at room temperature, tightly wrapped in aluminum foil, for up to 3 days. Heat before serving. These pastries may be frozen (see "Refreshing Yeasted Coffee Cakes," page 213).

strudel: then and now

TRADITIONAL STRUDELS

Hand-Pulled Strudel Dough

Old-Fashioned Apple Walnut Strudel

Sweetened Bread Crumbs

Pear and Dried Cranberry Strudel

Cheese Strudel

Sour Cherry Cheese Strudel

Pineapple Cheese Strudel

NEW WORLD STRUDEL—PHYLLO

Cherry Phyllo Triangles

Phyllo Triangles with Stewed Fruit Filling

STRUDEL, THEN AND NOW

Strudel, the favorite dessert of so many, is a pastry that has been made for centuries. Through migration and travel, Central Europeans were introduced to this tissue-thin dough. In fact, Hungarian and Austrian bakers became famous for creating their own method of preparing and stretching strudel dough. While the craft is still practiced, today it is a fading art. It has been replaced with phyllo, the ready-made dough that is convenient to use. This chapter presents both forms—the art of "then" and the method of "now."

A few years ago, my good friend Joanna Pruess, food writer and cookbook author par excellence, had just returned from a business trip to Vienna, Austria, and raved to me about the incredible pastries that she had the good fortune to sample. Little did Joanna know that my secret passion had been to travel to Vienna to learn about Viennese pastries, and especially the art of making strudel. Through the contacts that Joanna had made, I had the privilege of learning this marvelous craft with Dietmar Fercher, head pastry chef for the renowned Bristol Hotel and Café Central Coffeehouse.

When I returned from Vienna, I began to teach the art of hand-pulled strudel. The experience of stretching a small ball of dough into an enormous paper-thin sheet is more fun than you can imagine. I have been teaching my strudel class for many years, and every time I offer it, the class is sold out. In class, groups of four to six students stretch their dough to form a huge sheet that can cover a table. I have often suggested that three or four couples get together and have a strudel-pulling party.

For this book, I have scaled down the recipes to one-third of the amount that I teach in class. This smaller quantity will make pulling the dough by yourself easier. Whether you do this alone or choose to invite some baking buddies over for a strudel-pulling party, you are going to have a blast.

REHEATING STRUDEL

To restore crispness, all strudel requires reheating before serving. Place the strudel on a cookie sheet and heat in a 325°F oven for 6 to 8 minutes. Let stand at room temperature a few minutes before serving. Add an additional 5 minutes or more, as needed, for strudel that has been refrigerated.

ABOUT HAND-PULLED STRUDEL

Here are some tips on working with strudel dough.

• Remember, the filling of your choice must be made before you stretch the dough. Once stretched, the dough must be filled immediately, otherwise it becomes too brittle.

• A bridge table or a rectangular kitchen table makes an ideal surface for stretching the dough. You must be able to move around all sides of the stretching area.

• Use a patterned tablecloth or a doubled flat twin bed sheet to cover the stretching surface. The pattern helps to determine the thick and thin areas of the dough.

• Before stretching the dough, remove all jewelry (watches, wedding bands, etc.) because the slightest snag will tear the dough.

• Brushing the dough with clarified butter will prevent it from drying out. While a large (at least 2-inch) pastry brush may be used, it's easier to sprinkle the butter on with your hand. Dip your fingertips into the butter and spritz it as you would water, gently patting the surface.

• To prevent the strudel dough from springing back, weight the perimeter with heavy objects such as a rolling pin, kitchen wraps like aluminum foil or plastic, a bag of beans, etc. These objects can be moved as needed.

• If small holes appear, immediately pinch them together. As you continue to stretch, avoid those areas, returning to them toward the end of the stretching period.

• As the dough becomes larger, weight two ends, lift the two opposite ends, and "shimmy" them gently, moving the dough up and down, while carefully pulling it toward you. Shimmying it is a great way to thin the dough.

• Ideally, the dough should be stretched into a rectangle about 24 inches wide and 30 inches long. However, the overall shape is less important as long as the dough has an area large enough to spread an 18-inch strip of filling.

• If the dough develops large holes during the final stretching, cut pieces from the irregular edges and set them in the spaces without pinching them to the main piece of dough. As the dough is rolled, no one will notice the patchwork.

hand-pulled strudel dough

MAKES ENOUGH FOR ONE 20-INCH STRUDEL

1⅓ cups (6 ounces) sifted bread flour

2 teaspoons sugar

½ teaspoon salt

½ cup lukewarm water

2 tablespoons vegetable oil, such as canola or safflower

½ teaspoon white vinegar

⅔ cup unsalted butter, clarified (see page 382)

MAKE THE DOUGH

Stand Mixer Method

1. Place the flour, sugar, and salt in the large bowl of an electric mixer fitted with the paddle attachment and blend on medium-low speed. In a small bowl, combine the water, vegetable oil, and vinegar, and with the machine off, add the liquids all at once to the flour mixture. With the mixer on low speed, mix the ingredients to form a rough dough. Change to the dough hook, and continue mixing on low speed until the dough is smooth and elastic. This will take 8 to 10 minutes.

2. Remove the dough from the mixer bowl, shape it into a ball, and place it in a clean bowl greased with 2 teaspoons of vegetable oil. Turn the dough to coat the surface with the oil. Cover the bowl with plastic wrap, and let the dough rest in a warmish place for 1 to 3 hours. *Resting time is required to relax the gluten to enable the dough to be stretched without too much elasticity.*

Hand Method

1. Place 1 cup of the flour, the sugar, and salt in a large mixing bowl, and blend together with a whisk. (Reserve the remaining ⅓ cup flour for kneading.) Make a well in the center. In a small bowl, combine the water, vegetable oil, and vinegar, and pour the liquids into the well. Using a wooden spoon, gradually draw the flour into the liquids, working the mixture as best you can, until a rough dough is formed.

2. Place the remaining ⅓ cup flour on the corner of a pastry board or other flat work surface. Sprinkle the board with a little of this flour. Empty the dough onto the floured surface, and with the help of a dough scraper, knead it for about 15 minutes, gradually working in the remaining flour. As the dough reaches the end of its kneading time, it should be smooth and elastic. Place the dough in a clean bowl lightly

greased with 2 teaspoons of vegetable oil. Turn the dough to coat it with oil. Cover with plastic wrap, and let it rest in a warmish place for 1 to 3 hours. *Resting time is required to relax the gluten to enable the dough to be stretched without too much elasticity.*

STRETCH THE DOUGH

3. Cover a work surface such as a bridge table, a kitchen island, or a table with a table-cloth or a doubled twin-size flat bed sheet. While a surface that you can reach from all four sides is preferable, the dough can be stretched successfully on three sides of a kitchen island (see "About Hand-Pulled Strudel," page 287).

4. Sprinkle 3 to 4 tablespoons of flour over the entire surface of the cloth, and rub it into the fabric with your hands. Place the dough in the center of the cloth and flatten it into a small rectangle with your hands. Using a floured rolling pin, roll the dough from the center out into a larger rectangle measuring 8 × 10 inches. Rest the dough for a few minutes. Roll the dough again, until it measures 10 × 14 inches.

5. Slide floured hands palm side down under the dough, toward the center. Carefully and gently start to stretch the dough from the center out, slowly spreading your hands apart as you stretch. Sprinkle the dough with tepid clarified butter from time to time, patting the butter into the surface with the palm of your hand. The butter will prevent the dough from becoming brittle and cracking. Continue to stretch the dough as thinly as possible, working it very carefully to avoid tearing. If small holes appear, immediately pinch them together. For ease of handling, let the dough rest every few minutes to relax the gluten.

6. As the dough becomes larger, anchor one of the corners over a corner of the work surface. This will help facilitate the stretching. Continue stretching and buttering the dough, moving around the work surface so you can reach all sides of the dough. "Balloon" the dough from time to time by repeatedly lifting it up and down. Ballooning helps to stretch the dough more thinly. It's okay if the edges of the dough remain thick. When the dough measures approximately 24 × 30 inches, trim the thick edges with a pair of scissors and discard the selvage as it cannot be rerolled. The dough is now ready to be filled.

old-fashioned apple walnut strudel

MAKES ONE 20-INCH STRUDEL, 10 TO 12 SERVINGS

PLAN AHEAD: Prepare dough 1 to 3 hours

before stretching

Crispy thin layers of hand-pulled strudel dough encase sweet apples, rum-soaked raisins, and crunchy walnuts. To appreciate this delicacy to the fullest, the strudel should be eaten when freshly baked, accompanied by cool, softly whipped cream.

FILLING

1½ pounds Golden Delicious apples
(about 4 medium)

2 teaspoons fresh lemon juice

½ cup coarsely chopped toasted walnuts
(see pages 391–392)

¼ cup golden raisins, plumped (see page 389),
steeped in 2 tablespoons dark rum for
30 minutes, drained

¼ cup granulated sugar

½ teaspoon freshly grated lemon zest

¼ teaspoon ground cinnamon, or to taste

Sweetened Bread Crumbs (opposite)

Hand-Pulled Strudel Dough (page 288),
stretched

2⅓ cup unsalted butter, clarified (see page 382)

Powdered sugar, for garnish

MAKE THE FILLING

1. Peel the apples, cut them in half, and remove the cores with a melon ball cutter. Slice each half into four pieces, and cut across the slices into generous ½-inch pieces. Place the apples in a large bowl and toss them with the lemon juice.

2. Just before assembling, add the remaining filling ingredients to the apples along with ½ cup of the sweetened bread crumbs and toss the mixture with your hands to combine.

STRETCH, FILL, AND BAKE THE STRUDEL

3. Position the rack in the middle of the oven. Heat the oven to 400°F. Line a rimmed cookie sheet with baking parchment.

4. Proceed with Stretch the Dough (page 289).

5. Generously butter the dough. Sprinkle with 3 to 4 tablespoons of the bread crumbs. Starting at the 24-inch side of the dough, 4 to 5 inches from the edge, mound the apples in a 20 × 3½-inch strip. Lift the 4-inch side of the dough over and stretch it to cover the apples, compacting them well to eliminate air pockets.

6. Take the tablecloth in your hands and roll it up until you almost reach the strudel log. With two hands, lift the cloth up and flip the log over several times until you reach the end, keeping the seam on the bottom. Take care to roll the pastry loosely. Trim the ends, leaving about 1 inch of dough. To seal in the filling, pull the bottom of the dough up over the fruit and pull the top over the bottom, tucking it under the roll.

7. Lift the log onto the baking pan, stretching it back to its original size, and curve it into a crescent. Brush the surface of the dough with melted clarified butter. Pierce the log several times with the tip of a paring knife to create air vents.

8. Bake the strudel for 40 to 45 minutes, or until golden brown and the juices begin to run, brushing the log with additional clarified butter two or three times during baking.

9. Remove the strudel from the oven, and brush it again with clarified butter. With a serrated knife, partially cut through the top of the strudel at 2-inch intervals to release the steam. This keeps the pastry crisp. Cool for at least 30 minutes before slicing. Just before serving, dust the top of the strudel heavily with powdered sugar.

STORAGE: Strudel is best eaten the day it is made. Leftover strudel should be refrigerated and covered lightly with aluminum foil, for up to 3 days. Reheat before serving (see page 286).

sweetened bread crumbs

MAKES ABOUT 1 CUP

¾ cup packaged plain dry bread crumbs

3 tablespoons sugar

Scant ¼ teaspoon ground cinnamon

Few drops pure vanilla extract

4 teaspoons clarified butter (see page 382)

1. Position the rack in the middle of the oven. Heat the oven to 350°F.

2. Place all the ingredients in the bowl of a food processor fitted with the steel blade. Pulse until well blended.

3. Spread the crumb mixture in an even layer on a rimmed cookie sheet. Toast in the oven for 15 minutes, or until the crumbs begin to lightly brown around the edges, stirring occasionally. The toasted crumbs may be stored in the refrigerator or freezer.

pear and dried cranberry strudel

MAKES ONE 20-INCH STRUDEL, 10 TO 12 SERVINGS

PLAN AHEAD: Prepare dough 1 to 3 hours before stretching

Fresh pears combined with Kirsch-soaked dried pears and cranberries make a tasty variation on the strudel theme. Mixing fresh fruit with dried heightens the flavor of the filling. Try it with a dab of whipped cream.

AT A GLANCE
PAN: Rimmed cookie sheet
PAN PREP: Line with parchment
OVEN TEMP: 400°F
BAKING TIME: 40 to 45 minutes
DIFFICULTY: ♟ ♟ ♟

FILLING

2 ounces (scant ½ cup) dried cranberries (not organic)

4 ounces (about 6 halves) dried pears (not organic)

⅓ cup Kirsch or dark rum

5 to 6 ripe Anjou pears (about 2½ pounds)

2 teaspoons fresh lemon juice

⅓ cup granulated sugar

½ teaspoon ground ginger

⅛ teaspoon ground allspice

1 teaspoon freshly grated lemon zest

Sweetened Bread Crumbs (page 291)

Hand-Pulled Strudel Dough (page 288), stretched

2⅓ cup unsalted butter, clarified (see page 382)

Powdered sugar, for garnish

MAKE THE FILLING

1. Place the dried cranberries in a small bowl and cover with boiling water; soak for 3 to 4 minutes to soften. Drain well and place on a double thickness of paper towels and dry thoroughly. Cut the dried pears into ¾-inch pieces. Place them in a separate small bowl and cover with boiling water; soak for 15 minutes to soften. Drain well and place on a double thickness of paper towels and dry thoroughly. Combine the plumped cranberries and pears, add the Kirsch, cover, and macerate for at least 30 minutes. Drain well and blot dry with paper towels.

2. Peel the fresh pears, cut them in half, and remove the cores with a melon ball cutter. Slice each half into four pieces, and cut across the slices into generous ½-inch pieces. Place the pears in a large bowl and toss them with the lemon juice. Combine the granulated sugar, ginger, and allspice in a small bowl. Set aside.

STRETCH, FILL, AND BAKE THE STRUDEL

3. Just before filling the strudel, place the pears, dried fruit, sugar mixture, and lemon zest in a large bowl. Add ½ cup of the bread crumbs and mix well with your hands.

4. Position the rack in the middle of the oven. Heat the oven to 400°F. Line a rimmed cookie sheet with baking parchment.

5. Proceed with Stretch the Dough (page 289).

6. Generously butter the dough. Sprinkle with 3 to 4 tablespoons of the bread crumbs. Starting at the 24-inch side of the dough, mound the fruit mixture in a 20 × 3½-inch strip. Lift the 4-inch side of the dough over and stretch it to cover the fruit, compacting it well. Having the fruit mixture fit snugly firms the filling and eliminates air pockets.

7. Take the tablecloth in your hands and roll it up until you almost reach the strudel log. With two hands, lift the cloth up and flip the log over several times until you reach the end, keeping the seam on the bottom. Take care to roll the pastry *loosely*. Trim the ends, leaving about 1 inch of dough. To seal in the filling, pull the bottom of the dough up over the fruit and pull the top over the bottom, tucking it under the roll.

8. Lift the log onto the baking pan, stretching it back to its original size, and curve it into a crescent. Brush the surface of the dough with melted clarified butter. Pierce the log several times with the tip of a paring knife to create air vents.

9. Bake the strudel for 40 to 45 minutes, until golden brown, brushing the log with additional clarified butter two or three times during baking.

10. Remove the strudel from the oven and brush it again with clarified butter. With a serrated knife, partially cut through the top of the strudel at 2-inch intervals to release the steam. This will help to keep the pastry crisp. Let the strudel cool for at least 30 minutes before slicing into individual pieces. Just before serving, dust the top of the strudel heavily with powdered sugar.

STORAGE: Strudel is best eaten the day it is made. Leftover strudel should be refrigerated and covered lightly with aluminum foil, for up to 3 days. Reheat before serving (see page 286).

cheese strudel

MAKES ONE 20-INCH STRUDEL, 10 TO 12 SERVINGS

PLAN AHEAD: Make the cheese filling 6 to 8 hours in advance. Prepare the dough 1 to 3 hours before stretching.

Those of you who crave a good piece of cheese strudel will love this recipe. A trio of cheeses—cream cheese, ricotta, and farmer—is flavored with orange and lemon zests and golden raisins. The best part is that the filling doesn't run, a common problem with cheese fillings. (Don't miss the variations of fruit and cheese strudels included in this chapter.) Whether you combine this filling with fruit or eat it on its own, it makes a wonderful strudel.

When I make the cheese filling, I like to press the cheeses through a food mill, a technique that gives the filling its smooth, creamy texture. While a wide-gauge strainer will do in a pinch, a food mill has many uses and is well worth the investment.

> **AT A GLANCE**
> **PAN:** Rimmed cookie sheet
> **PAN PREP:** Line with parchment
> **OVEN TEMP:** 400°F
> **BAKING TIME:** 40 to 45 minutes
> **DIFFICULTY:** 🥄 🥄 🥄

CHEESE FILLING

1 (15-ounce) container whole milk ricotta

1 pound cream cheese, at room temperature

2 (7.5-ounce) packages farmer cheese

¼ cup all-purpose flour, spooned in and leveled

¾ cup granulated sugar

2 large egg yolks

1½ teaspoons pure vanilla extract

1 teaspoon freshly grated navel or Valencia orange zest, or to taste

1 teaspoon freshly grated lemon zest, or to taste

¼ teaspoon lemon oil

¼ teaspoon salt

6 tablespoons golden raisins, plumped (see page 389)

Hand-Pulled Strudel Dough (page 288), stretched

½ recipe Sweetened Bread Crumbs (page 291)

⅔ cup unsalted butter, clarified (see page 382)

Powdered sugar, for garnish

MAKE THE FILLING

1. Arrange two linen or 100 percent cotton dish towels (do not use terry cloth) on top of each other on the kitchen counter. Spread the ricotta cheese lengthwise on the doubled towels into a rectangle measuring about 14 × 5 inches. Bring the sides of the towels to the center and roll the cheese up tightly in the towels, jelly roll fashion. Let stand for 30 minutes.

2. Press the ricotta, cream cheese, and farmer cheese through a food mill or a wide-gauge strainer into a bowl, and blend in the flour.

3. Add the granulated sugar, egg yolks, vanilla, zests, lemon oil, and salt, blending until smooth. This is a thick mixture, but it should not be overmixed. Gently fold in the raisins. Chill for 6 to 8 hours or overnight.

STRETCH, FILL, AND BAKE THE STRUDEL

4. Position the rack in the middle of the oven. Heat the oven to 400°F. Line a rimmed cookie sheet with baking parchment.

5. Proceed with Stretch the Dough (page 289).

6. Generously butter the dough. Sprinkle with 3 to 4 tablespoons of the bread crumbs. Starting at the 24-inch side of the dough, mound the cheese filling in a 20 × 3½-inch strip. Lift the 4-inch side of the dough over and stretch it to cover the cheese. Gently smooth out the covered cheese filling with your hand.

7. Take the tablecloth in your hands and roll it up until you almost reach the strudel log. With two hands, lift the cloth up and flip the log over several times until you reach the end, keeping the seam on the bottom. Take care to roll the pastry *loosely*. Trim the ends, leaving about 1 inch of dough. To seal in the filling, pull the bottom of the dough up over the cheese mixture and pull the top over the bottom, tucking it under the roll.

8. Lift the log onto the baking pan, stretching it back to its original size, and curve it into a crescent. Brush the surface of the dough with melted clarified butter. Pierce the log several times with the tip of a paring knife to create air vents.

9. Bake the strudel for 40 to 45 minutes, until golden brown, brushing the log with additional clarified butter two or three times during baking.

10. Remove the strudel from the oven and brush it again with clarified butter. With a serrated knife, partially cut through the top of the strudel at 2-inch intervals to release the steam. This will help to keep the pastry crisp. Let the strudel cool at least one hour before slicing into individual pieces. Just before serving, dust the top of the strudel heavily with powdered sugar.

STORAGE: Strudel is best eaten the day it is made. Leftover strudel should be refrigerated and covered lightly with aluminum foil, for up to 3 days. Reheat before serving (see page 286).

sour cherry cheese strudel

MAKES ONE 20-INCH STRUDEL, 10 TO 12 SERVINGS

PLAN AHEAD: Make the cheese filling 6 to 8 hours in advance. Drain the cherries several hours in advance. Prepare the strudel dough 1 to 3 hours in advance.

The pairing of sour cherries with cheese is a perennial favorite in the world of pastry. Whether in Danish pastry, cheesecake, or strudel, its popularity has never waned. Here we have this tasty combination encased in the thin layers of crisp strudel. For those of you who crave cherries and cheese, this strudel will more than satisfy.

AT A GLANCE
PAN: Rimmed cookie sheet
PAN PREP: Line with parchment
OVEN TEMP: 400°F
BAKING TIME: 40 to 45 minutes
DIFFICULTY: 🍶 🍶 🍶

When you prepare the cherries for the filling, use Morello cherries, a Middle European sour cherry with dark red skin. Don't confuse these cherries with sweet eating varieties like Bing. I generally purchase these cherries in specialty stores like Trader Joe's, some supermarkets, or ethnic stores.

CHEESE FILLING

7 to 8 ounces whole milk ricotta (not low-fat)

1 (7.5) ounce package farmer cheese

8 ounces cream cheese, at room temperature

2 tablespoons all-purpose flour

6 tablespoons granulated sugar

1 large egg yolk

¾ teaspoon pure vanilla extract

½ teaspoon freshly grated navel or Valencia orange zest, or to taste

½ teaspoon greshly grated lemon zest, or to taste

⅛ teaspoon lemon oil

⅛ teaspoon salt

3 tablespoons golden raisins, plumped (see page 389)

CHERRY FILLING

1 (28 to 32 ounce) jar pitted Morello cherries packed in light syrup or imported dark sour cherries in light syrup or water-packed (3 to 3½ cups)

¼ cup strained powdered sugar

¼ cup whole, unskinned, toasted almonds

¼ teaspoon ground cinnamon

¼ teaspoon grated lemon zest

1 recipe Sweetened Bread Crumbs (page 291)

1 recipe Hand-Pulled Strudel Dough (page 288), stretched

⅔ cup unsalted butter, clarified (see page 382)

Powdered sugar, for garnish

MAKE THE CHEESE FILLING

1. Arrange two linen or 100 percent cotton dish towels (do not use terry cloth) on top of each other on the kitchen counter. Spread the ricotta lengthwise on the doubled towels into a rectangle measuring about 8 × 5 inches. Bring the sides of the towels to the center and roll the cheese up tightly in the towels, jelly roll fashion. Let stand for 30 minutes.

2. Press the ricotta, farmer cheese, and cream cheese through a food mill or a wide-gauge strainer into a bowl, and blend in the flour.

3. Add the granulated sugar, egg yolk, vanilla, zests, lemon oil, and salt. Stir until smooth, being careful not to overmix. Gently fold in the raisins. Chill for 6 to 8 hours or overnight.

MAKE THE CHERRY FILLING

4. Drain the cherries for several hours in a colander placed over a bowl. Discard the liquid.

5. Place the powdered sugar, almonds, and cinnamon in the bowl of a food processor fitted with the steel blade. Process until the nuts are chopped medium-fine.

6. Just before assembling, combine the drained cherries, nut mixture, and lemon zest with ¼ cup of the bread crumbs and toss the mixture with your hands to combine.

STRETCH, FILL, AND BAKE THE STRUDEL

7. Position the rack in the middle of the oven. Heat the oven to 400°F. Line a rimmed cookie sheet with baking parchment.

8. Proceed with Stretch the Dough (page 289).

9. Generously butter the strudel dough. Sprinkle with 3 to 4 tablespoons of the bread crumbs. Starting at the 24-inch side of the dough, 4 to 5 inches from the edge, spoon the cheese filling onto the dough in a 20 × 2-inch strip. Even the sides as best you can. Using a teaspoon, make a 1-inch channel down the length of the cheese filling to hold some of the cherry filling in place. Spoon the cherry mixture on top of the cheese filling. Lift the 4-inch side of the dough over, and stretch it to cover the fillings, compacting them gently.

10. Take the tablecloth in your hands and roll it up until you almost reach the strudel log. With two hands, lift the cloth up and flip the log over several times until you reach the end, keeping the seam on the bottom. Take care to roll the pastry loosely. Trim the ends, leaving about 1 inch of dough. To seal in the filling, pull the bottom

recipe continues

continued from previous page

of the dough up over the filling, and pull the top over the bottom, tucking it under the roll.

11. Lift the log onto the baking pan, stretching it back to its original size, and curve it into a crescent. Brush the surface of the dough with melted clarified butter. Pierce the log several times with the tip of a paring knife to create air vents.

12. Bake the strudel for 40 to 45 minutes, until golden brown, brushing the log with additional clarified butter two or three times during baking.

13. Remove the strudel from the oven, and brush it again with clarified butter. With a serrated knife, partially cut through the top of the strudel at 2-inch intervals to release the steam. This will help to keep the pastry crisp. Let the strudel cool for at least 1 hour before slicing into individual pieces. Just before serving, dust the top of the strudel heavily with powdered sugar.

STORAGE: Strudel is best eaten the day it is made. Leftover strudel should be refrigerated and covered lightly with aluminum foil, for up to 3 days. Reheat before serving (see page 286).

THE WEIGHT OF SOFT CHEESES

The package weight of ricotta and farmer cheese may vary in different supermarkets throughout the United States. In the New York metropolitan area, ricotta is commonly packaged in 15-ounce containers, and farmer cheese is sold in 7.5-ounce packages. Whether the container or package of cheese is 15 or 16 ounces, or 7 or 8 ounces, by all means use the entire amount. A little less or a little more cheese will not alter the recipe.

pineapple cheese strudel

MAKES ONE 20-INCH STRUDEL, 10 TO 12 SERVINGS

PLAN AHEAD: Make the cheese filling 6 to 8 hours in advance. Prepare the dough 1 to 3 hours in advance

Cheese with sweet-tart pineapple is one of the favorite yin/yang duos of the dessert world. Don't worry if the pineapple filling spills over the cheese. When the strudel dough is rolled, the fillings will come together beautifully.

PINEAPPLE FILLING

2 (20-ounce cans) pineapple chunks in heavy syrup (3 cups)

3 tablespoons cornstarch

¼ cup granulated sugar

¼ teaspoon salt

2 to 3 teaspoons fresh lemon juice

1 teaspoon freshly grated navel orange zest

½ teaspoon pure vanilla extract

Hand-Pulled Strudel Dough (page 288), stretched

½ recipe Sweetened Bread Crumbs (page 291)

Cheese Filling for Sour Cherry Cheese Strudel (page 296)

⅔ cup unsalted butter, clarified (see page 382)

Powdered sugar, for garnish

MAKE THE PINEAPPLE FILLING

1. Drain the pineapple chunks in a colander set over a bowl. Reserve 1⅓ cups of the syrup. Spread the pineapple on a double thickness of paper towels, and blot dry with two more layers of towels.

2. Cut the pineapple into ½-inch pieces and place them in a large mixing bowl lined with a double thickness of paper towels.

3. Whisk the cornstarch, granulated sugar, and salt together in a heavy 2-quart saucepan. Slowly whisk in the reserved syrup, mixing until smooth. Cook on low heat *gently* stirring with a wooden spoon until the mixture comes to a slow boil. Reduce the heat to simmer and cook for 15 to 20 seconds. Off the heat, *gently* mix in the lemon juice, orange zest, and vanilla.

4. Remove the paper towels from under the pineapple pieces and fold in the thickened pineapple syrup. Cool completely before using.

recipe continues

continued from previous page

STRETCH, FILL, AND BAKE THE STRUDEL

5. Position the rack in the middle of the oven. Heat the oven to 400°F. Line a rimmed cookie sheet with baking parchment.

6. Proceed with Stretch the Dough (page 289).

7. Generously butter the strudel dough. Sprinkle with 3 to 4 tablespoons of the bread crumbs. Starting at the 24-inch side of the dough, 4 to 5 inches from the edge, spoon the cheese filling onto the dough in a 20 × 2-inch strip. Even the sides as best you can. Using a teaspoon, make a 1-inch channel down the length of the cheese filling to hold some of the pineapple filling in place. Spoon the pineapple filling on top of the cheese filling. Lift the 4-inch side of the dough over and stretch it to cover the fillings, compacting them gently.

8. Take the tablecloth in your hands and roll it up until you almost reach the strudel log. With two hands, lift the cloth up and flip the log over several times until you reach the end, keeping the seam on the bottom. Take care to roll the pastry *loosely*. Trim the ends, leaving about 1 inch of dough. To seal in the filling, pull the bottom of the dough up over the filling and pull the top over the bottom, tucking it under the roll.

9. Lift the log onto the baking pan, stretching it back to its original size, and curve it into a crescent. Brush the surface of the dough with melted clarified butter. Pierce the log several times with the tip of a paring knife to create air vents. Bake the strudel for 40 to 45 minutes until golden brown, brushing the log with additional clarified butter two or three times during baking.

10. Remove the strudel from the oven and brush it again with clarified butter. With a serrated knife, partially cut through the top of the strudel at 2-inch intervals to release the steam. This will help to keep the pastry crisp. Let the strudel cool at least one hour before slicing into individual pieces. Just before serving, dust the top of the strudel heavily with powdered sugar.

STORAGE: Strudel is best eaten the day it is made. Leftover strudel should be refrigerated and covered lightly with aluminum foil, for up to 3 days. Reheat before serving (see page 286).

NEW-WORLD STRUDEL—PHYLLO

In these busy days we can still have a taste of the past by making strudel with phyllo. This flaky, tissue paper–thin dough is ready-made and makes an easy alternative to the hand-pulled dough made from scratch. All of the fillings for the strudel recipes can be used with phyllo. This delicate dough is manufactured in large sheets measuring 18 × 14 inches and in smaller sheets that are 9 × 14 inches. While I don't recommend the smaller sheets for making large strudel rolls, the half-size sheets are perfect for fruit- or cheese-filled triangles.

Phyllo sold in larger sheets is primarily available in stores specializing in Middle Eastern foods, while smaller sheets can be found in the freezer section of most supermarkets. The advantage to seeking out the larger sheets of phyllo is that the package generally has not been frozen. Phyllo that has not been frozen is far superior and easier to handle; therefore, seek out fresh whenever possible. When frozen sheets are thawed, they sometimes stick together. For this reason, it is a good idea to buy more than you need. That extra box may come in handy.

ABOUT WORKING WITH PHYLLO

Here are a few tips to help you work with phyllo:

- If the phyllo was frozen, thaw it in the refrigerator overnight.
- Before opening the package of dough, assemble the other ingredients and utensils called for in the recipe.
- Have the filling prepared and ready for use.
- Place a large sheet of wax paper into a large jelly roll pan. Remove the phyllo from the package and unroll the dough onto the pan, laying it flat.
- To prevent the dough from cracking and drying, lay another sheet of wax paper on top of the phyllo. Cover this layer of paper with a moist dish towel or two layers of damp paper towels.
- As you use the sheets of phyllo, always keeps the unused portion covered.
- Always brush the melted butter on the edges first because they dry more quickly than the center.
- Use a wide pastry brush because it will cover more surface in less time.
- Unused fresh phyllo dough can be rerolled in plastic wrap and stored in the refrigerator for up to 1 week, or frozen according to manufacturer's directions. If the dough was purchased at a supermarket previously frozen, refreezing is not recommended.

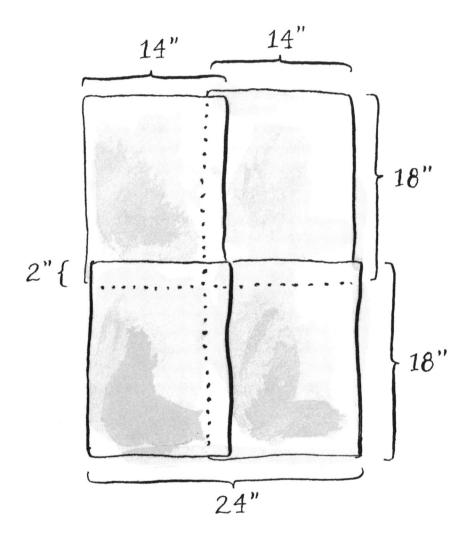

PIECING PURCHASED PHYLLO SHEETS FOR STRUDEL

Follow the directions below to use 14 × 9-inch sheets of phyllo in place of hand-pulled strudel dough.

• Start with four sheets of phyllo. On a cloth-covered surface, arrange two of the sheets next to each other, with the 14-inch side across the top. The sheets should overlap each other by 2 inches. Secure the seam by brushing it with melted clarified butter.

• Lay two more sheets of phyllo, again with the 14-inch side at the top directly under the first sheets, with a 2-inch overlap on each of the sides. Secure all of the seams with a brushing of more clarified butter. You should now have a large rectangle measuring approximately 24 × 32 inches (see illustration). Brush the entire surface of the phyllo with clarified butter to keep it moist.

Refer to the recipe of your choice for further instructions. If you are making a large phyllo roll, arrange the filling across the 24-inch side, leaving a 2-inch margin on either end.

cherry phyllo triangles

MAKES SIXTEEN 4½-INCH TRIANGLES

PLAN AHEAD: Drain cherries several hours in advance

Morello cherries make a perfect filling to use with small phyllo sheets. Because the color of jarred cherries is not vibrant, I like to lift the color of the cooked filling with a few drops of red food coloring. When you bite into the buttery layers of the crisp dough, you will taste a mouthwatering, sweet-tart cherry filling. If you wish, these baked triangles can be cut in half for smaller size servings.

AT A GLANCE

PANS: Rimmed cookie sheets
PAN PREP: Line with parchment
OVEN TEMP: 375°F
BAKING TIME: 18 to 20 minutes
DIFFICULTY: 🥄 🥄

CHERRY FILLING

1 (28- to 32-ounce) jar pitted Morello cherries, 3 to 3½ cups (see headnote, page 296)

⅔ cup granulated sugar

3 tablespoons cornstarch

1 tablespoon unsalted butter, softened

1 teaspoon fresh lemon juice

½ teaspoon almond extract

¼ teaspoon red food coloring

1 (1 pound) package 9 x 14-inch phyllo dough, thawed

⅔ cup unsalted butter, clarified (see page 382)

⅔ cup Sweetened Bread Crumbs (page 291)

Powdered sugar, for dusting

MAKE THE FILLING

1. Drain the cherries for several hours in a colander placed over a bowl. Reserve 1 cup of the juice. You should have about 3 cups of cherries.

2. In a heavy-bottomed 2-quart saucepan, whisk together the granulated sugar and cornstarch. Blend in 3 tablespoons of the reserved cherry juice, whisking until smooth. Stir in the remaining juice. Place over low heat, and stir constantly with a wooden spoon until the mixture comes to a slow boil. Cook for 15 to 20 seconds longer, but stir only occasionally. The mixture should be thick and clear.

3. Remove from the heat and *gently* fold in the cherries, butter, lemon juice, almond extract, and food coloring. Do not overmix. Set aside to cool.

ASSEMBLE THE TRIANGLES

4. Dab the corners of rimmed cookie sheets with butter, line with baking parchment, and set aside. Working with half of the package at a time, unroll the phyllo onto a jelly roll pan or cookie sheet lined with wax paper. To prevent the phyllo sheets from drying out, lay another sheet of wax paper on top of the phyllo, and cover with a moist dish towel. Have ready the clarified butter, bread crumbs, and filling.

5. Place one sheet of phyllo on a pastry or cutting board. Brush the sheet of phyllo with clarified butter, and sprinkle it with 1 teaspoon of the bread crumbs. Arrange a second sheet of phyllo over the first. Brush again with clarified butter and sprinkle with 1 teaspoon of the crumbs.

6. Cut the phyllo lengthwise into two long even strips. Place a generous tablespoon of the filling about 1 inch above the lower edge of the phyllo on each strip. Fold the bottom corner of the strip diagonally across to the opposite edge to cover the filling, forming a triangle. Then fold the triangle over on itself as you would fold a flag. *Do not fold too tightly.* When you reach the end, either trim any extra dough with a pizza wheel or brush with clarified butter and tuck it under the triangle to form a neat package.

7. Place the triangle seam side down on the prepared pan and brush the top with clarified butter. Make air vents by piercing the top of the triangle three or four times with the tip of a sharp knife. Repeat with the remaining phyllo and filling. (If any filling remains, store it in the refrigerator. It can be spooned over a slice of your favorite cheesecake.)

BAKE THE TRIANGLES

8. Position the racks in the upper and lower thirds of the oven. Heat the oven to 375°F.

9. Bake the triangles for 18 to 20 minutes, or until the tops are golden brown. Rotate the pans top to bottom and front to back toward the end of the baking time. Remove from the oven and let cool for about 5 minutes on the pans, then transfer to cooling racks and cool completely. Dust with powdered sugar before serving.

STORAGE: These triangles are best eaten the day they are made. Leftover triangles should be refrigerated and covered lightly with aluminum foil, for up to 3 days. Reheat before serving (see page 286).

phyllo triangles with stewed fruit filling

MAKES SIXTEEN 4½-INCH TRIANGLES

PLAN AHEAD: Make fruit filling at least 2 hours in advance

Mixed dried fruits make a marvelous filling for baking. Most supermarkets offer a medley of dried fruits like apples, apricots, cherries, pears, and prunes all in a single package. I like to simmer these fruits with a Granny Smith apple, a slice each of orange and lemon, and a cinnamon stick. Avoid using dried organic fruits; these do not soften during cooking.

> **AT A GLANCE**
> **PANS:** Rimmed cookie sheets
> **PAN PREP:** Line with parchment
> **OVEN TEMP:** 375°F
> **BAKING TIME:** 18 to 20 minutes
> **DIFFICULTY:** ♨ ♨

When you prepare these turnovers, the dried fruit filling should be made at least 2 hours before you assemble the triangles. In fact, the filling can be made days in advance, and the best part is that it gets better with age. These cooked fruits also make a terrific topping for ice cream or your favorite pound cake.

STEWED FRUIT FILLING

1½ cups mixed dried fruit (not organic), cut into ¾-inch dice

1 cup peeled and diced Granny Smith apple (¾-inch dice)

1 orange slice, ¼ inch thick

1 lemon slice, ¼ inch thick

1 cup water

½ cup granulated sugar

1 cinnamon stick

1 (1-pound) package phyllo dough, 9 x 14 inches, fresh or frozen and thawed

⅔ cup unsalted butter, clarified (see page 382)

⅔ cup Sweetened Bread Crumbs (page 291)

Powdered sugar, for dusting

MAKE THE FILLING

1. At least 2 hours before making the triangles, prepare the filling. In a 2-quart saucepan, combine the dried fruit, apple, orange and lemon slices, water, granulated sugar, and cinnamon stick. Bring to a slow boil, stirring occasionally to dissolve the sugar. Cook, covered, over low heat for 45 minutes, or until tender and the liquid is almost absorbed. Remove the cover for the last few minutes and reduce the liquid if too much remains. Cool completely, discarding the orange and lemon slices and cinnamon stick.

ASSEMBLE THE TRIANGLES

2. Dab the corners of rimmed cookie sheets with butter, line with baking parchment, and set aside. Working with half of the package at a time, unroll the phyllo onto a jelly roll pan or cookie sheet lined with wax paper. To prevent the phyllo sheets from drying out, lay another sheet of wax paper on top of the phyllo, and cover with a moist dish towel. Have ready the melted clarified butter, bread crumbs, and filling.

3. Place one sheet of phyllo on a pastry or cutting board. Brush the sheet of phyllo with clarified butter, and sprinkle it with 1 teaspoon of the bread crumbs. Arrange a second sheet of phyllo over the first. Brush again with clarified butter and sprinkle with 1 teaspoon of the crumbs.

4. Cut the phyllo lengthwise into two long even strips. Place a generous tablespoon of the filling about 1 inch above the lower edge of the phyllo on each strip. Fold the bottom corner of the strip diagonally across to the opposite edge to cover the filling, forming a triangle. Fold the triangle over on itself as you would fold a flag. *Do not fold too tightly.* When you reach the end, either trim any extra dough with a pizza wheel or brush with clarified butter and tuck it under the triangle to form a neat package.

5. Place the triangle seam side down on the prepared pan and brush the top with clarified butter. Make air vents by piercing the top of the triangle three or four times with the tip of a sharp knife. Repeat with the remaining phyllo and filling. If any filling remains, store it in the refrigerator. It can be spooned over a slice of your favorite pound cake or ice cream.

BAKE THE TRIANGLES

6. Position the racks in the upper and lower thirds of the oven. Heat the oven to 375°F.

7. Bake the triangles for 18 to 20 minutes, or until the tops are golden brown. Rotate the pans top to bottom and front to back toward the end of the baking time. Remove from the oven and let cool for about 5 minutes on the pans, then transfer to cooling racks and cool completely. Dust with powdered sugar before serving.

STORAGE: These triangles are best eaten the day they are made. Leftover triangles should be refrigerated and covered lightly with aluminum foil, for up to 3 days. Reheat before serving (see page 286).

coffee break bites

Super-Moist Brownies

Macadamia Fudge Squares

Apricot Walnut Bars

Maple Oatmeal Meringue Bars

Black Raspberry Jam Squares

Miniature Faux Strudel Rolls

Chocolate Pistachio Thumbprints

Lemon Shortbread

Glazed Orange Ricotta Cookies

Chocolate Orange Biscotti

Powdered Sugar Italian Slices

Nut-Crusted Rugelach

VARIATION: Cinnamon Raisin Rugelach

VARIATION: Chocolate Chip Rugelach

Cinnamon Pecan Crescents

Apple Strips

Black Chocolate Madeleines

Kirsch Krisps

ABOUT COFFEE BREAK BITES

In this chapter you will find a large selection of cookies, from bar cookies, biscotti, and drop cookies to others made from dough that is rolled and filled. To help you along, here are some tips to ensure successful results.

• Watch brownies carefully toward the end of baking time. Even 1 or 2 minutes can make a difference between rich, moist brownies and ones that are dry and overdone.

• Remember that brownies continue to bake when taken out of the oven. Even if the center of the bar appears underdone, it will firm up upon standing.

• When making layered bar cookies, when pressing the dough into the pan for the bottom crust, if the dough for the bottom crust feels too oily, let it rest for 5 minutes to allow the flour to absorb the butter. This will make it easier to handle.

• Distribute the dough evenly for the bottom crust by dividing it into eighths, then place two rows down each side of the pan. Use a batarde, flat-bottomed glass, or the heel of your hand to flatten the dough. If the utensil sticks to the dough, cover it with plastic wrap.

• Insert a cake tester, toothpick, or the tip of a small knife randomly in the bar cookie dough to test for even thickness.

• Use a small offset spatula to smooth the surface of the bar cookie dough.

• When making layered bar cookies, to be sure the top layer adheres to the bottom layer, always place your topping on a warm crust.

• If the cookie dough is too soft to hand-shape into balls, chill the dough for about 30 minutes, or until firm enough to handle. Do not allow it to become too cold, or it will crumble.

• To reduce the stickiness of dough when it is to be rolled or hand-shaped into balls, allow it to rest for a few minutes. This standing time permits the flour to absorb the fat.

• When shaping biscotti dough, if the dough sticks to your palms, wet them with cold water, rub lightly with bland cooking oil, or dust with flour. It's okay if the sides are somewhat irregular when shaping.

• Because biscotti are twice-baked, do not overbrown them on the initial baking. The top should feel firm to the touch, and the bottom should be light brown.

• If you like softer biscotti, toast only on one side, and reduce the baking time.

• Cutting biscotti on the diagonal will give you larger slices, while cutting the loaves straight across will make smaller slices.

- If rugelach dough is made with cream cheese and butter, be sure that the consistency of both is of equal softness. If they are not the same, cream the firmer one first.
- If rugelach dough is ready to roll, it should yield to the touch when pressed with a finger. If the dough is too cold, it will crack and be difficult to roll.
- When rolling filled cookies, do not roll them too tightly. It's important to leave room for steam to form, which causes the layers of dough to expand and the centers to bake through.
- When rolling cookie dough, to ensure even thickness, give the dough a quarter turn every so often.
- When rolling cookie dough, always form the dough into the shape into which it will be rolled. For example, dough that is to be rolled into a rectangle should be formed into an oblong shape before rolling.
- Avoid the temptation to overfill dough. Too much filling results in the dough cracking and the filling leaking during baking.
- For refrigerated doughs, remove only one piece of dough at a time for rolling.

super-moist brownies

MAKES THIRTY-TWO 1½ × 2-INCH BARS

For me there is no time of day that's a bad time of day (or night) to enjoy a brownie. This terrific recipe comes from Kathleen Sanderson, my teaching partner for more than eighteen years in the Principles of Cooking Series at King's Cooking Studio. Here's a friendly reminder: baked goodies continue to cook even when removed from the oven. You want your brownies to be super moist, so pay special attention not to overbake them.

<table>
<tr><td colspan="2">AT A GLANCE</td></tr>
<tr><td>PAN:</td><td>9 × 13 × 2-inch baking pan</td></tr>
<tr><td>PAN PREP:</td><td>Line with foil/butter</td></tr>
<tr><td>OVEN TEMP:</td><td>350°F</td></tr>
<tr><td>BAKING TIME:</td><td>26 to 28 minutes</td></tr>
<tr><td>DIFFICULTY:</td><td>🍵</td></tr>
</table>

- 1 cup (2 sticks) unsalted butter
- 10 ounces fine-quality bitter- or semisweet chocolate, such as Lindt, coarsely chopped
- 2½ ounces unsweetened chocolate, coarsely chopped
- 5 large eggs
- 1¾ cups sugar

- 1½ teaspoons pure vanilla extract
- ½ teaspoon salt
- 1¼ cups all-purpose flour, spooned in and leveled
- 1½ cups medium-chopped toasted pecans or walnuts (see pages 391–392)

1. Position the rack in the middle of the oven. Heat the oven to 350°F. Line a 9 × 13 × 2-inch pan with aluminum foil and butter the foil (see the sidebar).

2. Place the butter and chopped chocolates in a medium bowl and set it over a pot of simmering water. (Be careful that the bottom of the bowl does not touch the water.) Heat until the chocolates are almost melted, then remove the bowl from the pot and stir to form a smooth mixture.

3. In a large mixing bowl, whisk the eggs to blend, then add the sugar in a steady stream. Blend in the vanilla, then add the chocolate mixture along with the salt and mix well.

4. Place the flour in a large strainer. Sift it over the chocolate mixture in three or four additions, folding with a large rubber spatula after each addition. Fold in the nuts.

5. Pour the batter into the prepared pan, spreading it evenly into the corners, and bake for 26 to 28 minutes. A toothpick inserted into the center of the brownie should come out slightly moist, with a few crumbs on the toothpick. *Do not overbake.*

6. Cool the brownies in the pan for at least 2 hours. *Note:* These brownies will cut better if allowed to rest several hours or overnight before cutting (see "Cutting Bar Cookies," page 317). Lift the brownies from the pan and place on a large cutting board. Pull down the sides of the foil and cut into $1\frac{1}{2} \times 2$-inch bars using a long thin-bladed knife.

STORAGE: Store in an airtight container, layered between strips of wax paper, for up to 5 days. These brownies may be frozen.

PREPARING FOIL-LINED PANS FOR BAR COOKIES

Invert the baking pan. Center an 18-inch sheet of heavy-duty aluminum foil over the top of the pan. Allow 2 inches of foil to extend beyond the edge where the pan meets the counter. Smooth the foil against the pan, pressing it down the sides. Remove the foil shell and turn the pan right side up. Place the foil into the pan and press it evenly across the bottom and smoothly against the sides. Bend your index finger to press it into the corners. Working with very soft (not melted) butter, carefully butter the bottom and sides of the pan with a pastry brush. Take care not to tear the foil.

macadamia fudge squares

MAKES 4 DOZEN 2-INCH SQUARES

This pretty bar cookie is another play on a brownie. Dark brown sugar and a hint of cinnamon are perfect partners for the robust flavor of the chocolate. The top is generously sprinkled with macadamia nuts and has a chocolate webbed finish that's guaranteed to catch your eye.

AT A GLANCE
PAN: 10½ x 15½ x 1-inch jelly roll pan
PAN PREP: Line with foil/butter
OVEN TEMP: 375°F
BAKING TIME: 13 to 15 minutes
DIFFICULTY: ☕

1 cup all-purpose flour, spooned in and leveled

¼ teaspoon ground cinnamon

¼ teaspoon salt

1 cup (2 sticks) unsalted butter

4 ounces unsweetened chocolate, coarsely chopped

1 cup (lightly packed) *very fresh* dark brown sugar

1 cup granulated sugar

4 large eggs, well beaten

1 teaspoon pure vanilla extract

1½ to 1¾ cups coarsely chopped, salted macadamia nuts

1 small recipe Midnight Chocolate Glaze (page 363)

1. Position the rack in the middle of the oven. Heat the oven to 375°F. Line a 10½ x 15½ x 1-inch jelly roll pan with aluminum foil and butter the foil (see the sidebar on page 313).

2. In a medium bowl, thoroughly whisk together the flour, cinnamon, and salt. Set aside.

3. In a large bowl set over a pot of barely simmering water, slowly melt the butter and the chocolate. Stir occasionally. Remove from the heat and, using a whisk, blend the brown sugar into the mixture, stirring until melted. Gradually mix in the granulated sugar. Stir in the eggs and the vanilla. Add the dry ingredients, stirring just until combined. Do not overmix.

4. Spread the batter evenly in the prepared pan, smoothing it with the back of a tablespoon. Sprinkle the surface with the macadamia nuts and press them gently into the batter. Bake for 13 to 15 minutes, or until the top is set and the bar begins to pull away from the sides of the pan. *Do not overbake.* The squares should remain slightly moist on the inside. (Note: If the batter rises in the pan during baking, prick the bub-

bles gently with a fork to release the air.) Remove from the oven and let stand until almost cool.

5. While the bar is cooling, make the glaze. To web the bar, dip a small whisk into the glaze and squiggle it across the pan. If the glaze becomes too thick, thin it with a little *very hot* water. Let stand until the glaze is set.

6. Carefully lift the bar from the pan by grasping the foil on both sides and place it on a large cutting board. Pull down the sides of the foil and cut into 2-inch squares using a thin-bladed, sharp knife (see "Cutting Bar Cookies," page 317).

STORAGE: Store in an airtight container, layered between strips of wax paper, for up to 5 days. These cookies may be frozen.

"I cannot remember when I first ate a macadamia, but I was hooked. . . . They were beautiful—so lumpy, Macadamian, salty golden! I can still sense its complete Macadamianimity."

M. F. K. FISHER

apricot walnut bars

MAKES 2 DOZEN 1¼ X 2-INCH BARS

One day during lunch, one of my assistants, Deb Barrett, brought in a terrific bar cookie for us to enjoy. It was made with chewy apricots and lots of walnuts, highlighted with Triple Sec and orange zest. As I began to nibble on one, just to taste, my willpower deteriorated rapidly, and before I knew it, the entire cookie was gone. The flavors blend beautifully and this cookie gets better with age.

AT A GLANCE
PAN: 9 x 9-inch square baking pan
PAN PREP: Line with foil/butter
OVEN TEMP: 350°F
BAKING TIME: 35 to 40 minutes
DIFFICULTY: ♥

1½ cups all-purpose flour, spooned in and leveled

1 teaspoon baking powder

½ teaspoon salt

½ cup (1 stick) unsalted butter, slightly firm

1 teaspoon freshly grated navel orange zest

1½ cups (lightly packed) *very fresh* light brown sugar

2 large eggs

1 tablespoon orange liqueur, such as Triple Sec

1 cup (6 ounces) very fresh dried apricots (not organic), cut into ¼-inch pieces

1 cup broken walnuts (see page 392)

2 teaspoons sparkling sugar (see page 380)

1. Position the rack in the lower third of the oven. Heat the oven to 350°F. Line a 9 × 9-inch pan with aluminum foil and butter the foil (see the sidebar on page 313).

2. In a large bowl, thoroughly whisk together the flour, baking powder, and salt. Set aside.

3. In the bowl of an electric mixer fitted with the paddle attachment, mix the butter and orange zest together on medium speed until smooth, about 1 minute. Gradually add the brown sugar, taking about 2 minutes, then beat for 2 minutes longer.

4. Add the eggs, one at a time, mixing to blend after each addition. Scrape down the side of the bowl, then mix in the liqueur.

5. With the mixer on low speed, add the flour mixture, mixing only until combined. Add the apricots and walnuts, and mix for 20 seconds.

6. Spoon the batter into the prepared pan and smooth the top with an offset spatula. Sprinkle the top with sparkling sugar.

7. Bake for 35 to 40 minutes, or until the top is firm to the touch and golden brown. Remove from the oven and place on a cooling rack. When the bar is cool, grasp the foil on either side of the pan and lift the bar onto a cutting board. Pull down the sides of the foil and lay flat. Using a thin-bladed, sharp knife, cut into two dozen 1¼ × 2-inch bars (see "Cutting Bar Cookies," below).

STORAGE: Store between sheets of wax paper in a tightly covered cookie tin for up to 1 week. These bars may be frozen.

CUTTING BAR COOKIES

Always cool bar cookies completely before cutting. Some cookies, such as brownies, actually cut better the day after baking. Cut bar cookies with a thin, sharp 10-inch slicing or 12- to 14-inch serrated knife. Longer-bladed knives allow you to cut through the cookie in one motion. Very thick bar cookies can be cut with a small spatula or dough scraper, inserting the spatula straight down into the bar.

When cutting the bar, do not use a sawing motion. Instead, cut straight down through the cookie. Paper towels moistened with hot water are handy for wiping the knife between cuts. Replace the towels as needed, because a clean blade will give you a cleaner cut. Measure the bar evenly with a ruler, preferably before you begin cutting. Your knife should be periodically rinsed with hot water to thoroughly clean it. Dry it well, and begin again.

maple oatmeal meringue bars

MAKES THIRTY-TWO 2 X 1½-INCH BARS

This bar cookie is made with a tasty cookie crust containing ground oats, brown sugar, maple extract, and cinnamon, all bound with butter. A maple-flavored brown-sugar meringue coats the top along with a blanket of chopped toasted walnuts.

AT A GLANCE
PAN: 9 x 13 x 2-inch baking pan
PAN PREP: Line with foil/butter
OVEN TEMP: 350°F for crust, 325°F for topping
BAKING TIME: 17 to 18 minutes for crust, 30 to 32 minutes for topping
DIFFICULTY: 🥄 🥄

CRUST

⅔ cup (1⅓ sticks) unsalted butter

¼ cup (lightly packed) *very fresh* light brown sugar

3 tablespoons granulated sugar

½ teaspoon maple extract

1 cup unsifted all-purpose flour, spooned in and leveled

⅔ cup quick-cooking oats

½ teaspoon salt

½ teaspoon ground cinnamon

¼ teaspoon baking powder

TOPPING

3 large egg whites, at room temperature

¼ teaspoon cream of tartar

¼ teaspoon salt

¾ cup (lightly packed) *very fresh* light brown sugar

1 teaspoon maple extract

½ teaspoon pure vanilla extract

½ teaspoon ground cinnamon

1¼ cups toasted walnuts, coarsely chopped (see pages 391–392)

1. Position the rack in the middle of the oven. Heat the oven to 350°F. Line a 9 × 13 × 2-inch pan with aluminum foil and butter the foil (see the sidebar on page 313).

MAKE THE CRUST

2. Put the butter in a 2-quart saucepan and place over low heat. When the butter is almost melted, remove the pan from the heat. Cool to tepid.

3. Place the sugars and maple extract in the work bowl of a food processor fitted with the steel blade. Pulse 2 to 3 times, then process for 5 to 6 seconds, until well blended. Add the flour, oats, salt, cinnamon, and baking powder. Pulse 5 to 6 times,

then process for 8 to 10 seconds, until the mixture is the consistency of fine meal. Empty into the cooled butter and stir with a fork until a crumb mixture forms.

4. Squeeze the crumbs in your hands to form larger clumps of crumbs and scatter them evenly in the bottom of the prepared pan. Press down with a flat bottom meat pounder or a glass to flatten and form a smooth crust. Clean the edges of the pan by using a dough scraper or small spatula inserted between the dough and foil. Bake the crust for 17 to 18 minutes, remove from the oven, then *reduce the oven temperature* to 325°F. While the crust is baking, prepare the meringue topping.

MAKE THE TOPPING

5. Place the egg whites in the bowl of an electric mixer fitted with the whip attachment. Whip the whites on medium-low speed until frothy, then add the cream of tartar and salt. Increase the mixer speed to medium-high and whip to firm peaks (see "Beating Egg Whites," page 385). Add about 2 tablespoons of the brown sugar at a time, taking about 2 minutes. Add the extracts and the cinnamon, and beat for 10 to 15 seconds longer. Remove the bowl from the machine and fold in 1 cup of the walnuts using an oversize rubber spatula.

BAKE THE BARS

6. Spoon the meringue over the warm crust, smoothing the top with a small offset spatula. Sprinkle with the remaining walnuts. Bake for 30 to 32 minutes, or until the bar begins to pull away from the sides of the pan. The top will feel soft. Remove from the oven and place on a wire rack. When cool, grasp the sides of the foil and carefully lift the bars onto a cutting board. Pull down the foil and lay flat. Cut into 2 × 1½-inch bars with a thin-bladed sharp knife (see "Cutting Bar Cookies," page 317).

STORAGE: Store in a container with the cover askew, layered between strips of wax paper, for up to 1 week. Freezing is not recommended.

black raspberry jam squares

MAKES THIRTY-TWO 2 X 1½-INCH BARS

At the end of a baking class that I taught at the Institute for Culinary Education in New York City, my assistant, Sarah Abrams, told me about a recipe of her mother's that was a favorite of hers since childhood. Maida Abrams, Sarah's mom, made her bar cookie with Damson plum preserves, a product that is difficult to obtain these days. For convenience, I substituted black raspberry jam with excellent results, but if

> **AT A GLANCE**
> **PAN:** 9 x 13 x 2-inch baking pan
> **PAN PREP:** Line with foil/butter
> **OVEN TEMP:** 350°F
> **BAKING TIME:** 23 to 25 minutes for crust, 23 to 25 minutes for topping
> **DIFFICULTY:** 🥄 🥄

you can locate Damson plum preserves, by all means use it. The jam is spread on a warm shortbread crust and has a crunchy meringue topping.

CRUST

1 cup (2 sticks) unsalted butter, softened

2 teaspoons finely grated lemon zest

½ cup strained powdered sugar, spooned in and leveled

4 large egg yolks

2 cups all-purpose flour, spooned in and leveled

¼ teaspoon salt

½ cup pure seedless black raspberry jam or preserves

TOPPING

4 large egg whites

Pinch of salt

1 cup granulated sugar

½ teaspoon ground cinnamon

½ teaspoon pure vanilla extract

2 cups coarsely chopped walnuts (see page 392)

1. Position the rack in the lower third of the oven. Heat the oven to 350°F. Line a 9 × 13 × 2-inch pan with aluminum foil and butter the foil (see the sidebar on page 313).

MAKE THE CRUST

2. In the bowl of an electric mixer fitted with the paddle attachment, on medium-low speed, mix the butter with the lemon zest just until smooth. Add the powdered sugar and mix again. Add the egg yolks, two at a time, scraping down the side of the bowl as needed.

3. Reduce the mixer speed to low and add the flour in two additions along with the salt, mixing until almost incorporated. It's okay if some of the flour remains visible.

4. Divide the dough into eight portions and place two rows across and four down in the prepared pan. With the palm of your hand, press the dough evenly across the bottom. Smooth the top of the dough with a small offset spatula or the bottom of a graduated dry measuring cup. Using a dough scraper or small metal spatula, neaten the edges of the dough by carefully inserting the scraper between the dough and foil, working around the pan.

5. Bake for 23 to 25 minutes, or until lightly browned around the edges. Remove the crust from the oven and let stand for 5 minutes. Spread the preserves evenly over the warm crust with a small offset spatula. Set aside.

MAKE THE TOPPING

6. In the bowl of an electric mixer fitted with the whip attachment, beat the egg whites on medium speed until frothy. Add the salt. Increase the speed to medium-high and beat until firm peaks form (see "Beating Egg Whites," page 385). Add the granulated sugar, 1 to 2 tablespoons at a time, taking about 2 minutes. Add the cinnamon and vanilla, and beat for 15 seconds longer to form a shiny meringue. Remove the bowl from the machine. Using an oversize rubber spatula, fold in the walnuts.

BAKE THE SQUARES

7. Spoon the meringue over the preserves, and smooth the top with a small offset spatula. Bake for 23 to 25 minutes, or until firm to the touch. Let stand on a wire rack until completely cooled.

8. When the bar is cool, grasp the foil on both sides and carefully remove it from the pan and place on a cutting board. Pull down the sides of the foil and lay flat. Using a warmed, long, thin-bladed knife, cut into 2 × 1½-inch bars. (See "Cutting Bar Cookies," page 317.) Let the cookies air-dry for 3 to 4 hours before storing.

STORAGE: Store in a container with the cover askew, layered between strips of wax paper, for up to 5 days. Freezing is not recommended.

miniature faux strudel rolls

MAKES 8 DOZEN 2 X 1¼-INCH COOKIES

When I was growing up in Memphis, one of the most popular sweets that I remember being served at family celebrations was a little strudel-like pastry, generously filled with flavorful dried fruits and nuts that had been macerated in liqueur. This recipe is my adaptation of one that was shared with me many years ago by my cousin, Charlotte Bilsky.

AT A GLANCE
PANS: Cookie sheets
PAN PREP: Butter/line with parchment
OVEN TEMP: 325°F
BAKING TIME: 30 to 35 minutes
PAN PREP: Difficulty: 🥄 🥄 🥄

FILLING

2¾ cups golden raisins (1-pound box)

2½ cups halved dried apricots (not organic)

1¼ cups quartered dried peaches (not organic)

1¼ cups whole pitted prunes

1⅓ cups flaked sweetened coconut

⅓ cup halved red glacéed cherries

⅓ cup halved green glacéed cherries

2 teaspoons freshly grated lemon zest

1 (12-ounce) jar thick peach preserves

2 cups coarsely chopped toasted pecans or walnuts (see pages 391–392)

⅔ cup strained powdered sugar, spooned in and leveled

¼ cup **Grand Marnier liqueur**

DOUGH

4 cups sifted, all-purpose flour, spooned in and leveled

1 teaspoon baking powder

½ teaspoon salt

¾ cup warm water

½ cup canola or safflower oil

2 large eggs, lightly beaten

½ cup granulated sugar

1 teaspoon ground cinnamon

MAKE THE FILLING

1. Place the raisins, apricots, peaches, and prunes in a large bowl. Add enough boiling water to cover. Soften for 10 minutes. Drain the fruits well and place them on several layers of paper towels. Cover with more towels and press to remove excess water.

2. In a large bowl, combine the drained fruits, coconut, red and green cherries, and lemon zest. In the work bowl of a food processor fitted with the steel blade pulse the mixture in batches until medium-fine. Empty into a large bowl and stir in the peach preserves, chopped pecans, powdered sugar, and liqueur. (The filling may be made up to 1 week ahead.)

MAKE THE DOUGH

3. Heat the oven to 200°F for 2 to 3 minutes. Turn the oven off. In a large bowl, thoroughly whisk together the flour, baking powder, and salt. Make a well in the center and add the water, oil, and eggs. Using a wooden spoon, mix briefly to blend, then knead gently in the bowl until smooth. Place the dough in a clean bowl, cover it tightly with plastic wrap, and set in a pan of warm water. Place in the warmed oven and let rest for 30 minutes.

FILL THE STRUDEL

4. Position the racks in the upper and lower thirds of the oven. Heat the oven to 325°F. Dab the corners of cookie sheets with butter, then line with baking parchment.

5. Combine the granulated sugar and cinnamon in a small bowl. Remove the dough from the oven, and using a dough scraper or a sharp knife, divide it into eighths. Keep the unused portions in the unlit oven in the water bath. Working with one piece at a time, place the dough on a lightly floured board and roll it into a 14 × 9-inch rectangle, keeping the 9-inch side parallel to the countertop. The dough should be very thin. Spread one-eighth of the filling over the dough, leaving a 2-inch border on the far side. Sprinkle the filling with 1 teaspoon of the cinnamon/sugar mixture.

6. Starting with the edge closest to you, roll the dough into a log and pinch the seam well. Do not roll too tightly. Roll the log back and forth until it measures about 15 inches. Cut into twelve 1¼-inch pieces. Dip the top of each piece in the remaining cinnamon/sugar mixture. Place the pieces seam side down on the prepared cookie sheets, spacing them about 1 inch apart. Repeat the procedure until all of the dough and filling have been used.

BAKE THE STRUDEL

7. Bake for 30 to 35 minutes, or until golden brown. To ensure even browning, toward the end of baking time, rotate the sheets top to bottom and front to back. Remove from the oven and let rest on the cookie sheets for 5 minutes, then loosen with a thin-bladed metal spatula and transfer to cooling racks. These are best if they are allowed to mellow for a few days before serving.

STORAGE: Store in an airtight container, layered between strips of wax paper, for up to 3 weeks. These cookies may be frozen.

chocolate pistachio thumbprints

MAKES 32 COOKIES

Before baking, these cookies are dipped in beaten egg white, then rolled in crunchy, toasted, chopped pistachio nuts and sparkling sugar. The thumbprint in the center is filled with a rich chocolate glaze. This eye-catching cookie is perfect for entertaining as well as for a casual family treat.

AT A GLANCE
PANS: Two rimmed cookie sheets
PAN PREP: Line with parchment
OVEN TEMP: 350°F
BAKING TIME: 12 minutes, plus 3 to 5 minutes
DIFFICULTY: ♟

1¾ cups all-purpose flour, spooned in and leveled

¼ cup strained Dutch-process cocoa powder, spooned in and leveled

¼ teaspoon salt

1 cup (2 sticks) unsalted butter, slightly firm

¾ cup granulated sugar

2 large egg yolks

1½ teaspoons pure vanilla extract

1 cup medium-chopped toasted pistachios (see pages 391–392)

3 tablespoons sparkling sugar (see page 380)

2 large egg whites, lightly beaten with 2 teaspoons water

Midnight Chocolate Glaze (page 363)

1. Position the racks in the upper and lower thirds of the oven. Heat the oven to 350°F. Line two rimmed cookie sheets with baking parchment and set aside.

2. In a large bowl, thoroughly whisk together the flour, cocoa powder, and salt. Set aside.

3. Place the butter in the bowl of an electric mixer fitted with the paddle attachment. Mix the butter on medium speed until smooth, about 2 minutes. Add the granulated sugar in a steady stream, mixing just until incorporated. Blend in the yolks and vanilla, scraping down the side of the bowl as needed.

4. Remove the bowl from the machine, and using a wooden spoon, blend in the flour mixture in two additions, mixing just until incorporated after each addition. Do not overmix or the dough will become oily.

5. Taking a scant tablespoon of dough, roll it in your hands into a large, walnut-size ball. Place on a large sheet of wax paper. Repeat until all of the dough has been formed.

6. In a small bowl, combine the pistachios and sparkling sugar. Place one-half of the mixture in a low, flat dish, such as a pie plate. Dip each ball into the egg white, then

into the nut mixture, adding more of the mixture as needed. Place the balls 2 inches apart on the prepared pans.

7. Make a deep indentation in the center of each cookie using the tip of a wooden spoon handle. Choose a spoon with a rounded handle about ½ inch wide. (If the dough starts to stick, dip the handle of the spoon in flour before pressing.)

8. Bake for 12 minutes, then remove the cookies from the oven and press each indentation again. Return to the oven, rotating the pans top to bottom and front to back, and bake for another 3 to 5 minutes, or until the cookies are firm to the touch.

9. Remove from the oven and let rest on the pan for 5 to 6 minutes. While the cookies are resting, prepare the glaze. When cool enough to handle, transfer to cooling racks. When the cookies are tepid, fill each indentation with ½ teaspoon glaze.

STORAGE: Store in an airtight container, layered between strips of wax paper, for up to 1 week. These cookies may be frozen.

lemon shortbread

Shortbread makes a perfect nibble to enjoy with coffee, tea, or milk. These buttery cookies, made with lots of lemon zest and a touch of orange as well, are impossible to resist.

AT A GLANCE

PANS: 9 x 9-inch square baking pan/cookie sheet
PAN PREP: Line with foil/butter
OVEN TEMP: 300°F
BAKING TIME: 45 to 50 minutes, plus 10 to 12 minutes
DIFFICULTY: ☕

1½ cups all-purpose flour, spooned in and leveled

⅓ cup rice flour, spooned in and leveled

½ teaspoon ground cardamom

¼ teaspoon salt

¾ cup (1½ sticks) unsalted butter, slightly firm

2 tablespoons finely grated lemon zest

1 teaspoon finely grated navel orange zest

6 tablespoons superfine sugar

1. Position the rack in the center of the oven. Heat the oven to 300°F. Line a 9 × 9-inch square pan with aluminum foil and butter the foil (see the sidebar on page 313).

2. In a large bowl, thoroughly whisk the all-purpose and rice flours, cardamom, and salt. Set aside.

3. In the large bowl of an electric mixer fitted with the paddle attachment, cream the butter with the lemon and orange zests until smooth, about 1 minute. Add the sugar in a steady stream and beat for another 2 minutes.

4. Reduce the mixer speed to low and add half of the dry ingredients, mixing until almost incorporated. Add the remaining dry ingredients and mix just until clumps begin to form. Remove the bowl from the machine and knead the mixture with your hands until it forms a dough. Do not overwork the dough.

5. Place the dough on a lightly floured surface and shape into a 5-inch square. Divide the dough into nine equal pieces and arrange them evenly in the prepared pan, with three pieces across in each direction.

6. Place a piece of plastic wrap on top of the dough and press it evenly into the pan using a meat batarde or the flat bottom of a glass or measuring cup. Be sure the dough

is pushed into the corners of the pan. Clean the edges of the pan by using a dough scraper or a small spatula inserted between the dough and the foil.

7. Using a table fork dipped in flour, press around the edges of the dough to create a design, then prick the dough with the fork at 1-inch intervals to create steam vents and prevent it from cracking. Bake for 45 to 50 minutes, or until just beginning to brown. Keep the oven on.

8. Remove the shortbread from the oven and let rest for 10 minutes. Have ready a cookie sheet without sides. Grasp the foil on each side and carefully lift the shortbread from the pan and place it on the cookie sheet. Pull the aluminum foil down to release it from the sides of the shortbread and smooth the foil over the cookie sheet. Using a long, serrated knife, cut five 1½-inch strips. Give the cookie sheet a quarter turn and cut five more strips, forming twenty-five squares. Spread the cookies apart with a small metal spatula. Return to the oven for 10 to 12 more minutes to dry and crisp the cookies. Remove from the oven and let cool for 5 to 10 minutes. Using a small offset spatula, transfer the cookies to a cooling rack.

STORAGE: Store in an airtight container, layered between sheets of wax paper, for up to 1 week. These cookies may be frozen.

glazed orange ricotta cookies

MAKES ABOUT 4 DOZEN 2½-INCH COOKIES

This cookie is made with soft ricotta, the versatile Italian cheese that is used in many desserts. The ricotta is added to a buttery dough, giving it a softer crumb. For added texture, the dough is made with stone-ground cornmeal. To heighten the flavor, I have added orange zest to the cookie and topped it with orange glaze. With the stroke of a wand a simple cookie is transformed into Cinderella-at-the-ball!

2 cups unsifted all-purpose flour, spooned in and leveled

¼ cup yellow cornmeal, preferably stone-ground

½ teaspoon baking powder

½ teaspoon baking soda

½ teaspoon salt

¾ cup (1½ sticks) unsalted butter, slightly firm

1 tablespoon freshly grated navel orange zest

½ cup whole milk ricotta

1 cup superfine sugar

2 large egg yolks

1½ teaspoons pure vanilla extract

Orange Glaze (page 362)

½ cup toasted pine nuts (see page 391)

1. Position the racks in the upper and lower thirds of the oven. Heat the oven to 350°F. Moderately butter two cookie sheets.

2. In a large bowl, thoroughly whisk together the flour, cornmeal, baking powder, baking soda, and salt.

3. In the bowl of an electric mixer fitted with the paddle attachment, mix the butter and orange zest on medium-low speed until creamy and lightened in color, about 2 minutes. Add the ricotta and mix until well blended, about 1 minute. Add the sugar in three parts, mixing well after each addition, then add the egg yolks and vanilla. Scrape down the side of the bowl as needed.

4. Reduce the mixer speed to low and add the flour mixture in two additions, mixing just until blended.

5. Using a teaspoon, drop small walnut-size mounds of dough onto the cookie sheets, spacing them about 2 inches apart.

6. Bake the cookies until the edges are golden and the tops begin to brown, 14 to 16 minutes. To ensure even browning, toward the end of baking time, rotate the pans

top to bottom and front to back. Remove from the oven and let stand for 2 to 3 minutes. Loosen with a thin metal spatula and place on cooling racks set over wax paper.

7. While the cookies are still warm, spread ½ teaspoon of the glaze across the top of each cookie. (The whole top of the cookie does not have to be covered.) Immediately sprinkle with a few toasted nuts. Let stand until the glaze hardens.

STORAGE: Store in an airtight container, layered between strips of wax paper, for up to 2 weeks. These cookies may be frozen.

chocolate orange biscotti

This recipe for this favorite sweet snack features the irresistible combination of orange, chocolate, and pecans. Once again, I tapped the talents of my assistant, Deb Barrett, when she brought in a batch of these to share with us. Her recipe was so good that I wanted to share it with my baking audience. I think that you, too, will find these biscotti to be the perfect "coffee break bite."

AT A GLANCE
PAN: Rimmed cookie sheet
PAN PREP: Line with parchment
OVEN TEMP: 325°/300°F
BAKING TIME: 25 to 30 minutes, plus 15 minutes
DIFFICULTY: ♨

---

2 cups all-purpose flour, spooned in and leveled

1 teaspoon baking powder

¼ teaspoon salt

½ cup (1 stick) unsalted butter, slightly firm

2 teaspoons freshly grated navel orange zest

½ teaspoon orange oil

½ cup sugar

2 large eggs

1 cup (about 5 ounces) finely chopped, fine-quality bittersweet chocolate, such as Lindt

1 cup lightly toasted pecans, coarsely chopped (see pages 391–392)

1. Position the rack in the middle of the oven. Heat the oven to 325°F. Lightly butter the corners of a rimmed cookie sheet and line with baking parchment.

2. In a large bowl, thoroughly whisk together the flour, baking powder, and salt. Set aside.

3. In the bowl of an electric mixer fitted with the paddle attachment, mix the butter, orange zest, and orange oil on medium speed until smooth. Add the sugar in a steady stream and mix until lightened in color. Blend in the eggs, one at a time. Scrape down the side of the bowl as needed.

4. Reduce the mixer speed to low and blend in the flour mixture in two additions, mixing only to incorporate. Remove the bowl from the machine, and using an over-size rubber spatula, fold in the chocolate and the nuts.

5. Divide the dough in half. With well-floured hands, form each half of the dough into a log measuring 14 inches long and 1½ inches wide, placing the logs about 4 inches apart on the prepared pan. (The logs will spread.) Flatten the logs slightly and square off the ends to neaten them.

6. Bake for 25 to 30 minutes, or until set and lightly browned. Remove the logs from the oven and reduce the oven to 300°F. Allow the logs to cool on the pan for at least 20 minutes.

7. Using a spatula, carefully loosen the logs from the parchment. Being careful to support the middle, transfer one log to a cutting board. (The logs are very tender and will crack if not moved carefully.) Cut into ½-inch-wide diagonal slices using a serrated knife. Return the slices to the pan placing them cut side down, and bake for 15 minutes, or until lightly browned. Let rest on the pan for 5 minutes, then transfer the slices to a cooling rack.

STORAGE: Store in an airtight container, layered between strips of wax paper, for up to 2 weeks. These biscotti may be frozen.

"Begin the day by dipping a biscotti in your coffee . . ."
EMILY LUCHETTI

powdered sugar italian slices

MAKES FORTY 3½-INCH COOKIES

The recipe for these vanilla-flavored biscotti came to me from my good friend Linda Bogan, who works for the school system in Bergen County, New Jersey. Linda has an artistic flair and is known for her extraordinary origami. These cookies are a favorite of the teachers in Linda's school, and she was eager to share the recipe with me. The buttery biscotti will appeal to children and adults alike.

AT A GLANCE
PANS: Two rimmed cookie sheets
PAN PREP: Line with parchment
OVEN TEMP: 350°/300°F
BAKING TIME: 25 to 28 minutes, plus 15 to 18 minutes
DIFFICULTY: ☕

---

3 cups all-purpose flour, spooned in and leveled

I teaspoon baking soda

I teaspoon baking powder

⅛ teaspoon salt

I cup (2 sticks) unsalted butter, slightly firm

I cup granulated sugar

2 large eggs

⅓ cup sour cream

I tablespoon pure vanilla extract

½ cup strained powdered sugar, spooned in and leveled, for sprinkling

1. Position the racks in the upper and lower thirds of the oven. Heat the oven to 350°F. Lightly dab the corners of two rimmed cookie sheets with butter and line each with baking parchment.

2. In a large bowl, thoroughly whisk the flour, baking soda, baking powder, and salt. Set aside.

3. In the bowl of an electric mixer fitted with the paddle attachment, mix the butter on medium-high speed until softened. Add the granulated sugar and mix until lightened. Reduce the mixer speed to medium and add the eggs one at a time, then blend in the sour cream and vanilla. Scrape down the sides of the bowl as needed.

4. On low speed add the flour mixture, mixing just until combined. (The dough will be sticky.) Spoon the dough onto one of the rimmed pans, forming two strips about 15 inches long and 2½ inches wide, placing the strips 3 inches apart. With floured hands reshape each strip of the dough into the correct measurement.

5. Bake on the lower shelf for 25 to 28 minutes, or until slightly firm. Remove from the oven and let rest on the pan for 5 minutes. Reduce the oven temperature to 300°F.

6. Using a large offset spatula, carefully transfer one of the loaves onto a cutting board. Using a serrated knife, cut the loaf into ½-inch-thick slices. Place the slices on the second rimmed pan and repeat with the remaining strip. (If needed, use the original pan so the slices are not crowded when baking.)

7. Return to the oven for 10 minutes to bake, then turn the slices over and bake for another 5 to 8 minutes, or until the cookies are lightly browned around the edges. Remove from the oven and, when cool enough to handle, transfer the cookies to a cooling rack set over a sheet of wax paper. Place the powdered sugar in a strainer and sprinkle the slices heavily on both sides.

STORAGE: Store in an airtight container, layered between strips of wax paper, for up to 3 weeks. These cookies may be frozen.

nut-crusted rugelach

MAKES 4 DOZEN 2 X 1¼-INCH COOKIES

PLAN AHEAD: *Refrigerate dough 4 hours or overnight*

Rugelach are one of the most popular sweets on any dessert table. These rugelach have a bit of extra pizzazz. The pastry is filled with preserves, cinnamon, sugar, nuts, and raisins. The logs of dough are cut into pieces and dipped in beaten egg white, then rolled in chopped walnuts to form a wonderfully crunchy crust.

> **AT A GLANCE**
> **PANS:** Two rimmed cookie sheets
> **PAN PREP:** Line with parchment
> **OVEN TEMP:** 350°F
> **BAKING TIME:** 25 to 30 minutes
> **DIFFICULTY:** 🥄 🥄

Check out the variations that follow. And feel free to play around with the fillings but be careful not to overfill the dough. The wonderful pastry will complement most any combination you choose.

DOUGH

2¼ cups all-purpose flour, spooned in and leveled, plus additional for kneading and rolling the dough

1 tablespoon granulated sugar

¼ teaspoon salt

¼ teaspoon baking powder

3 ounces cream cheese, very soft

1 cup (2 sticks) unsalted butter, very soft

1 large egg yolk

⅓ cup sour cream

FILLING

3 cups finely chopped walnuts (see page 392)

½ cup granulated sugar

1½ teaspoons ground cinnamon

½ cup thick preserves, such as apricot, Morello cherry, or seedless red or black raspberry

1 teaspoon freshly grated navel orange zest

½ cup golden raisins, plumped (see page 389)

1 large egg white, lightly beaten with 1 teaspoon water, for egg wash

Powdered sugar, for dusting

MAKE THE DOUGH

1. In a large bowl, thoroughly whisk together the flour, granulated sugar, salt, and baking powder. Set aside.

2. Place the cream cheese in the bowl of an electric mixer fitted with the paddle attachment. Mix on medium-low speed until smooth, about 30 seconds. Blend in the butter in four additions, mixing until smooth.

3. In a small bowl, whisk together the egg yolk and sour cream, then blend into the butter mixture. The mixture will look separated. Scrape down the side of the bowl as needed.

4. With the mixer off, add about one-third of the flour mixture. On low speed, mix just until blended. Add the remaining flour in two more additions, turning the mixer off before each addition. Do not overmix.

5. Remove the bowl from the machine and empty the dough onto a lightly floured pastry board or other flat surface. With floured hands, knead briefly until smooth. Divide the dough in half, dust with flour, and shape each half into a $3\frac{1}{2} \times 5$-inch rectangle. Cover each piece tightly in plastic wrap and refrigerate for at least 4 hours or up to 3 days. (This dough may be frozen for up to three months.)

MAKE THE RUGELACH

6. Position the racks in the upper and lower thirds of the oven. Heat the oven to 350°F. Line two rimmed cookie sheets with baking parchment and set aside.

7. Remove 1 full cup of walnuts and place in a shallow dish, such as a pie plate. Set aside.

8. Combine the granulated sugar and cinnamon in a small bowl. In another bowl, combine the preserves and orange zest. Have ready the remaining 2 cups of walnuts, the raisins, and egg white.

9. Remove one piece of dough from the refrigerator, divide it in half (the cut surface of the dough will be sticky and should be lightly floured), and reshape each half into a small rectangle. Working with one piece at a time, place the dough on a lightly floured pastry board or other flat surface and roll into an 8×10-inch rectangle. Arrange the dough so the 10-inch side is parallel to the edge of the board or countertop.

10. Using a small offset spatula, spread the rectangle with 2 tablespoons of preserves, leaving a ¾-inch margin on the far side of the dough. Sprinkle with a generous tablespoon of the cinnamon/sugar mixture. Top with a scant ½ cup of the remaining chopped nuts and 2 tablespoons of raisins.

11. Brush the far edge and the sides of the dough with the egg white wash, then roll into a log, gently stretching the dough on either end as you roll. When the log measures approximately 12 inches long, use a dough scraper or a thin-bladed sharp knife to cut into twelve 1-inch pieces. Place on the prepared pan and chill while shaping the remaining dough.

12. Dip the top of each piece into the egg wash, then into the reserved nuts. Return to the pan and press the nuts gently into the top to adhere, flattening the cookie slightly.

recipe continues

continued from previous page

13. Bake for 25 to 30 minutes, or until the rugelach are golden brown. To ensure even baking, toward the end of baking time, rotate the pans from top to bottom and front to back. Remove from the oven and let cool on the pans for about 10 minutes, then loosen with a thin-bladed metal spatula and transfer to cooling racks. Dust with powdered sugar before serving.

STORAGE: Store in an airtight container, layered between strips of wax paper, for up to 1 week. These cookies may be frozen.

VARIATIONS

cinnamon raisin rugelach

Prepare the dough for Nut-Crusted Rugelach as directed above, omitting the walnuts and increasing the raisins to 1 cup. Brush the tops of the rugelach with the egg wash and sprinkle with a mixture of 2 tablespoons of sugar and a scant ½ teaspoon of cinnamon. A sugar shaker works best here. Proceed with the recipe as written.

chocolate chip rugelach

Dough for Nut-Crusted Rugelach
  (page 334)

½ cup sugar

1 tablespoon plus 1 teaspoon strained
  cocoa powder

1 teaspoon ground cinnamon

½ cup preserves, such as apricot, Morello
  cherry, or seedless red or black
  raspberry

1 teaspoon freshly grated navel orange
  zest

1 cup mini chocolate chips

¾ cup medium chopped walnuts or
  pecans (optional)

Follow the directions for making Nut-Crusted Rugelach, making the following changes: (1) Combine the sugar, cocoa powder, and cinnamon in a small bowl. In a separate small bowl, combine the preserves with the zest. Set aside. (2) Prepare and roll the rugelach dough as directed in the above recipe. (3) Spread each rectangle of dough with 2 tablespoons of preserves, then sprinkle with 2 tablespoons of the sugar/cocoa mixture, followed by ¼ cup of chocolate chips and nuts, if using. (4) Proceed with the recipe as written, brushing the tops with egg wash and omitting the nut crust. When ready to serve, dust the top with powdered sugar.

"Nothing is really work unless you'd rather be doing something else."

J. M. BARRIE, *PETER PAN*

cinnamon pecan crescents

MAKES SIXTY-FOUR 3-INCH COOKIES

PLAN AHEAD: *Refrigerate dough at least 4 hours*

The inspiration for these yummy crescents came from my good friend Lori Fink. Her recipe called for using grape preserves, a flavor that I had never used for spreading on this type of pastry. I took the plunge, and loved the result.

Here we have a simple yeasted-style cookie dough thinly rolled on sugar and cinnamon instead of flour. Rolling on sugar and cinnamon adds a delightful finish to these crescents. Don't be surprised by the amount of sugar called for—they aren't too sweet, I promise

AT A GLANCE
PANS: Two rimmed cookie sheets
PAN PREP: Line with parchment
RISING TIME: 30 minutes
OVEN TEMP: 350°F
BAKING TIME: 18 to 20 minutes
DIFFICULTY: ♟ ♟

DOUGH

2 tablespoons plus 1 teaspoon sugar

½ cup warm water (110° to 115°F)

1 package active dry yeast

4 cups all-purpose flour, spooned in and leveled, plus additional for kneading

1 teaspoon salt

1½ cups (3 sticks) cold butter, cut into ½-inch cubes

2 large eggs, lightly beaten

ROLLING AND FILLING

1¾ cups sugar

1 tablespoon plus 1 teaspoon ground cinnamon

1 (12-ounce) jar (1 cup) grape preserves or jelly

3 cups finely chopped pecans (see page 392)

MAKE THE DOUGH

1. Rinse a small bowl in hot water to warm it. Add 1 teaspoon of the sugar and the warm water. Sprinkle the yeast over the water. *Do not stir.* Cover the bowl with a saucer and let the mixture stand for 5 minutes. Stir it briefly with a fork, cover again, and let it stand for 2 to 3 minutes, or until bubbly.

2. Place the flour, the remaining sugar, and the salt in the work bowl of a food processor fitted with the steel blade. Add the butter and pulse 6 to 8 times, then process for 6 to 8 seconds until meal-size pieces are formed. Empty the mixture into a large mixing bowl.

3. Stir the eggs into the yeast mixture. Make a well in the center of the flour mixture and pour in the yeast mixture. Combine the ingredients with a wooden spoon, mixing until a rough dough begins to form. With floured hands, work the dough in the bowl until it comes together.

4. Transfer the dough to a floured work surface and knead it lightly 6 to 8 times, or until fairly smooth. Shape it into a ball, then divide into quarters using a dough scraper or a sharp knife. Shape the quarters into rounds and dust lightly with flour. Wrap the pieces in plastic wrap and refrigerate for at least 4 hours, overnight, or up to 3 days. (This dough may be frozen; see "Freezing Yeasted Doughs," page 225.)

SHAPE THE CRESCENTS

5. Position the racks in the upper and lower thirds of the oven. Heat the oven to 350°F. Line two rimmed baking sheets with baking parchment and set aside.

6. Working with one round of dough at a time, remove it from the refrigerator and divide it in half. With lightly floured hands, shape each piece into a disk.

7. Combine the sugar and cinnamon in a small bowl. Sprinkle a pastry board or other flat surface with about 2 tablespoons of the cinnamon/sugar mixture. Working with one disk at a time, roll it in the cinnamon/sugar mixture into a 10-inch circle, turning the dough over as needed. Using a small offset spatula, spread the dough with 2 tablespoons of grape preserves, then sprinkle with $1\frac{1}{2}$ tablespoons of the cinnamon/sugar mixture. Scatter a generous $\frac{1}{3}$ cup of chopped pecans over the filling.

8. Using a fluted pastry cutter, cut the circle into eight wedges. Working from the wide edge, roll each wedge to the center. Place it on the baking pan, making sure that the tip is on the bottom, and shape it into a crescent. Repeat with the remaining dough and filling, being sure to clean the work surface after rolling and shaping each disk. Cover the crescents with a tea towel and let rest in a warmish place for 30 minutes.

BAKE THE CRESCENTS

9. Bake for 18 to 20 minutes, or until the tops are golden brown. To ensure even baking, toward the end of baking time, rotate the pans from top to bottom and front to back. Remove from the oven and let cool on the pans for 8 to 10 minutes, then transfer to cooling racks.

STORAGE: Store in an airtight container, layered between strips of wax paper, for up to 5 days. These cookies may be frozen.

apple strips

AT A GLANCE
PANS: Two rimmed cookie sheets
PAN PREP: Line with parchment
OVEN TEMP: 350°/325°F
BAKING TIME: 35 minutes
DIFFICULTY: ♨ ♨

These apple cookies, which have been in my baking repertoire since my catering days, were among my most requested pastries. A delicate crust envelops fresh apples, raisins, and walnuts. During baking, the sugar and juices of the apples caramelize, resulting in flavors reminiscent of apple pie. Serve these slightly warm for a little slice of heaven on a plate.

DOUGH

3 cups all-purpose flour, spooned in and leveled, plus additional for kneading and rolling

⅓ cup granulated sugar

1½ teaspoons baking powder

¾ teaspoon salt

1 cup (2 sticks) unsalted butter, chilled and cut into ½-inch cubes

2 large eggs, lightly beaten

¼ cup milk

1 teaspoon pure vanilla extract

FILLING

4 large tart apples, such as Granny Smith (about 1¾ pounds)

¾ cup coarsely chopped walnuts (see page 392)

½ cup golden raisins (not organic), plumped (see page 389)

½ cup (lightly packed) *very fresh* light brown sugar

¼ cup granulated sugar

2 teaspoons freshly grated lemon zest

1 teaspoon ground cinnamon

Pinch of ground nutmeg

ASSEMBLING AND FINISHING

2 tablespoons unsalted butter, melted and cooled

1 large recipe Vanilla Glaze (page 359)

¼ cup chopped walnuts

MAKE THE DOUGH

1. Combine the flour, granulated sugar, baking powder, and salt in the work bowl of a food processor fitted with the steel blade. Pulse 3 to 4 times to combine. Add the chilled butter and process for 8 to 10 seconds to produce fine crumbs. Empty the crumbs into a large bowl and make a well in the center.

2. In a small bowl, whisk together the eggs, milk, and vanilla.

3. Add the liquids to the crumbs and blend together with a wooden spoon to form a soft dough. Empty the dough onto a lightly floured pastry board or other flat surface and, with floured hands, knead six to eight times to smooth, then shape into a large round. Using a dough scraper or sharp knife, divide the dough into quarters, lightly

flour each quarter, and shape each quarter into 3 × 4-inch rectangles. Cover each with plastic wrap and refrigerate overnight.

MAKE THE FILLING

4. Position the racks in the upper and lower thirds of the oven. Heat the oven to 350°F. Line two rimmed cookie sheets with baking parchment and set aside.

5. Peel the apples, cut in half, and remove the core with a melon baller. Lay the apples on a cutting board cut side down, and cut across the stem end into ⅛-inch-thick slices. Place in a large bowl and add the walnuts, raisins, sugars, lemon zest, cinnamon, and nutmeg. Toss gently to blend.

ASSEMBLE THE STRIPS

6. Working with one piece at a time, place the dough on a lightly floured pastry board or other flat surface. Roll the dough into a 14 × 8-inch strip. Brush a 3-inch-wide strip of melted butter in the center, down the length of the strip. Mound one-fourth of the apple filling over the butter.

7. Enclose the filling by lifting the dough on either side with a dough scraper, over-lapping one of the sides by about ¾ inch. *Pinch the seams well.* Lay the strip seam side down slightly to the right of the center of the prepared pan. Repeat with the remaining dough and filling, placing two strips on each of the pans.

BAKE AND FINISH THE STRIPS

8. Using a paring knife, cut ten to twelve 1-inch slashes lightly across the top of each strip to allow steam to escape. Bake at 350°F for 20 minutes, then reduce the temperature to 325°F. Bake for another 15 minutes, or until golden brown. It's okay if the strips form a crack across the top. To ensure even baking, toward the end of baking time, rotate the pans from top to bottom and front to back.

9. Remove from the oven, let stand for 5 minutes, then loosen the strips with a long, thin spatula. While the strips are cooling, make the glaze. Cool for 15 minutes. When cool, using the back of a soupspoon, spread the glaze on the sides and top of each strip, then sprinkle with the chopped walnuts. Cut each strip diagonally into twelve 1-inch pieces.

STORAGE: Store in a container with the cover slightly askew, layered between sheets of wax paper, for up to 3 days. These cookies may be frozen.

black chocolate madeleines

MAKES ABOUT 2 DOZEN COOKIES

Here is a delectable chocolate version of the well-known petite cake, the madeleine. The crumb of the teacake has a rich chocolate flavor that is complemented with shaved bits of bittersweet chocolate. Before folding in the chocolate shavings, be sure to let the batter stand a few minutes after preparing it to allow it to thicken slightly. This will help to keep the chocolate shavings evenly distributed throughout the batter.

> **AT A GLANCE**
> **PANS:** Madeleine pans with 3-inch cavities
> **PAN PREP:** Butter generously/dust with cocoa powder
> **OVEN TEMP:** 375°F
> **BAKING TIME:** 12 to 13 minutes
> **DIFFICULTY:** 🥄 🥄

A great advantage to making these madeleines is that the batter can be made ahead and refrigerated for up to 3 days, then used as needed. Also, if you have only one pan, this allows you to bake them in batches.

⅔ cup (1⅓ sticks) unsalted butter

¼ cup honey

¾ cup all-purpose flour, spooned in and leveled

⅔ cup strained Dutch-process cocoa powder, spooned in and leveled

1 teaspoon baking powder

¼ teaspoon baking soda

¼ teaspoon salt

4 large eggs

⅔ cup granulated sugar

2 teaspoons pure vanilla extract

¼ cup shaved fine-quality bittersweet chocolate, such as Lindt (about 1 ounce)

Powdered sugar, for dusting

1. Position the rack in the middle of the oven. Heat the oven to 375°F. Using softened butter and a pastry brush, generously butter madeleine pans, being sure to reach into the grooves. Dust with cocoa powder, then invert over a sink and tap two or three times to shake out the excess. Dust with cocoa a second time, again shaking out the excess. Note: If using nonstick pans, they must be greased and dusted with cocoa as well. They will need only one dusting of cocoa. To prevent sticking, the interiors of the molds should be completely coated with no metal visible. Chill the pans until ready to use.

2. Over low heat, in a heavy 1-quart saucepan, melt the butter and honey together, stirring to combine. Cool until tepid.

3. In a medium bowl, thoroughly whisk together the flour, cocoa, baking powder, baking soda, and salt.

4. In the bowl of an electric mixer fitted with the whip attachment, beat the eggs on medium speed for 2 minutes. Add the granulated sugar, 1 tablespoon at a time, beating until light in color and thickened, about 2 minutes, then blend in the vanilla.

5. On low speed, add the flour mixture alternately with the *tepid* butter mixture, dividing the flour into three parts and the butter into two, beginning and ending with the flour. Increase the speed to medium and beat about 10 seconds longer. Remove the bowl from the machine. Let the batter stand for 10 minutes to thicken, then fold in the shaved chocolate with a rubber spatula. (*Note:* The batter may be prepared up to 3 days ahead and spooned into the pans immediately before baking. It is not necessary to bring the batter to room temperature.)

6. Using a 1-tablespoon measuring spoon, drop 2 level tablespoons of batter into each cavity of the prepared pans. Be careful not to overfill the pans. They should be about two-thirds full. Do not smooth the tops, as the cakes should dome during baking. Bake for 12 to 13 minutes, or until the tops are springy to the touch. If using a nonstick pan, reduce baking time to 10 to 11 minutes. Do not overbake.

7. Remove from the oven and let cool for 1 minute. Invert the pan, and tipping the pan toward you, give a few firm taps on the counter. The cakes should pop out. Use the tip of a small knife to release any that stick. Dust the madeleines with powdered sugar and serve at once.

STORAGE: Store in an airtight container, layered between strips of wax paper, for up to 3 days. Before serving, refresh the madeleines in a 300°F oven loosely covered with aluminum foil for 6 to 7 minutes. While madeleines may be made ahead or frozen, they are best eaten freshly made.

kirsch krisps

Several years ago, when I lived in Bergen County, New Jersey, I paid a visit to my seamstress, Marguit, at holiday time. When I walked in the door, Marguit was busily deep-frying her fabulous Swiss wafer cookies, which she called Marveilles. Wow! was my first reaction. These light-as-a-feather, crisp wafers absolutely melt in your mouth.

AT A GLANCE

PANS: 10-inch sauté pan/several rimmed cookie sheets

PAN PREP: Line with heavy-duty brown paper

DIFFICULTY: 🍶 🍶 🍶

Some tips before you begin: *While this dough can be put together within minutes, it must be fried immediately after rolling or it will become sticky and difficult to handle. Don't forget to add some additional vegetable shortening from time to time. This will prevent the fat from smoking and keep it from breaking down. Be mindful of the temperature. If it gets too hot, the cookies will overbrown.*

3 tablespoons unsalted butter, melted

2 tablespoons plus 2 teaspoons granulated sugar

1 large egg

⅛ teaspoon salt

⅓ cup Kirsch or whiskey

1⅔ cups all-purpose flour, spooned in and leveled, sifted, plus additional for rolling

1½ pounds solid vegetable shortening, such as Crisco

Powdered sugar, for dusting

1. Line several rimmed cookie sheets with heavy-duty brown paper, such as clean grocery bags.

2. Place the butter, granulated sugar, egg, and salt in a large mixing bowl. Stir well to blend, then mix in the Kirsch.

3. Sift 1 cup of flour over the liquid and beat with a wooden spoon until very smooth. Gradually add another ½ cup flour. Work the dough until smooth, then turn it onto a floured pastry board or countertop and knead in the remaining flour. Bang the dough on the board several times to relax the gluten.

4. Have ready eighteen 8-inch squares of wax paper. Using a dough scraper or a sharp knife, divide the dough into eighteen pieces (each about the size of a large walnut). Let the pieces of dough rest, lightly covered with a sheet of wax paper, for about 15 minutes.

5. On a lightly floured pastry board or other flat surface, roll each piece of dough as thinly as you can. The dough should measure about 6 inches and will be a somewhat irregular circle. Place the circles of dough between the squares of wax paper to prevent them from sticking together or drying out.

6. Have ready a can to pour the used frying oil into. Also have two table forks to handle the cookies, as well as the paper-lined rimmed cookie sheets. Just before frying restretch each piece of dough with your fingertips.

7. In a heavy 10-inch skillet, add enough shortening to measure about ¼ inch deep when melted. Heat until very hot. Test the temperature of the oil by breaking off a small piece of dough and dropping it carefully into the oil. The oil should bubble up and the edges of the dough should start to brown.

8. Working with one piece of dough at a time, carefully place the dough into the hot oil. Quickly take the table forks and press the dough into the oil. The cookie will bubble and form a crinkled shape. To make sure the center of the cookie browns, press the cookie with the forks so the hot oil flows over the middle. As soon as the cookie becomes golden brown, in 10 to 15 seconds, turn over with the forks. Fry for about 5 seconds on the second side, taking care not to overbrown the cookie, then remove to the prepared pan to drain. Let cool for about 2 minutes. While still hot, sprinkle lightly with powdered sugar. Repeat with the remaining dough. Be sure to refresh the oil after frying 3 or 4 cookies.

9. When cool, sprinkle the cookies again with powdered sugar, this time more heavily. These cookies will keep for several weeks and do not need to be frozen. To serve, break off small pieces and enjoy.

STORAGE: Store in an airtight container with wax paper between each cookie to keep them from breaking. These cookies are very fragile.

"*Remember, you're all alone in the kitchen and no one can see you.*"
JULIA CHILD

streusels, glazes, frostings & spreads

SPREADS

Apple Cider Caramel Spread

Cranberry Orange Spread

Maple Pecan Spread

Orange Honey Butter

Dried Pear, Toasted Walnut, and Blue Cheese Spread

Crystallized Ginger and Macadamia Nut Cream Cheese

ABOUT STREUSEL TOPPINGS

The quantity of streusel topping that you use is a matter of personal taste. Some bakers like a thick layer while others prefer a lighter coating. Pound cake batters and yeasted doughs are good candidates for thicker streusel toppings. Thinner coatings are okay on softer batters.

• The amount of moisture in the flour, the humidity in the air, and the time of year (summer vs. winter) all influence the amount of butter needed to make good streusel crumbs.

• When melting butter for streusel, choose a pot large enough to get your hand into so you can form the crumbs.

• The key is to be able to take a handful of the crumbs and squeeze them together into a clump. They should hold together. If not, soften by reheating the crumbs briefly over low heat. If the mixture still falls apart or breaks up too easily, add more butter sparingly, 2 to 3 teaspoons at a time.

• Streusel toppings can be made in the pan that the butter was melted in. If the amount of butter has to be increased, push the flour mixture aside and add another 2 to 3 teaspoons of butter. Place the pot back on the burner, positioning it so only the butter is over the heat. It will take only a few seconds for it to melt. Be careful that the butter does not get too hot.

• Let the streusel mixture stand in the pot for 10 to 15 minutes to allow the flour to absorb the butter.

• Streusel that stands too long may become too dry. Correct this by placing the saucepan on very low heat. This warms the butter in the crumb mixture and will eventually bring it back to the proper consistency. When the mixture is over the heat, use a heatproof spatula or the side of a fork to move the streusel around the pan.

• Streusel toppings are not recommended for use on very fluid batters because they will sink through the surface during baking.

• Chilling a muffin batter before you apply the streusel helps to prevent the crumbs from sinking as they bake.

carole's favorite streusel

MAKES ENOUGH FOR ONE 8-INCH SQUARE OR 9-INCH ROUND COFFEE CAKE,

OR 12 MUFFINS (SMALL RECIPE);

OR ONE 9 X 13 X 2-INCH OR 10-INCH ROUND COFFEE CAKE,

OR 16 TO 18 MUFFINS (LARGE RECIPE)

This has been my tried-and-true streusel recipe for as long as I can remember. The key here is to melt the butter, but only to the point where it does not overheat. Once the butter has cooled to tepid, the remaining ingredients are added. If the crumb mixture appears to be too dry or too crumbly, add a bit more butter (see "About Streusel Toppings," page 349).

Making the streusel in the same pot in which the butter was melted is very convenient. If the crumb mixture requires additional butter, push some of the crumbs aside and place the butter in the cleared spot. Place the saucepan on low heat, positioning it so that the butter is over the heat.

SMALL RECIPE

6 to 7 tablespoons unsalted butter

I cup all-purpose flour, spooned in
   and leveled

$\frac{1}{2}$ cup sugar

$\frac{1}{2}$ teaspoon ground cinnamon

$\frac{1}{4}$ teaspoon baking powder

$\frac{1}{4}$ teaspoon salt

3 tablespoons finely chopped walnuts
   or pecans (optional)

LARGE RECIPE

$\frac{2}{3}$ cup (10$\frac{2}{3}$ tablespoons) unsalted butter

1$\frac{1}{2}$ cups all-purpose flour, spooned in
   and leveled

$\frac{3}{4}$ cup sugar

$\frac{3}{4}$ teaspoon ground cinnamon

$\frac{1}{2}$ teaspoon baking powder

scant $\frac{1}{2}$ teaspoon salt

$\frac{1}{4}$ cup finely chopped walnuts
   or pecans (optional)

1. Place the butter in a 2-quart heavy-bottomed saucepan for small recipe or 3-quart for large recipe and heat until almost melted; remove from the heat and cool to tepid.

2. Whisk together the flour, sugar, cinnamon, baking powder, salt, and nuts if using. Add to the butter and stir with a fork until blended and mixture begins to form crumbs. Gently squeeze the mixture with your hand to form larger lumps, then break them apart with your fingertips. Before using, let the streusel stand for 10 to 15 minutes.

almond crunch streusel

MAKES ENOUGH FOR ONE 10-INCH ROUND OR 9 X 13 X 2-INCH COFFEE CAKE, OR 12 TO 14 MUFFINS

This crunchy streusel is laced with a sweet, toasted almond crunch—making it absolutely perfect for those who crave nuts in their crumb toppings. In the variation of my Favorite Vanilla Muffins (page 86), it not only crowns the top of the muffin, but enlivens the batter. It can also be used with fruit muffins and coffee cakes.

ALMOND CRUNCH

I large egg white

I tablespoon sugar

¾ cup unblanched sliced almonds

STREUSEL

⅓ cup (⅔ stick) unsalted butter

½ cup all-purpose flour, spooned in and leveled

6 tablespoons sugar

½ teaspoon ground cinnamon

½ teaspoon ground cardamom

¼ teaspoon baking powder

¼ teaspoon salt

¼ teaspoon almond extract

MAKE THE ALMOND CRUNCH

1. Place the butter in a 2-quart heavy-bottomed saucepan for small recipe or 3-quart for large recipe and heat until almost melted; remove from the heat and cool to tepid.

2. Whisk together the flour, sugar, cinnamon, baking powder, salt, and nuts if using. Add to the butter and stir with a fork until blended and mixture begins to form crumbs. Gently squeeze the mixture with your hand to form larger lumps, then break them apart with your fingertips. Before using, let the streusel stand for 10 to 15 minutes.

MAKE THE ALMOND CRUNCH STREUSEL

3. Place the butter in a heavy bottomed 2-quart saucepan and heat until almost melted. Remove from the heat and cool to tepid.

4. Place half of the almond crunch in the work bowl of a food processor fitted with the steel blade. Add the flour, sugar, cinnamon, cardamom, baking powder, salt, and almond extract. Process until the almonds are finely ground and the mixture resembles fine meal. Add to the tepid butter and stir with a fork to combine.

5. Place the remaining almond crunch in a plastic freezer bag, release the air, and secure the top. Break up the nuts into smaller pieces by hitting them 10 times with a rolling pin, or the bottom of a small saucepan. Stir into the streusel.

brown sugar whole wheat streusel

I highly recommend this crunchy streusel with the Crumb-Topped Whole Wheat Peach Muffins (page 112).
It is also an excellent topping for most cakes and muffins made with fresh or dried fruits.

⅓ cup (⅔ stick) unsalted butter

½ cup old-fashioned oatmeal

⅓ cup *very fresh* light brown sugar

⅓ cup stone-ground whole wheat flour,
  spooned in and leveled

⅓ cup all-purpose flour, spooned in and leveled

¾ teaspoon ground cinnamon

½ teaspoon baking powder

¼ teaspoon salt

1. Place the butter in a heavy-bottomed 3-quart saucepan and heat until almost melted; remove from the heat and cool to *tepid*.

2. Place ¼ cup of the oatmeal, the brown sugar, flours, cinnamon, baking powder, and salt in the work bowl of a food processor fitted with the steel blade. Pulse to blend, then add the remaining ¼ cup oatmeal. Empty the oat mixture into the butter, then toss with a fork until crumbs are formed.

3. Gently squeeze the mixture with your hand to form larger lumps, then break them apart with your fingertips. Before using, let the streusel stand for 10 to 15 minutes.

butter-nut streusel

I like to call this my anytime streusel. It comes together so quickly in the food processor, it's perfect anytime!
Think about it for buttery coffee cakes, vanilla or fruit muffins, or fruit coffee cakes.

½ **cup (1 stick) unsalted butter**

½ **cup sugar**

⅓ **cup slivered almonds**

¼ **teaspoon almond extract**

1 ⅓ **cups all-purpose flour, spooned in and leveled**

⅛ **teaspoon salt**

1. Position the rack in the lower third of the oven. Heat the oven to 325°F. Line a baking sheet with Silpat or Release aluminum foil. Set aside.

2. Beat the egg white in a small bowl until foamy. Add the sugar and almonds and toss to coat. Spread the almonds on the prepared pan and bake for 10 minutes. Remove from the oven, and using a spatula, turn the almonds over and break up the large pieces as best you can. Bake for another 8 minutes, or until crisp and golden brown. When cool enough to handle, break the nuts into smaller pieces.

chocolate streusel

MAKES ENOUGH FOR ONE 9-INCH ROUND OR 9 X 13 X 2-INCH COFFEE CAKE, OR 12 TO 14 MUFFINS

Have you ever tried a chocolate streusel? If not check out this recipe. While it is used with Chocolate Chocolate Streusel Squares (page 44), it would be equally delicious with Favorite Vanilla Muffins (page 86) or Jeff's Chocolate-Glazed Midnight Muffins (page 88).

6 to 7 tablespoons unsalted butter

1 cup all-purpose flour, spooned in and leveled

¼ cup granulated sugar

¼ cup (lightly packed) *very fresh* dark brown sugar

2 tablespoons strained Dutch-process cocoa powder

¼ teaspoon baking powder

¼ teaspoon salt

¼ teaspoon ground cinnamon

1. Place the butter in a 2-quart heavy-bottomed saucepan and heat until almost melted; remove from the heat and cool until tepid. Whisk together the flour, sugars, cocoa powder, baking powder, salt, and cinnamon. Set aside.

2. Add the dry ingredients, tossing with a fork until crumbs are formed. Gently squeeze the mixture with your hand to form larger lumps, then break them apart with your fingertips. Before using, let the streusel stand for 10 to 15 minutes.

toasted coconut streusel

MAKES ENOUGH FOR ONE 10-INCH ROUND OR 9 X 13 X 2-INCH COFFEE CAKE, OR 18 TO 20 MUFFINS

This streusel makes an especially nice topping for cakes made with pineapple or citrus flavors.

1 cup flaked, sweetened coconut

6 tablespoons unsalted butter

½ teaspoon freshly grated navel orange zest

1 cup all-purpose flour, spooned in and leveled

½ cup strained powdered sugar, spooned in and leveled

⅛ teaspoon freshly grated nutmeg

1. Position the rack in the center of the oven. Heat the oven to 325°F. Place the coconut in a shallow pan and bake for 8 to 10 minutes, or until golden brown. Watch carefully and stir occasionally, as it burns quickly. When the coconut has cooled, crush into smaller pieces with your hand.

2. Place the butter and orange zest in a 3-quart heavy-bottomed saucepan and heat until almost melted; remove from the heat and *cool to tepid.*

3. Add the crushed coconut, flour, powdered sugar, and nutmeg, then stir with a fork to form coarse crumbs. Before using, let the streusel stand for 10 to 15 minutes.

country crumb topping

MAKES ENOUGH FOR ONE 10-INCH ROUND OR 9 X 13 X 2-INCH COFFEE CAKE, OR 16 TO 18 MUFFINS

This topping is loaded with old-fashioned farmhouse textures and flavors. Chopped walnuts and oatmeal combined with nutty whole wheat flour are blended with dark brown sugar and cinnamon to form the perfect topping for fruit muffins or coffee cakes.

¾ cup all-purpose flour, spooned in and leveled

½ cup medium-chopped walnuts or pecans (see page 392)

¼ cup whole wheat flour

¼ cup *very fresh* dark brown sugar

¼ cup granulated sugar

¼ cup old-fashioned oatmeal

¾ teaspoon ground cinnamon

½ teaspoon baking powder

¼ teaspoon salt

7 tablespoons unsalted butter, softened

1. Combine the all-purpose flour, nuts, whole wheat flour, sugars, oatmeal, cinnamon, baking powder, and salt in a large mixing bowl.

2. Add the softened butter and work through with your fingertips until the mixture begins to form coarse crumbs. Gently squeeze the mixture with your hand to form larger lumps, then break them apart with your fingertips. Before using, let the streusel stand for 10 to 15 minutes.

rustic maple pecan streusel

MAKES ENOUGH FOR ONE 10-INCH ROUND OR 9 X 13 X 2-INCH COFFEE CAKE, OR 18 TO 20 MUFFINS

Not only does this topping pair beautifully with the Maple Pecan Sweet Potato Muffins (page 110), it is great with any batter that is made with fresh or dried apples or pears. When autumn leaves begin to fall, and you want to top off your muffins with a treat in keeping with the season, try this rustic streusel.

7 tablespoons unsalted butter

½ teaspoon maple extract

1¼ cups all-purpose flour, spooned in and leveled

⅓ cup *very fresh* dark brown sugar

⅓ cup granulated sugar

¼ teaspoon baking powder

¼ teaspoon salt

½ cup toasted broken pecans

1. Place the butter in a 3-quart heavy-bottomed saucepan, and heat until almost melted; remove from the heat and add the maple extract. Set aside to *cool to tepid.*

2. In a large bowl, whisk together the flour, sugars, baking powder, and salt. Add the dry ingredients and pecans to the butter and mix with a fork until crumbs are formed. Gently squeeze the mixture with your hand to form larger lumps, then break them apart with your fingertips. Before using, let the streusel stand for 10 to 15 minutes.

ABOUT GLAZES

Many cakes and pastries are enhanced with glazes in a variety of flavors. To successfully apply the glaze, always add it while the cake is still warm. The warm surface allows the glaze to spread evenly, have a better sheen, and adhere well. The glaze should be of a semi-fluid consistency to spread easily. To check this, place some of the glaze in a spoon and pour it back into the bowl. The stream should not break when the glaze is poured.

If coating an entire cake, use the back of a spoon or a small offset spatula. For webbing or drizzling, use the tines of a fork, the tip of a teaspoon, a whisk, or a plastic squeeze bottle. Hold the utensil a few inches above the cake or pastry and move it rapidly back and forth to produce the desired effect.

Remember that the time of year and your kitchen temperature will affect the consistency of the glaze. Here are some of my favorite tips:

• If the glaze is too fluid, chilling it will help to firm it. Also, if powdered sugar is used in the recipe, adding a bit more will help thicken it.

• If the glaze is too thick, thin it with a few drops of hot water.

• Placing the bowl holding the glaze in a skillet filled with an inch of hot water will help maintain its consistency while you work.

• If the glaze becomes too thick, place it in a microwave-safe container and warm it briefly on the defrost setting.

• Glazes are always thinly applied.

• Glazes made with powdered sugar are best made shortly before using because, upon standing, they form a crust.

vanilla glaze

MAKES ENOUGH FOR ONE 9-INCH ROUND OR 8-INCH SQUARE COFFEE CAKE,
OR 12 TO 14 PASTRIES (SMALL RECIPE); OR ONE 10-INCH ROUND OR 9 X 13 X 2-INCH COFFEE CAKE,
OR 16 TO 18 PASTRIES (LARGE RECIPE)

This simple glaze is the one you will use the most throughout this book to finish your pastries. From pound cakes to cinnamon buns to Danish, it is literally the icing on the cake. Do not make this glaze ahead of time because it thickens as it stands and develops a crust. The amount of liquid varies in each recipe depending on how thick you like your glaze. Be sure to have your water very hot.

SMALL RECIPE	LARGE RECIPE
⅔ cup strained powdered sugar	1 cup strained powdered sugar
2 to 3 teaspoons very hot water	3 to 4 teaspoons very hot water
1½ teaspoons light corn syrup	2 teaspoons light corn syrup
⅛ teaspoon pure vanilla extract	¼ teaspoon pure vanilla extract
Few drops lemon juice	⅛ teaspoon lemon juice
Pinch of salt	2 pinches of salt

Place the powdered sugar in a medium bowl. Add 2 teaspoons of the hot water for the small recipe, 3 teaspoons for the large, the corn syrup, vanilla, lemon juice, and salt. Stir until smooth. Add 1 additional teaspoon hot water or more as needed to make a thin glaze. Using a small whisk, fork, or tip of a teaspoon, drizzle the glaze over the pastry by moving the utensil rapidly back and forth to create a light coating.

VARIATION

enriched vanilla glaze

If you like a more opaque finish to your glaze, try substituting dairy products such as milk, half-and-half, or light or heavy cream in place of the hot water—the richer the dairy product, the whiter the glaze. The liquid should be heated so it will thoroughly combine with the sugar.

clear shiny glaze

MAKES ¼ CUP, ENOUGH FOR THREE 8 X 3¾ X 2½-INCH OR TWO 8½ X 4½ X 2¾-INCH LOAVES, OR 12 TO 14 PASTRIES

If you want to give a professional finish to your pastry, use this glaze. While it adds a touch of sweetness, it has no color, but has a beautiful sheen. Not only does it bring out the natural color of the pastry, it is also handy for securing nuts to the top of the pastry.

3 tablespoons sugar
3 tablespoons water

1½ teaspoons corn syrup

Combine the sugar, water, and corn syrup in a small saucepan. Bring to a boil over medium heat. Cook for 2 to 3 minutes. Keep warm.

applejack glaze

MAKES ENOUGH TO GLAZE ONE 9 X 13 X 2-INCH OR 10-INCH ROUND CAKE, OR 16 TO 18 MUFFINS

Use this snappy glaze for cakes and muffins featuring apples or other spice cakes.

1 cup strained powdered sugar, spooned in and leveled
1 tablespoon boiling water

2 teaspoons applejack, Calvados, or rum
2 teaspoons light corn syrup
Pinch of salt

Combine the powdered sugar, boiling water, liqueur, corn syrup, and salt in a medium bowl. Stir until smooth. (Note: If the glaze is made ahead of time, you will have to thin it with a few drops of boiling water. Use the water sparingly; a little goes a long way.)

caramel glaze

MAKES ENOUGH FOR ONE 10-INCH BUNDT OR 9 X 13 X 2-INCH CAKE, OR 16 TO 18 MUFFINS

This flavor of caramel marries perfectly with Blackberry Jam Cake (page 60), but it also complements spice cakes or cakes made with fruits and nuts. Caramel is easier to make than you think, but you must pay attention to the directions and be sure to watch the color as it begins to change. It can become too dark and bitter in a matter of seconds.

¼ **cup superfine sugar**

¼ **teaspoon fresh lemon juice**

¼ **cup heavy cream**

I **cup strained powdered sugar, spooned in and leveled**

½ **teaspoon pure vanilla extract**

1. Have ready a pastry brush and glass of cold water. Combine the superfine sugar and lemon juice in an 8-inch skillet set over low heat. (Wet the brush and gently brush the side of the pan occasionally to remove any stray sugar crystals.)

2. Continue to cook the sugar on low heat until it is melted and turns a caramel color. As the edges begin to deepen in color, do not stir the syrup. Instead, carefully tilt the skillet and slowly swirl the syrup around the pan until it is evenly browned. Remove from the heat and add the cream, stirring constantly until the mixture is smooth. (*Caution: The mixture will bubble up at first. Do not touch! It is dangerously hot.*) Blend in the powdered sugar, then the vanilla. Keep warm until ready to use in a skillet filled with 1 inch of hot water.

thin lemon glaze

ENOUGH FOR ONE 9 X 5-INCH LOAF OR ONE 8-INCH SQUARE OR 9-INCH ROUND CAKE, OR 12 MUFFINS

Here is a glaze that will add just a bit of tang to your pastry. It is a pleasant alternative to dusting with powdered sugar. Pair this with recipes that use fresh or dried fruits.

½ cup strained powdered sugar, spooned in and leveled

1½ teaspoons fresh lemon juice

1½ teaspoons light corn syrup

1 to 1¼ teaspoons *very hot* water

⅛ teaspoon pure vanilla extract

Pinch of salt

Combine the powdered sugar, lemon juice, corn syrup, hot water, vanilla, and salt. Whisk until smooth. Pour the glaze on the hot cake or muffins.

orange glaze

MAKES ENOUGH TO GLAZE ONE 9 X 13 X 2-INCH CAKE, OR 16 TO 18 MUFFINS

Try this flavorful glaze on Kugelhopf (page 211), as well as a finish for "Too Good to Be True" Bran Muffins (page 114) or Cape Cod Cranberry Muffins (page 102).

1 cup strained powdered sugar

4 to 5 tablespoons orange juice, hot

1½ teaspoons light corn syrup

⅓ teaspoon orange oil

⅛ teaspoon pure vanilla extract

Combine the powdered sugar, orange juice, corn syrup, orange oil, and vanilla. Whisk until smooth. Pour or spoon the glaze on the warm cake or muffins.

midnight chocolate glaze

MAKES ENOUGH FOR ONE 10-INCH BUNDT CAKE OR 9 X 13 X 2-INCH COFFEE CAKE, OR 16 TO 18 MUFFINS

Here is a glaze that has a beautiful, glossy shine and wonderful, rich chocolate flavor. While I think the best results are achieved if the glaze is applied when it is made, it can be made ahead and either refrigerated or frozen. The glaze will keep its sheen for up to eight hours, depending on your room temperature and weather conditions. When I tested the recipe, it was impossible not to lick my fingers when scraping the pot clean.

½ cup water

¼ cup granulated sugar

2 tablespoons light corn syrup

4 ounces fine-quality bittersweet chocolate, such as Lindt, finely chopped

¼ cup strained powdered sugar

1 tablespoon Dutch-process cocoa powder

1 teaspoon pure vanilla extract

¼ teaspoon lemon juice

Pinch of salt

1 tablespoon unsalted butter, *soft*

1. Place the water in a 3-quart heavy-bottomed saucepan. Add the granulated sugar and corn syrup, but *do not stir*. Cover and bring to a slow boil on medium-low heat. After 1 minute, check to see if any sugar crystals remain. If so, *gently* stir the mixture. Continue to cook the syrup uncovered for 3 to 4 minutes. (Large bubbles will form on the surface.)

2. Remove the pan from the heat and sprinkle the chopped chocolate over the syrup. Push the chocolate gently into the syrup, but *do not stir*. Let stand for 2 to 3 minutes, until the chocolate is melted, then stir gently with a small whisk.

3. When smooth, stir in the powdered sugar and cocoa powder, then blend in the vanilla, lemon juice, and salt. Stir gently with the whisk until smooth, then blend in the butter. If the glaze is not pourable, add 3 or 4 teaspoons of very hot water until the desired consistency is reached. *Note:* This glaze is best used immediately.

STORAGE: Leftover glaze can be refrigerated for several weeks. This glaze may be frozen. To use, reheat, adding very hot water to thin the glaze as needed.

ABOUT FROSTINGS

Frostings differ from glazes as they are richer and are applied thickly rather than in a thin layer. Glazes are spread on cakes and pastries that are still warm, while frostings should always be used after the baked goods have cooled completely. A small offset spatula (see page 374) is the ideal tool for applying frosting; however, for casual cakes the back of a large soupspoon makes a satisfactory alternative.

cream cheese frosting

MAKES ENOUGH FOR ONE 8-INCH SQUARE OR 9 X 5 X 2¾-INCH LOAF, OR 12 TO 14 MUFFINS (SMALL RECIPE); OR ONE 9-INCH SQUARE OR TWO 8½ X 4½ X2¾-INCH LOAVES, OR 20 MUFFINS (LARGE RECIPE)

This recipe for a classic cream cheese frosting will surely bring back childhood memories. It is the perfect topping for Old-Fashioned Carrot Muffins (page 100), and will pair beautifully with cakes, muffins, and quick breads made with fruits and spices. Use it often and enjoy!

SMALL RECIPE	LARGE RECIPE
(SCANT I CUP)	(1⅓ CUPS)
4 ounces cream cheese, *cold*	6 ounces cream cheese, *cold*
4 tablespoons unsalted butter, *soft*	6 tablespoons unsalted butter, *soft*
I cup strained powdered sugar	1½ cups strained powdered sugar
¾ teaspoon pure vanilla extract	I teaspoon pure vanilla extract
¼ (generous) teaspoon freshly grated navel orange zest	½ teaspoon freshly grated navel orange zest

Combine all the ingredients in the work bowl of a food processor fitted with the steel blade. Pulse 3 to 4 times, then process for 3 to 4 seconds. Stop the processor, scrape down the side of the bowl, and empty into a small bowl. Cover with plastic wrap and refrigerate until ready to use.

STORAGE: Store in the refrigerator for up to 3 days, or freeze in a plastic container for up to 3 months.

ABOUT SPREADS

What better way to top off some freshly baked biscuits, muffins, or scones than with a homemade spread! Tastes vary as to how much spread to use, but as a general rule, allow about 1 tablespoon per serving for spreads made with cream cheese. For those made with butter or a combination of butter and cream cheese, figure on half a tablespoon per serving. The Apple Cider Caramel is the exception; a little goes a long way.

apple cider caramel spread

MAKES ½ CUP

This rich cider reduction is the perfect accompaniment to corn and fruit muffins as well as biscuits and scones. In fact, it's good on brioche and croissants as well. You can make it during apple cider season, and because it has an extremely long shelf life, you can enjoy it almost until spring comes along!

4 cups apple cider   **2 cinnamon sticks**

1. Place the cider and cinnamon sticks in a heavy 3-quart saucepan. Bring to a boil over medium-high heat. Reduce the heat to medium-low and cook on a high simmer for 30 minutes.

2. Remove the cinnamon sticks and continue to simmer until reduced to ½ cup.

3. Strain the caramel into a heatproof pitcher or jar to cool. After cooling, the mixture will reach spreading consistency.

STORAGE: Refrigerate for up to 6 months. Freezing is not necessary.

cranberry orange spread

MAKES ABOUT 1⅓ CUPS

Here's the perfect addition to your holiday table. Pair it with muffins, quick breads, biscuits, and scones. Whether served at breakfast, brunch, lunch, or dinner, it's sure to please.

¼ cup fresh orange juice

2 tablespoons Grand Marnier or other orange-flavored liqueur

6 tablespoons dried cranberries (not organic), plumped (see page 389)

½ cup (1 stick) unsalted butter, softened

6 ounces cream cheese, softened

¼ cup sifted powdered sugar

1 teaspoon freshly grated navel orange zest

Pinch of salt

1. Combine the orange juice and Grand Marnier in a 1-quart saucepan. Warm over low heat, then add the cranberries and steep for 5 minutes. Drain the cranberries and pat dry on paper towels.

2. Place the cranberries in the work bowl of a food processor fitted with the steel blade and pulse until finely chopped.

3. Add the butter, cream cheese, powdered sugar, zest, and salt. Process until combined. Remove from the processor, place in a small bowl or a ramekin, and refrigerate. Let soften slightly before serving.

STORAGE: Refrigerate, tightly covered with plastic wrap, for up to 5 days. Freezing is not recommended.

"I am not a glutton—I am an explorer of food."

ERMA BOMBECK

maple pecan spread

MAKES ½ CUP

Indulge your sweet tooth with this simple, crunchy spread—perfect for most any coffee break snack.

4 ounces cream cheese, softened

1 tablespoon powdered sugar

2 tablespoons medium-chopped toasted pecans (see pages 391–392)

4 teaspoons pure maple syrup

Place the cream cheese and powdered sugar in a small bowl, and using a wooden spoon, blend until smooth. Add the pecans and maple syrup, and stir until combined. Transfer to a small serving bowl or a ramekin and refrigerate. Let soften slightly before serving.

STORAGE: Refrigerate, tightly covered with plastic wrap, for up to 5 days. Freezing is not recommended.

orange honey butter

MAKES ⅔ CUP

This spread is perfect with a fresh-from-the-oven biscuit or scone. I must admit to indulging in a dollop (or two) on a croissant, as well!

½ cup (1 stick) unsalted butter, softened

3 tablespoons honey

½ teaspoon freshly grated navel orange zest

Combine the butter, honey, and zest in a medium bowl. Stir with a spoon until well blended. Place in a ramekin or a small bowl and refrigerate. Let soften to spreading consistency before serving.

STORAGE: Refrigerate, tightly covered with plastic wrap, for up to 1 week. This butter may be frozen.

dried pear, toasted walnut, and blue cheese spread

MAKES ABOUT 1¼ CUPS

Dried pears and rich blue cheese combined with crunchy walnuts make this spread one of my favorites. For a special treat, try it with Classic Brioche (page 230) or Angel Biscuits (page 140).

3 ounces cream cheese, softened

3 ounces dried pears, plumped (see page 389) and cubed

¼ cup sour cream

1 tablespoon honey

3 ounces blue cheese, crumbled and softened

½ cup medium-chopped toasted walnuts (see pages 391–392)

Pinch of salt

Combine the cream cheese, pears, sour cream, and honey in the work bowl of a food processor fitted with the steel blade. Pulse 8 to 10 times, then process for 10 seconds. Add the blue cheese, pulse 2 times, then add the walnuts and pulse 2 more times. Remove from the processor, place in a small bowl or ramekin, and refrigerate. Let soften slightly before serving.

STORAGE: Refrigerate, tightly covered with plastic wrap, for up to 5 days. Freezing is not recommended.

crystallized ginger and macadamia nut cream cheese

MAKES ABOUT ¾ CUP

Indulge your taste buds with this lavish spread. Piquant crystallized ginger and buttery macadamia nuts are swirled through mellow cream cheese.

6 ounces cream cheese, softened

3 tablespoons finely chopped crystallized ginger

3 tablespoons medium-chopped macadamia nuts (see page 392)

½ teaspoon fresh lemon juice

¼ teaspoon freshly grated lemon zest

Pinch of salt

Combine the cream cheese, ginger, nuts, juice, zest, and salt in a medium bowl. Stir with a wooden spoon until well blended. Place in a ramekin or small bowl and refrigerate. Let soften slightly before serving.

STORAGE: Refrigerate, tightly covered with plastic wrap, for up to 5 days. Freezing is not recommended.

about equipment

Using the correct equipment will reduce the amount of time and effort spent in the kitchen, and increase your enjoyment of baking. While many of the items used are already in your kitchen, when you add to your baking gear, remember that it will receive a workout and that quality equipment always pays dividends.

DRY AND LIQUID MEASURES

Graduated and/or dry measures should be used for measuring dry ingredients. The standard set includes ¼-, ⅓-, ½-, and 1-cup capacities, while some sets include ⅛-, ⅔-, ¾-, and 2-cup measures.

Choose quality stainless steel measuring spoons. Standard sets come in measures of ¼, ½, 1 teaspoon, and 1 tablespoon. Oval or rectangular spoons make it easier to reach into narrow spice bottles.

Most liquid measures available in 1-, 2-, and 4 (1-quart)-cup capacity are heatproof glass or plastic with a spill-proof pouring spout. Choose a more pointed spout for neater pouring. To double-check the accuracy of your liquid measure, fill a dry measuring cup to the brim with water and pour it into your new measuring cup. If the volumes are not comparable, adjust the liquid accordingly.

KITCHEN SCALES

A good-quality digital scale is a solid investment and is especially useful for weighing yeasted dough. For small quantities, a spring scale manufactured by Cuisinart with a 10-ounce limit is very handy.

THERMOMETERS

A regular oven thermometer and an instant-read thermometer are essential in your baker's kitchen. An oven thermometer allows you to make minor adjustments in the thermostat. An instant-read thermometer is useful in gauging the temperature of liquids for dissolving yeast.

DOUGH SCRAPER

A dough scraper performs many tasks. An essential tool when I prepare dough, it has many uses, including cutting and portioning dough, releasing pastry that may stick to the rolling surface, cleaning the rolling surface, and moving and turning pastry. Avoid purchasing dough scrapers with metal handles as they are slippery and hard to grip.

PASTRY CLOTH AND ROLLING PIN COVER

Using a pastry cloth virtually eliminates sticking, tearing, or breaking of dough. My custom-made canvas pastry cloth and knitted rolling pin cover (stocking) are available by mail order from Ateco, manufacturers of specialty baking equipment (see "Specialty Sources," page 400). Complete directions for use and care are included in the package.

ROLLING PINS

For rolling yeasted dough, because of its elasticity, I recommend a quality, heavy-duty rolling pin. The standard size has a 12-inch wooden barrel and bearing set handles. For laminated doughs, like croissants and Danish, choose a rolling pin with the larger 15-inch wooden barrel, as well. Avoid less expensive bearing set handles as they lack the weight and stability of the more expensive pins.

ROLLING SURFACES

The surface you choose may help or hinder your efforts. My favorite rolling surface is a large wooden pastry board, approximately 18 × 24 inches. Anchor the board with a large piece of rubber shelf liner or a dampened cloth towel to keep it from sliding while working. If you don't have a pastry board, roll the dough on a large polyethylene cutting board or on a kitchen counter.

SILPAT

A flexible nonstick French baking mat, this is ideal for rolling smaller pieces of dough, baking cookies, and making caramelized brittles. While pricey, it is worth the investment.

PASTRY DOCKER

This 5-inch-long cylinder with sharp spikes on its entire surface is used for piercing holes in sheets of dough to reduce elasticity and relax the gluten. A four-pronged table fork is an acceptable alternative.

GRATERS

A four-sided box grater will cover most of your needs. The side with the larger moon shaped or scalloped edge is ideal for shredding almond paste, fruits, and vegetables. Essential to every kitchen is the Microplane grater, used for grating citrus zests and whole nutmeg.

STRAINERS AND SIFTERS

It is smart to have a variety of sizes and mesh densities on hand for various uses. Invest in those that are well constructed, as the mesh on less-expensive equipment is easily bent out of

shape. For sifting, I recommend an 8-inch double-mesh medium-gauge strainer, made by Cuisipro or Best. If you own a sturdy sifter, you should wipe it with damp paper towels; never wash it. Use it only for flour, never powdered sugar or cocoa powder. A strainer is recommended for these ingredients.

KNIVES

No kitchen is complete without high-quality, high-carbon, no-stain, steel knives. Brands such as Wüsthof and Victorinox will cover your needs. Sizes include 8- or 10-inch chef's knives for chopping nuts and cutting dried fruits; a $10\frac{1}{4}$-inch bread knife for slicing pound and other firm cakes and yeasted breads; a 12-inch slicing knife for cutting bar cookies; a 6-inch utility knife for slicing soft cakes and cakes made with fresh fruits; a $3\frac{1}{2}$-inch paring knife; and a stainless-steel swivel peeler for removing zests from citrus fruits and skins from fresh fruit.

FOOD PROCESSORS

A food processor is an indispensable piece of kitchen equipment. The model and age of your machine will affect the timing of a procedure, while differences in motors among models will affect the size of crumbs when making pastry doughs and streusels, as well as chopping nuts and chocolate. Blades may dull over time and should be replaced as necessary. Both Cuisinart and KitchenAid make well-designed units, each having different features. For most needs, the 9-cup capacity is ideal.

ELECTRIC MIXERS

There are two categories of electric mixers: stand mixers and hand mixers. The best stand mixer for home use is the 325-watt, 5-quart,

KitchenAid Artisan Tilt-Head mixer, especially useful for mixing batters and when kneading doughs over extended time. Other brands are acceptable as long as they have adequate horsepower for mixing dense batters. Hand-held mixers are fine for light mixing but are not recommended for heavy-duty work.

POTS AND PANS

Well-constructed cookware will contribute to the success of a recipe. Recommended manufacturers include All-Clad, Calphalon, and KitchenAid. For these recipes, I do not recommend Teflon or nonstick cookware.

Baking Pans

When baking, it is crucial to use high-quality baking pans of the size specified in the recipe. Look for reliable manufacturers, as inferior brands are often not sized accurately. Quality aluminum pans are good conductors of heat and heavy enough not to warp. Stainless steel, while easy to clean, is expensive and not a good conductor of heat. Teflon (nonstick) pans are acceptable, but avoid less expensive brands as they are thin and the coating wears off with age.

When purchasing bakeware, look for brands with the newer nonstick, *silver-coated* interior surface and dark outer coating, such as Kaiser Noblesse Bakeware. Avoid bakeware with dark interior surfaces because they overbrown most baked goods. Recommended brands are All-Clad, Calphalon, Chicago Metallic, Doughmakers, Kaiser Noblesse, Magic Line, Nordic Ware, Village Baker, and Vollrath.

If using nonstick bakeware with dark interiors, prevent overbrowning by reducing the oven temperature by 25°F. This also applies to oven-tempered glass bakeware such as Pyrex or Anchor Hocking.

Layer Cake Pans

Sizes most frequently used include the 8- or 9-inch round pan. The sides should be at least 2 inches high, and the pans should have a solid, heavy feel, with no seams on the inside.

Springform Pans

These are round pans with a spring-loaded hinge on the side, allowing the side to be released while the cake or pastry remains on a bottom disk. The most commonly used sizes are 9 and 10 inches.

Tube or Angel Food Cake Pan

This is a 10-inch pan with a center tube that allows heat to circulate through the middle. Also available is a useful, half-size pan manufactured by Wilton. Look for shiny aluminum, and choose a pan with little "feet" standing on the edge of the rim of the pan, making it great for inverting. Avoid a pan with an extra-long center tube.

Bundt and Other Ornamental Pans

These pans are decoratively fluted around the sides and have center tubes that allow the heat to circulate through the middle. Imported fluted ring (Kaiser Noblesse) pans are usually higher and more tapered and measure 10 inches across. The classic Bundt pan, which has a more rounded top and measures approximately 9 inches across, is manufactured by Nordic Ware and is extremely popular. Also manufactured by Nordic Ware are ornamental theme pans, which make unusual and beautiful presentations.

Kugelhopf Pan

A round pan similar to, but higher than, a Bundt pan. This pan is made of heavy, tinned-steel and is generally imported from Germany.

Muffin Pans

Metal pans for baking muffins, sticky buns, and small cakes are available in three sizes: mini muffin pans (usually 12 or 24 cavities), standard size (12 muffin cavities), and large or jumbo (6 muffin cavities). A standard muffin pan cavity should be 2¾ inches across and have a ⅓-cup capacity. Look for heavy-gauge aluminum pans, such as Nordic Ware or Silverstone (Farberware). Having two standard-size (12-cup) muffin pans is useful since many recipes make more than 12 muffins.

Brioche Molds

These round 8-inch fluted molds are designed especially for traditional French knot-topped buttery bread and are best when made of tinned steel. Small ones 2½ inches wide are perfect for individual buns.

Madeleine Pans

This French baking pan has individual, shallow cavities shaped similar to a scallop seashell, ranging in sizes from standard 3 inches across to minis. Choose tinned steel pans over nonstick.

Fluted Removable-Bottom Tart Pan

This classic tinned steel, 11-inch French pan is perfect for unmolding baked coffee cake rings.

Rimmed Cookie Sheet or Jelly Roll Pan

Frequently used for large and individual pastries and cookies, rimmed cookie sheets are rectangular pans, preferably made of heavy-weight shiny aluminum, with 1-inch sides. The sides allow the dough to be contained, while the aluminum bottom provides even baking without warping.

Square and Retangular Pans

Look for pans made of heavy, shiny aluminum to ensure even baking. Older pans have slightly sloped sides while the newer pans are straight sided. The recipes in this book were tested in sloped-sided pans, therefore if your pans have straight sides, reduce your baking time by a few minutes.

Cookie Sheets

Look for cookie sheets that are made of heavyweight, shiny aluminum, which is the best conductor of heat. When purchasing, look for cookie sheets with one or two lips for easy grasping. A large cookie sheet, 17 × 14 inches, manufactured by Ware-Ever Professional or Vollrath, is an excellent investment. Keep in mind your oven size when purchasing large cookie sheets and be sure to allow 2 inches of oven space around the sheet.

Loaf Pans

Dark pans are not recommended for more delicate pound cakes and tea breads, as the crusts can easily overbrown. Suggested sizes include 9 × 5 × 2¾ and 8½ × 4½ × 2¾.

Aluminum Foil Pans

Because heavy metal medium-size loaf pans are no longer manufactured, at times 8 × 3¾ × 2½-inch aluminum foil loaf pans can act as substitutes. Other useful sizes are 8 × 8 × 2-inch square pans and the 8-inch pie pan. These disposable pans are ideal to use for freezing baked and unbaked yeast cakes; Danish, pound, and creamed butter cakes; and for gift giving. For ease of handling, place foil pans on rimmed cookie sheets or in a metal pan of similar size to encourage browning on the bottom.

BAKING PAN SUBSTITUTIONS

For creamed butter cakes, it is easy to make baking pan substitutions as long as the capacity is the same as the pan given in the recipe. To ensure successful pan substitution, follow these guidelines:

• Always choose a pan as close in size as possible to the one called for in the recipe.

• To determine the size of the pan, measure across the inside of the top for length and width and vertically for depth.

• To measure the volume of the pan, determine how many cups or quarts of water it takes to fill the pan to the rim. It can be used if the volume is the about the same. Adjust the baking time accordingly.

• Pans should be filled about two-thirds full.

• Fluted, Bundt, Turk's head, or kugelhopf pans can usually be used interchangeably as long as the capacity is about the same.

CAKE RACKS OR COOLING RACKS

Stainless steel or nonstick cooling racks with small rectangular grids are my preference. Choose racks that are stable, with high legs for good air circulation. Thin-wired racks, imported from France, are excellent. Cake racks are also useful to set cakes and pastries on when glazing so the excess can drip through the openings onto wax paper.

MISCELLANEOUS TOOLS

Offset Spatula

This is a spatula with the metal blade set lower than the handle. Convenient for releasing pastries from pans and smoothing the surface of cakes, bar cookies, and glazes. Recommended sizes are $3\frac{1}{2}$ inch and 6 inch.

Rubber Spatulas and Bowl Scrapers

Sometimes referred to as scrapers, these come in the following sizes: small 1-inch spatula, handy for scraping out the inside of small containers and measuring cups; 2-inch medium size, good for stirring, blending, and scraping the bottom of bowls; $2\frac{3}{4}$-inch oversize, essential for folding in beaten egg whites, nuts, chocolate chips, and chopped fruits into batters and doughs. Those made by Rubbermaid with a plastic or wooden handle flex well. Heatproof rubber spatulas are also useful, but some are not good for folding. An inexpensive and useful item is a palm-held plastic bowl scraper, professionally called a pastry corn. The curved side is especially useful for cleaning bowls and lifting heavy doughs.

Whisks

The longer, tapered sauce whisk is indispensable for combining dry ingredients with leavening, or for blending and stirring; also great for removing lumps from batters and cooked fillings. Look for graduated sizes; also invaluable is an 11- to 13-inch balloon whisk for whipping.

Pastry Cutting Wheels

Also called jaggers, pastry wheels come in two styles: a straight-bladed variety, frequently referred to as a pizza cutter, and one with a jagged or fluted edge. The fluted wheel gives an attractive zigzag edge to the finished product; however, the best choice for cutting doughs layered with butter (such as croissant and Danish) is the straight-blade pastry wheel. Choose a stainless steel pastry cutter with a sturdy wheel.

Biscuit Cutter

Biscuit cutters come in a variety of sizes. Choose one with a sturdy handle, made of quality metal. Good sizes are 2 and 2¼ inches.

Pastry and Goosefeather Brushes

These are indispensable accessories for making all pastries. Uses include greasing pans, buttering as well as brushing excess flour from dough, and glazing. Quality, flat natural-bristle brushes, with tight ferrules secured with metal or rubber bands, are recommended. Commonly used sizes are widths of 1, 1½, and 2 inches. Clean pastry brushes by soaking them in very hot, soapy water, changing the liquid a few times to remove grease. Goosefeather brushes are made from tightly wrapped feathers and are useful for removing excess flour from croissant and Danish dough.

Decorating Equipment

For this book, you will need a 14- or 16-inch canvas-lined pastry bag for holding pastry fillings and for piping the pastry fillings; also, large plain round tips nos. 805 and 806. The brand that I recommend is Ateco (see "Specialty Sources," page 400).

Food Mill or Potato Ricer

Available in varying sizes, food mills are made of either tin-plated or stainless steel. Look for one that has interchangeable cutting plates. Either tool is ideal to use when a smooth consistency is necessary, such as for cheese-style fillings.

OTHER TOOLS

18-inch Artist's Ruler

Accurately measures rolled dough.

Batarde (flat-bottomed meat pounder)

For smoothing and evening dough in the bottom of pans.

Square Metal Mini Offset Spatula (2¼ x 2¼ inches)

For cutting bar cookies.

Ice Cream Scoop

The no. 16 scoop (¼-cup capacity) with a spring-release, cog-regulated blade for portioning muffin batter.

Cupcake Liners

Paper cups are best for muffin batters that are going to be baked immediately, while aluminum foil liners are better for longer keeping. Available in the baking section of most supermarkets. (See "Muffins in Minutes," page 83.)

Baking Parchment

For lining baking pans.

Aluminum Foil

Regular, Release (nonstick), and 18-inch heavy duty foil.

Two-Sided Melon Ball Cutter

Smaller side, ⅜ inch to larger side, 1¼ inches for coring apples.

Sugar Shaker

For garnishing baked pastries with powdered sugar.

Pastry Blender

For cutting fat into flour.

about ingredients & techniques

FLOURS AND GRAINS

Flour, the cornerstone of baking, provides structure for butter, sugar, and eggs as well as other important ingredients. Wheat flour—the most common flour used for baking—is harvested from the wheat stalks as tiny kernels, or wheat berries. Each berry is made up of three parts: the bran (outer shell), the endosperm (starchy center), and the germ (heart), the latter of which is highly perishable. Whole wheat flour is milled from the entire kernel, while all-purpose flour comes only from the starchy center.

The ability of flour to absorb liquid is determined by its protein content—that is, the greater the amount of protein, the more liquid it absorbs. The type of wheat and the variables of soil and climate conditions all impact the protein level and the moisture content.

Protein counts, listed on the side of the package on the nutritional label, range from ¼ cup to ⅓ cup of flour. It is always wise to check the protein content when trying a new brand of flour. While flour should be used within several weeks of purchase, the shelf life can be extended if it is refrigerated in an airtight container or frozen for up to one year. Once opened, whole wheat, as well as other specialty flours, should be stored in the freezer. All flours should be brought to room temperature before using.

Wheat Flours

Bleached All-Purpose Flour (3 grams protein per ¼ cup flour): An enriched white flour, milled from the center or starchy part of the wheat kernel, has been whitened with chlorine dioxide or benzyl peroxide or chlorine gas. Bleached all-purpose flour may be used interchangeably with unbleached all-purpose flour.

Unbleached All-Purpose Flour (3 grams protein per ¼ cup flour): This flour is milled without chemical bleaching agents, resulting in a flour with a slight cream or ivory color. Although the flour can contain slightly more protein than bleached flour, it can be used interchangeably.

Bread Flour (3 to 4 grams protein per ¼ cup): This high-protein flour, made from hard red winter or spring wheat, is usually associated with hard-crusted yeasted breads. The high protein content provides structure to the dough, giving the elasticity needed for stretching strudel dough. Bread flour is available in most supermarkets and grocery stores.

Cake Flour (2 grams protein per ¼ cup): Milled especially for cakes and tender pastries, enriched white cake flour is produced from high-quality soft wheat. Packaged in 2-pound boxes, cake flour is usually located in the flour section of your supermarket or sometimes among the cake mixes. Look for plain cake flour, not self-rising, which contains leavening and salt.

Self-Rising Flour (3 grams protein per ¼ cup): Self-rising flour is a soft, white wheat flour premixed with leavening (baking powder) and salt; it is best used for recipes written for this type of flour.

Whole Wheat Flour (3 to 5 grams protein per ¼ cup flour, depending on the brand): This nutritious, high-fiber flour is milled from the entire wheat kernel—the bran, the endosperm, and the germ. Stone-ground whole-wheat flour retains more nutrients and vitamins. Oil released from the germ during milling makes these flours highly perishable. They should be stored in the refrigerator or freezer.

Semolina (3¼ grams protein per ¼ cup flour): Similar to cornmeal, semolina has a coarse texture and a golden color. It is made exclusively from durum wheat that has been chipped or sliced, instead of ground. Although high in protein content, durum wheat does not form the same quality gluten as other types of wheat flour.

Non-Wheat Flours and Meals

Cornmeal Made from either white or yellow corn kernels, cornmeal is frequently combined with wheat flours to achieve texture and enhance the flavor of baked goods. Stone-ground cornmeal is more temperature-sensitive and should be stored in the refrigerator or freezer. Regular cornmeal may be stored at room temperature.

Cornstarch Cornstarch, the starchy center (endosperm) of the corn kernel, is sometimes combined with wheat flour to lessen the strength of the protein and achieve a more delicate finished product. Cornstarch also provides an excellent dusting for surfaces to be used for rolling doughs. As a thickener, cornstarch produces a clear gel and has twice the thickening power of wheat flours.

Nut Flours Frequently found in ethnic pastries, nut flours are commonly made from non-wheat products such as almonds, chestnuts, and hazelnuts. These fine, powdery flours are used either alone or in combination with wheat flour. The best nut flours are commer-

cially produced; however, you may replicate the process by grinding nuts in the processor or blender with the addition of flour or sugar. Nut flours are highly perishable; store them in the refrigerator or freezer.

Rice Flour Made from white rice, this very soft, powdery flour contains protein, but does not form gluten. It is available in some supermarkets and most Asian and health food stores.

Rolled Oats (Oatmeal) This healthy grain is high in protein, fiber, and unsaturated fats. In baking, oatmeal adds flavor, texture, and nutrition to the finished product. Steel-cut oats are not suitable for baking.

Is Sifting (Straining) Flour Really Necessary?

Whether passed through a sifter or a strainer, flour should be free of lumps and light, resulting in better blending with other ingredients, more accurate measuring, and, most important, thorough incorporation with chemical leavenings. When choosing a strainer, look for one that is well made (see page 371). I find most sifters do not hold up well; therefore, I generally prefer a strainer.

Although a bag of flour may be labeled "pre-sifted," if a recipe calls for sifting, it is best to ignore the label and sift, since the flour has stood over time and become heavy and compacted.

Many bakers are confused about whether to measure before or after sifting. "One cup flour, *sifted*," means to measure first, then sift. If the recipe calls for "one cup sifted flour," sift first and then measure. Some recipes specify no sifting at all—only whisking to combine the flour with leavenings, salt, spices, or other dry ingredients. Use an appropriate size whisk to thoroughly incorporate the leavening.

Getting the Flour into the Cup

Begin with a standardized set of graduated or dry measuring cups. Place a sheet of wax paper on a flat surface. Strain or sift the flour as directed in the recipe. If the recipe does not call for sifting the dry ingredient before measuring, just fluff it lightly with a spoon, then measure.

Never dip the measuring cup into the flour; always spoon the flour in. When the cup is dipped in, the flour is compacted and results in too much flour in the recipe, which then throws off the balance of ingredients and causes dryness.

After the cup has been filled, sweep a straight-bladed utensil over the top of the cup to level the flour. Do not shake the measuring cup as you spoon the flour into it. (Note: For quantities less than ¼ cup, it's okay to dip the measuring spoons directly into the dry ingredient.)

Incorporating Leavening with Dry Ingredients

Ideally, I prefer to blend leavenings with the flour by sifting or straining them together. Place two sheets of wax paper next to each other. Set a medium-gauge strainer over one of the sheets and strain the flour and leavenings through the strainer three times, alternating between the pieces of paper. Lift the paper up and form a funnel, pouring the ingredients back and forth. (When using a food processor, this procedure is unnecessary.)

If using grain flours, such as cornmeal or whole wheat, it is best to strain the leavening through the white flour first, then whisk in the grain flour. Because of its coarse texture, straining grain flour is not recommended.

LEAVENINGS: CHEMICAL AND AIR

Pastries must have some form of leavening to make them rise. That leavening can be chemical, yeast, or air. *Baking powder*, a fast-rising leavening agent, is made with cream of tartar, an acid, and baking soda, an alkaline, along with a small amount of cornstarch to prevent lumping. Pure *baking soda*, also fast rising, is used to neutralize the acid in batters that contain cultured products, some fresh fruits, chocolate, molasses, and honey. *Yeast* is slow-acting and is used primarily for sweet and savory breads, croissants, and Danish. See the yeast section that follows.

Air, the other leavening, is the invisible ingredient that enables whipped eggs to form the structure for some cakes, in addition to forming foamy peaks for meringues and whipped creams.

Chemical Leavenings

Double-Acting Baking Powder This leavening agent releases gas in two stages. The first is when it comes into contact with liquid when assembling a recipe; the second occurs during baking. Recipes in this book refer to double-acting baking powder.

Single-Acting Baking Powder The gas in single-acting baking powder is released upon coming into contact with liquid. Batters and dough made with this should be baked as soon as possible, since they lose their rising power as they stand.

Baking Soda Baking soda, also known as sodium bicarbonate, is an element of baking powder. Possessing four times the leavening power of baking powder, it is used as a neutralizing agent for batters that contain acidic ingredients (buttermilk, yogurt, or sour cream).

Cream of Tartar Another element of baking powder, cream of tartar is made from the residue formed inside wine casks during fermentation. It stabilizes beaten egg whites and prevents the crystallization of sugar while caramelizing.

Yeast

There are three forms of yeast familiar to the home baker: cake (fresh or compressed) yeast, active dry yeast, and quick yeast. In this book, when yeast is called for, the product of choice is active dry yeast. When working with yeast, remember that it is a living organism with particular needs. To thrive, yeast needs moisture, food (sugar or starch), and a warm temperature (70° to 85°F is optimal).

Cake, Fresh, or Compressed Yeast Formed when excess water is removed from cream yeast, cake yeast is packaged in 0.6-ounce squares or 2-ounce foil-wrapped packages. It can be refrigerated for up to 6 to 8 weeks or frozen for up to 3 months.

Active Dry Yeast Active dry yeast is dormant and must be hydrated ("proofed") in warm liquid (110° to 115°F) before using. Sold in strips of three ¼-ounce (2¼ teaspoons) packets, active dry yeast should be stored at room temperature until its expiration date or frozen for longer shelf life. Once opened, unused yeast may be stored in its original envelope (tightly closed and well wrapped) for up to 3 months in the refrigerator or 6 months in the freezer.

Instant Active Dry Yeast, Rapid-Rise Yeast, Quick Rise Yeast A very active strain of yeast that requires only one rising. However, this sometimes compromises the finished flavor and is not recommended for recipes in this book. (See "Working with Yeast," page 186.)

SUGARS AND OTHER SWEETENERS

Standard Baking Sweeteners

Brown Sugar The combination of molasses and refined white sugar creates brown sugar. Light brown sugar contains less molasses than dark brown sugar. It has a more subtle flavor than dark brown sugar; however, the sugars may be used interchangeably. When used in large amounts, the flavor of the finished product can be affected. For successful results, these sugars must be *very fresh*. Granulated brown sugar may be substituted for the nongranulated type, but it is expensive and the advantage does not seem to justify the cost. To store, tightly reseal the bag, secure with tape, and return it to the box. Place it in a large zipper plastic bag and refrigerate. Refreshing stale brown sugar in the microwave is *not* a solution. Don't jeopardize the quality of your pastry by adding something bad to something good. Save the hardened brown sugar for the candied sweets and open a fresh box for the sticky buns!

Powdered Sugar (Confectioners' Sugar) Powdered, or confectioners', or 10x, sugar is a blend of 3 percent cornstarch and granulated sugar processed to a fineness ten times that of granulated sugar. When used in baking, this sugar produces a very fine, velvety texture. Powdered sugar should always be strained before measuring.

Corn Syrup Corn syrup is made from cornstarch and comes in two varieties: light and dark. Light corn syrup is clear, sweet, and flavorless, while dark corn syrup is flavored with caramel, which contributes to its rich dark color. Store corn syrup at room temperature. Do not substitute light corn syrup for dark corn syrup.

Golden Syrup This honey-colored liquid sweetener, imported from England, may be used in place of corn syrup and provides a unique, toasty flavor to baked goods. It is sold under the Lyle's label and can be purchased domestically in specialty food stores and some supermarkets. (See "Specialty Sources," page 400.)

Molasses A dark, thick syrup made from the remnants of sugar crystals during refining, molasses imparts flavor, moistness, and color to baked goods. Sulfured molasses has a strong, rich flavor while the unsulfured variety is milder.

Granulated Sugar The all-purpose sweetener of choice in the American home is granulated sugar. While providing sweetness in baked goods, sugar also contributes texture, moisture, tenderness, and color. The finer the crystal, the more easily the sugar will dissolve and incorporate air when beaten with butter or eggs. If your sugar has large crystals, grind it, preferably in a blender; however, a food processor may also be used. Sugar will keep indefinitely in an airtight container.

Superfine Sugar This finely grained premium cane sugar, packaged in 1-pound boxes, is used because the smaller crystals melt quickly during baking. It may be used interchangeably with regular granulated sugar. Store superfine sugar in an airtight container to prevent lumps from forming.

Honey Honey purchased in supermarkets will likely have come from the nectar of clover, orange blossom, or lavender flowers. While honey may be substituted for sugar in syrup-style recipes, making this substitution for baked goods is not recommended as the flavor, texture, and consistency of the finished product will be altered.

Maple Syrup Pure maple syrup is distilled from the sap of mature maple trees and is graded by the USDA according to color and flavor; deeper color indicates more intense flavor. Maple syrup should be kept in the refrigerator to prevent it from forming mold.

Decorative Sugars

A variety of decorative sugars are available for sprinkling atop baked goods. Sources for these and other specialty products are listed on page 400.

Coarse Sugars Available in brown (Demerara) and sparkling white, these lend an attractive finish and crunch to baked goods.

Pearl Sugar With super-white large, irregular-shaped sugar grains, pearl sugar's main attraction, beyond appearance, is that it does not melt in baking.

Sparkling Sugar These clear, large crystal sugar grains, commonly from Scandinavia, are slow-melting and used for finishing Danish pastries and for decorating cookies.

Working with Sugars and Other Sweeteners

Along with flour, butter, and eggs, sugar is one of the four primary baking ingredients. In addition to contributing sweetness, moisture, and tenderness to baked goods, it also encourages browning. For best baking results, always use the sugar called for in the recipe. If you wish to use substitutes, refer to books written for those particular products.

Measuring White Sugars A set of dry or graduated measuring cups is essential for measuring white sugar. Use a large spoon or the dip method to fill the cup to the brim, then level the sugar using a straight-bladed utensil, such as a dough scraper or the dull side of a knife.

Measuring Brown Sugar Measure brown sugar in dry or graduated measuring cups. When measuring *lightly packed* brown sugar, the sugar should be lightly pressed when filling the measuring cup. When inverted, the sugar will have some open spaces, but gently retain its shape. Firmly *packed* brown sugar should be pressed firmly into the measuring cup; when inverted, it will have no open spaces and have a solid shape.

Once measured, brown sugar should be covered with plastic wrap to prevent a crust from forming on the surface. Do not let the measured brown sugar sit uncovered for any length of time.

Measuring Thick Syrups Molasses, corn syrup, maple syrup, Lyle's Golden Syrup, and honey are best measured in graduated or dry measuring cups or spoons. Before measuring, lightly grease the container with nonstick cooking spray or vegetable oil to allow the liquid to flow without sticking.

FATS

Types of Baking Fats
Butter Butter is made up of about 80 percent animal fat and 10 to 16 percent water, with the remaining amount curds and minerals. While European-style butters are available, you will receive excellent results using butters such as Land O Lakes.

In baking, butter provides color, flavor, and tenderness, and helps retain freshness. For baking purposes, unsalted butter is far superior because its flavor is more fresh and pure than that of salted butter. If salted butter is used, reduce the salt in the recipe. Never use whipped or "lite" butter in baking because these products are usually aerated or have added moisture. If dietary laws are a consideration, unsalted margarine may be used as a substitute.

Butter should always be refrigerated to prevent it from becoming rancid. It should also be well wrapped so it does not absorb refrigerator odors and flavors. Take note of the expiration date on the package; butter may be frozen for up to 6 months.

Hydrogenated Vegetable Shortening The classic solid vegetable shortening is neutral flavored and pure white; however, a butter flavored product has been introduced in recent years. While shortening can be stored at room temperature, I find that refrigeration helps maintain freshness and color.

Vegetable and Other Oils Many oils can successfully be used in baking. Choose those with the more neutral flavors, such as canola or safflower oil. Oil should not be substituted for solid fats because it does not aerate and the texture of a batter or dough will be adversely affected.

Working with Butter, Solid Shortening, and Oils
Semi-solid fats such as butter and margarine, as well as solid fats like vegetable shortening, have the ability to hold air. Liquid fats, such as oils, are unable to hold air and cannot be creamed with regular kitchen equipment. Most pastry recipes in this book rely on the clean, fresh flavor of butter, therefore pay attention to quality and freshness.

The protein in wheat flour is converted into gluten when it comes in contact with fat or moisture. When butter is used, the fat coats the wheat flour's starch granules and the gluten strands are shortened, resulting in the delicate, melt-in-your-mouth texture so prized by bakers. The fluidity of oil actually *moistens* the starch granules, creating a softer dough that is more difficult to handle.

Substituting Butter for Vegetable Shortening

I am frequently asked if butter and vegetable shortening are interchangeable. While possible, it must be remembered that vegetable shortening is 100 percent fat, while butter is 80 percent fat and 20 percent water and milk solids. *If you do replace butter with vegetable shortening, reduce the liquid in the recipe by 1 tablespoon for every 4 tablespoons (one-half stick) of butter.*

Using the Right Temperature

When preparing batters and doughs, remember that the temperature of the butter, shortening, or margarine is key. Recipes referring to *room temperature* can be very confusing, since indoor room temperatures can vary, depending on the time of year.

I prefer the term *slightly firm*. To check this, hold a wrapped stick of butter in your hand and press it firmly with your thumb. There should be a slight indentation. If the butter is too soft, the butterfat and milk solids will separate and the dough will be difficult to handle. On the other hand, butter that is too firm will not blend easily with other ingredients, resulting in a rough-textured dough. If using margarine, it should be somewhat firmer when used.

Measuring Fats

Recipes in this book specify measurements by cups and/or sticks. While stick butter and margarine are wrapped in pre-marked 4-ounce bars, be sure to double-check the marking on the packaging, since the measurements are not always aligned properly. I suggest opening the wrapper and measuring the sticks accordingly. Always use a liquid measuring cup for oil.

Many recipes call for cubed or sliced butter. Start with *cold* butter or margarine, unwrap the stick, but do not discard the outer wrapping (it will keep your hands from becoming oily). To form cubes, position a dough scraper or long sharp knife parallel or lengthwise to the butter or margarine and cut down firmly through the center. While still on the wrapper, give the bar a quarter-turn and cut down again lengthwise, forming four long sticks. Cutting across, make ½-inch cubes.

For slicing butter or margarine into slivers, unwrap the *cold* stick, keeping it on the wrapping, and use a dough scraper or sharp knife to cut it crosswise into ⅛-inch pieces.

Clarifying Butter

Clarified butter is butter that has been cooked to a point where it forms three distinct layers. The first is a white foam containing milk solids or whey proteins that rise to the top of the pot; the second is a clear, golden liquid free of impurities that is 100% fat (the clarified butter), and the third is a watery substance that is milk protein and salts and that settles to the bottom of the saucepan.

To clarify butter, place the butter in an appropriate size, heavy-bottomed saucepan deep enough to allow for any splatters. Simmer until white foam forms over the top. Carefully remove and discard the foam, continuing until it no longer accumulates. Simmer over low heat until the watery liquid evaporates and brown sediment *begins* to form on the bottom of the pot. This can take from 15 to 30 minutes, depending on the amount you are clarifying and the weight of the saucepan. Watch it carefully to avoid burning. Let the butter stand until tepid, then pour it through a small fine-mesh strainer into a jar. Cover the jar and refrigerate for 4 to 6 months or freeze indefinitely.

When just a few tablespoons of butter are needed, the microwave is convenient to use. However, the flavor of the butter is not as intense as the stove-top method above. Using a microwave-proof container, such as a glass measuring cup, add enough butter to allow for the loss of 20 to 25 percent of the volume. Using medium power, melt the butter, stopping from time to time to skim off the foam. When the foam stops forming, let the butter stand at room temperature for 2 to 3 minutes so the impurities can sink to the bottom. Pour off the clear butter, discarding the milky liquid at the bottom.

Using Browned Butter

Browned butter, or *beurre noisette,* is butter that has been cooked to a rich, golden brown to have an intense, nutty flavor. Pay careful attention to the *color* toward the end of the cooking time, as the flavor can quickly change from being richly nutty to burned.

DAIRY PRODUCTS

Milk and Cream

In baking, lactose (milk sugar) caramelizes to contribute color and texture to the finished product. In yeast doughs, milk sugars enhance fermentation by feeding the yeast, while the liquids help develop gluten. Milk and other dairy products also contribute to the texture of baked goods by moistening the dry ingredients and helping them bind together, while the fats and proteins help develop a tender crumb.

Milk Whole milk has about 3½ percent milk fat, low-fat milk has from 1 to 2 percent, and skim (nonfat) milk has less than ½ percent milk fat. Whole milk and low-fat milks are interchangeable in most recipes, unless otherwise indicated. Evaporated whole or skim milk may also be substituted as long as they are reconstituted with 50 percent water.

Purchase milk well in advance of the expiration date. Refrigerate in tightly sealed cartons or containers, and keep away from strong odors.

Buttermilk Buttermilk is produced by the addition of special bacteria to nonfat or low-fat milk. Its distinctive tangy flavor provides a welcome balance to the sweetness in many cakes, muffins, and quick breads. Buttermilk's acidity also activates the leavening power of baking soda. Use only when specified.

Cream Cream is the high-fat milk product separated from milk. *Heavy whipping cream* and *light whipping cream* are most often used in baking and are available in pasteurized and ultra-pasteurized form. Because of its longer shelf life, ultra-pasteurized cream is more readily available; however, my preference is to use pure cream because this cream does not contain additives and stabilizers. Be sure to use the type of cream specified in a recipe because altering the fat content may not produce successful results.

Eggnog Eggnog, a traditional holiday beverage, is made by blending milk or cream with eggs, sugar, nutmeg, and sometimes a liquor such as rum, brandy, or whiskey. Commercial eggnogs contain 1 percent egg solids by weight and do not contain liquor.

Powdered Buttermilk Powdered buttermilk is dehydrated buttermilk that is used almost exclusively for baking. It performs in the same manner as liquid buttermilk; however, like other powdered milk products, it lacks the taste of fresh buttermilk.

Cheese

Many soft cheeses contribute flavor and texture to a variety of rich batters, flaky doughs, and creamy spreads.

Brie Brie from France is considered the standard to which all others are compared. This full-flavored cow's milk cheese, with an edible white rind, has a cream-colored interior that is meltingly soft when fully ripened.

Camembert Made from cow's milk, named for the village of origin in France, Camembert is characterized by an edible white rind and a smooth, creamy, mild-flavored interior.

Cheddar Cheese Originally produced in the English village of Cheddar, this firm cow's milk cheese is now produced stateside in Vermont, Wisconsin, New York, and California. An excellent grating cheese, its color ranges from creamy white to bright orange, with mild to sharp flavor.

Cream Cheese Made from cow's milk, this unripened cheese by law must contain at least 33 percent milk fat and no more than 55 percent moisture. Whipped cream cheese should not be substituted for conventional cream cheese in baking because it is aerated. Light, low-fat, and fat-free cream cheeses also should not be substituted.

Farmer Cheese The tiny curds of this fresh, dry unripened cow's milk cheese are commonly pressed into 7.5-ounce rectangles. Frequently used in Central and Eastern European pastries and desserts, it is a key ingredient in cheese strudel. Farmer cheese is available in most supermarket dairy departments.

Jarlsberg Cheese This cheese is marketed as either a Swiss or Norwegian Emmentaler type. A good melting cheese, Jarlsberg is made from cow's milk and has a rich buttery texture and a sweet nutty flavor. Its fat content is slightly lower than Swiss cheese.

Ricotta This fresh Italian cheese, now manufactured in the United States, is made from the whey (by-product) of provolone or mozzarella and whole or skim milk. Whole milk ricotta has a certain sweetness to it which is lost in the nonfat version. Once opened, this cheese should be used within a day or two.

Sour Cream Containing 18 to 20 percent butterfat, sour cream has lactic acid culture added to provide its familiar tang. It contributes a moist texture and a tanginess that complements the sweetness in pastries. At times it can be substituted for yogurt or buttermilk. Light sour cream should not be used unless specified in recipes. Sour cream is best used within 1 week of the date indicated on the carton. If it develops mold on its surface, discard it.

Yogurt Creamy and thick, yogurt is the result of milk's being invaded by "friendly" bacteria that cause it to ferment and thicken. Its tangy flavor and moistness make yogurt a popular baking ingredient. Low-fat and fat-free yogurts are not acceptable substitutions because of the addition of sugar, gum, stabilizers, and thickeners. Greek yogurt, a superior product, is not always an acceptable substitute because it is richer and the moisture content is different.

EGGS

Eggs are among the most crucial baking ingredients because they perform a variety of roles. The yolk is high in fat and adds richness, tenderness, and color to baked goods. The white is high in protein and provides structure and moisture. When eggs are added to beaten butter and sugar, they form cells that expand and multiply to lighten the mixture. Beaten eggs are also a major leavening agent, with or without a chemical leavener. This action incorporates air, creating millions of tiny air cells that expand during baking to make the cake rise.

Most recipes, unless otherwise specified, call for large eggs. White and brown eggs have the same nutritional value and flavor—the difference in color is simply the result of the breed of chicken laying the egg.

Handling Eggs

Remove eggs from the refrigerator 20 to 30 minutes before baking. Room-temperature eggs will blend better and have greater volume when beaten than those used straight from the refrigerator. If you need to use the eggs immediately, remove the chill by placing them in a bowl of tepid water for a minute or two.

Storing Eggs

Eggs must be stored and handled properly to avoid salmonella poisoning. Refrigerate eggs in their cartons because eggshells are porous and can absorb bacteria and odors easily. They should be stored pointed end facing down, in a colder part of the refrigerator. Discard any eggs that have cracked shells and do not taste batter containing raw eggs. To avoid cross-contamination, be sure to wash your hands after handling raw eggs, and keep measuring and mixing utensils clean.

Shelled whole eggs, egg yolks, and whites may be stored in the refrigerator, tightly covered with plastic wrap. Whole eggs and yolks will keep up to 3 days and the whites for up to 4 days. Egg whites can be frozen for several months but freezing can cause egg whites to pick up a bit of moisture, so they may not be ideal for meringues.

Separating Eggs

Separate eggs while cold, using the three-bowl method. Use one bowl to crack the egg over, a second bowl to empty the whites into, and the third to hold the yolks. Crack the eggshell by giving it a firm tap across the center with a table knife. Hold the egg upright and remove the top shell, allowing the white to flow over the side into the empty bowl. Pass the yolk back and forth between the two shells. Tip the yolk a bit to remove as much of the white as possible. Do not allow *any* of the yolk to fall into the whites. If any pieces of the shell fall into the egg, for sanitary reasons, remove them with a spoon, not the eggshell.

Two protein-rich, cordlike strands called chalazae hold the yolk to the center of the egg. When heated, the chalazae toughens and becomes marble-like. Larger chalazae may be pulled from the egg yolk with your fingertips.

Beating Eggs and Egg Whites

Many recipes call for eggs to be *lightly beaten* before adding them to other ingredients (usually butter and sugar). Whisking the eggs helps them blend in more readily. For proper aeration, if whole eggs are to be beaten in a stand mixer, always use the whip attachment. Begin on medium-low speed and increase gradually to medium-high.

For greater success when beating egg whites, always start them at room temperature. Be sure your mixing bowl and beater have no oil on the surfaces. While a copper bowl is best for whipping whites, stainless steel bowls perform very well. Avoid bowls made of reactive metal such as aluminum.

To prevent overbeating the whites, refer to the four stages below.

Stage 1—Frothy: the whites have developed a foamy surface, and are no longer clear. This is when salt and cream of tartar are frequently added.

Stage 2—Soft Peak: ridges are visible on the surface and the whites are shiny and moist.

Stage 3—Firm Peak: the ridges are very defined; they somewhat resemble the spokes on a bicycle wheel. The whites are still moist and shiny. If making a stiff or hard meringue, now is the time to add the sugar. Remember, egg whites pass from stage 2 to stage 3 in a matter of seconds.

Stage 4—Stiff Peak: the sugar has been added at stage 3, and the whites are now beaten to stiff, shiny peaks.

Start beating the egg whites on medium speed. When the whites are frothy, add the salt and cream of tartar if used. Gradually increase the mixer speed to medium-high, and whip to the desired stage. Avoid using high speed as this will result in egg whites with large, unstable air cells that will burst because of too much friction. *Overly beaten egg whites may be corrected by adding one egg white (for up to six whites) and whipping it in briefly.*

Folding and Lightening Mixtures

When two mixtures of different consistencies are blended together, the process is referred to as *folding.* To prevent air loss, one-quarter to one-third of the lighter mixture is usually blended into the heavier, denser mixture to lighten its consistency. Always fold by hand, using an appropriate size rubber spatula in a bowl large enough to blend the mixtures without crowding. Cut through the center of the mixture to the bottom of the bowl, then sweep the spatula up the side of the bowl and over the top, cut-

ting through the center again. Move the bowl in a circular motion as you fold.

When combining ingredients, determine their degree of firmness ahead of time. If one is firmer than the other, mix the harder one first to bring it to the same consistency as the softer one. Chilled items like butter and cream cheese will blend more readily if allowed to soften at room temperature.

LIQUIDS

Milk and other dairy products are the most commonly used liquids in cakes; however, water, fruit juices, fruit purees, and coffee are sometimes used as moistening agents. Liquid in a batter serves two essential purposes. It changes the protein in flour to gluten and it begins the chemical reaction of leaveners. These two actions, alone or combined, allow carbon dioxide to develop, which makes the cake rise. Additionally, during baking, liquid gives off steam, a major contributor to the texture of baked goods.

Water Use room-temperature tap water unless a recipe directs you to heat the water.

Fruit Juices, Purees, and Canned Fruits Fruit juices and purees play a dual role in baking, contributing moisture as well as good taste. When purchasing canned fruits, seek out quality name brands. However, some stores do carry quality items packaged under their own labels. Your best bet is to try them and see.

Citrus Fruits and Juice Nothing can surpass the flavor of fresh orange or lemon juice. Seek out fruits that are blemish free and feel heavy in the hand, as they will have more juice.

Measuring Liquids Liquid (fluid) measuring cups should be used to measure liquids. My preference is ovenproof glass because the measurements are clearly marked. Choose a measuring cup nearest to the amount you are measuring —that is, when measuring quantities under ½ cup, don't choose a 2- or 4-cup measure.

Zesting Citrus Fruits

Zesting citrus fruits refers to removing only the colored outer portion of the skin; the underlying white pith should not be grated. There are many varieties of zesters on the market today, each producing a different size and shape of zest. Because larger pieces of zest release very little oil, they give the least amount of flavor, while more finely grated zest releases more oils and has a more pungent taste.

Navel or Valencia oranges are the preferred fruit for zesting. Do not try to zest a juice orange, as the skin is too thin. The larger thick-skinned lemons are wonderful for zesting and offer more intense flavor. Thin-skinned lemons yield more juice but will not give you as much zest.

The Microplane zester is the most popular zester used today. It produces a more feathery shred, which should be gently pressed into the measuring spoon. When zesting, use short strokes on the Microplane to produce smaller shreds, while longer strokes will result in threadlike strips. If the shreds are too long, place them on a cutting board and chop them with a chef's knife

Before zesting, wash and dry the fruit well. Grate the zest onto a piece of wax paper or parchment. Be careful to grate only the colored peel, not the bitter white pith. Once a fruit is zested, it will deteriorate rapidly. Squeeze the juice and use when needed. Kept in a tightly sealed container, the juice will keep for about 1 week.

Juicing Citrus Fruits Please do not microwave your fruit to help release the juice! Roll the fruit on a flat surface, pressing gently to help soften the pulp.

CHOCOLATE

Whether chocolate is melted, chunked, or chipped in a dough or batter, no baking book would be complete without a healthy dose of this seductive ingredient. The longest-lived chocolates are unsweetened, bittersweet, and semisweet. Double-wrapped in aluminum foil and plastic wrap, and properly stored in a cool, dry place, they will keep for years. Milk chocolate and white chocolate are far more perishable. Milk chocolate should be used within one year and white chocolate within 8 months of purchase. During storage, a "bloom" may appear on chocolate, meaning that its color has changed. Chocolate that has experienced bloom can be used for baking.

Types of Chocolate

Bittersweet and Semisweet By federal regulation, chocolates labeled bittersweet or semisweet must contain no less than 27 percent cocoa butter and at least 35 percent cocoa liquor. Both semisweet and bittersweet chocolates contain sugar, chocolate liquor, cocoa butter, lecithin (a natural soybean product), and vanilla. Well-known domestic brands include Nestlé, Baker's, and Ghiradelli. Premium domestic chocolates include Guittard, Scharffen Berger, Mercken's, and Peter's Burgundy. Widely available, imported premium chocolates include Lindt Bittersweet or Surfin, from Switzerland; Callebaut Semisweet or Bittersweet from Belgium; Valrhona from France; and Perugina from Italy. Should you have difficulty locating premium chocolate in your supermarket's baking aisle, try the candy aisle or check online sources.

Milk Chocolate Also termed a real chocolate, milk chocolate is easily recognized by its lighter color. Milk chocolate must be made from at least 10 percent chocolate liquor and 12 percent milk solids.

Unsweetened Chocolate This chocolate contains between 53 and 55 percent cocoa butter and 45 to 47 percent chocolate liquor. It does not contain sugar and cannot be substituted for bittersweet or semisweet chocolate.

Chocolate Chips Chocolate chips are available in sizes and shapes that are different from the original, familiar dollop. Mini chips or morsels give you more chocolate pieces per measure. Jumbo chips and chocolate chunks are also available. Different types of chocolate are used to make chips and include semisweet, milk, and white chocolate. When purchasing chocolate chips, be sure to select real chocolate.

Unsweetened Cocoa Powder Two types of cocoa powder are available for bakers: nonalkaline and alkaline (commonly called Dutch-process). The most popular cocoa sold in the United States is nonalkaline cocoa manufactured by Hershey's, Baker's, or Ghiradelli. This acidic cocoa has a strong, full-bodied flavor. In alkaline or Dutch-process cocoa, favored by baking professionals for its rich, delicate flavor, the acid is neutralized with alkali. Popular Dutch-process brands are Dröste, Valrhona, Poulain, Feodora, and Van Houten, along with Hershey's, which has introduced its own Dutch-process cocoa powder packaged in a silver tin.

How to Chop Chocolate

To ensure even melting, always chop chocolate into small pieces. This will guarantee flavor and texture retention. It's especially important to break up larger pieces of chocolate because the outer surface overheats before the center has a chance to melt. Consider the texture of the chocolate before chopping it. Hardest of all chocolates is unsweetened, followed by bittersweet and semisweet. Large pieces of bulk or block chocolate can be broken into smaller pieces with an ice pick. It can also be shaved on a cutting board with a chef's knife (shave it at an angle into slivers). When the chocolate must be ground in a food processor, cut into pieces no larger than 1 inch before chopping. This will protect the blade and help achieve even consistency. Dark chocolates are firm enough to chop in a food processor because they can tolerate the heat. Milk and white chocolates are very heat sensitive and should be cut on a cutting board with a chef's knife.

Some recipes suggest using 3.5-ounce chocolate bars. To dice these bars, unwrap the chocolate and place it on a cutting board. Use a chef's knife to dice the bar into appropriate size cubes. Also, an ice pick is a handy tool for easily breaking small bars of chocolate. To do this, do not unwrap the chocolate to be chopped. Place the paper-wrapped chocolate on a cutting board and pierce it several times with the ice pick. When you remove the paper, the chocolate will be chopped into pieces, ready to melt with no mess! Cut-up chocolate can be used in place of chocolate chips, or as desired.

Melting Dark Chocolates (Unsweetened, Bittersweet, and Semisweet)

Stove-Top Method Fill an appropriate size saucepan with no more than 2 inches of water. Choose a stainless steel or glass heat-proof bowl that fits snugly over the pan. The bowl should not be wider than the pot, and the bottom should not touch the water. Bring the water to a simmer. Place the chopped chocolate in the bowl and set it over the water. When almost melted, allow the chocolate to slowly finish melting *off the heat. Gently* stirring from time to time will ensure that the chocolate melts evenly. Chocolate should not be covered during or after melting.

Microwave Melting Melt small amounts of chocolate in the microwave on the defrost setting. Using this low setting will melt the chocolate more evenly, reducing the risk of overheating. The chopped chocolate should be placed in a heatproof glass bowl and heated for about 1 minute. Stir gently with a rubber spatula, then microwave for another 30 seconds. For larger amounts, use the medium setting for about 1 minute, stir gently with a rubber spatula, and continue melting in 15- to 20-second increments. The overall time will depend upon the wattage of your microwave and the amount of chocolate being melted. Chocolate melts from the inside out, therefore it *retains its shape* even when melted.

Melting Chocolate in Liquid The rule to remember when melting chocolate in liquid is that it hates a little and loves a lot. There is a myth that chocolate cannot be melted with liquid— not so! As long as enough liquid is present, it's okay to combine these ingredients.

FRUITS

Using Dried Fruits

Raisins, currants, prunes, dates, figs, and apricots are the traditional and most familiar dried fruits. Pineapple is sold in two varieties: dried, with a sugared surface; and shiny and prepared with corn syrup. If you can't find it in the supermarket, refer to Specialty Sources, page 400.

I do not recommend purchasing organic dried fruits. While they are fine for eating out of hand, no amount of soaking will improve their leathery texture. Additionally, the color of organic fruit is often dull and unappealing. Instead, seek dried fruits that are grown in places where pesticides and herbicides are monitored, and that have a minimum of chemical additives. Fruits treated with sulfur dioxide have more vibrant color, softer texture, often better flavor, and cook into a softer puree.

After opening dried fruit, seal the package tightly, expelling as much air as possible and cover with plastic wrap or place in plastic airtight bags. If the fruit is not used within 2 or 3 weeks of purchase, put it in the refrigerator, where it will keep for up to 3 months.

Plumping Dried Fruit Plumping dried fruit before use provides better flavor and texture, and prevents the fruit from drawing moisture from the batter. Fruits that are commonly plumped are raisins, apricots, cranberries, and cherries.

To plump fruit, place it in a heatproof bowl and pour boiling water over the surface, covering the fruit by about 1 inch. The fresher the fruit, the less time it will take. Also, small pieces plump more quickly than larger ones. When the fruit has softened, empty it into a strainer and rinse briefly under cool water. Spread on a double layer of paper towels, then blot dry with another double layer of towels.

Macerating Dried Fruit Follow the directions above for plumping and drying but *do not rinse with cool water.* Empty the fruit into a bowl. The warm fruit will absorb the flavor of the liqueur more efficiently. Proceed with the recipe as written.

Cutting Dried Fruit Plumped dried fruit should be chopped, sliced, or diced on a cutting board using a chef's knife, not in a food processor. Occasionally, rinse the knife with warm water or lightly coat it with unflavored vegetable oil to prevent sticking. Fruits that have not been plumped may be cut with scissors, a paring knife, or a chef's knife. Again, rinse the utensil with warm water or coat lightly with unflavored oil to prevent sticking.

Using Fresh Berries

To wash berries, place the berries in a strainer or colander. Rinse under cool running water. Spread the berries evenly on a rimmed cookie sheet lined with a double layer of paper towels. Shimmy the pan back and forth a few times, then blot the berries dry with more paper towels. Note: firm berries, such as blueberries, may be refrigerated after drying. Raspberries should be washed and dried immediately before using.

Using Fruit Preserves, Jams, Spreads, and Butters

Fruit preserves are a delicious component of many pastries. Preserves contain chunks of fruit, while jams are thick purees. Less expensive brands have higher quantities of water, so seek out those laden with fruit. I prefer to use those made with sugar because of the less smooth texture and stronger color. An excellent brand of fruit spread, though pricey, is St. Dalfour, imported from France. It is available in most upscale supermarkets.

NUTS

The most popular nuts in baking are walnuts, pecans, and almonds. Nuts form the foundation of dough when ground into nut meal, while larger pieces act as "spacers" by changing the density of baked products. Given the increasing prevalence of food allergies (and because some adults and children just don't like textured foods), it is certainly acceptable to omit nuts and seeds from a recipe. Be aware, however, that the end product may have a very different result. Think about substituting another ingredient, such as chocolate chips, for the ingredient being omitted.

The flavor of nuts is derived from the natural oil they contain. These oils cause nuts to become rancid if not properly cared for. Store in a cool, dark place until opened. After opening, refrigerate in a well-sealed container for up to 3 months or freeze for up to one year. Always date your packages and rotate your stock.

Almonds The almond is the kernel of the fruit of the almond tree. Almonds can be purchased unblanched or blanched (with or without skin), whole, sliced, slivered, and chopped.

Peanuts The two most common varieties of peanut are the large oval Virginia peanut and the smaller, round, red-skinned Spanish peanut. Shelled peanuts, in vacuum-packed containers, can be stored for up to one year. Open jars can be refrigerated for up to 3 months.

Pecans The pecan, a member of the hickory family, has the highest fat content of all nuts. Grown primarily in the southern states, pecans are available year-round. They are sold shelled and unshelled, in halves or pieces. It is best to store these rich nuts in the refrigerator or freezer to prevent rancidity.

Pistachios Pistachios, grown in the Mediterranean, the Middle East, and California, are sold with shells that are pale tan or dyed red. The color of the nut can range from a brownish green for the salted variety to a beautiful bright green for the unsalted. While pistachios are available in many forms, for baking use the unsalted skinned ones, available at Trader Joe's or Whole Foods Market.

Walnuts The English walnut is most familiar and most frequently used in baking. Walnuts are available year-round, shelled and unshelled. Look for shelled nuts that are plump, meaty, and crisp; dark-colored, shriveled walnuts are past their prime and often have a bitter overtone. Shelled walnuts can be purchased whole, broken, or chopped. Refrigerate or freeze to keep them from turning rancid.

Coconut The most common type of coconut used for baking is sweetened packaged or canned coconut, sold either flaked or shredded. Unsweetened or desiccated coconut, while in previous years were sold only in heath food stores, can now be found in many supermarkets. Both sweetened and unsweetened coconut should be well sealed after opening and stored in the refrigerator or freezer to retain freshness.

Using Coconut

In this book, recipes call for sweetened, flaked coconut. To measure, lightly pack the coconut into a graduated or dry measuring cup.

Nut Pastes and Spreads

Almond Paste Almond paste, a dense nut paste made from finely ground blanched almonds, sugar, water, and sometimes glucose or egg white, is a frequently used ingredient in Scandinavian baking. Look for the Love N' Bake or Solo brand, which are sold in cans rather than the plastic-wrapped, imported almond pastes. Leftover almond paste should be well wrapped in plastic to keep it soft and refrigerated or frozen for later use. Avoid using hardened almond paste as it does not perform well in baked goods. Do not confuse almond paste with marzipan, which has a smoother consistency and sweeter flavor.

Peanut Butter In its most natural form, peanut butter, either chunky or smooth, is a blend of ground shelled peanuts and sometimes salt and sugar. The peanut butter used in this book is smooth and you can use a kid-friendly supermarket brand.

Working with Almond Paste

The consistency of almond paste is very dense; therefore, it is best to use it at room temperature. To ensure that it will blend smoothly with other ingredients, break it into small pieces (or shred it on a box grater). The almond paste may sometimes be mixed in an electric mixer or chopped in the work bowl of a food processor using the steel blade. Once almond paste has dried out, it becomes very hard. Softening it in a microwave may prove helpful; if it doesn't soften and is a major ingredient in a recipe, I suggest discarding it and beginning with a fresh batch.

Toasting Nuts

Toasting nuts not only enhances flavor by enlivening their oils but also adds extra crunchiness. Toast nuts before they are chopped. *Be sure to let them cool completely before using.* Cooling allows the oils to be reabsorbed into the nutmeat. Also, chopping nuts before cooling can cause them to become pasty; adding warm nuts to batters or doughs may melt the butter.

Oven Toasting Line a heavy-gauge rimmed cookie sheet with aluminum foil. Toast the nuts in a single layer in a moderate to low oven (300° to 325°F). The length of toasting time will depend on the volume, size, and oil content of the nut. Color and fragrance are the best guidelines for determining when the nuts are done. In a blanched or skinless nut, look for a slight change in color. Fragrance is the best test for unskinned nuts. As soon as the nuts begin to release their aroma, remove them from the oven. Once nuts become overly toasted, they are bitter and should be discarded.

Remember that nuts with a high oil content toast much more quickly than those with a low oil content. Never toast nuts with different oil contents on the same pan. (For example, pecans and almonds.) High-fat nuts like cashews and macadamias take 6 to 8 minutes, while pecans and walnuts take 8 to 10 minutes. Pistachios, while small, are soft, so I recommend toasting for 6 to 8 minutes. Hard, less oily nuts like almonds take 12 to 15 minutes or longer to toast.

Stovetop Toasting This method is sometimes used for small nuts like pine nuts (pignolis), as well as sliced or slivered almonds. However, although this is a satisfactory solution when time is an issue, nothing can replace the color or flavor of oven-toasted nuts.

Chopping Nuts

Chopping nuts to the correct size can sometimes determine the difference between the success and failure of a recipe. Chopping nuts by hand produces uniform pieces while losing the least amount of oil. Nuts chopped in the food processor will be irregular in size and more oily. Here are suggestions for the best way to chop nuts.

Broken Nuts are broken by hand into large, irregular pieces ³⁄₈ to ½ inch. Softer nuts like walnuts and pecans are the best candidates.

Coarsely Chopped Place the nuts on a cutting board and use a chef's knife to chop them into the size of dried chickpeas, ¼- to ³⁄₈-inch pieces. If you don't have a chef's knife, you may place the nuts in a wooden bowl and chop them with a crescent-shaped hand chopper.

Medium Chopped Nuts should be chopped by hand into pieces slightly smaller than ¼ inch,

about the size of dried lentils or split peas.

Finely Chopped Nuts should be chopped by hand into barley-size pieces, about ⅛ inch.

Nut Meal Pulverize or grind the nuts to a meal-like texture. A Mouli grater is the ideal home tool for making nut meal because it produces the most powdery consistency with a minimal amount of oil loss.

While food processors are super time-savers for chopping nuts, care must be taken not to overprocess:

• For most chopping purposes, use the steel blade.

• For medium-chopped nuts, try the shredding disc, which will produce more uniform pieces.

• Do not overfill the work bowl. Chop the nuts in small quantities, ½ cup to 2 cups at a time, depending on the size of the processor.

• To achieve more evenly chopped nuts, use the pulse button.

• If making finely chopped nuts or nut meal, add a small amount of sugar or flour to the nuts to help absorb the oils released during chopping.

It will take longer to chop hard nuts such as almonds than soft nuts like walnuts and pecans. Always stop the processor and check the size of the nuts when chopping over a period of time; scrape around the edge of the bowl, if necessary.

To separate larger pieces of nuts from nut dust, empty the chopped nuts into a wide-gauge strainer or colander placed over a sheet of wax paper or baking parchment. Shake the strainer to separate the smaller particles of dust. Reuse these particles in recipes calling for finely chopped nuts.

When chopping smaller quantities of nuts, a great time-saver is to place them in a plastic bag and use a batarde, mallet, or the bottom of a heavy saucepan to crush them. Press the air out of the bag and seal it well before crushing.

Measuring Nuts

Use graduated measuring cups when measuring nuts. There is some confusion regarding recipe terminology and chopped nuts. When a recipe calls for "1 cup nuts, chopped," you should measure the nuts first and then chop them. If the recipe calls for "1 cup chopped nuts," *chop the nuts first*, then measure. The measurement between the two will differ because chopped nuts are reduced in volume and the spaces between larger pieces disappear. For 1 cup chopped nuts, measure 1 generous cup whole nuts.

SEEDS

Seeds contribute flavor and texture to baked goods, and enhance appearance as well. Purchase seeds in small jars or packages instead of in bulk because they go stale quickly. Seeds are best stored in cool, dark places. Refrigerate or freeze for long-term storage.

Pepita Seeds These edible, dark green pumpkin seeds, with their white shells removed, have a delicately sweet and nutty flavor that is heightened by toasting and salting. For baking, look for seeds that are raw, hulled, and unsalted. While roasted seeds can be used, raw pepitas have more color.

Poppy Seeds Tiny bluish-gray poppy seeds provide a crunchy texture and nutty flavor to many baked goods. Poppy seeds can be purchased at most supermarkets. Their high oil content makes them prone to rancidity; therefore, after opening, storage in the refrigerator or freezer is recommended.

Sunflower Seeds High in nutrients, with a crunchy texture and mildly nutty flavor, sunflower seeds have become a popular addition to muffins and quick breads. Sunflower seeds can be purchased plain or salted, and dried or roasted. Be sure to use the type indicated in your recipe.

Toasting Seeds

Toast the seeds in a small skillet over low heat until they begin to brown and are fragrant. To ensure even browning, shake the pan occasionally. Cool the seeds before using.

SPICES

Spices play an important role in baking, but should be used judiciously to provide balance and nuance. Their flavors should be subtle and never distracting to the finished product. Purchase spices in small amounts so they will be used within a reasonable time. Heat and light hasten the deterioration of spices, so store them in a cool, dark place and make sure they are tightly capped.

Allspice With a flavor reminiscent of cinnamon, cloves, and nutmeg, allspice is used to season both sweet and savory dishes.

Cardamom Native to India, and a member of the ginger family, ground cardamom comes from a seed with a spicy-sweet flavor and distinctly pungent aroma. Because of its intensity, a little cardamom goes a very long way.

Cinnamon Cinnamon is the inner bark of a tropical evergreen. Native to Southeast Asia, cassia cinnamon, with its strong, spicy-sweet flavor, is most familiar.

Cloves The pungent, peppery clove is the dried unopened, pink flower bud of the evergreen clove tree. It is sold either whole or ground and should be used sparingly.

Crystallized (or Candied) Ginger Fresh ginger is peeled, cut, cooked in sugar syrup, and tossed in coarse sugar. It is fiber-free, and especially good to use in baking. Australian ginger is of finer quality than Asian.

Dried Ground Ginger This peppery, slightly sweet, tropical spice is popular for desserts and pastries. Dried ground ginger should not be used interchangeably with fresh ginger.

Mace Derived from the fruit of the nutmeg tree (a tropical evergreen), mace is the thin, orange, lacey covering of the nutmeg seed. With a flavor more delicate than nutmeg, mace is most often sold ground.

Nutmeg Native to the Spice Islands, nutmeg is the seed of a tropical evergreen tree. The hard, egg-shaped seed is sold whole or ground. Freshly ground nutmeg has superior flavor to pre-ground. If substituting ground nutmeg, reduce the amount by one-third to one-half because of its finer grain.

SALT

Sodium chloride, or salt, is used to enhance the flavor of other ingredients, adding depth and brightness to all it touches. Use ordinary table salt when baking, unless otherwise indicated.

In yeasted doughs, salt plays the role of regulator. By slowing the rate of yeast's fermentation, the dough rises more slowly and develops a tighter gluten structure. As a result, the end product will have better elasticity and texture. Be careful to measure salt correctly; too much can be harmful to yeast. Always add salt where indicated in the recipe and never have it come in direct contact with yeast.

FLAVORINGS

Coffee and Espresso Coffee or espresso, when used in concentrated form, is a wonderful fla-vor accent, especially for chocolate. Freeze-dried instant coffee, such as Taster's Choice, is acceptable, as is instant espresso powder, such as Medaglia d'Oro. Store opened jars in the refrigerator to maintain freshness.

Vanilla Of all the flavorings available to the baker, none is more important than vanilla, with its unique ability to enhance, mellow, and deepen other flavors. Pure vanilla extract is made from vanilla beans combined with at least 35 percent alcohol, water, and sugar. Vanilla flavor extract and natural vanilla flavor are weaker in flavor than pure vanilla extract. Imitation vanilla flavorings or vanillin, a by-product of paper making, do not compare with natural vanilla and should be avoided. Bourbon vanilla beans—the gold standard— are grown on the Indian Ocean islands of Madagascar, Réunion, and the Comoros.

Vanilla extract is very concentrated and should be measured carefully to avoid over-whelming your baked goods. A 2-inch piece of vanilla bean equals 1 teaspoon of vanilla extract.

Flavored Extracts Check out your supermarket's baking aisle or any cook's catalog and you will find a wide variety of pure and imitation fla-vors. Pure almond, lemon, orange, banana, raspberry, hazelnut, spearmint, and pepper-mint are available, as well as imitation maple and coconut. Always choose pure extract when available, though an imitation can be substituted.

Flavored Oils Made by squeezing the oil from the rind of lemons, limes, and oranges, fla-vored oils are highly concentrated and intense in flavor. A few drops of these citrus oils go a long way. The Baker's Catalogue sells dropper caps, which screw onto bottles and can pre-cisely measure a drop or two when ¼ teaspoon is too much. Flavored oils, as with all extracts and flavorings, should be added off direct heat. After opening, it is best to store them in the refrigerator.

LIQUEURS, BRANDIES, SPIRITS, AND FORTIFIED WINES

Liqueurs (Cordials) Liqueurs and brandies can add a fruity nuance to baked goods. Some of the more commonly used liqueurs in baking are the orange-flavored Grand Marnier, Cointreau, and Triple Sec. Other liqueurs are Amaretto, Kahlúa, and brandy.

Brandies A potable spirit aged in wood, brandies are obtained from the distillation of wine or a fermented mash of fruit. Popular brandies used in baking include Kirschwasser (from wild black cherries), Calvados and applejack (from apples), Framboise (from raspberries), and Poire William (from pears).

Spirits Rum is an alcoholic spirit distilled from fermented sugarcane, sugarcane syrup, sugarcane molasses, or other sugarcane by-products. Scotch, made only in Scotland, uses barley for flavoring and is characterized by a smoky flavor.

Fortified Wines A wine to which brandy or another spirit has been added is a fortified wine. Such wines include port, sherry, and Marsala, Italy's most famous fortified wine (available sweet and dry).

PREPARING PANS FOR BAKING

All pastries can be baked using pans prepared with butter, margarine, vegetable oil, cooking spray, baking parchment, Release nonstick or regular aluminum foil, paper or foil muffin cups, and treated liners such as Silpat. Occasionally, an ungreased pan is used. Here are recommendations for baking pan preparation:

Butter For doughs and batters requiring moderate greasing, my preference is butter. Butter encourages even browning, protects the finish of the pan, and allows for easier cleaning.

Butter and Flour or Cocoa Powder This combination is ideal for batters and doughs that are more difficult to release, such as those baked in Bundt pans. The flour coating strengthens the sides of the cake, making it less likely to stick to the pan's ridges.

Margarine Recommended only for those observing dietary laws.

Vegetable Shortening and Oils Not only are these are not pleasing to the palate but they also leave a baked film on the surface of the pan that is difficult to clean.

Nonstick Cooking Spray Use only when necessary. An alternative is a nonstick cooking spray containing flour, such as Baker's Joy.

Baking Parchment Ideal for baked goods that tend to stick to the pan, like those made with brown sugar, fresh fruit, and preserves. It is sometimes necessary to butter the paper. Best used on rimmed cookie sheets. For a quick clean-up, use it for lining the bottom only.

Aluminum Foil Use 18-inch heavy-duty aluminum foil (either the dull or shiny side) for lining the bottom and sides of square and oblong pans. Aluminum foil at times is coated with butter. Nonstick aluminum foil is great to use. Always place the nonstick side up.

Ungreased Pans Cookie sheets and rimmed baking sheets may be used ungreased when the biscuit, pastry, or cookie has a high percentage of butter.

How to Butter Pans

One of the major mistakes that bakers make is the improper buttering of the pan. To ensure success, follow the guidelines below.

Lightly Buttered Spread a thin, barely visible layer of butter evenly on the pan with a pastry brush.

Moderately Buttered Use a pastry brush to spread very soft butter on the pan. The butter should be more visible. Melted butter should not be used.

Generously Buttered Using a pastry brush, spread a thicker coating of very soft butter on the pan. The metal surface of the pan should be slightly visible. Avoid over buttering, which causes smoking in the oven.

Generously Buttered and Floured Follow the above procedure for generously buttering. Using a flour shaker filled with all-purpose (not cake) flour, sprinkle the bottom and sides of the pan thoroughly. If using a tube pan, be sure to butter and flour the tube portion as well. Invert the pan over the sink and give a firm tap to remove any excess flour. Alternatively, place the flour in a small, medium-gauge strainer and tap it over the pan.

Lining Pans with Aluminum Foil See sidebar, page 313.

Lining the Bottom of a Tube Pan or Angel Cake Pan Butter the bottom and sides of the pan as directed in the recipe. Use pre-cut parchment liners available in kitchen shops. Alternatively, place a 12-inch square of parchment on the countertop, and using a pencil, trace around the bottom and inner tube of the pan. Fold the paper into quarters, aligning the lines. Cut around the outside arc, then cut the inside arc. Open the parchment and press into the bottom of the pan. Butter the paper if directed.

Lining the Bottom of a Round, Square, Loaf, or Springform Pan Butter the bottom and sides of the pan as directed in the recipe. Cut a piece of parchment at least 2 inches larger than the pan. (For example, for a 9-inch pan, cut an 11-inch piece.) Place the pan on the parchment and use a pencil to trace around the bottom of the pan. Fold the paper into quarters, aligning the pencil lines. Cut around the lines, then unfold the paper and press it onto the bottom of the pan. Butter the paper if directed to do so. Wax paper may be substituted, but it should always be buttered.

Muffin Pans Most of the muffin recipes in this book use paper liners or double liners that are aluminum foil on the outside and paper on the inside. You can separate the double liners and save the sturdier aluminum foil cups for Muffins in Minutes (page 83). For muffin pans that need to be buttered, follow the above directions for generously buttering.

USING BAKING PANS AND OTHER EQUIPMENT

Cookie Sheets: Rimmed Versus Unrimmed In many instances, rimmed and unrimmed cookie sheets are used interchangeably. The two pans, however, are not the same. A cookie sheet is flat except for a lip at one side for easy handling. A rimmed cookie sheet, also known as a jelly roll pan or half sheet pan, has 1-inch sides. Baking on rimmed cookie sheets can take somewhat longer because the sides of the pans buffer the heat. These cookie sheets are easy to line with baking parchment because the sides prevent the parchment from sliding off.

When baking large pastries, choose a flat cookie sheet because you can slide the cake from the pan without cracking the cake. Without the sides, it is easy to place a spatula under the pastry. In addition, flat cookie sheets have a larger capacity. When lining a flat cookie sheet with parchment, butter each corner of the sheet to hold the parchment in place.

Baking in Aluminum Foil Pans Some recipes in this book use disposable aluminum foil baking pans. For best baking results, to help conduct heat, always place the filled pans on a rimmed cookie sheet before baking. Placing them on a rimmed sheet also enables you to handle the cakes more easily.

Filling Baking Pans To achieve a beautifully shaped finished cake, take care when filling the pan. Pour thin batter into the pan and gently tilt the pan so the batter moves evenly into the edges and corners. If the batter has air bubbles, tap the pan firmly on the counter to burst them. Spoon thick batters evenly into the prepared pan, then spread with the back of a soupspoon. It's especially important to spread the batter evenly into the corners.

The batter should fill one-half to two-thirds of the cake pan. When substituting pans, it is essential that the pan be filled to this capacity. If the pan is too large, the cake will be too flat; you also risk overbaking, which results in a dry cake. If the pan is too small, the batter will overflow. This will not only create a mess in the oven, it can cause the cake to sink in the center.

Spreading Doughs Doughs such as those used for the base of bar cookies can be difficult to spread in an even layer. Here is an easy way to resolve this: Instead of emptying the entire batch of dough into the pan, spoon it in mounds, spacing them evenly. Then spread the dough with a small offset spatula, taking care to reach all the corners.

Rolling Surfaces Pastry, biscuit, scone, and cookie dough can be rolled on a variety of surfaces. The optimum piece of equipment is a wooden pastry board, about 18 × 24 inches. Secure the board on the countertop by placing an appropriate size piece of rubberized shelf liner underneath the board (available in most houseware departments). Alternatively, a damp dish towel may be used. In lieu of a pastry board, a large cutting board is an adequate substitute.

For rolling buttery dough, as for croissants and Danish, marble or granite make excellent surfaces because they are cooler than a countertop or pastry board.

Using a Pastry Cloth and Rolling Pin Cover This cloth is a specially treated rectangular piece of canvas that prevents the dough from sticking. A rolling pin cover (or stocking) slips over the barrel of a 12-inch ball-bearing rolling pin. Flour is rubbed into the weave of the cloth and the stocking, which keeps too much flour from being absorbed into the dough while rolling (see "Specialty Sources," page 400).

As an alternative to a pastry board, lay a pastry cloth on a piece of rubberized shelf liner. Do not lay the cloth directly on your kitchen counter because it will slide, making rolling awkward.

Before rolling, rub 2 to 3 tablespoons of flour deeply into the weave of the cloth and rolling pin cover. Be sure to flour an area on the cloth that is larger than you plan to roll the dough. Re-flour as needed.

Using a Pastry Bag In this book, a pastry bag is used to pipe fillings for Danish pastry. Never fill the bag to more than one-third of its capacity. Place the appropriate pastry tip in the bag, then insert the bag in a tall jar or glass to make it easier to fill.

FINISHING TOUCHES

Egg Wash Egg washes produce color and shine on finished baked goods, seal pieces of dough together, and help secure trimmings and sugars to dough before baking. Egg whites provide the least amount of color, but the greatest amount of shine and crispiness. Egg yolks produce a deep golden color, while whole eggs give a light gold color. Always dilute any part of the egg with tap water, about 2 teaspoons per egg. To prepare the egg wash, lightly beat the egg in a small bowl with a fork to break up the albumen, then beat in the water and/or optional salt or sugar.

Doneness To tell when cakes are done, look for three signs: (1) When pressed gently with your fingertip, the cake springs back without leaving an indentation; (2) light-colored batters turn golden brown; (3) the cake begins to release from the side of the pan. If all of these requirements are met, remove the cake from the oven. If not, immediately close the oven door (to keep the oven hot) and retest the cake in 2 or 3 minutes.

Firm-textured cakes, such as pound cakes and some homestyle coffee cakes, are not always springy and can be more difficult to judge doneness simply by touch. (See "About Pound Cakes," page 6.)

Releasing Cakes from Pans A freshly baked cake is fully expanded with heat and extremely fragile. Most cakes must stand at least 10 minutes to stabilize and shrink slightly before they can be successfully removed from the pan. It's okay to remove the cake while it is still warm; once cool, it may stick to the pan. Here are some helpful guidelines:

• If the cake sticks, a thin, sharp knife may be run gently around the side to help release it.

• When baking cakes in decorative pans, such as Bundt, or other large cakes, allow them to stand for 10 to 15 minutes before removing the pan.

• To prevent cakes from sticking to the cooling rack, spray it first with nonstick cooking spray.

• When cakes are served top side up, after removing them from the pan onto the rack, place another rack over the cake and invert it top side up to prevent indentations on the presentation side of the cake.

• For releasing cakes with streusel toppings, see "About Home-style Coffee Cakes," page 34.

STORING CAKES, PASTRIES, AND COOKIES

When storing any type of cake or pastry, maintaining freshness and moisture for as long as possible is of primary importance. Depending on the type of baked goods you are storing, there are many ways to accomplish this. Refrigeration tends to dry out baked goods and impair flavor. Refrigeration is necessary only when the pastry has been made with pastry cream or some cheeses. I store cakes that keep at room temperature under a glass dome because it is airtight and maintains freshness. Cake boxes, such as those used by bakeries, are also great storage containers (see "Specialty Sources," page 400). These are porous and allow the right amount of air to circulate around the cake. Cakes baked in oblong and square pans are sometimes stored directly in the pan, to be cut at will for snacking.

Muffins and quick breads may be covered with plastic wrap or aluminum foil, depending on the ingredients. Those made with fresh fruits or vegetables should be wrapped in aluminum foil because the higher moisture content creates condensation, which can cause mold to form. Biscuits and scones may be stored in heavy-duty plastic freezer bags, aluminum foil, or other airtight containers.

About Freezing and Defrosting

Unfrosted Cakes, Coffee Cakes, and Yeasted Pastries Completely cool the cake or pastry. Place it on a cardboard disk (or other nonstick surface) and partially freeze. After it is firm, wrap it in heavy-duty aluminum foil using a butcher's fold, similar to covering a package with gift wrap. Turn the ends under the cake and seal with tape. Place in a plastic bag (not zip-top), remove as much air as possible, and secure with a twist tie. Label and date the package. Cakes or pastries that are baked in disposable aluminum pans can be wrapped before freezing in their container.

Defrosting frozen cakes and pastries in the oven gives the best results. The pastry will taste almost freshly made. Remove the cake or pastry from the plastic bag, remove the tape, and pull the folded ends from underneath it. Do not unwrap the cake completely. Place the foil-wrapped cake in a 300° to 325°F oven, allowing 20 to 30 minutes or more for thawing, depending upon the size and thickness of the cake. Cakes and pastries may also be defrosted at room temperature or overnight in the refrigerator; either way, refresh them in the oven.

Test the cake or pastry by pressing gently on the foil. It should feel soft. To double-check, insert a toothpick or wooden skewer through the foil. If the toothpick shows resistance, or is not slightly warm, heat the cake a bit longer. Once thawed, tear the foil to expose the top of the cake to the heat of the oven. Bake for another 5 minutes to crisp or firm the surface; the cake should be warm, not hot. Place on a cooling rack and remove the foil. Glazes should be used while the cake is still warm. Powdered sugar should be applied after the cake or pastry is cool.

Baked Cookies and Small Pastries These may be frozen in airtight containers such as cookie tins or well-sealed aluminum foil containers. If the container is not completely filled, eliminate the air space by placing aluminum foil directly on top of the baked goods. Label and date your containers.

Defrost frozen crisp cookies and small pastries at room temperature. Soft and chewy cookies, iced cookies, or those with sticky surfaces should be removed from their container, arranged on rimmed cookie sheets, and covered lightly with a piece of aluminum foil or wax paper. Plastic wrap should be avoided because condensation forms underneath the surface.

specialty sources

A COOK'S WARES
211 37th Street
Beaver Falls, PA 15010
www.cookswares.com
800-915-9788

Gourmet foods, such as honey, Lyle's Golden Syrup, pure
maple syrup, Nielsen-Massey vanilla, high-quality chocolate,
and spices. Baking equipment includes spatulas (straight and
offset), Nordic Ware and All-Clad bakeware, springform pans,
brioche molds, pastry blenders, cookie sheets, Microplane
graters, measuring equipment, and bowls. Catalog available.

ATECO
August Thomsen Corporation
36 Sea Cliff Avenue
Glen Cove, NY 11542-3699
888-645-7171

Carole Walter's custom heavy-weight pastry cloth with rolling
pin cover, and 12-inch barrel solid Rock Maple ball-bearing
rolling pin. High quality cake decorating equipment, pastry
scrapers, pastry brushes, biscuit cutters, pastry wheels, straight
and offset spatulas, palm-held bowl scraper, baking pans.

THE BAKER'S CATALOGUE
P. O. Box 876
Norwich, VT 05055-0876
www.bakerscatalogue.com
www.bakingcircle.com
800-827-6836

High-quality flours, sparkling sugar, nuts, dried and candied fruits,
crystallized ginger, pure maple syrup, Nielsen-Massey vanilla,
extracts, and oils. Quality chocolate. Wide range of baking equipment, including cookie sheets, half and quarter sheet pans, cooling racks, biscuit cutters, pastry boards, Silpat mats, measuring
equipment, assorted baking pans, and dough scrapers.

BRIDGE KITCHENWARE
214 East 52nd Street
New York, NY 10022
www.bridgekitchenware.com
800-274-3435

Bridge, a chef and restaurant supplier open to the public,
offers a total line of imported and domestic cookware and
bakeware, including baking equipment, baking parchment
(available in sheets) sold in bulk, strainers, cookie sheets, and
rolling pins. Catalog available ($3.00 refundable with first
order).

LINDT CHOCOLATE
www.lindt.com/USA
Premium chocolate for baking.

NEW YORK CAKE AND BAKING DISTRIBUTORS
56 West 22nd Street
New York, NY 10010
www.nycakesupplies.com
212-675-2253

Specialty baking pans, cookie sheets, cake boxes and cake
rounds, Silpat mats, rolling pins, small cupcake
liners. Stocks bulk chocolate. Catalog available.

SUR LA TABLE
1765 Sixth Avenue South
Seattle, WA 98134
www.surlatable.com
800-243-0852

This upscale kitchenwares chain offers a varied line of specialty baking pans and accessories, as well as rolling pins,
cookie sheets, cookware, kitchen gadgetry, small appliances,
and gift items. Catalog available.

WILLIAMS-SONOMA
Mail Order Department
P. O. Box 7456
San Francisco, CA 94120-7456
www.williams-sonoma.com
800-541-2233

Williams-Sonoma's "A Catalog for Cooks" features cutting-
edge equipment, including baking accessories such as cake pans,
cookie sheets, measuring equipment, Nielsen-Massey vanilla,
and premium baking chocolate. Some items are catalog only.

acknowledgments

WRITING A COOKBOOK is seldom the work of one person. The process engenders a circle of professionals and friends who are passionate about food, and in this case coffee cakes. For more than two and a half years, prep trays were organized, batters and doughs were mixed, the kitchen sink brimmed with stacks of dishes and pans, page after page of notes were taken, the keyboard on the computer hummed with the rhythm of tapping fingers, and in the end a cookbook was born.

I began the journey of this book with Chris Pavone, the acquiring editor of the project at Clarkson Potter. I thank him for getting the ball rolling and then passing it into the gifted hands of senior editor Rica Allannic. Rica and I labored over an appropriate title for this book for more than a year. It was Rica's passion for sticky buns that led to the final name, along with the book's tempting cover. I never realized that these sweet little buns had such a huge audience. How intuitive of you, Rica, to have pointed me in the right direction! Thank you also for helping me fine-tune my manuscript. Your baking knowledge and standard for perfection helped make this book what it is today. A big thank-you to Kathleen Fleury, Rica's assistant, for being so accommodating to me. You are a fabulous worker and one terrific gal Friday.

I cannot say enough in behalf of my literary agent, Judith Weber. Over the many years of our association, Judith has wisely guided me through many frustrating moments with a cool head and good judgment. Thank you so much, Judith, for your sound advice and friendship. Her assistant, Adia Wright, who is a terrific asset to Judith's office and a pleasure to work with, also deserves my appreciation.

In writing this book, I was blessed to have had three outstanding assistants. Kathie Finn-Redden, to whom this book is dedicated, viewed the world from a vantage point that is not the norm. Anyone who knew her will agree that not only did she have an outstanding sense of taste, but her sense of humor kept you in stitches with her pranks and off-the-cuff remarks. Kathie had nicknames for everything and everybody. I answer to "Felix," taken from the *The Odd Couple* team of Felix and Oscar, because my criteria for accuracy often drove her crazy. Kathie's dedication to seeing this book completed was without measure. Sadly, just before publication, Kathie lost her battle with breast cancer.

Judy Epstein, who has managed my office for almost four years, quietly stays the course through thick and thin. Not only is she a whiz at the computer, but she's terrific in the kitchen as well. Throughout this entire book, the only thing that really rattled Judy's cage was when I first told her to prepare a batch of yeasted sweet dough. I knew you could do it, Judy! Thank you for standing by my side for these many years. I also tip my hat to Judy for raising two teens with such sophisticated palates. Cory and Hannah Epstein made terrific tasters for dozens of recipes.

No author of a baking book could have asked for a more talented assistant than Debbie Barrett. Deb is a sensational baker, a marvelous cook, and equally great at the computer. The word *no* does not exist in her vocabulary. Whether it's a trip to Trader Joe's or a quick stop at her local Asian market, whatever I need, I know Deb will be there. How can I ever begin to thank you for stepping up to the plate every time you were needed?

Maureen Rosin, who came on board toward the later days of this book, proved to be a valuable teammate. She jumped right in and barely missed a beat. Other invaluable help came from Chiaki Romano, whom I can always count on, regardless of the task. From schlepping my bundles to preparing a proper cup of tea, she has truly spoiled me. Also there for me was my former teaching partner and friend Kathleen Sanderson. When in need, Kathleen will always come through. To John Cappalbo and Roann Green, my appreciation for your time when I was shorthanded. Arlene Sarappo left no stone unturned when she researched the ingredient and equipment sections of this book. Thank you, Arlene, for a job well done. To proofreaders Judith Bernhaut and Janice Godfrey, my sincerest thanks for helping with this tedious job.

My talented photographer, Duane Winfield, never ceases to amaze me. With a fractured foot, Duane stood for hours snapping picture after picture. Thank you, Duane, for your endurance and for making every cake crumb come alive in your photos. Thank you also to Kimberlee Piper, Duane's skillful assistant, who had to work twice as hard to keep him from hopping about without his crutches, and to Dolores Feinswog and Judy Bernhaut, who graciously loaned me china and linens for photography props.

There were many others behind the scenes who were eager to lend a helping hand. Lorette Cheswick, my computer technician for many years, continues to dazzle me with her scope of knowledge. Thank you, Lorette, for your help and for keeping me supplied with stone-ground cornmeal. Other assistance came from Mary Ann Castronovo Fusco of the *Star-Ledger*; Doug Schneider, vice president of August Thomsen Corporation; and Dean Kleinhans, vice president of engineering for Nordic Ware. A special thanks to Susan Konzen for her artistic talent and for the fine job she does with maintaining my Web page.

The credit for the design and layout of this book belongs to Maggie Hinders, senior designer at Clarkson Potter. Maggie is a great talent and was a joy to work with. Thank you, Maggie; I could not have wished for better. The fabulous illustrations were created by Meredith Hamilton, who so perfectly transcribed my visions on paper. A special thank-you to the brilliant Marysarah Quinn, Potter's creative director, for bringing me to Maggie and Meredith.

Other members of the talented Clarkson Potter team that have made this publishing house the "best of the best" are Lauren Shakely, senior vice president and publisher of Potter; Doris Cooper, editorial director; Sibylle Kazeroid, senior production editor; Joan Denman, senior production manager; Alice Peisch in publicity; Katherine Sungarian, marketing manager; and my copy editor, Carole Berglie, who did a meticulous job. My sincerest thanks to each and every one of you.

I will forever be grateful for the continued support that I receive from the entire Kings Super Markets family. My sincere appreciation to Pat Mickell, director of marketing, and Cherry Huntoon, manager of the cooking studios. Cherry is also the skillful manager of the Short Hills cooking studio. I know I can always count on her support and understanding and her willingness to lend a helping hand. I also give thanks to former manager of the cooking studios Susan Loden and Bedminster studio manager Ellen Taylor. To my teaching partner, Michael Salvatore, I give a great big hug for making the hours we spend together such a pleasure. Along with Michael, accolades go to my outstanding assistants, who helped me through my classes while I was under the stress of writing this book.

To Morgan Larsson, pastry chef extraordinaire of the famed Russian Tea Room, thank you for sharing your knowledge of Danish pastry with me. I give special thanks to food maven Arthur Schwartz for his input on babkas and for his support, friendship, and faith in me as his baking guru. My deepest gratitude goes to Lila Gault and Roy Finamore, who have wisely given me such good advice throughout the years. To Annellen Guth, Joan Rothbell, and Dr. Harvey Schor, my appreciation for scanning family recipe collections to help perpetuate the yeasted cakes of the 1940s and 1950s. Other invaluable help came from my family, friends, and students, who graciously shared treasured recipes with me. I will always be indebted to my terrific students, whose curiosity and thirst for learning encourages me to continue teaching and writing. They are a tremendous source of inspiration.

To my husband, Gene, you are a very special mate to have your home turned into a three-ring circus for two and a half years. I know my children, Frank and Marla and Pam and Andy, and my grandchildren, Zach, Samantha, Jeffrey, and Neil, will be happy to have their mother and grandmother back. Thank you for your understanding. I love each of you more than I can say.

index